FOOD AND REVOLUTION

PITT LATIN AMERICAN SERIES

CATHERINE M. CONAGHAN, EDITOR

FOOD AND REVOLUTION

FIGHTING HUNGER IN NICARAGUA, 1960–1993

CHRISTIANE BERTH

UNIVERSITY OF PITTSBURGH PRESS

Published by the University of Pittsburgh Press, Pittsburgh, Pa., 15260
Manufactured in the United States of America
Printed on acid-free paper
10 9 8 7 6 5 4 3 2 1

Cataloging-in-Publication data is available from the Library of Congress

ISBN 13: 978-0-8229-4604-5
ISBN 10: 0-8229-4604-1

Cover art and design: Melissa Dias-Mandoly

CONTENTS

CHAPTER SIX.

CHAPTER SEVEN.

EPILOGUE.

ACKNOWLEDGMENTS

Numerous people in Nicaragua, Guatemala, Costa Rica, Switzerland, Germany, and the United States have contributed with their support to the research and writing of this book. My research was supported by generous funding from the Swiss National Science Foundation, which allowed me to do archival research at different places, present my findings at international conferences, and dedicate sufficient time to writing. I owe my interest and passion for Central American history—and more specifically for my research on food and consumption in Nicaragua—to Volker Wünderich, who served as one of my PhD supervisors.

I would like to thank Corinne Pernet, who initiated a Swiss National Science Foundation research project on food policies in Latin America and invited me to participate. She supported the idea of my research on Nicaragua from the beginning. Our intense exchange on food and the activities of international organizations in Latin America strengthened my analysis for the book. Corinne contributed to the further development of the project and the chapters of this book with numerous helpful comments.

Numerous librarians and archivists contributed helpful advice. I would like to thank especially the staff of the Instituto de Historia de Nicaragua y Centroamérica (IHNCA) library in Nicaragua, the Institute of Nutrition of Central America and Panama (INCAP) library in Guatemala, the New York Public Library, the Ibero-American Institute Library in Berlin, the Food and Agriculture Organization (FAO) archives and library in Rome, the Bundesarchiv in Bern, and the Bundesarchiv and Politisches Archiv des Auswärtigen Amtes (BArch) in Berlin.

I started this research project at the University of St. Gallen and benefited from the support of the researchers and administrative staff there. In the next stage, the project moved to the Institute for European Global Studies at the University of Basel where the helpful staff and my quiet office with a view into the greenery facilitated my work significantly. I especially thank

Isabella Löhr, Patricia Hertel, Cornelia Knab, and Tamar Lewinsky for the discussions and advice during our monthly meetings in Basel. I thank Christian Büschges and Christian Gerlach at the University of Bern, for their friendly welcome and their advice. Finally, during a difficult resettlement period at the University of Costa Rica I appreciated the support of Cátedras Internacionales staff, and I thank Baruc Chavarría Castro for revising the footnotes and the bibliography.

For support during my two research periods in Nicaragua, I would like to especially thank Miguel Ayerdis and Ligia Peña. Yuridia Odalis Mendoza deserves special thanks as she supported my research as an assistant with the transcription of Nicaraguan newspaper articles and helpful bibliographic information from Nicaraguan libraries. I wish to thank Monika Strasser in León for her warm reception and hospitality as well as her help in establishing contacts to interviewees. I owe many thanks to all of my interviewees for their patience and willingness to share their stories, anecdotes, and recipes.

After the periods of archival research and traveling, I entered a period of intense writing during which the support of Héctor Jiménez Guzmán was crucial for finishing the manuscript. He contributed to the success of this endeavor with his patience, advice, critical reading, and delicious food. I am very grateful for the helpful comments of Annika Hartmann, Patricia Hertel, Mona Nikolić, Corinne Pernet, and Heike Wieters to the different chapters of the manuscript's first version. I wish to thank the two anonymous reviewers for their detailed comments and suggestions for restructuring, which provided useful directions for revisions. In addition, I would like to thank Margaret Puskar-Pasewicz for her careful editing of my English writing, her forbearance to my unpredictable schedule during my move overseas, and her numerous helpful questions, which improved the final version of the text. Finally, I thank the University of Pittsburgh Press for making this book possible, particularly Josh Shanholtzer for his patience and advice during revision.

ABBREVIATIONS USED THROUGHOUT THIS BOOK

AFA	Arroz, Frijoles, Azúcar
AMNLAE	Asociación de Mujeres Nicaragüenses Luisa Amanda Espinoza
BArch	Bundesarchiv
BICU	Bluefields Indian and Caribbean University
CAFTA	Central America Free Trade Agreement
CARE	Cooperative for Assistance and Relief Everywhere
CAT	Centro de Abastecimiento para los Trabajadores
CDS	Comité de Defensa Sandinista
CEPAL	Comisión Económica para América Latina y el Caribe
CIA	Central Intelligence Agency
CIERA	Centro de Investigaciones y Estudios de la Reforma Agraria
ENABAS	Empresa Nacional de Alimentos Básicos
FAO	Food and Agriculture Organization
FSLN	Frente Sandinista de Liberación Nacional
GDR	German Democratic Republic
IDNND	The Interdepartmental Committee on Nutrition for National Development
IADB	Inter-American Development Bank
IFAD	International Fund for Agricultural Development
IHNCA	Instituto de Historia de Nicaragua y Centroamérica
INCAP	Institute of Nutrition of Central America and Panama
INCEI	Instituto Nacional de Comercio Exterior e Interior
INIDE	Instituto Nacional de Información de Desarrollo
MICOIN	Ministerio de Comercio Interior
PA AA	Politischcs Archiv des Auswärtigen Amts
PAHO	Pan American Health Organization
PAN	Programa Alimentario Nicaragüense
PLC	Partido Liberal Constitucionalista

RAAN   Región Autónoma del Atlántico Norte
UCA   Universidad Centroamericana
UNAG   Unión Nacional de Agricultores y Ganaderos
UNICEF   UN International Children's Emergency Fund
UNO   Unión Nacional Opositora
UNRISD   UN Research Institute for Social Development
URACCAN   Universidad de las Regiones Autónomas de la Costa Caribe
                Nicaragüense
USAID   US Agency for International Development
WFP   World Food Programme
WHO   World Health Organization

MAP OF NICARAGUA

FOOD AND REVOLUTION

INTRODUCTION

In April 2011 in Matagalpa, at the Centro Cultural Heroes y Mártires in the city center, a food competition takes place. Shortly before Easter week, the event promotes traditional Semana Santa dishes. Under Nicaraguan flags and a photo remembering the final Frente Sandinista de Liberación Nacional (FSLN) offensive in Matagalpa in June 1979, women present their food to the jury and visitors of the fair.[1] Outside, a large statue of the Nicaraguan revolutionary leader Augusto César Sandino overlooks the scene. The colorful dishes are carefully decorated: *sopa de queso* mixes with *buñuelos*, tamales with fish, and pineapple desserts with milk pudding. All these dishes belong to Central and Pacific Nicaraguan food culture that since Spanish conquest has incorporated a large variety of cultural influences. The jury wanders around, tasting the different dishes, while musicians and the local mayor take over the stage. The mayor summarizes: "We have deep roots. We must remember, for example, that corn, corn is a fundamental grain, the grain of the gods, they say, as a grain original to our America, original to Nicaragua. This corn, among our other foods, is the fundamental one that has allowed us to exist."[2]

At the end of his speech he argues staunchly that it is necessary to rescue Nicaraguan culinary traditions for future generations. According to him, ancestral culinary knowledge represents an important cultural heritage and has formed part of Nicaraguan food sovereignty. In 2011 Nicaragua was among the first Latin American countries with a food sovereignty law (approved in 2009). Nevertheless, malnutrition still affected more than one million Nicaraguan people. In the northern departments of Nueva Segovia, Jinotega, and Madriz, more than 27 percent of children under the age of five were suffering from chronic malnutrition.[3] These people lacked the money and the ingredients to prepare the typical dishes presented at the festival.

After the jury concludes its tour, I leave the event and wander around the plaza. Between the cathedral and the restaurants and shops surrounding it a different culinary landscape becomes visible: small stands selling chips, ice cream, hot dogs, and *sopa maruchan* (an instant soup produced by the Japanese firm Toyo Suisan, which has appeared in different Latin American countries since the 1970s). This scene shows two seemingly opposed culinary worlds: the world of "traditional" Nicaraguan food and the world of global fast food.

In between these two worlds, however, Nicaraguans have carved out spaces to create their own food practices and traditions. They have invented new recipes, made substitutions for scarce products, and even incorporated into their diets foreign foods acquired through international aid. Sometimes, they also rejected substitutes or new foods because of their taste, texture, or high price. While Nicaraguans struggled with dietary choices during periods of food insecurity, nutritionists, medical professionals, and politicians debated the best strategies for improving the Nicaraguan diet. Their visions of the ideal Nicaraguan diet changed significantly from the 1950s to the 1990s.

Access to food became a central political matter during the second half of the twentieth century. Depending on the particular political circumstances, Nicaraguans depicted foreign influences and "traditional" foods in many different ways. Corn, for example, acquired dual meanings. It was a traditional food related to preconquest history as well as a revolutionary food that represented national self-sufficiency in times of counterrevolutionary aggression. For the Sandinistas, corn linked the precolonial past with their political revolution in the late twentieth century. As the opening vignette shows, FSLN politicians well into the early twenty-first century continued to make connections to Nicaragua's pre-Hispanic food practices. However, the Ortega government's food policy was far less radical than the Sandinista policy of the early 1980s.

After the Sandinistas lost the 1990 elections, Nicaragua was governed by a broad oppositional alliance—the Unión Nacional Opositora (UNO), the National Opposition Union, and two subsequent Liberal Party presidents until 2006. At that time, Daniel Ortega Saavedra, the former coordinator of the revolutionary government junta in the 1980s, was reelected, and he has governed the country ever since. The FSLN, however, had changed significantly in the meantime. For over a decade it has promoted an ambiguous form of Christian socialism and has abandoned earlier Sandinista ideals such as a redistributive policy and anti-imperialism. At the same time, the government limited electoral democracy and changed the constitution's prohibition on a president's reelection, which has enabled Daniel Ortega to continue in the presidency after his original term would have ended in 2011. Both political opponents and international observers accused the government of electoral manipulations at the local and national levels. Nevertheless, the government won over supporters through its social policy directed toward poor Nicaraguans. Backed by Venezuelan economic support, the FSLN promoted social reforms in health, education, and agriculture that benefited its followers and reduced poverty. In 2017 Nicaragua was the country with the third highest economic growth rate in Latin America.[4]

Nevertheless, recent statistics and oppositional press reports indicate an increasing number of undernourished people.[5] The deep economic crisis in Venezuela from 2013 onward has weakened the Ortega government and affected Nicaragua's economy. In its last report on global food security, the Food and Agriculture Organization (FAO) diagnosed a food crisis in Nicaragua for 2018.[6] It is very likely that the nutritional situation has worsened between 2016 and 2019 although the Ortega government has not published any recent information.

In April 2018 a broad protest movement challenged the Ortega government. At first, people protested against a reform of the pension system. In response to the violent repression of these protests, Nicaraguans organized further marches, occupied university buildings, and blocked important roads throughout the country. Protesters mobilized with the slogan "Ortega y Somoza son la misma cosa" (Ortega and Somoza are the same thing) for mass demonstrations in April and May 2018. State and partisan violence against these protests claimed more than 320 lives by early 2020, and 96,000 Nicaraguans have left the country.[7] Although the regime had stabilized once again by July 2018, it has been unable to silence the protesters completely. At the time of writing (late 2019), the political future of Nicaragua remains highly uncertain.

The Ortega government still faces opposition, along with the increasing challenge of supplying Nicaraguans with enough food. In 2018 the economy shrank by 3.8 percent, and unemployment was on the rise. In addition, a drought seriously affected food production in the Central and Pacific lowlands, also known as the dry corridor.[8] These economic and political conditions provide a striking parallel with the final stages of the Somoza dictatorship in the 1970s. For almost fifty years Nicaraguan political leaders have struggled to ensure a stable food supply despite natural disasters, adverse economic conditions, and unequal land distribution.

The focus in this book is on the overlooked story of how food and its scarcity shaped contemporary Nicaraguan history between the 1950s and 1993. Insufficient access to food contributed to both the rise and the demise of the Sandinista revolution. The dictatorship of the Somoza clan (1936–1979) promoted agro exports, which accelerated land conflicts and affected basic grains production. Contrary to other historical accounts that depict the 1972 earthquake as the decisive moment for the weakening of the Somoza regime, in this account I argue that the dictatorship was already weakened by the crisis of the Nicaraguan food system during the early 1970s. From then on, tensions over food prices contributed to the erosion of the dictatorship. After the 1972 earthquake, massive aid misappropriations demonstrated the fraudulent character of the regime, and although it weathered the storm, its power was seriously undermined. Despite increasing social tensions, the regime continued to promote US culture including food practices although most imported foods were an option only for small minorities within Nicaraguan society.

The success of the 1979 Sandinista revolution generated enormous hope for social change. To make food accessible for all Nicaraguans, the revolutionaries introduced a new distribution system. They supported basic grains production and promoted corn as a revolutionary grain. Corn represented an ideal revolutionary food because it established historical continuity between the country's Mesoamerican past, a past free from colonial rule, and the 1979 revolution liberating Nicaragua from US imperialism. The Sandinistas chose corn as the emblematic local grain for their food campaigns based on its strong presence in Nicaraguan literature, music, and art. At the same time, they attempted to steer Nicaraguans away from mass consumption by promoting austere and frugal consumption practices that favored local products. By the 1980s food policy and consumption were intrinsically linked, as the promotion of self-sufficiency required changes in daily personal consumption. Although Sandinista political propaganda insisted on giving priority to locally produced food, consumers did not change their habits as fast as the government wanted. They continued to demand wheat, powdered milk, maggi soups, Gerber baby foods, and breakfast cereals. All of these foods were imported and, except for wheat, produced by foreign multinational companies.

From the early years of the revolution, external aggression by the United States accelerated the need for self-sufficiency measures. However, the Contra War soon undermined efforts to increase local food production. By 1984 Nicaragua had converted into a "shortage economy" affected by the chronic lack of food and consumer goods. At the same time the Sandinistas failed to adequately address specific regional needs and thus failed to convince large sectors of the Nicaraguan peasantry to follow the new strategy. Disappointed by low prices for basic grains and slow agrarian reform, peasants increasingly joined the Contras.[9]

As a result of the war, the US trade embargo, and Sandinista economic policy, the Nicaraguan economy entered a serious crisis in 1985 from which it never fully recovered. People struggled to provide three daily meals for their families. Malnutrition and the scarcity of basic foods were widespread. By 1988 people were exhausted; they wanted an end to the war and increasingly lost faith in the revolutionary project. Ordinary Nicaraguans were forced to reduce their consumption to the bare minimum, but some Sandinista leaders displayed luxury goods in public, which was another important cause of disillusionment.

Contemporary observers were surprised when the FSLN lost the 1990s elections to the oppositional candidate Violeta Chamorro. The new government reestablished close relations with the United States. The US Agency for International Development (USAID) reappeared on the scene and provided conditional support for a neoliberal restructuring of the economy. Simultaneously, a large influx of expensive consumer goods and cheap imported food started in the early 1990s generating debates about globalization. Although consumer credit was reintroduced, expensive products such as large refrigerators, color TVs, and premium liquor brands remained inaccessible for most Nicaraguans. During the early 1990s, many Nicaraguans survived on limited diets only alleviated by international food aid and remittances from emigrated family members.

REVALUING NICARAGUAN CONTEMPORARY HISTORY

Researchers and intellectuals have struggled over historical caesura and elements of continuity in recent Nicaraguan history. At first they identified the revolution as an event that interrupted the long tradition of dictatorial rule and US dominance over the country.[10] As I argue, a rupture also occurred in food supply and consumption. The Sandinistas conceived of Nicaragua as a self-sufficient country and prioritized the consumption of local foods.

Scholarly works on Nicaragua experienced a boom with the Sandinista revolution. In the early 1980s Nicaragua was at the center of global attention. Thousands of solidarity activists traveled to the country along with international experts interested in the revolution's social projects. The revolution attracted historians, political scientists, and economists who analyzed the revolutionary changes. This first generation of researchers reported on the FSLN, mass organizations, media, gender relations, economic organization, agrarian reform, and culture. Many works focused on Pacific Nicaragua, and anthropologists and historians discussed the situation at the Caribbean Coast separately. In particular, the works on the Contra War show evidence of the Cold War political polarization. Testimonies published during the 1980s highlighted the heroic fight for the revolution's survival but remained silent on political doubts, fatigue, or disillusionment.[11] When the revolution experienced a serious crisis in the late 1980s, international interest faded, only to experience a short revival after the Sandinista's historic electoral defeat.

The electoral loss in 1990 provoked a new wave of disagreements about the revolution and the reasons for its downfall. The struggle over the revolution was a struggle over memories, accelerated by political divisions within the FSLN. After 1990 several former FSLN leaders published their autobiographies. Given the incomplete holdings of the Nicaraguan state archives, these publications have become an important source for historical research. In addition, researchers have collected testimonies from groups whose memories remained at the margins, such as Contra members, peasants at the agrarian frontier, and middle- and low-rank Sandinista supporters.[12] The testimonies of a heroic revolutionary struggle gave way to new, more ambivalent memories. With increasing temporal distance and the growing authoritarianism of the Ortega government, issues came to light that were unutterable in the 1980s, among them accounts of abuses committed by the Sandinista police and army, the corruption and authoritarian behavior of the FSLN leaders, and ongoing food scarcity as well as gender inequalities.

The authoritarian tendencies of the Ortega government after 2007 have led to more critical evaluations of revolutionary history.[13] Again, the debate on continuities and caesura in contemporary Nicaraguan history broke out. Some scholars have pointed out that social organizing after 1979 has provided an important foundation for community participation and social movements up to the present. Others have highlighted enduring trends such as the concentration of wealth and power, informal political agreements, and strict control over police, army, and public administration throughout the last century of Nicaraguan history.[14] The political struggle over the revolution's heritage is still ongoing, but recent historical works have moved on to other areas such as the health sector, foreign policy, and the solidarity movement.[15]

I argue that social and economic history are important for explaining political changes. We need more studies that follow up on the research from the 1980s. This means analyzing, for example, long-term economic transformations and the history of enterprise, labor movements, the social basis of the FSLN, and corruption.[16] My analysis of food policies shows that the revolutionaries were unsuccessful in finding a balance between the needs of urban consumers and those of rural Nicaraguans, between industrial agriculture and small farmer production, and between agro exports and basic grains cultivation. The historian Hilary Francis has recently argued that the Sandinistas failed to take into account Nicaraguan diversity in terms of sexuality and peasants' desires.[17] This is also true for the area of food. By ignoring the special needs of people in the Caribbean and rural communities, state food distribution alienated these sectors from the revolution.

Until now historians have mainly situated the Nicaraguan revolution within the contexts of US dominance and the Cold War. In this book I argue for including other foreign actors into Nicaragua's revolutionary history—namely, relief agencies, European development assistance, and international organizations. It was their staff, together with Nicaraguan actors, that negotiated and implemented food policy in the field, far away from headquarters where new strategies for global food problems had been designed.

Traditionally, historians have analyzed the revolution's history using categories such as mass organizations, the state sector, students, peasants, and elites. The consumer as a category and a political figure has been absent in scholarly analyses, but here I introduce the consumer as a social identity to be used in food struggles, as an ascription that became increasingly important in supply politics, and as an important historical actor. Distribution rules, as well as the food offered and its quality, frequently clashed with consumers' desires. Faced with adverse conditions Nicaraguans carved out in-between spaces to defend their food choices. By doing so, they creatively incorporated new ingredients and found alternative solutions for scarce products.

How did competing visions of consumption as well as the scarcity of certain food products contribute to the demise of the revolution? Broad definitions of consumption and consumer cultures are necessary for such an analysis. In this sense, consumption includes related rituals, emotions, discourses, and sociability. In anthropological research the emphasis has been on the symbolic dimension of consumer goods, as people use them to spread messages about their social status and lifestyle.[18] The same is true for food items: the ingredients of meals and the choice of dishes reveal information about wealth and social aspirations. To understand how food cultures changed, sometimes based on local creativity and sometimes based on global nutrition transitions, we need to apply transcultural approaches.

The stories of Nicaraguan food consumption resist easy categorizations, such as the homogenization of consumer habits through globalization. Books such as *The McDonaldization of Society* have strongly promoted this perspective, which is still present in contemporary debates.[19] In Nicaragua, fast food ascended in the 1950s but was first promoted by the local enterprise Pollo Tip Top, which adapted US trends to Nicaraguan consumption patterns. At the same time, local fast food sold at the street *fritangas* dominated urban public spaces.

Food insecurity, migration, and food aid also inspired Nicaraguans to design new recipes or to try different combinations of ingredients. For example, they invented dishes such as potato pizza with chicken, soy cookies, and hamburgers with corn tortillas in place of wheat bread. In many cases, scarcity jolted creativity into motion—or as one interviewee expressed it, "in times of crisis, creativity keeps us afloat."[20] Historians and anthropologists have made a strong case for a more nuanced analysis that would take into account the large corpus of theoretical works on cultural change. Alluding to the concepts of hybridity, creolization, and transculturality, these scholars depict changes in food habits as a continuous process of negotiation.[21] Reactions vary to standardized global food such as the processed food distributed by multinational firms or food aid rations: some people resist its introduction while others integrate it into the preparation of traditional dishes or they invent brand new recipes. In this sense, the anthropologist Richard Wilk has argued that globalization actually produces local culture such as the emergence in an improvised way of new styles of food, music, and clothing. Hence, essentialism of local food cultures has to be avoided. Transcultural approaches emphasize the ways in which cultural exchange creates new dishes and cooking styles.[22] Although some transcultural theorists have generated the impression that in a globalized world everything was available to everybody, this was certainly not the case, as power asymmetries persisted.[23]

During severe food crises in Nicaragua, however, creativity reached its limits. People survived on monotonous diets of tortillas, beans, reptiles, or bananas. This happened, for example, when people lost land during the agro-export boom of the 1950s, after the 1972 earthquake, during the Contra War, and in rural communities in Northern Nicaragua in the early 1990s. The micro level of daily consumption was situated in a wider structure of power relations that limited consumers' options. In his reflections on food and power, anthropologist Sidney Mintz distinguishes between an inner and an outer sphere of consumption. The "inner sphere" of daily consumption routines was surrounded by the "outer sphere" of economic, social, and political conditions that set limits to consumers' decisions through working hours, purchasing power, or war. For example, on plantations or in institutional feeding, food was introduced by force. Depending on the geographical location and the work regulations of a plantation, workers had no choice in terms of their food rations and the products offered at the plantation store. Inmates had to accept the food served in prisons or hospitals.[24]

The plantation economy radically changed Caribbean economies and food cultures. The presence of slaves, Chinese migrants, and foreign merchants also influenced local food cultures. The Caribbean has been an important cultural contact zone where people invented new technologies and songs as well as new patterns of social and economic organization.

Consequently, it was also a zone of significant culinary exchanges that has inspired research on global food cultures.[25]

The Nicaraguan Caribbean should be included in ongoing historical scholarship. It occupies more than 50 percent of national territory but has remained for long periods at the margins of the mestizo nation.[26] Its separate history of colonization and its ethnic heterogeneity have characterized the region until today. Consequently, the stronger state presence in the region since the 1960s met with resistance from the indigenous and Creole communities. People perceived mestizo state representatives as outsiders attempting to implement projects designed in Pacific Nicaragua. Unlike in the rest of the country, tensions over land or food prices did not develop into broader social protests. As a result, the Sandinistas never built up a strong basis of support at the Coast, and they ignored regional particularities. People here viewed state intervention in the food supply more critically than in the rest of the country.

Culinary culture at the Caribbean Coast also differs profoundly from that in Central Nicaragua in terms of consumption habits. While mestizo Nicaraguan nutrition is based on maize, beans, and rice as basic staples, food cultures at the Atlantic Coast integrated roots, tubers, spices, and seafood from the wider Caribbean region. While Central Nicaraguan culinary habits affected Coast regions between the 1960s and the 1990s, the influence of Caribbean food on Central Nicaragua remained limited.

Contrary to Mexican or Peruvian food, Nicaraguan cuisine has never received large global attention. Instead, it was the political turmoil that suddenly captured the world's attention. The story of a corrupt and aged dictator challenged by young guerrilleros in olive uniforms quickly circulated around the globe in the late 1970s.

FOOD AND COLD WAR IN GLOBAL SOUTH COUNTRIES

Nicaragua represents the many small countries with dependent economies in the Global South that experienced regime changes and became Cold War flash points in the twentieth century. Food and consumption had a strong Cold War dimension. Both superpowers were eager to show that their political model was superior, and in this competition, access to consumer goods became an important indicator.[27] In Latin America, Cold War tensions intensified after the United States supported a coup against a left-wing government in Guatemala in 1954 and after the Cuban Revolution of 1959. Since then, the US government has tried hard to prevent radical groups from gaining support in Nicaragua and other Central American countries.[28] The distribution of food aid was one means by which the United States tried to stifle political radicalization and ensure stability.

During the early years of the Cold War, many Global South countries struggled to supply their growing urban population with sufficient food and to overcome dependency on a few export commodities. High-yielding seeds seemed to offer a way out but also bore the risk of dependency on foreign seed and fertilizer companies. Since the 1950s a paradoxical coexistence of food aid, demands for self-sufficiency, and the spread of Green Revolution technologies has emerged in numerous Global South countries. During the 1950s and 1960s, for many African and Asian countries, the early Cold War years overlapped with decolonization. New political leaders took over the government in the postcolonial nations while developing a common identity as "Third World" countries. Political independence was linked to economic independence and the control of food resources.[29]

In Latin America the situation was different. Most countries—among them Nicaragua—had already become independent during the early nineteenth century. Hence, debates over self-sufficiency in Latin America revolved around economic independence. Leading theorists of dependency theory argued that Latin American economies needed to break with the colonial legacy of agro-export dependency. Since the 1950s the Comisión Económica para América Latina y el Caribe (CEPAL), the UN economic commission for Latin America, promoted import-substituting industrialization within the framework of dependency theory. By building up the local production of cars, household appliances, and cement, Latin American nations would avoid further imports and promote economic development with less dependence on agro exports. For example, in Argentina and Venezuela politicians promoted self-sufficiency as an important goal of economic policy. For these countries with strong industries and a large internal market, this was far easier than for small economies that were more dependent on agro exports such as Nicaragua.

During the post–Second World War years, a focus on self-sufficiency has coincided in many countries with increased dependence on international food aid. From early on, food aid was intrinsically linked to Cold War conflicts; thus, it converted into a strong instrument of foreign policy. The 1966 US Food for Peace Act declared food aid an instrument of development aid, and it allowed the inclusion of other commodities beyond surplus production. In the course of the 1960s, Asian countries became the main recipients of US food aid while Latin America also gained ground.[30]

Food aid in Central America began with milk distribution. With the foundation of the UN International Children's Emergency Fund (UNICEF) in 1946, a new actor appeared on the global scene that strongly engaged in school milk programs on multiple continents. In Central America from the 1950s onward, FAO and UNICEF advocated on behalf of milk powder.[31] Food aid expanded throughout the 1970s but escalated in the 1980s when the region became a prime location for Cold War conflicts. Researchers during the 1980s focused mainly on the political implications of US food aid.[32] Consumption habits received less attention. I argue that the impact of food aid on consumption habits should be researched as food aid was a powerful force in changing global consumer preferences.

As part of its Cold War efforts to expand its influence, the United States exported high-yielding modern agricultural techniques to Global South countries, including Nicaragua. In what was eventually known as the Green Revolution, US scientists had been working on the development of high-yielding seeds and plants since the nineteenth century. The breakthrough occurred in the 1940s when the North American biologist Norman Borlaug bred high-yielding and disease-resistant wheat varieties. In Nicaragua the use of Green Revolution seeds expanded under the Somoza regime and was supported by US aid. This is in line with historian Nick Cullathers's understanding of the Green Revolution as a combined US development effort in the 1950s and 1960s. The aim was to guarantee the supply of food for the world's growing population and to contribute to stable nation-building and the modernization of the peasantry. Green Revolution methods required large investments for seeds, irrigation technology, and fertilizers, thus favoring large producers over individual peasants. In Nicaragua, as elsewhere in Latin America, the Green Revolution strongly benefited large landholders. It fostered the agro-export sector, contributing to the enrichment of the business elites. President Anastasio Somoza Debayle proudly referred in his speeches to high-yielding seeds and the application of fertilizers, although these supplies had been financed to a high degree by Alliance for Progress money.[33]

The application of Green Revolution strategies varied in different places and time periods with ups and downs according to donor strategies, available resources, and public debates on hunger. The Green Revolution reached its global height in the 1970s. After growing criticism of its ecological consequences, however, international donors' support for Green Revolution projects declined during the 1980s. In Nicaragua, part of the Sandinista leadership promoted an agricultural strategy influenced by Green Revolution premises: large-scale production relying on agricultural supplies and technology. The Cold War dimension of development aid became visible again as Eastern bloc aid supported many of these large agricultural projects.

External financial aid and development assistance were important for the survival of the revolution between 1979 and 1989. The Sandinista revolutionaries were successful in attracting support from external donors for many of the government's social projects. Diverse donors, such as Western European countries, international organizations, Latin American nations, and the Eastern bloc contributed to health, education, and agriculture projects. After the 1985 US trade embargo, development aid also provided the resources for importing basic goods that had become scarce in Nicaragua.

Especially in the early period of the revolution, agency was not exclusively in the hands of the external donors, as some authors of development literature have suggested.[34] The Sandinistas used international conferences as a forum to launch political initiatives. They also organized international meetings in Nicaragua and capitalized on the presence of foreign delegates and international donors for their political campaigns. With the looming economic crisis, however, the Sandinista project depended even more on external support, which required adapting to the agendas of political leaders from both Cold War blocs as well as different international organizations and NGOs. Although publicly rallying for autonomy, in fact the Sandinistas pursued a policy of diversified dependency. As I argue in this book, Sandinista food policy combined both idealism and pragmatism. Sandinista politicians successfully promoted self-sufficiency as an important strategy in the fight against hunger in the Global South. At the same time, however, they were aware that Nicaragua's economic situation made it impossible for them to reach self-sufficiency within a short time. The pragmatic way out was to support both agro exports and the cultivation of basic grains and to acquire as much external funding as possible. Throughout the 1980s, statistics on deficiencies in caloric consumption were used to support arguments for international food aid.

FROM THE INVENTION OF THE CALORIE TO GLOBAL FOOD SECURITY

The late nineteenth-century discovery of the calorie has shaped global evaluations of the nutritional situation until today. Historical research has revealed that the calorie was converted into a powerful political tool during the first half of the twentieth century. After its discovery in the United States in 1896, the unit of measure soon became an instrument for defining living standards, minimum wages, and food rations. The calorie prompted the first "scientific" comparisons between the diets of different social groups and countries. Measuring calories formed part of a general trend to map the world by numbers and statistical charts.[35]

Consequently, food policy relied on consumption surveys, tables with the caloric value of different foods, and dietary recommendations—a trend reinforced by the discovery of vitamins. Hence, some governments incorporated special ministries of food, which became a playground for nutritional scientists. In other cases, such as Nicaragua, the government created special institutions for nutrition in response to pressure from international actors. Scientists, doctors, nutritionists, and health planners constructed dietary ideals throughout the twentieth century. Although scientific publications promoted the new requirements for good nutrition as objective truth, they actually reflected middle-class experts' contemporary ideals.[36]

Latin American governments had become aware of nutrition problems beginning in the 1930s. Several countries established national nutrition councils, as governments were concerned about high child mortality levels and workers' low living standards. The initiatives mainly came from larger Latin American countries with reform-oriented governments such as Chile, Peru, or Uruguay.[37] In Central America similar concerns arose later as authoritarian regimes dominated the 1930s political scene. There, the Guatemalan reform government of Juan José Arévalo (1945–1951) finally launched an initiative for a regional nutrition institute, the Instituto de Nutricion de Centroamérica y Panama (INCAP), the Institute of Nutrition of Central America and Panama. Founded in 1949, its four main tasks were: (1) to elaborate a diagnosis of the regional nutrition situation, (2) to conduct research to find solutions for local nutrition problems, (3) to act as an advisor to regional governments, and (4) to facilitate the education of Central American experts. INCAP initiated the first scientific nutrition survey in Nicaragua in the 1950s, followed by a large Central American study in the 1960s.

Scientists, intellectuals, and politicians evaluated Nicaraguan food in new and sometimes contradictory ways between the 1950s and the 1980s. Scientists expressed their concerns in accounts of deficiencies of protein, calories, and nutrients while intellectuals praised emblematic dishes, special flavors, and historical tradition. After the revolution, the government no longer ignored malnutrition and introduced a political evaluation of Nicaraguan diets. Sandinista leaders promoted affordable prices and locally produced basic grains. All of these actors inscribed their moral values on new dietary ideals.

Anthropological researchers have questioned whether hunger is a clearly definable state and instead suggest understanding it as an unstable phenomenon that can be expressed in many different forms.[38] However, quantifiable definitions are still attractive as they nurture the illusion that technical solutions can resolve the problems. As historical source for analyzing nutrition habits, however, statistical data poses two challenges. One is the general concern as to whether numbers can describe hunger, malnutrition, and consumption in an adequate way. One of the main global actors for distributing a quantitative approach to hunger and elaborating global mappings is the Food and Agriculture Organization. Until very recently, the categorization of a country as "food insecure" depended on average caloric intakes alone.

During the 1970s, international actors introduced the concept of food security to the debates on malnutrition, but in Nicaragua the concept did not influence food politics before the 1979 revolution. FAO was one of the main actors diffusing the concept of food security on a global scale. In the early 1970s, the World Food Crisis had brought the subject of hunger back to the global political agenda. In 1974, the FAO convened the World Food Conference in Rome to open a forum for debate on food problems. One important outcome was the rise of the concept of food security in global politics.[39] As the Sandinista government cooperated closely with the FAO in the early 1980s, food security became a part of Nicaraguan policy. In 1987 the Nicaraguan constitution included food security—in the form of a state guarantee for adequate availability and equitable distribution of food—as a political right for all Nicaraguans.[40] In internal political debates, however, the concept of self-sufficiency remained more significant.

THE HISTORICAL STATISTICS, SOURCES, AND THE STRUCTURE OF THIS BOOK

Statistics inform us about large trends in food production and consumption, but the numbers fail to capture heterogeneous local realities, flavors, plant varieties, and people's perceptions of the nutritional situation. Statistics do not differentiate between bean varieties, for example. For Nicaraguan consumers, however, there was an important distinction between cooking with local red beans or being forced to use imported beans that they strongly disliked. Statistics were also designed for Central Nicaraguan consumption habits and did not include Caribbean staples. Thus, statistical averages often hide regional disparities as well as inequalities in inter-household food distribution.

The lack of resources and qualified personnel as well as the occurrence of natural disasters also pose significant challenges to reliable statistical data for Nicaragua.[41] For researchers in the past and the present, this situation constitutes a dilemma as the data is in many cases incomplete and contradictory. As it was beyond my aims and capacities to engage with an intense documentation of all statistical data, I finally made the decision to work mainly with FAO statistics as they were available for the whole research period.[42]

The source material for this book draws on a large variety of archival sources that I collected both inside and outside of Nicaragua. At the time of my research in Nicaragua, documents on Nicaraguan food policy after 1979 were unavailable in the state archives, which prevented my analysis of internal government correspondence on the matter of food policy and supply issues.[43] I followed two strategies to compensate for this deficiency. First, I consulted the archives of actors engaged in projects to support Nicaraguan food policy, such as the FAO, the Cooperative for Assistance and Relief Everywhere (CARE), and German and Swiss development assistance archives. Second, I focused on grey literature and press coverage to shed light on government campaigns, political priorities, and institutional settings.

In the book I have followed a chronological structure to examine how food and consumption shaped Nicaraguan history from the 1950s to the early 1990s. The six chronological chapters are followed by a separate chapter on the Nicaraguan Caribbean, in which I examine the region's unique history and local opposition to Sandinista food policy. In the epilogue I discuss how the Nicaraguan revolution contributed to the recognition that food security is a basic right and the rise of peasant movements for food sovereignty.

In the first chapter, on the Somoza dictatorship, I argue that urbanization and the agro-export economy challenged the production, distribution, and consumption of food in Nicaragua beginning in the 1950s. Corn, rice, and beans were basic staples of the Nicaraguan diet, combined in many ways in traditional dishes and daily cooking. When it was moved to marginal and less fertile soils, basic grains production became insufficient to feed the growing urban population. Because of their work obligations, urban Nicaraguans consumed more processed foods and street food in order to save time. High food prices created social tensions within Nicaraguan society. These were temporarily alleviated by US economic aid in the 1960s. In the late 1960s, however, the United States lost interest in the Alliance for Progress, and the world food supply entered a crisis. Both of these factors significantly affected Nicaragua.

Beginning in the 1960s, nutritionists and doctors perceived that malnutrition was a serious health problem and a threat to national development. The focus of the first nutritional surveys was on quantitative evaluations of the Nicaraguan diet in calories, vitamins, and micronutrients. This language challenged the intellectual discourse of a rich and varied Nicaraguan cuisine. It also ignored people's creativity in providing simple foods with flavor in times of scarcity. The hospitals filled with patients suffering from malnutrition, but politicians paid no attention to the problem. Foreign actors intervened through food aid, basic grains production projects, and nutrition education. The nutritional surveys demonstrated, however, a stagnation of the nutrition situation. More than 50 percent of Nicaraguan children suffered from malnutrition; average caloric intakes varied between 1,800 and 2,100 kilocalories.

Access to food became a key problem in 1970s Nicaragua, as demonstrated in Chapter Two. International actors used the first nutrition surveys to demand measures from the Somoza regime to improve the nutritional situation. Although the government had introduced some nutritional institutions around 1965 because of this international pressure, politicians continued unwilling to take food policy seriously. They mainly used the efforts of international organizations and NGOs as examples of the regime's successful governance. Between 1965 and 1970, food donations increased and temporarily eased the pressure on the Nicaraguan food system. At the same time, food aid strengthened the consumption of imported grains, thus increasing foreign dependence. Rising food prices in the early 1970s provoked social protests and controversies over the agro-export focus in Nicaraguan society.

During these controversies, the popular consumer with rights became an important social category. The repression of social protests further radicalized urban and rural people. During the severe food crisis after the 1972 earthquake, the regime misappropriated foreign aid and consequently lost support among elites and the middle class. The 1972 earthquake also increased already existing social gaps. During post-disaster reconstruction, Managua became a more divided city. Advertisements for imported goods invaded newspapers and public spaces, but for most Nicaraguans these products remained unaffordable. While the regime publicly celebrated luxury dinners, ordinary people lacked access to food. This increasing chasm between rich and poor strengthened the position of the revolutionaries.

In Chapter Three the focus is on how, between 1979 and 1982, the Sandinistas combined idealism and pragmatism to improve food distribution, strengthen basic grains production, and promote local foods. They envisioned Nicaragua as a self-sufficient revolutionary country but were aware of economic dependency on agro exports and hence established alliances with large-scale private producers and foreign development aid. The Sandinistas' willingness to take food policy seriously inspired support from a wide range of actors, among them international organizations, food activists, and diplomats. The initiative to request foreign support came in all cases from the Sandinistas. Food was part of their public diplomacy campaign for revolutionary Nicaragua, especially after US president Ronald Reagan canceled the loans for wheat imports in early 1981.

The Sandinistas implemented fundamental reforms in a short time, but they also faced enormous challenges. The Somoza regime had left a difficult heritage of high debts and an economy oriented toward agro exports. A major dilemma was the need to rely on export production for financial reasons while politically wanting to support basic grains production. In the case of land redistribution, the revolutionaries did not fulfill the peasants' hopes for individual access to land, which became a serious problem later on. The inefficiency of large state farms affected the availability of milk and meat. Finally, the food program was split between different ministries and government institutions, which weakened its impact. Hence, although ordinary Nicaraguans' access to food improved, they still experienced uncertainties because of speculation and the temporary unavailability of certain foods.

In Chapter Four we follow the Sandinista campaigns for self-sufficiency that went hand in hand with increasing US aggression. Self-sufficiency required Nicaraguans to switch to locally produced foods and consume less imported products. Hence, the revolutionaries gave new political meanings to food and consumption. The consumer was an important figure in these campaigns: he or she was a frugal, disciplined individual who subordinated personal desire to revolutionary survival. At the same time, ordinary Nicaraguans used the figure of a consumer with rights—already present in 1970s social movements—to frame their demands for an improved food supply.

From 1982 onward, natural disasters and the Contra War significantly affected the already limited food supply. The Sandinistas strengthened rationing, introduced supply priorities, and increased revolutionary vigilance. Rationing and food speculation increased tensions among different social groups and regions within Nicaraguan society. People had to invest more time in acquiring sufficient food and to revive traditional survival methods. At the same time, an enormous gap in the food supply between rural and urban areas persisted, which further alienated rural people from the revolution. In failing to address women's double burden and to campaign for an equal distribution of household work, the Sandinistas missed out on a chance to transform gender relations in Nicaragua more profoundly. Overall, the Sandinista campaigns prompted mixed responses, as they failed to take into account regional and social diversity as well as gender inequalities. The government also failed to fully understand people's food priorities and desires, which limited the success of its campaigns.

Chapter Five is a chronicle of the growing disillusionment in the years 1985 and 1986 when the economic crisis worsened and the Contra War began to seriously affect the national food supply. During this period Nicaragua became more dependent on external aid and food donations. The US economic blockade had shrunk economic possibilities to a minimum. At first the strategy for diversified dependency once again proved successful, and the Sandinistas rapidly procured donations and established new commercial links. However, the general supply situation remained difficult, speculation continued, and wages lost purchasing power because of accelerating inflation. As a result, the Sandinistas established their first economic adjustment package, which among other things, devalued the currency, reduced the budget for social projects, and eliminated food subsidies. In the end, these reforms did not alleviate the crisis.

Also, the government's relationship to the peasants remained contradictory, as an important part of the Sandinista leadership favored large-scale food production based on Green Revolution technologies. During the economic crisis, the gap increased between their ambitious visions and actual local realities. The improvement in land distribution in 1986 came too late for many peasants who by this time had started supporting the Contras. From 1985 onward the Sandinista policy turned ever more into crisis management, which disillusioned both Nicaraguans and external advisers.

In Chapter Six, I explain how the 1988 adjustment programs also alienated Sandinista allies from the revolutionary project. Scarcity, hyperinflation, and a natural disaster culminated in an overall crisis. Critical voices became louder although they seldomly resulted in open protests. Despite widespread scarcity, some Sandinista leaders displayed luxury consumption in public. Consequently, they lost credibility when calling for personal austerity and revolutionary discipline. The transition back to a capitalist market economy began with the 1988 economic reforms. Severe budget cuts and the dismissal of state employees as well as the strengthening of market mechanisms in food distribution put an end to the vision of a self-sufficient Nicaragua with democratic access to food resources. During transition Nicaraguans suffered increasingly from hunger, especially in the northern rural regions, and the Sandinistas did not recognize this publicly until after the elections. All of these factors contributed to their electoral defeat in 1990.

During the whole transition period from 1988 to 1993, food policy deteriorated into crisis management. The governments handled emergency aid but lacked the capacity for any ambitious reform projects. The new UNO government neglected food policy and put off international donors with its lack of interest. Despite significant international aid the situation did not improve for ordinary Nicaraguans, who suffered from price shock and malnutrition. The new political and economic elites promoted US consumer ideals as a model and fostered the foundation of shopping centers as well as the granting of loans. Once again, controversies about consumption and US influences broke out in Nicaraguan society. At the same time, nutritional campaigns lost political militancy. They promoted local food as healthier and cheaper and assigned individual responsibility to people for improving their dietary choices.

In Chapter Seven, I argue that Caribbean people rejected Sandinista food policy to a much greater degree than Pacific Nicaraguans did. Long-term residents, new settlers, and local indigenous communities reacted negatively to state intervention in the Coast's food supply. Food prices increased at the Coast more than anywhere else in Nicaragua because of inadequate transport infrastructure and broken international trade relations, and this prompted more negative feelings. In addition, the Contra War seriously affected local food production. Moreover, the Sandinistas did not take local culinary habits into account until negotiations on regional autonomy started.

The Coast's negative reactions to the revolution have deep historical roots. The Caribbean has a different history of colonization than Central Nicaragua. In addition, it is a region with a very heterogeneous population. British and Caribbean cultural influences dominated local power relations until the nineteenth century. The booming plantation economy and lumber industry attracted numerous US firms to the region, which led to a broad availability of imported goods from the late nineteenth to the mid-twentieth century, a period that local people still remembered with nostalgia during the 1980s. From the 1960s onward, settlers from Central Nicaragua influenced local food production and consumption. By contrast, Pacific people only seldom incorporated Caribbean dishes into their diet. The autonomy process strengthened the documentation of local recipes and gave new value to Caribbean food culture. Nevertheless, wood and seafood extraction has remained a challenge for the local food system across the different political regimes.

In the epilogue, I show that the Sandinista revolution left an ambivalent legacy for future food policy. After food security was established in the constitution under the Sandinistas in 1987, it was easier to establish a food sovereignty law. More important, the revolution had empowered peasants to mobilize for their own concerns and organize a peasant-to-peasant education network. These peasant networks, connected throughout Central America, contributed to the rise of the global peasant network called La Vía Campesina, which promoted the concept of food sovereignty at a global scale. This concept took up important elements of Sandinista food policy, such as the preference for local production and agrarian reform. However, the concept also advanced beyond the limitations of Sandinista food policy in promoting peasants' autonomy and control over seeds and water.

The Nicaraguan food sovereignty law that was approved on June 18, 2009, includes some of these elements of food sovereignty but was deradicalized by FAO and the new Ortega government. Since the 1980s FAO has established close links with government officials in promoting a food

security policy. Part of the Sandinista leadership had favored industrial agriculture in the 1980s, and some of these leaders went on to shape food
policy in the early twenty-first century, which facilitated cooperation with
FAO. Despite the new food sovereignty law and the Zero Hunger program
established in 2007, many challenges to food security continue, including
access to land, high food prices, and ecological problems related to soil
degradation and natural disasters as well as resource extraction at the Caribbean Coast.

CHAPTER ONE

GROWING TENSIONS

THE AGRO-EXPORT ECONOMY, FOOD CULTURE, AND NUTRITION SURVEYS, 1950–1965

In 1952 Nicaraguan doctors traveled to Ciudad Darío in Matagalpa department to investigate an outbreak of night blindness, an illness caused by vitamin A deficiency. Local peasants had been surviving for months on a diet limited to tortillas, coffee, and beans. Hesitantly they admitted that they had even substituted maize with millet for tortilla production, which aggravated the situation. In particular, peasants who had lost land because of the expansion of agro exports were struggling for survival. Once newspapers reported on the case, the Somoza regime denounced the accusations as a political maneuver. In a situation where Nicaragua proudly presented high economic growth rates to international funding institutions, the regime feared any negative publicity and was unwilling to hear the experts' critical statements. Nonetheless, the reports put the drama of rural malnutrition on the political agenda. Shortly afterward, an INCAP technician made a survey of the region and diagnosed acute hunger. By 1960 experts were publicly denouncing malnutrition in Nicaragua. The Nicaraguan doctor Emilio Álvarez Montalván even compared the situation to hunger crises in tsarist Russia and India. By doing so, he indirectly linked the Somoza regime to authoritarian rule and colonialism. The regime, however, still contradicted the experts' reports and maintained that Nicaraguans were well nourished.[1]

This incident reveals two trends: the political establishment's unwillingness to acknowledge the problem of malnutrition and the new authority gained by experts such as doctors and nutritionists to evaluate Nicaragua's food situation. INCAP expert teams in the 1950s traveled to every Central American country and published the first science-driven evaluations of local diets. They expressed these evaluations in the powerful new language of calories, vitamins, and nutrients. According to contemporary nutrition science wisdom, they frequently diagnosed lack of protein as a main problem, but they also emphasized the socioeconomic origins of malnutrition. The struggle between the experts who denounced widespread malnutrition and a political establishment that denied the existence of any problem at all shaped the debates over food in Nicaragua for the next two decades.

Social tensions over the nutritional situation and consumption developed in Nicaragua from the early 1950s to 1965. Culinary change accelerated in this period because of three factors: the agro-export boom, the growth of the middle classes, and urbanization. All of these factors also challenged the prevailing organization of food production and supply. Because of the rapid expansion of the cotton and cattle industries, social conflicts intensified concerning land distribution in the countryside and food prices in urban areas. During the mid-1960s, Nicaragua became the most urban country in Central America with 40 percent of the population living in cities.[2] The fact of living in urban environments changed Nicaraguans' daily diet. In the growing cities, rural migrants from different parts of the country met, integrated new foods into their everyday meals, and participated in a vivid street food culture. By analyzing culinary literature and oral testimonies, I identify important flavors, dishes, and ingredients for Nicaraguans in the second half of the twentieth century. Both Nicaraguan intellectuals and interviewees highlighted culinary creativity; nutrition experts criticized limited diets that lacked micronutrients and protein.

With the first Central American nutrition survey in 1965, experts' findings on malnutrition in Nicaragua reached broader international audiences. The survey demonstrated that children, in particular, suffered severely from malnutrition in the mid-1960s when the food supply was generally insufficient. Nevertheless, the Somoza regime resisted all pressure to give food policy a higher priority. US support in the early years of the Cold War still allowed the Somoza regime to mitigate tensions through food aid. At the same time, the dictatorship repressed peasant protests and political opposition.

As social inequality increased and low-income sectors struggled with high food prices, Nicaraguan elites and members of the middle class embraced US consumption models. Their public display of wealth through imported goods made social gaps in Nicaraguan society more obvious. Their profligate consumption became visible in the late 1950s, in the first supermarkets and fast food restaurants. The high prices impeded the ability of most Nicaraguans to participate in these new establishments, which strengthened feelings of exclusion. Overall, by the mid-1960s social tensions over food were manifested in land conflicts and public criticism of malnutrition from experts and conservative intellectuals, as well as in growing urban support for the FSLN. Nevertheless, economic aid in the framework of the Alliance for Progress still alleviated pressure on the Nicaraguan food system until the late 1960s, which allowed the Somoza regime to maintain its long-term rule.

MECHANISMS OF POWER AND THE INTERNATIONAL CONTEXT, 1940S TO 1960S

The Somoza regime was one of the most long-lasting dictatorships in Latin America. Its rule in Nicaragua started in 1936, when Anastasio Somoza García deposed the elected president, Juan Bautista Sacasa. With a short interruption from 1947 to 1951, Somoza García remained in power until his assassination in 1956. Throughout his rule, he created a system of domination based on various elements. It was strongly focused on the person of the president, who according to the 1939 constitution should "personify the nation."[3] His rule relied on continuous manipulation of the constitution, the political institutions, and the electoral process. The regime based its power on a "pyramid of corruption" that extended throughout Nicaraguan society.[4] Finally, the Somozas employed the National Guard as a repressive force in times of political crisis.[5]

The United States welcomed these developments because of the fear of the rise of left-wing social movements in Latin America. Throughout the 1930s and 1940s the United States intervened frequently in Central American politics and in Nicaragua inserted itself into politics and stationed US Marines in the country from 1912 to 1933. Although US military presence remained limited, a group of Wall Street bankers controlled Nicaraguan public finances. Shortly before retiring from the country, the United States supported the buildup of the Nicaraguan National Guard whose first commander was the later president Anastasio Somoza García.

The US campaign to intern and expropriate "enemy aliens" during the Second World War fostered the self-enrichment of the Somoza clan. Although US–Latin American relations had temporarily improved during the 1930s with the era of the Good Neighbor Policy, the 1940s witnessed renewed US interventions on the continent.[6] During the Second World War, the United States abandoned the principles of the Good Neighbor Policy and intervened in Latin American nations' sovereignty. Overestimating Nazi influence but also interested in eliminating German economic competition, beginning in 1941 the United States pressured Latin American governments to intern and expropriate German, Italian, and Japanese nationals. Once the governments had yielded, local political leaders used the measures for their own interests. Anastasio Somoza García, for example, benefited personally from the expropriation of German coffee plantations.[7] These US wartime interferences in Latin American affairs were a prelude to later Cold War interventions.

Although most of Latin America became more democratic during the 1940s, US interventions strengthened authoritarian rule in some places on the continent. The year 1944 marked a political rupture for Central America when the long-term dictatorships fell in Guatemala and El Salvador.[8] Nicaragua, however, remained an exception. By 1946 it was among the five remaining Latin American countries with authoritarian presidents. Although this overall political trend toward democracy raised hopes for a more egalitarian future throughout Latin America, these hopes were soon shattered. In the postwar period the United States declared the fight against communism as its central mission. It provided military support to those governments promising to fight left-wing organizations. The United States perceived the Somoza regime as a guarantor of regional stability and consequently reinforced its military training as well as economic aid to Nicaragua.

Throughout the 1940s and early 1950s, the United States supported Nicaraguan agriculture and health programs. Following up on sanitary projects executed in Nicaragua during the Second World War, the United States pursued Nicaraguan public health schemes in the postwar period. In the early 1950s US advisers also exerted influence on key political decisions in related Nicaraguan ministries. Between 1953 and 1957, Nicaragua received $8.9 million of nonmilitary aid from the United States, mainly for health, education, and agricultural programs.[9]

The Cuban Revolution in 1959 reinforced US support for anticommunist dictatorships in Latin America, among them the Somozas. After the assassination of Somoza García in 1956, his son Luis Somoza Debayle took over the presidency, but his administration marked no significant change from his father's regime. He continued the brutal suppression of the opposition and engaged in anticommunist activities so as to attract further US economic and military support. This tactic was quite successful as his presidency coincided with the Cuban Revolution and the start of the Alliance for Progress in 1961.

The Cuban Revolution was a watershed for Latin America. The United States redesigned foreign policy for the hemisphere so as to prevent any similar insurrections. It evaluated all governments based on their position regarding Cuba and their repression of left-wing social movements. US officials frequently overestimated communist influence and hence misjudged the political character of these movements. Based on unsubstantiated suspicions the United States intensified support for authoritarian regimes and extended training capacities for Latin American police and military. Simultaneously, the United States launched a huge economic assistance project for the continent—the Alliance for Progress, which temporarily mitigated tensions in the Nicaraguan food system. After the presidency of René Schick (1963–1966) and a short interim, Somoza García's second son, Anastasio Somoza Debayle, took over the presidency in 1967.[10]

The Somozas benefited from US support and used their position of power for personal gain. Over the decades the clan built an economic imperium based on plantations and industrial firms. Calculating the exact value of the family's properties has always been difficult as the Somozas used a complex network of straw men and established companies with foreign domiciles and bank accounts all over the globe to hide their assets. In 1979 the family owned one-fifth of all cultivatable land in Nicaragua, which contributed to the family's reported wealth of least one billion US dollars. The Somoza clan was omnipresent in commerce, industry, and agro exports and also controlled important sectors of Nicaraguan food production, such as industrial meat production and the milk industry.[11]

THE RISE OF AGRO EXPORTS, SOCIAL CHANGE, AND INCREASING TENSIONS OVER FOOD

In the 1950s and 1960s social structures in Nicaragua changed with the expansion of the agro-export economy. First, the number of landless laborers increased, which accelerated urbanization. Second, the Nicaraguan population grew quickly at approximately 3 percent annually.[12] Third, more and more women were entering the workforce; women's share in the economically active population rose from 14 percent in 1950 to nearly 29 percent in 1977. Fourth, the urban middle class increased, as the expanding state bureaucracy needed more employees. In 1960 the middle class made up 11 percent of the Nicaraguan population, including state employees, professionals, and small business owners.[13] The rise of the middle class contributed to the growth of a consumer goods market, but its size remained small compared to that in other Latin American countries.

Changing social structures in Nicaraguan society also influenced food policy and consumption habits. Population growth and urbanization required a long-term strategy for ensuring food supply; however, the government neglected strategic planning and depended increasingly on food imports. The challenge for the regime was to provide the growing urban population with enough food at accessible prices. For the regime's leaders this was less a social compromise than a means to avoid protests. However, the government was only partially successful, as unrest about food prices intensified in the early 1970s. In addition, the official intent to cheapen food for urban workers happened at the cost of the peasants. Insufficient income from basic grains sales and less access to hacienda land forced them to rely on salaried work on farms. Owing to the cotton boom in Northern Nicaragua, many peasants lost their land and their employment stability; hence, land invasions increased.[14]

The agricultural policy favoring agro exports had deep roots in the nineteenth century. At that time the Nicaraguan economy had become in-

FIGURE 1.1. Food production in different Nicaraguan regions, 1980. This map is based on a map developed for the 1980 report of the International Fund for Agricultural Development. It shows the status of food production after three decades of intense agro-export cultivation. The map indicates the geographical distribution of Nicaragua's main agricultural products but neglects regional varieties at the agricultural frontier and at the Caribbean Coast.

creasingly dependent on the export of agricultural products such as coffee. From the 1950s onward coffee exports decreased, and cotton, cattle, and sugar exports began their ascendancy. Coffee production was concentrated in the interior mountain regions of Matagalpa, Jinotega, and the Segovias as well as in the southern uplands in the departments of Managua and Carazo. In those regions with a village structure where coffee was produced on smaller farms, peasants could still cultivate basic grains on small plots. This changed during the rapid expansion of cattle and cotton in the 1950s. Cattle and cotton production expanded mainly in the Northern and Central Pacific's fertile volcanic soil as well as in the Pacific interior (see figure 1.1).[15] In 1950, cotton already occupied nearly 40 percent of all arable land and deeply transformed landscapes, mainly the surrounding areas of the cities León and Chinandega.

In Chinandega department, where 46 percent of all Nicaraguan cotton was cultivated, the expansion produced a major social rupture. Prior to the 1950s most hacienda owners provided agricultural workers access to small plots of land where they grew corn and held cattle. In addition, the owners supplied their workers with milk or cheese. Rural women contributed to survival with the collection of fruits and wild plants.[16] In the 1950s landowners expanded cotton cultivation and hence denied workers access to land. At the same time hacienda owners appropriated municipal lands for cotton farming that peasants had used traditionally for hunting and subsistence agriculture. More and more peasant families were cut off from land, which worsened their supply situation. By the 1960s rural workers increasingly relied on salaries of around six Córdobas per day, which were insufficient for acquiring enough milk, cheese, rice, and beans for their families' survival.[17] The scanty wages created growing social unrest in the Nicaraguan countryside. Over the long run, the regime leaders' ignorance of rural people's needs contributed to the outbreak of the revolution. The FSLN guerrillas managed to get a foothold in some rural communities throughout the 1960s.

Cotton, meat, and sugarcane production displaced peasants and moved them to the agricultural frontier between 1950 and 1965. Given the difficult ecological conditions, peasants produced fewer basic grains in disconnected areas, which affected Nicaraguan food supply. At the same time as the cotton boom, meat exports to the United States increased, which meant that more land was assigned to livestock farming. Sugarcane production expanded slightly later than cotton production and concentrated on the Pacific Coast and in the southern interior. The exports of all three products soared by more than 300 percent between 1960 and 1979.[18] This expansion required immense areas of land, and basic grains production had to move into the country's interior. Peasants who had previously engaged in subsistence agriculture were forced either to work on export plantations or to move inland or directly to the cities. Although the areas cultivated with basic grains did not diminish between 1952 and 1960, the yields decreased by 30 percent, as the soil quality was lower. Compared to other Central American countries, Nicaraguan agricultural productivity was relatively low, especially in corn production. All peasant migrants struggled with the different climate and inferior soil at the agricultural frontier. In addition, these regions lacked access to transport infrastructure.[19]

Settlements at the agricultural frontier especially changed food production and social relations in the sparsely populated Caribbean departments. Basic grains production increased, but farmers also faced difficulties because of climate and isolation. The massive influx of settlers in the Caribbean regions provoked conflicts over land use. The Somoza regime actively encouraged the resettlement of peasants in the interior from the 1960s onward. With financial support from the World Bank and the Inter-American Development Bank, the government designed a colonization program and assigned peasants small areas of land in the interior. Between 1963 and 1971 the Caribbean departments' population increased by 63 percent. Also, large cattle owners expanded landholdings in the region, causing additional land conflicts. Families that had independently moved to the interior were often forced to move a second time.[20] Hence, the tensions in the Nicaraguan food system expanded regionally by the mid-1960s. The colonization project provided no sustained solution to supply problems, as soils at the agricultural frontier were inferior and peasants struggled to adapt to the new environment.

Despite difficult living conditions in the countryside, the Nicaraguan economy was characterized by high growth rates during the 1950s and 1960s. Although the decline of coffee prices after 1955 caused a short recession, economic growth rates remained around 7 percent in the early 1960s.[21] Industrial expansion was limited, however, and the Nicaraguan economy continued to depend on agro-export products. Government-supported export agriculture was increasingly dominated by technological innovations such as machinery, fertilizers, and pesticides; basic grains production continued to be neglected. Although strengthening productivity, the increased use of technology reinforced dependency on imported seeds, spare parts, and chemical fertilizers.

Rising food prices increased social tensions in the 1950s, which were mitigated temporarily by price regulation and increased regional trade in the 1960s. The consumer price index shows rapidly rising prices in the first half of the 1950s. The food price index (100=1955) rose from 57 in 1950 to 100 in 1955 and decreased slightly to 90.5 in 1960.[22] This data shows how social tensions evolved in the Nicaraguan food system by the 1950s. Within a decade, food prices increased around 40 percent. In 1960 Nicaragua founded the Instituto Nacional de Comercio Exterior e Interior (INCEI), the National Institute of Foreign and Internal Trade, to regulate basic grains prices, but the lack of financial resources undermined its work.[23]

At the same time, basic grains production stagnated and was replaced by increasing food imports. According to FAO statistical data, the imports of basic grains were on the rise, especially during the mid-1960s. Although regional food trade within Central America increased in the 1960s, this development failed to deter dependency on imports from abroad and the effects of strong US economic influence. Between 1960 and 1964, Nicaragua processed only around 20 percent of its food imports from Central

America.[24] During the whole decade, external financial support and food aid alleviated the increasing costs for imports. After Alliance for Progress aid declined, social conflicts related to food prices broke out in the 1970s. High prices prevented Nicaraguans from acquiring important ingredients for their favorite dishes.

NICARAGUAN FOOD CULTURES IN THE SECOND HALF OF THE TWENTIETH CENTURY

For most of the twentieth century, the diet of almost all Nicaraguans was based on rice, beans, and corn. Nicaraguans consume maize mainly in the form of tortilla or tamales. As one of my interviewees put it, "a meal without tortilla was useless," showing the importance of tortillas for daily nutrition.[25] Equally important was gallo pinto, a dish that combines rice and beans. Similar combinations have spread from the Caribbean all over Latin America reaching as far as Mexico and Brazil. By contrast to other preparations, Nicaraguans fry the ingredients and prefer red beans. Both Costa Rica and Nicaragua claim gallo pinto as their national dish, which shows how important it is to the national identity of different peoples.[26] To vary their daily diet, rural Nicaraguans combined gallo pinto with dried fish or *cuajada*, when available. Nicaraguans have their own expression for the side dish: *bastimento*. Typical bastimentos in Nicaraguan cuisine are tortillas, plantains or bananas, and bread. Beyond these basic staples, my interviewees identified two elements as being typical for Nicaraguan food: the combination of bell pepper, onions, and bitter oranges and the use of spices and herbs such as achiote, oregano, or peppermint.

Between the 1950s and the 1980s people's daily nutrition in Pacific Nicaragua had some standardized elements with individual and regional variations. Generally, people would start their day with a breakfast consisting of gallo pinto, bread, tortilla, or fruit with some black coffee or *pozol*, a corn drink with milk. A typical workday lunch would include dishes such as *carne desmenuzada* (shredded meat) or ground meat with vegetables, rice, and beans. If meat was unavailable or unaffordable, people had rice and beans or tortilla for lunch, accompanied by cuajada, plantains, or vegetables. Soups were quite common, for example, bean-based soups. At the end of the day families met for a light dinner with bread, gallo pinto, or tortilla, accompanied either by coffee or by traditional beverages such as the corn drinks *tiste* or *pinol*. Tiste is generally flavored with cocoa or clove. However, these traditional corn drinks have faced strong competition from soft drinks, as most interviewees mentioned. Aside from imported soft drinks such as Coke and Pepsi, several Nicaraguan enterprises produced local alternatives such as Kola Shaler.[27] Hence, rice, beans, bread, and maize were essential for Nicaraguans' diets. Their absence seriously affected people in times of food scarcity, but people also missed common ingredients such as salt and spices or herbs that provided dishes with their particular flavor. Finally, meat had a special value among Nicaraguans as press reports in the 1970s and consumer surveys in the 1980s demonstrated.

Throughout the second half of the twentieth century, there were sharp differences between rural and urban food consumption. In general, urban diets contained more processed foods such as stock cubes, cookies, powdered milk, and breakfast cereals. However, many urban Nicaraguans frequently supplied themselves from their patios. In these backyard gardens they cultivated fruits, vegetables, and herbs. Sometimes, several families shared a common patio. Ximena Cubero, one of my interviewees, described the family patio as "a small farm in the city."[28]

Rural people mainly relied on food produced in the village. During seeding period, people agreed on the plants they would seed to ensure adequate supply. In addition, some farmers held pigs and some women produced cuajada. Rural women prepared tortillas relying on the traditional and very laborious method. First, they selected the corn, then added lime, soaked it in water, and washed it again. Finally, women either ground the corn or brought it to the local corn mill. When a city was nearby, people would sell their harvest on the local market and buy some processed food such as canned fish, or spaghetti, which was incorporated as a side dish and combined with rice and cream.[29]

In times of crisis throughout the second half of the twentieth century, people skipped meals and cut back on meat. Nicaraguans frequently judged the nutritional situation by considering whether a family was able to have three meals a day. My interviewees remembered how their mothers between the 1950s and the 1970s enriched simple dishes with small details such as herbs from their gardens or fried tomatoes. Also, people prepared fried yuca or plantain balls with cheese or cuajada. Women sold lunches or traditional beverages within their neighborhood to improve their families' income. Mothers shared their culinary knowledge with their daughters who cherished them as an important resource for their own cooking.[30]

Food memories introduce us to a culinary repertoire of simple dishes for daily use, meals for festive seasons, and dishes considered as typically Nicaraguan. Throughout the twentieth century, Nicaraguans passed on most recipes by oral tradition. Although the Nicaraguan cookbook tradition is historically weak, there is a canon of national dishes that were frequently mentioned by my interviewees and are included in most cookbooks. These include *nacatamales*, *indio viejo*, *carne en vaho* (steamed meat), and *sopa de mondongo* (soup of organ meats). Many of the traditional dishes are based on pork meat and use lard as fat.[31]

In times of scarcity the preparation of many traditional dishes was complicated, as they required a large number of different ingredients. The writer Sergio Ramírez characterizes typical Nicaraguan dishes as "baroque," given their varied ingredients with decorative elements, sauces, and fillings.[32] For example, the Nicaraguan nacatamal is known for its combination of pork, corn dough, a sauce including achiote, and a stuffing with vegetables, rice, raisins, and olives. Commonly, the corn dough is covered by a banana leaf, which dates back to pre-Hispanic traditions when people needed to take food on long journeys. Other famous national dishes such as indio viejo combine plantains, rice, corn, and meat. The meat is first cooked, then shredded and fried together with vegetables, such as onion, tomato, or bell pepper. Next, a dough of soaked corn tortillas or corn flour is added. Finally, bitter oranges, peppermint, and achiote provide the typical flavorings. Generally, the dish is accompanied by plantains and rice.[33] Many regional and family variations of these dishes existed, which shows that culinary habits were in constant motion. With increasing US influence on consumer culture, however, some Nicaraguan writers have expressed concerns about the potential loss of these traditional dishes.

Some Nicaraguan intellectuals have tried to establish a stable, authentic Nicaraguan cuisine as a response to fears of globalization while others have recognized culinary change as inherent of Nicaraguan food culture. José Coronel Urtecho, for example, has described Nicaraguan cuisine as an original, genuine "mestizo cuisine"; Sergio Ramírez has characterized it as a "hybrid of ceaseless alloys."[34] Based on research through interviews, culinary writing, and public debates, I argue that Nicaraguans found their own way in-between culinary heritage, global food transformations, and interventions from development assistance such as food aid or nutrition education. This reinforces Sergio Ramírez's portrayal of Nicaraguan food culture as being constantly in flux because of migration, food availability, prices, climate, and people's preferences. Coronel Urtecho, by contrast, depicts a cuisine that incorporated different cultural influences in colonial times and since then has experienced little change. He argues that food had converted different ethnic groups into Nicaraguans, hence establishing food culture as critical for nation-building.[35]

Given the dominant self-perception of Nicaragua as a mestizo nation, culinary writing has mostly ignored different food cultures at the Nicaraguan Caribbean. Not until the early twenty-first century have Nicaraguan cookbooks started to include Caribbean dishes. As early as the 1950s, however, scientific evaluations of Nicaraguan food practices started to challenge culinary writings about a single national cuisine using the language of nutrition.

THE FIRST NUTRITION SURVEYS

In the 1950s nutritionists and medical experts emerged on to the stage of Nicaraguan food debates. They presented sober, numerical evaluations of the Nicaraguan diet and challenged the historical discourse of a rich national cuisine. During this period of rapid agricultural expansion, national food surveys revealed that the nutrition of workers, peasants, and the urban poor did not benefit from the economic boom. These were the first science-driven evaluations of the Nicaraguan diet, determining nutritional quality through calories, proteins, and vitamins.

At this time the global trend of mapping the world based on caloric and protein intakes reached Nicaragua via INCAP. Nicaragua joined the institute comparatively late, in 1954, which reflects the Somoza regime's opposition to the Guatemalan reform governments and its ignorance of nutrition problems. INCAP's research considerably advanced the knowledge on Central American food habits; however, the institute's nutrition experts differed with experts from other international organizations in their assessment of regional diets. INCAP argued that local staples had a nutritional value and should be used. Other international actors insisted on the deficiencies in animal protein in local diets. These new, contradictory nutritional ideals trickled into Nicaragua in the 1950s and 1960s, recommended by the first generation of INCAP nutritionists and advocates of development cooperation. INCAP's program for local expert education took off in the 1960s. The Escuela de Nutrición (the school of nutrition) was founded in 1966, which educated the first Nicaraguan nutritionists. On the one hand, calories and nutritional statistics became a weapon to attack the regime's ignorance of social realities; on the other hand, international organizations and NGOs used both calories and nutritional statistics to validate their interventions. Regional governments resisted interference and perceived even the publication of statistical data on malnutrition to be damaging to their nation's public image.

An INCAP research team completed the first local nutrition surveys in Nicaragua in 1954.[36] The study focused on the municipality of San Isidro in Matagalpa department and the low-income district of San Luis in Managua. The researchers spent a week in each place analyzing the daily nutrition of thirty families in each location. Their findings about daily nutrition shared the following characteristics. The most frequently consumed basic grain was corn, followed by rice. In both places people consumed few fruits and vegetables, which gave rise to health problems related to insufficient vitamin intake. Instead, meat and milk products were very popular, which the researchers explained by the strong tradition of livestock farming.

To assess food consumption, researchers weighed food during their visits and interviewed the person responsible for cooking. As nutritionists have found out over the course of decades, food surveys based on self-reporting tend to underestimate caloric consumption.[37] By weighing the food, the researchers could verify these reports; however, families might have adapted their diet during the researchers' presence. Undoubtedly, in Nicaragua the political conditions and composition of the survey teams also mattered. Was the survey introduced as a government measure? Who administered the surveys, local nutritionists or foreigners? How were previous encounters with health staff and health surveys experienced? In most cases, archival evidence gives us no answers to these questions, but these factors nonetheless influenced the surveys and their outcomes.

The survey stood in the tradition of socioeconomic nutrition surveys introduced to Central America by FAO nutritionist Emma Reh in the 1950s. Reh, a chemist by training, had studied in the United States and done fieldwork with indigenous groups in Mexico and Central America during the 1940s. After FAO hired her for its nutrition division, she came to Guatemala and participated in long field trips to study food habits in different Central American regions.[38] These surveys were an important basis for the formulation of dietary standards for Central American countries that were published by INCAP from 1953 onward. The first guidelines aimed to establish quantitative recommendations for "good nutrition for nearly the whole population."[39] Following up on these traditions, the two Nicaraguan surveys first analyzed the social situation in both areas of study. Among other things, the authors highlighted that many families in San Isidro had lost access to land during the expansion of coffee production. At the time of the survey, only 40 percent of local inhabitants possessed their own land.

In both case studies, people reached averages of caloric intake between 1,800 and 1,900 kilocalories (kcal). This is close to the FAO's definition of hunger at 1,800 kcal that was used between the late 1960s and the early twenty-first century. These averages hide the fact that, in both regions, around 50 percent of the families did not consume the estimated daily needs of calories and proteins.[40] In addition, the research did not address the distribution of food within the household. Overall, the nutritionists were most concerned about the deficiencies in vitamin A and C, which they attributed to low vegetable consumption. Contrary to other surveys, the authors abstained from any references to hunger, "bad" nutrition habits, the superiority of animal proteins, and so on. Most likely, authors used language carefully as the surveys were published in an official journal of the Nicaraguan Ministry of Health in a period when the regime tried to suppress any public references to malnutrition.

The two 1954 INCAP surveys illustrate the situation at the beginning of the cotton boom, whose detrimental effects on nutrition became more visible afterward. Although these surveys focused on only two regions, it was the first time that international nutrition standards had been applied to the diets of Nicaraguans. The surveys provided some valuable evidence for those who were concerned with the nutritional situation. However, data for the country at large was still nonexistent. In his 1960 article in *Revista Conservadora*, ophthalmologist Emilio Álvarez Montalván argued: "Therefore, now is the time for Nicaragua's food shortage problem to be directed beyond a tight circle of technicians, to become an active and permanent concern of all Nicaraguans and their leaders."[41]

Alarm about Nicaraguans' nutritional situation grew increasingly throughout the 1960s once the negative implications of the agro-export boom for nutrition had become obvious. At the beginning of the decade, several doctors published short articles in *Revista Conservadora*, the main conservative periodical in Nicaragua. They based their arguments on limited statistical material as well as on observations from their medical practice. These physicians belonged to a group of conservatives in Nicaragua who were attempting to express some of the widespread concerns among medical and nutrition science experts at that time: the concern that poor nutrition had slowed economic development. Furthermore, these physicians assumed that poor nutrition was a consequence of inadequate diets including an insufficient intake of micronutrients. In their vision, malnutrition compromised the Nicaraguan nation, exposed it to external criticism, and made it fall behind other Latin American nations.

It had been Montalván who emphasized the link between economic development, progress, and good nutrition in 1960. If nothing was done, argued Montalván, a vicious circle of low wages and ongoing malnutrition would persist, affecting health, productivity, and living conditions. Montalván considered both the quality and quantity of the Nicaraguan diet to be deficient, which he attributed to low income levels and poor eating habits.[42] As a result, Montalván considered nutrition education to be of great necessity. Furthermore, he criticized Nicaraguan politicians and the broader society for trusting in the myth of a wonderful national diet, able to fulfill people's needs, while ignoring the evidence of malnutrition.[43]

Another voice was that of Dr. J. Ramiro Arcia who considered malnutrition a serious problem for the Nicaraguan population. He based his insights on his work at the Hospital General de Managua where he had seen many children with symptoms of severe malnutrition. He explained that malnutrition as a cause of death was not included in Nicaraguan health statistics, which made the numbers difficult to estimate. The existence of night blindness and endemic goiter, however, proved that nutritional problems originated for three reasons: low income, inadequate nutrition, and the lack of a food policy.[44] In his article he recommended increasing local food production, improving income opportunities, and introducing nutrition education.

Experts' negative evaluations of the nutrition situation in Nicaragua soon provoked intellectual resistance. Against these science-driven assessments Nicaraguan writers praised taste and culinary creativity. The poet Pablo Antonio Cuadra, for example, argued in his essay collection *El Nicaragüense*, first published in 1967: "And it's not a trivial thing, either, to have a delicious and developed cuisine. Instead, it's proof of a fertile imagination and cultural personality. In spite of the 'underdevelopment' that economists and technicians blame on lack of calories and vitamins, Nicaragua has a delectable cuisine: varied, imaginative, nuanced, strong and . . . nutritious." Cuadra characterized Nicaraguan cuisine as creative, diverse, and tasty, all of which, in his eyes, was an outcome of general Nicaraguan cultural richness. By contrast, Cuadra's other statements on Nicaraguan food were more critical: "This is a people who eat badly and while in transit. There's a disconnect between the way they actually eat and how they imagine they do."[45] Cuadra defended culinary imagination, but he admitted that daily nutrition suffered from deficiencies because people in urban environments with their fixed work schedules often lacked the time to prepare and consume elaborate meals at home. Cuadra was the only one who specified what he understood as deficient food practices, while doctors' and nutritionists' references remained vague.

URBAN FOOD CULTURES AND SHOPPING HABITS ON THE MOVE

With accelerating migration to the cities, more Nicaraguans started eating meals outside their homes. From the 1950s the Managuan population increased rapidly with the number of inhabitants doubling from 109,352 in 1950 to 234,580 people in 1963. By the 1960s Nicaragua was the most urbanized country in Central America. The exodus from the countryside was a reaction to the expanding cotton industry and to the concomitant rural poverty. The transformation of farmers into urban consumers contributed significantly to urbanization. During the process of moving to the city and adapting to the new living environment, people changed their food and consumption habits.[46]

Urbanization throughout twentieth-century Latin America fostered the consumption of processed foods and a tendency toward eating out. Nutritional research by scholars such as María Angélica Tagle and Marina Flores has highlighted various effects of urbanization on food consumption. First, people abandoned traditional rural diets for cheap industrialized food with less nutritional value. Time restraints in the new urban working environment led to increased consumption of street food—for example, dining at the famous fritangas.[47] The food-processing industry developed in tandem with urbanization, supported generously by Alliance for Progress funds and US food aid. At the same time, urban advertising and newspapers daily communicated the symbolic value of processed foods and foreign brands as signs of modernity.

Most of these products were inaccessible to large sectors of the Nicaraguan population, but the urban middle classes could afford a wider range of imported foods and consumer goods that were sold in the new supermarkets. In Nicaragua, national firms preceded foreign enterprises in establishing the first supermarkets and fast food restaurants. However, these firms reached only a very limited clientele since most Managuans preferred street food and conducted their daily shopping in small pulperías or went to the markets. This means that national entrepreneurs adapted global consumption trends for a national elite and a middle-class clientele. Although only small percentages of Nicaraguans actually consumed anything at these spaces, the vivid public debates indicate that people perceived the presence of supermarkets, fast food, and mass advertising as important changes.

Despite some initial resistance from consumers, Nicaraguan entrepreneurs established the first supermarkets during the 1950s. In 1956 the brothers Carlos and Felipe Mántica founded the first Nicaraguan supermarket in a district named after their family, Colonia Mántica. They remembered that it took beween ten and fifteen years before consumers became accustomed to shopping in a self-service supermarket.[48] Prior to the revolution, shopping at the supermarkets was a clear sign of an elite status, and supermarkets were exclusively located in Managua's upper-class districts.

Although the expansion of supermarkets occurred, the conditions in Nicaragua were less favorable than in more industrialized countries. In the United States, for example, supermarkets had surged during the 1930s. Supermarkets had less employees than smaller shops, where every client was attended personally. Self-service in supermarkets made consumers do this work, so the economic crisis in the 1930s was a means to economize on shopping by passing on the work of employees to the consumers. American consumers appreciated the lower prices and increased autonomy. The expansion of supermarkets was a process lasting over several decades, reinforced by the diffusion of cars and refrigerators in the United States, which allowed consumers to buy larger amounts of food and store them for longer periods. In Nicaragua, by contrast, this reliance on cars and refrigerators was only possible for a very small number of consumers, which limited the spread of supermarkets. Felipe Mántica identified advertising, discounts, and attractive offers as his main strategies for winning over clients.[49]

Intellectual critiques of the new shopping environment quickly arose. In 1960, only four years after the establishment of the first supermarket, the Nicaraguan intellectual José Coronel Urtecho criticized the United States for spreading its commercial culture and processed foods to Nicaragua: "The triumph of commercial vulgarity over the authentic elegance of the natural, is being extended over all of our national foods, with the same speed it's taking over other manifestations of Nicaraguan life. This is bad because it represents the disintegration of our culture. The modernization of food markets, and steady substitution of corner markets and street vendors with their trays, by 'groceries' and supermarkets. Those, along with the industrialization of food products demanded by such systems, tend to create a culinary situation similar to that of the United States."[50] Coronel Urtecho portrayed Nicaragua as being threatened by a new, commercial conquest that endangered local food culture. For him, the consumption of processed foods was an indicator of bad taste, and he depicted Nicaraguan food as authentic and natural. His perception of the conquest's speed, however, seems exaggerated, as supermarkets were far from dominant in Nicaragua at that time.

Coronel Urtecho belonged to the vanguard movement that was an important trend in Nicaraguan intellectual life from the 1930s until the 1960s. The movement was very heterogeneous; some of its members toyed with the idea of fascism while others opposed the Somoza regime. In general, its members promoted a vision for a Nicaraguan culture inspired by the indigenous past and peasant culture and largely in opposition to US influences.[51] While Coronel Urtecho focused on the possible loss of traditional cuisine, other poets criticized the influence of shopping centers advertising products that were unaffordable for most Nicaraguans. Similar types of literary criticism were visible in other Central American countries as well, especially from the 1950s onward, focusing on the consumption of imported goods, fast food, and an economic development model that increased social gaps.[52] The Nicaraguan political opposition took up this intellectual criticism in the 1960s, also influenced by cultural imperialism theories circulating at that time in Latin America.

Research on the change of consumption habits has frequently identified multinational fast food chains as being responsible for the homogenization of food consumption. In Nicaragua, however, local entrepreneurs established the first businesses before global chains arrived. For example, the first roasted chicken restaurant was founded nearly two decades before the first McDonalds franchise set up in 1975. The first Nicaraguan fast food chain gained success by relying on the popularity of US fast food and by incorporating references to local consumption habits.[53] In 1958 a Nicaraguan couple founded the fried chicken chain called Pollo Tip Top. First, they started by opening a chicken breeding farm, as the consumption of farm-raised chicken was still uncommon in Nicaragua. After the couple moved to Managua, they opened their first restaurant. The name Pollo Tip Top had US origins and referred to the expression "Tip of the Top." In 1968 the chain announced its services in a tourist guide for Managua with the slogan: "American Style 'Serve Yourself' Cafeteria. . . . Nicaragua's American colony top spot for a food meal. Fried and roast chicken in lunch boxes to go."[54] While this announcement was directed at the North American community, publicity in *La Prensa* addressed a Nicaraguan public. In these advertisements, the enterprise emphasized local elements such as the combination of menus with the popular Flor de Caña rum.[55] Unfortunately, historical data on the number of customers and food prices is not available for Pollo Tip Top or for its foreign competitors.

Fast food restaurants expanded slowly in the capital, and most Nicaraguans still frequented the local version: the street food fritangas scattered all over the city. Spanish colonizers had introduced the tradition of frying food, which has shaped Nicaraguan food culture up to today. Alberto Baldizón Vogl characterized Managua in one of his essays as "la ciudad de los puestos" (the city of stalls) with street food vendors as the most important source for workers' daily nutrition.[56] Until 1972 trade and markets were concentrated in the city center. From the markets in Central Managua, retailers and street vendors distributed food and consumer goods throughout the city.

Research on globalization and consumption habits has attributed culinary homogenization to the rise of supermarkets and fast food, but scholars have overlooked the influence of local food-processing industries. In many Latin American countries, fast food has become more prominent since the 1950s.[57] However, even if local criticism correctly perceived a risk of homogenization through fast food, developments within national food-processing industries also contributed to this trend. As Jeffrey Pilcher has shown for Mexico, the rise of a dehydrated tortilla flour industry standardized tortilla production. The flour mixture to which Mexican consumers only had to add water replaced the laborious work of soaking the corn in limewater and grinding it on a stone block called a *metate*. In consequence, the taste became more uniform, and so did the texture after the introduction of factory-pressed tortillas.[58]

In Nicaragua, a similar standardization process might have occurred through the introduction of *pinol* mills, but no systematic research on the food-processing sector has been undertaken. These mills contributed to a more homogenous cornmeal as the basis for the traditional *pinol* drink. The existence of twenty-three pinol mills, nine soft drink factories, eight distilleries, and one vegetable oil factory in Managua demonstrates the importance of processed foods and beverages in urban Nicaragua by 1946. In the 1960s food processing was the most important industrial sector contributing more than 50 percent to Nicaraguan manufacturing output.[59] This rapid rise of food processing was caused by a huge US economic assistance program for Latin America.

ECONOMIC AID AND NEW NUTRITION SURVEYS

During the 1960s the Alliance for Progress, a pan-American initiative, influenced development policy in Nicaragua. Launched in 1961 by President John F. Kennedy at the Organization of American States (OAS) Conference, the alliance aimed at strengthening Latin American economic and social development. However, for the United States, the alliance was also a mechanism to prevent the rise of communism in the Western hemisphere, which the United States perceived as a constant threat since the establishment of the Guatemalan left-wing governments (1944–1954) and the Cuban Revolution in 1959. The planned economic aid included $20 billion for the whole decade, mainly provided by the United States.[60]

Between 1960 and 1969 Nicaragua received $227 million of assistance: the US government provided $138 million of loans and other assistance; international organizations supplied an additional $89 million.[61] Although the alliance promoted social reforms and a more equal income distribution, there were no political commitments demanded from Latin American governments. Nicaraguan elites took advantage of the alliance's financial support and paid only lip service to promoting reforms or broader development goals. To attract funding, the government created reform proposals including the alliance's goals; however, the projects lacked effective measures imposed to achieve them.[62] In consequence, historian Paul Dosal has argued that the alliance strengthened the Somoza regime and its allies. The main achievements in Nicaragua were energy and road construction projects, whereas the impact on health, education, and nutrition remained limited. For example, Alliance for Progress funding was utilized to support the Nestlé powdered milk plant, Prolacsa, in Matagalpa. The regime promised Nestlé its support by investments in local infrastructure, a dairy cattle development program, and tax exemptions. In fact, Prolacsa concentrated on exports to neighboring countries. In 1971 the firm exported powdered milk worth $2.5 million, while from 1971 to 1972 only 7–10 percent remained for the Nicaraguan market.[63] In this case, Alliance for Progress funds supported the export plans of a Swiss multinational, and effects on local milk supply were marginal. Ultimately, the Alliance for Progress provided significant financial support for development projects and sustained the regime's strategy to promote the Green Revolution.

The Alliance for Progress reached its peak during the 1960s. When Richard Nixon assumed the US presidency in 1969, the alliance lost both popularity and funding. US foreign policy under Nixon prioritized other world regions, which was why the government reduced support to this development initiative.[64] The simultaneous decline of the Central American Common Market (CACM) and the Alliance for Progress in the late 1960s provoked a crisis in the Nicaraguan food system.

At the same time, INCAP published the results of its first regional nutrition survey, which situated Nicaragua within a regional mapping of malnutrition. It was also the first study to reach larger international audiences. The report combined a detailed nutrition survey with general suggestions for a regional food policy. Between 1965 and 1967 more than one hundred researchers traveled throughout Central America to undertake the first systematic regional nutrition survey. They conducted clinical examinations, took anthropometric measurements, interviewed thirty-eight hundred people about their food habits, and conducted a socioeconomic study. In Nicaragua, it was the first nationwide survey, including six hundred families. One hundred of the families lived in Managua; the other families were spread throughout the country, with the exception of the Caribbean region.[65]

The final report combines different narratives of malnutrition, its origins, and broad policy recommendations. The authors recommended a joint regional food policy including legal measures, food fortification, and nutrition education. The proposals encompassed very broad aims—from increasing local food production to raising the income of the poorest sectors.[66] Instead of presenting a coherent strategy, however, the long list appeared as a mixture of recommendations from which governments could choose the options most suitable to them. Through taking socioeconomic factors and food availability for individual countries into account, the report offered a nuanced narrative on the origins of malnutrition in Central America. According to the authors, the unequal income distribution and the focus of agricultural investments in the export sector had negatively affected the food supply.[67]

Similar to the 1954 survey results, the report identified the two most important nutritional concerns for Nicaragua: the limitations in protein and calorie supply and the dramatic lack of nutrients such as vitamin A and riboflavin. In identifying a variety of factors causing malnutrition, the research team advanced beyond the simplistic nutrition science notion of the "protein gap," which had been questioned since the 1950s and was finally abandoned around the mid-1970s. Overall, there was a dramatic lack of vitamin A. Only 11 percent of the people interviewed consumed sufficient levels. Vitamin A deficiency causes a number of serious health problems and increases susceptibility to sickness and diseases such as diarrhea and measles, which are especially dangerous for young children.[68]

Although the INCAP report meticulously listed average intakes of calories, proteins, and nutrients, the authors warned of precipitate judgments based on national averages. In Nicaragua, the average daily caloric intake was 2,108 calories in the cities and 1,986 calories in rural zones, which was 99 percent and 96 percent respectively of required levels recommended by FAO and WHO at that time.[69] The report highlighted, however, that average values "do not adequately describe the magnitude or nature of the problems."[70] Significant numbers of families failed to reach the averages; food in Nicaragua was distributed too unequally. In particular, the results showed deterioration in rural zones: 30 percent of the surveyed families reached less than 70 percent of the necessary daily caloric intake. From a projection of the anthropometric data sample for the whole country, the researchers estimated that there were 163,300 children under the age of five suffering from different degrees of malnutrition. Hence, in the mid-1960s malnutrition affected more than 56 percent of all Nicaraguan children from the same age group.[71]

Regarding food availability, the report concluded that the Nicaraguan food supply was "precarious," especially for eggs, meat, beans, vegetables, fruits, wheat, and rice. The data shows that availability was weakest for vegetables, with only 14 percent of the necessary quantities, followed by eggs (41 percent), and meat and wheat flour (both at 51 percent).[72] These conclusions were exactly those that the regime had tried to hide in the early 1950s: essential foods were scarce, hence vulnerable groups suffered from hunger, and malnutrition caused severe health problems. However, by the mid-1960s a larger community of experts with international reputations had already taken up their work in Central America.

The Somoza regime could not prevent the publication of INCAP's regional study in 1969. Unfortunately, the Nicaraguan government's direct reactions and debates with INCAP or within the Health Ministry were not documented in the archival material I consulted. The frequent insistence on the insufficiency of average values, however, might have been intended to impede the government from arguing there was no need for change. The international development community used the survey to request new projects. For example, USAID listed the study's results when justifying the loan for a nutrition improvement project for the Nicaraguan government in 1975.[73]

Shortly after finishing the survey, INCAP also published dietary recommendations for low-income groups in all Central American countries. The booklet for Nicaragua first introduces the hypothesis that the progress of a country was linked to its nutritional situation, which echoed concerns that had been raised by Nicaraguan doctors in the early 1960s. The authors provided several reasons for the nutritional problems, including the country's economic situation and local food habits. In the booklet the authors suggested daily quantities for seventeen different foods for different people, distinguishing between their sex, age, and residence in rural or urban areas.[74] On the one hand, the science-driven approach to nutrition led to quantitative recommendations for daily meals. On the other hand, the authors refrained from providing strict universal guidelines, which left room for adaptations. Unfortunately, archival evidence provides no information on the application of these recommendations. Hence, it is impossible to assess their impact on nutritionists' work and Nicaraguans food habits. Nevertheless, the conviction that nutrition had to contribute to economic progress and that people had to adapt their food habits accordingly shaped expert discourses on nutrition in the 1960s. At the same time, experts with elite or middle-class backgrounds frequently denigrated low-income Nicaraguans' food habits as "bad." Beyond the scientific assessment that these diets were lacking in nutrients, these statements also indicate a social gap between experts and poor Nicaraguans.

Since the 1950s important social transformations were underway in Nicaragua that challenged the existing systems of food supply, consumption, and politics. The agro-export economy deprived peasants of their landholdings and moved basic grains production to areas with less fertile land. The agro-export economy favored the trend toward urbanization, one major transformation that changed Nicaraguans' food habits. Urban people increasingly relied on processed foods and ate outside their homes. In this context, two social groups grew in importance: the urban middle classes and the landless peasants. The first group favored the consumption of imported brand products and processed food. The second group, often struggling to survive, moved to the agricultural frontier but also opted increasingly for land occupations. Hence, food gaps made inequality in Nicaragua more visible—between urban elites residing in spacious houses with access to modern supermarkets and inhabitants of improvised settlements at the margins of the cities or people in remote villages relying on subsistence agriculture. Soaring food prices in the 1950s increased the social gaps. Overall,

Nicaragua needed to supply more people with food in the 1950s and 1960s while the agro-export economy limited basic grains production.

Massive and rapid urbanization was a challenge for the Nicaraguan food system beginning in the 1950s. The countryside had to provide more food for the urban population while people were continuously leaving the country. Urban life changed consumer habits profoundly as more processed foods were available and time for cooking was limited. Over the decades, interactions among people from different cultural backgrounds and new products created new culinary habits. Contrary to common arguments in globalization literature, local entrepreneurs preceded foreign multinationals in spreading supermarkets and fast food in Nicaragua. Fritangas and street vendors remained an important factor for urban nutrition: they sold traditional dishes, such as nacatamales. Hence, fast food had an impact on Nicaraguan consumption habits but never became the homogenizing force that was predicted by many scholars of globalization.

Over the duration of the twentieth century, the nutrition of most people in Central and Pacific Nicaragua relied on maize, beans, and rice. Essential elements of food culture were tortillas, gallo pinto, and local corn drinks. In a country with a strong tradition of cattle production, the consumption of milk and meat was more widespread than in other Central American countries. In fact, people associated meat consumption with good nutrition throughout most of the twentieth century. The combination of bitter oranges, onions, and bell peppers created the flavor of Nicaraguan cuisine as well as oregano, peppermint, and achiote. People accompanied main dishes also with cuajada, plantains, and bread. They combined these ingredients in many creative ways in traditional dishes and in daily improvised cooking. However, these improvisations were not always able to overcome the scarcity of important ingredients such as maize, meat, or red beans. In particular, some of the traditional dishes required numerous ingredients that were difficult to substitute.

Medical and nutrition experts introduced a new, science-driven narrative of Nicaraguan food culture in the 1950s. They assessed the food situation in quantities of calories, proteins, and micronutrients. Inside the country, doctors who faced frequent cases of malnutrition in their daily work raised their voices and demanded political intervention. Outside the country, international organizations expressed similar concerns. INCAP had already initiated the first nutritional surveys in the 1950s and organized a nationwide study from 1965 to 1967. Overall, the nutrition surveys in Nicaragua from the 1950s to the 1970s demonstrated that hunger persisted in rural areas and poor urban neighborhoods. Hunger affected more than 50 percent of Nicaraguan children, and deficiencies in micronutrients caused

severe health problems throughout the country. Although nutritional surveys focused on quantitative evaluations, Nicaraguan intellectuals resisted
these sober, numerical descriptions. They praised the flavors, creativity, and
uniqueness of Nicaraguan food but also expressed concerns about the potential loss of culinary traditions. Both nutrition surveys and culinary writings either ignored or only reluctantly admitted influences from Caribbean
cultures.

The surveys' findings on caloric intake provided numbers to the state
bureaucracy and the international development community. Although the
government tried to ignore all data indicating the need for action in the
field of nutrition, international aid organizations used the surveys to request new projects. However, international experts differed on the strategies to take against malnutrition. INCAP experts valued the use of local
vegetable foods, and other international organizations promoted animal
proteins and powdered milk. INCAP staff identified both social inequality
and "bad" nutrition habits as key problems. Consequently, they perceived
nutrition education as a possible solution and published recommendations
for affordable diets. At the same time, INCAP staff also demanded a political intervention and rallied for nutrition planning from the 1960s onward.

Foreign aid allowed the Somoza regime to ease problems in food supply
during the 1950s and 1960s. In particular, US economic aid heavily influenced food production and consumption. After the long period of intervention from 1912 to 1933, the United States formally retired from Nicaragua
but continued monitoring and giving economic support during the Second
World War and the early years of the Cold War. The US government perceived the Somoza regime as assuring regional stability against left-wing
political alternatives. Economic aid concentrated on agro-export agriculture, the health sector, and food processing, and the expansion of economic
aid in the 1960s allowed the regime temporarily to alleviate tensions by
increasing food imports, expanding processed food production, and promoting colonization in the agricultural frontier. Nevertheless, tensions
continued over access to land. Confrontations with the National Guard
radicalized sectors of the Nicaraguan peasantry and opened up spaces for
cooperation with the FSLN in the late 1960s and 1970s.

CHAPTER TWO

TENSIONS REVEALED

FOOD POLITICS, NATURAL DISASTER, AND SOCIAL CONFLICTS, 1965–1979

On December 23, 1972, a fatal earthquake measuring 6.2 on the Richter scale hit the city of Managua. It destroyed 90 percent of the buildings in the city center. The number of victims was estimated at ten thousand people dead and twenty thousand people injured. Immediately afterward the water and electricity supply failed. At the same time the two main markets were on fire. The next day, a pall of smoke and red dust hovered over the city, and earthquake victims searched desperately for shelter, food, and water.

The international community reacted quickly. Within several hours planeloads with relief supplies were arriving at the Managuan airport. Representatives of humanitarian agencies from Costa Rica and Honduras arrived in the city with ten thousand loaves of bread, powdered milk, pots, pans, and plates. They reported that the Nicaraguan government was completely unprepared to deal with the disaster: there was no food inventory or any emergency distribution plans.[1] The government immediately formed a national emergency committee but then waited for four days with the first food distributions. President Anastasio Somoza Debayle himself headed the emergency committee. Under his command, emergency aid disappeared into a "black hole." Trucks transported food, medicine, and tents directly to nearby warehouses. More than 320,000 gallons of water delivered by the US Air Force just disappeared. Soon, speculators were selling relief supplies for exaggerated prices at local markets.[2]

The earthquake caused a temporary hunger crisis in Nicaragua and made the corruption of the Somoza regime more visible than ever. People were outraged and lost trust in their government, which had ignored their needs during the emergency. Although international donors were aware of the misappropriations, food aid reached new heights after the earthquake. The 1972 disaster reinforced social tensions over food that had been developing since the 1950s. Food and economic aid had temporarily alleviated the situation during the 1960s. By the mid-1960s several international relief organizations had taken up their work in Nicaragua. At that time they intensified food distributions to young children and expanded their activities into new regions. Thus, more Nicaraguans were exposed to imported food. With the end of the Alliance for Progress, however, the United States reduced donations in the late 1960s. At the same time, global basic grains production decreased, which contributed to higher food prices in many world regions. In Nicaragua, conflicts about land distribution in the countryside and rising food prices in urban areas intensified. Different social movements demanded affordable food and attacked the government for its inactivity. The earthquake accelerated the crisis.

While social inequality increased and low-income sectors struggled for survival after the disaster, Nicaraguan elites redesigned Managua according to US planning and consumption models. As a result social divisions increased in both shopping and housing between 1973 and 1979. This trend toward a more socially divided city provoked a new debate on US influences in Nicaraguan society. The strong trend toward Americanization was increasingly challenged by the political opposition to the Somoza regime. During the 1970s the Frente Sandinista de Liberación Nacional (FSLN), the Sandinista National Liberation Front, introduced a vision of personal austerity and argued for reversing "neocolonial penetration."[3]

As the political struggle intensified, Nicaraguan elites continued to display their wealth at elegant dinners and ostentatious receptions. For ordinary Nicaraguans, making ends meet remained difficult in the years after the earthquake. USAID characterized malnutrition in 1976 as "one of the most serious and widespread problems in Nicaragua."[4] More than 50 percent of Nicaraguan children were suffering from malnutrition, the food supply was precarious, and little political attention was paid to nutrition problems. Because members of the Somoza regime were focused on supporting the agro-export economy, they never accepted the bad nutritional situation as a political priority. Temporary—but severe—food crises occurred after natural disasters and in periods of high food prices and contributed to the fall of the dictatorship in 1979.

FOOD POLICY BETWEEN 1965 AND 1979, ALIBI INSTITUTIONS, AND DEVELOPMENT GOALS

Throughout the 1960s and 1970s government authorities in the Somoza regime remained reluctant to accept existing evidence concerning widespread malnutrition and hunger. Within the context of the UN decade for development and the Alliance for Progress, the pressure of international organizations on the Nicaraguan government had increased by 1965 but had limited effect until 1979. When the development machinery extended into Nicaragua, international aid workers faced a government that was unwilling to accept any reforms that would endanger the status quo. Instead, the Somoza regime introduced some alibi institutions and passed external aid off as its own success.

The Somoza regime changed its strategy around 1965. Responding to the demand to initiate a food policy, within a few years the government established five institutions that specialized in nutrition. In 1964 the government founded a nutrition division within the Ministry of Health, which was followed by the Comité Nacional Inter-Ministerial de Nutrición (the National Interministry Committee of Nutrition) to coordinate the nutrition activities of the Ministries of Health, Education, and Agriculture. Looking at the sheer numbers of institutions, one could conclude that food policy had become an important area of health policy by the mid-1960s. However, the institutions lacked qualified staff and financial resources; sometimes, they survived only for a few years. The development of several, sometimes competing, institutions was typical for that period in Central America when INCAP was pressing governments to include nutrition as a political priority. INCAP's reports show a growing frustration over the outcomes: whereas the establishment of new institutions was relatively easy, the development and implementation of more profound reforms were not.[5]

The regime's ignorance of and lack of interest in Nicaraguan's nutritional status became obvious at the First National Congress on Nutrition in 1970. In addition to Nicaraguan government officials and the president himself, members from FAO, INCAP, PAHO (the Pan American Health Organization), WHO, and CARE attended the meeting. In his speech, the Nicaraguan minister of health tried to convince the international community of the success of government programs, emphasizing progress toward the increased production of basic grains. However, FAO statistics reveal that this was only true for maize production. Beans and rice production increased slowly but still was not enough to feed a growing urban population. In fact, the 1965–1967 INCAP survey had demonstrated insufficient production of beans, vegetables, rice, and eggs.[6] At the meeting it became clear that the minister of health considered Nicaragua a less developed country: "Educational levels in more developed countries, make modern methods of food production, processing, and distribution viable. In our country, deep-rooted beliefs have hindered development and the utilization of clear agricultural advantages. Even more lamentable is that the very same malnutrition that keeps us in a cycle of poverty, has sapped the public will to improve its current state of economic and social development." In his opinion, traditional beliefs delayed development and prevented the consumption of food with high nutritional value. He went so far as to reproach the Nicaraguan people for a lack of will to improve the situation. Even more ignorant was the statement of President Anastasio Somoza Debayle, who claimed: "In Nicaragua, there has always been enough food, in the quantities and qualities that develop the human brain. Renowned examples are the poets, and the great oratorical skills of the Nicaraguans."[7] Somoza negated the existence of serious nutritional problems in his country. Instead, he highlighted the government's promotion of high-yielding seeds, fertilizers, and pesticides, the strategies promoted by Green Revolution advocates since the 1950s.

Josué de Castro, the Brazilian nutrition expert and author of *The Geopolitics of Hunger*, also participated in the conference.[8] In his speech, he argued for the need to fight hunger and underdevelopment: "Hunger is not a disease but a symptom of a much more complex social illness. Hunger is the biological expression of an economic disease at the deepest level. The fight against hunger is only authentic if it's carried out against underdevelopment, and on behalf of a comprehensive kind of development." According to Castro, hunger had its roots in the economic system and underdevelopment, which he characterized as a "social illness." Consequently, Castro argued, politicians had to stand up for fundamental economic change.[9]

Unfortunately, we do not know how discussions and interactions at this workshop evolved: if Josué de Castro attacked Somoza for his remarks or remained silent, if INCAP staff insisted on the findings of nutritional surveys, or if anyone questioned the Nicaraguan health minister. Only the speeches have been documented in a small report. In these speeches Nicaraguan officials mostly paid lip service to their international audience by discussing certain development goals. Despite the positive developments Nicaraguan politicians had announced during the 1970 conference, however, these new nutrition institutions never gained strength in Nicaragua as is clearly shown in a USAID report from 1976.[10]

In total, the nutrition division received only a sum of 857,000 Córdobas—that is, 1.7 percent of the Health Ministry's annual budget. From this amount, 48 percent was spent on personnel, 30 percent on equipment, and 13 percent on nutrition centers for undernourished children. It is remarkable that, among the fifty-nine employees of the division, only seven were trained nutritionists. The rest were administrative staff, presumably given the post as a reward for political loyalty. As a result the division lacked clear objectives and merely updated information on the nutritional situation throughout the country. The division limited its activities to supervision, nutrition education, and publishing nutritional guidelines.[11] Existing sources do not reveal whether the division was also involved in the supervision of food aid distributions.

THE INCREASING IMPORTANCE OF FOOD AID DURING THE COLD WAR

Food aid brought large quantities of imported foods into the Nicaraguan market. This aid increased around 1965 with new organizations taking up their work in Nicaragua, and food distributions temporarily alleviated the tensions in the Nicaraguan food system. At the same time, food distributions fostered the consumption of imported grains and processed food. Looking at the global context, food aid's expansion responded on the one hand to the growing agricultural surplus production in industrialized countries—namely, the United States, which led many of these early initiatives. On the other hand, the development of food aid programs originated from growing concerns about development after the Second World War. The Cold War powers were convinced that Global South countries need only to follow their particular path to economic development and declared the strategy of the other bloc dangerous. These powers considered food donations a means to shape local economies according to their political goals. Industrialized nations such as the United States, Canada, and Germany redirected wheat and other surplus products to the Global South, where they reinforced industrialization strategies based on cheap imported foods.[12]

The legal basis and development of US food aid has strongly influenced Nicaragua since the 1960s. US food aid from 1954 to 2008 was based on the 1954 Agriculture Trade Development Assistance Act, also known as Public Law 480.[13] In this framework there were three types of food aid. First, government-to-government food aid (Title I) comprised the largest share of US food aid. Recipient countries could sell this so-called program food aid on their internal market in order to earn additional revenue for the state budget. Title I food aid was sold to the recipients on concessional credit terms, which normally included a payment period of up to thirty years. In Nicaragua, it helped the Somoza regime to overcome shortages. Second, Title II food aid was provided during acute famines or after disasters; it was administered by USAID. Third, Title III regulated the distribution of donations within the United States but also managed the distribution of food aid abroad through NGOs.[14]

Since its introduction, US food aid reflected Cold War tensions. The United States perceived food aid as a legitimate means of influencing the governments of recipient nations. US policy makers considered food aid a means to alleviate social conflicts that could potentially lead to the establishment of socialist regimes.[15] They were convinced of the superiority of a diet based on industrialized food production as well as milk and wheat products. For instance, early on in the Cold War, wheat bread gained a strong symbolic significance for its superiority over the "dark bread" and the supply problems in Soviet Russia.[16] These trends are clearly visible in 1960s Nicaragua.

With the rise of the FSLN, Nicaragua was perceived in the United States as being a country endangered by international communism. Opposition intensified during the last two decades of the Somoza regime. In the early 1960s a group led by Carlos Fonseca, Tomás Borge, José Santos López, and Silvio Mayorga founded the FSLN. By 1963 the group had built up both an urban and a rural base for their guerilla fighters, and they began by organizing bank assaults and guerrilla activities in the northern mountains. The US representatives were concerned about the FSLN's insurgent potential and its links to Cuba.[17]

Combined US military and economic aid continued throughout the 1960s with food aid as an important element. Nicaraguan government institutions and NGOs managed and distributed the food donations. In general, US Title I food aid supported the Somoza dictatorship in stabilizing food prices and availability. US food aid expanded quickly and reached $1.9 million in 1964.[18] At that time, food aid consisted mainly of wheat, powdered milk, and new products designed by the food industry such as corn-soy milk. Nicaragua experienced a massive influx of imported foods, which influenced the preferences of Nicaraguan consumers. The Nicaraguan government resold Title I food aid to local enterprises and consumers, and humanitarian agencies concentrated on milk distribution. For example, Caritas had been engaged in food aid in Nicaragua since 1964. In 1966 the North American NGO CARE started its work in Nicaragua and became active in school feeding, nutrition education, making improvements to the public water systems, and constructing schools.[19] Both Caritas and CARE distributed powdered milk in school feeding programs and rural communities in the 1960s, and this contributed to the strong demand for powdered milk during the 1980s. The generation that had grown up with powdered milk also used it to feed their own children.

The fierce conviction of the superiority of animal protein among contemporary nutritional scientists led to massive milk distributions. The notion that cow's milk was an ideal children's food originated from new findings by early-twentieth-century nutritional scientists. Growing acceptance of the power of proteins and vitamins contributed to milk's "new profile as food for everybody."[20] During the Cold War, milk and wheat bread became the icons of a modern diet. The debate over milk distribution to children became linked to the debates over economic development; the lack of milk was identified as a key problem that could block economic success in the future. In Nicaragua, food distributions reinforced the consumption of powdered milk. Consequently, emotional debates and protests often erupted during periods of scarcity.

Compared to other Central American countries, Nicaragua had a strong tradition of local milk consumption owing to its cattle industry. Given the deficiencies in the potable water supply and the hot climate, however, both fresh and powdered milk consumption entailed considerable health risks.[21] The new spontaneous settlements at the urban margins as well as many rural communities lacked access to infrastructure and thus could not count on clean water. Nonetheless, Caritas and CARE organized powdered milk distributions for Nicaraguan school and preschool children throughout the 1960s. Their activities promoted milk consumption and the use of infant formulas in Nicaraguan rural zones. In 1967 Caritas operated a school milk program with ninety thousand recipients and a family feeding program with eighty-two thousand recipients. Milk products occupied the first rank among the distributed products in 1967, at more than 4.3 million pounds, outnumbering by far the second- and third-rank products (cornmeal with 3.65 million pounds and bulgur with 2.65 million pounds). CARE staff members observed in the 1970s that mothers were absolutely convinced that cow's milk was the best food for their children. Breastfeeding was not considered a viable alternative.[22]

Powdered milk received widespread acceptance, but corn-soy milk (CSM) faced more resistance. In the late 1960s CARE staff decided to increase educational activities for food aid distributions after CSM products had faced acceptance problems. The taste was off-putting, and the tropical climate meant that insects often attacked CSM bags. CARE increased educational activities for local nutritionists, cooks at the nutritional centers, and recipients to whom the NGO distributed recipes.[23] CARE also provided nutrition education for mothers and children because of the high level of child malnutrition. Volunteers, nurses, and doctors gave talks in the clinics, where they also showed educational films and distributed instructions for young children's nutrition. Sometimes they organized cooking demonstrations for mothers in an effort to promote, for example, donated oatmeal as a nutritious food.[24]

In the early 1970s US volunteers and CARE staff members tried to improve the nutrition of residents in newly colonized areas in the Caribbean departments. CARE staff members introduced canned food, oatmeal, and CSM products, but the mestizo settlers from Central Nicaragua longed for meat, vegetables, and milk.[25] The need for recipes based on local foods and technologies became obvious during the distribution of food donations. For example, Diane Trembly reported to CARE headquarters in 1977 that canned food had been distributed with instructions, but the recipes were not compatible with local realities: "The recipes suggested on the little fold out that comes with every can were all, however, inappropriate here, calling for ovens and refrigerators and for ingredients not available." As a result CARE volunteers were charged with taking one donated can home, conducting some experiments, and creating a recipe. CARE staff members then distributed these recipes with the cans, but they never knew if people made use of them.[26]

To sum up, food aid led to the greater availability of processed foods, which most likely increased the demand for high-priced canned foods and breakfast cereals. The fact that people could not afford recommended foods probably added to their discontent with living conditions in the colonized areas. However, some foods also faced resistance because of their taste or their unsuitability for the tropical climate.

Despite their knowledge of malnutrition in local communities, the first generation of CARE's staff workers in Nicaragua believed in President Somoza's promises for political change. Although the government used CARE's work to improve its own image, the CARE workers upheld an overly positive vision of the dictatorship. They expressed their first doubts only after the massive misappropriation of food aid in 1972.

Issues had come to light with the government's abuse of food aid for commercial sales. For instance, rumors circulated in 1966 that Caritas food aid was sold and exchanged all over Managua. This was in line with experiences throughout Central America where either beneficiaries or corrupt government functionaries resold donated food.[27] The documents on CARE's first negotiations with the Nicaraguan government shed light on the relationship between the government and the international humanitarian agencies. It is striking that the first CARE mission in Nicaragua had a positive impression of President Anastasio Somoza Debayle who had taken over the presidency in 1967. That same year a CARE report described the new president: "The General is a wealthy man, educated in the United States, a West Point graduate, friend of bankers, politicians, businessmen, and men of letters. . . . He has a charming manner that will undoubtedly attract investment funds solely through his personal contacts."[28]

Yet it was two years after the organization took up work before Somoza received the local CARE mission staff face-to-face. In 1967 Fred Anderson, chief of the CARE Nicaragua mission, tried to meet the president three times but always had to accept talking only to his ministers. CARE's archives document other failed efforts where the president even made four team members come to his office, "with coat and tie, and shoes duly polished," just for them to be informed that he had left spontaneously for the countryside. When CARE staff members finally managed to meet Somoza in May 1968, the evaluation was again, and perhaps surprisingly, positive.[29] The foreign cooperation worked well with the regime, not only because the government paid lip service to development goals but also because some staff members credulously believed those messages.

The overall picture of CARE's cooperation with the Nicaraguan government remains ambiguous. Other CARE reports showed the government's lack of interest and its use of projects for political gains. In October 1968 Ronald Burkard reported that the government distributed a CARE donation of hand pumps to local communities making the beneficiaries think it was part of a government project. Afterward, Nicaraguan newspapers attributed the donation to the president.[30] Clearly, the Somoza government was eager to portray foreign aid projects as its own success and to distract attention from its deficient social policy. It was not until 1972 that the director of CARE Nicaragua, James Puccetti, admitted frankly in a letter that "for political reasons the welfare of the uneducated rural masses is not of major political concern to the present MEP [Ministerio de Educación Pública] hierarchy."[31] By and large, the first generation of CARE staff maintained their illusions about the regime and even denied the existence of a dictatorship; however, in their daily work they had to fight against the government's ignorance, bureaucracy, and lack of interest. These became more obvious when social tensions over food increased in the early 1970s.

TENSIONS OVER FOOD PRICES IN THE EARLY 1970S

Food prices in Nicaragua doubled between 1972 and 1977.[32] Not surprisingly, the early 1970s witnessed growing unrest among the Nicaraguan population over the prices and availability of food. *La Prensa* since 1970 had been reporting the rising prices of salt, cooking oil, and corn. These were important for flavor, frying, and the preparation of typical Nicaraguan dishes. In August 1970 the state institution INCEI was at the center of public criticism. The institution had decided to export maize and beans to Costa Rica, even though basic grains were scarce throughout Nicaragua. Every day, long lines formed at the INCEI building, where people hoped to acquire maize at the reduced price of 25 Córdobas per quintal, but most of them had to leave empty-handed. *La Prensa* highlighted the danger of speculation and asked: "Why can't the government guarantee people their consumption?"[33] In light of the high prices, oppositional sectors asserted a claim for popular consumption (meaning low-income groups' rights to equal opportunities to purchase sufficient food), showing that this was already an accepted category in 1970s political debates.

At this time *La Prensa* divulged another corruption scandal exemplifying political favoritism in the food distribution sector. For the supply of the departments, there was a special program that allowed local mayors and politicians to acquire basic grains at reduced prices. They utilized this offer to enter into the lucrative food business and sold corn at the elevated price of 60 Córdobas per quintal in their regions. Sometimes they did not even transport the corn to their hometowns but just sold it on the Managuan markets.[34] It is unclear, however, if the scandal had any political consequences.

In May 1972 anger over high food prices erupted into protests throughout the whole country. After a strike against rising milk and gasoline prices, eighteen organizations founded the first Comité Nacional de Defensa Popular, the National Committee of Popular Defense. In the following days, members of the committee explained to people using public transportation the reasons for the rising prices—the government's emphasis on export agriculture, for example. Students joined the protests with slogans such as "Only the People Can Save Themselves" and "Bring Prices Down." Repressive measures by Nicaraguan authorities—where National Guard members beat up students and attacked them with tear gas or police patrols surrounded school buildings—intensified the protests.[35] In fact, student protests had started to gain strength beginning in 1967. Protesters' messages shifted from university issues to more radical critiques of the dictatorship and its political repression.[36] A comic strip illustrates this political atmosphere where food prices and repression grew hand in hand. The protagonist Nicasio first states that living conditions in Nicaragua are hard because of the rising prices. On his nightly walk through the streets of Managua, he specifies that prices for beans, rice, and clothes are increasing. In the background a police car approaches. In the last comic panel, the car stops and arrests Nicasio, which illustrates the regime's suppression of any complaints about high food prices.[37]

Protesters in Granada and Juigalpa, the capital of Chontales department, attacked the government's economic policy. At that time, criticism of high food prices turned into general opposition to the regime. In Juigalpa, the participants of a protest assembly argued in a local pamphlet: "The rising price of milk in our country is due to two fundamental reasons. First, based on the arguments for development, our agricultural and fish production has been channeled into obtaining the greatest profits for the developers themselves. It turns out that it's more productive for the ranchers to export meat than to produce milk. . . . It's not fair that the Nicaraguan people are paying the price for an economic policy that's so badly conceived, and even more badly managed."[38] The pamphlet shows a general political opposition toward both the economic policies and the development strategy of the Somoza government. The protesters also accused the agricultural industry of profit-seeking and depriving Nicaraguans of basic foods. Based on economic aid within the Alliance for Progress initiative, the foreign as well as the national food industry had expanded their activities significantly. Many of the large national processing firms belonged to the Somoza clan, which increased people's outrage. These debates show that the voice of the popular consumer was already present in contemporary political discussion. Ultimately, the movement reached a partial victory. On May 21, 1972, the management of the Compañía Nacional Productora de Leche S.A. (the national milk factory), also in the hands of the Somoza clan, announced a price reduction for milk sales in poor Managuan districts.[39] Despite this victory, however, tensions did not lessen in the following months.

Shortly before the 1972 earthquake, a global rise in grain prices and a local dry period intensified the crisis. Beginning in August 1972, concerns about a drought dominated newspaper coverage of national news. Most important, maize production had decreased significantly. By October, prices for basic grains at Central Managuan markets increased by 30 percent.[40] Parallel to the national crisis, the World Food Crisis (1972–1975) emerged on the global level, caused by decreasing world grain production, shrinking food reserves, the El Niño phenomenon, and higher consumption levels in countries such as the Soviet Union. Grain prices rose continuously for twenty months, causing famines in different countries such as Haiti, Ethiopia, and India. The crisis coincided with the oil price shock in 1973 and led to new efforts in international cooperation at the 1974 World Food Conference.[41] The World Food Crisis contributed to the downfall of regimes around the world, as in Niger (1974), Ethiopia (1974), and Bangladesh (1975). In Nicaragua, the protests against high food prices played a part in the erosion of the regime, but revolution did not occur until several years later.

The Nicaraguan press had been reporting on the international price increases since December 1972. The country depended on wheat imports; wheat was, in the words of *La Prensa*, "the main ingredient of our daily bread."[42] However, INCEI refrained from instigating any political measures to stabilize wheat prices and declared its powerlessness in the face of international rising prices.[43] Shortly afterward, the earthquake struck Managua, and the conflicts over food prices turned into a broader emergency.

THE 1972 EARTHQUAKE, ACCELERATING THE FOOD CRISIS

The fatal earthquake of December 1972 caused a temporary hunger crisis in Nicaragua. It destroyed 90 percent of all buildings in the city center, including hospitals, markets, government institutions, and basic infrastructure. Given the lack of food and water, many people fled to the countryside.

When the government failed to react quickly and then misappropriated donated goods, the crisis deepened the discontent throughout Nicaraguan society. As a result several historians have characterized the earthquake as the beginning of the end for the Somoza regime.[44] Tensions over the food supply had escalated earlier, however, and were then taken up by social movements, strengthening already existing opposition to the regime.

The situation was particularly difficult in the countryside, as a drought had affected food production for the eight months preceding the earthquake. FAO reported that maize production had declined by 36 percent and beans production by 25 percent during the 1972 harvest.[45] Most of the refugees went to Granada, Masaya, or León. In Managua, red flags were posted at houses (often from the windows) indicating that people were living in provisional shelters. These became frequent, alongside signs with the inscription "We are hungry."[46]

For Nicaraguan food distribution, Managua had always been the nodal point with its markets and infrastructure. The earthquake destroyed the two main markets in the city center, and in consequence distribution problems started to affect the whole country. At the same time the lack of food provoked violent outbreaks and peasant protests in several Nicaraguan regions. In June 1973 hundreds of peasants gathered in Carazo for an assembly to demand food; in the end they nearly attacked the mayor's office. As *La Prensa* reported, thousands of peasants in the region were suffering from hunger and had not received any food aid. After food aid distributions were reduced considerably, earthquake victims in Granada began to fight among themselves over the small amounts of food.[47] The tensions not only manifested in growing opposition to the government but also made victims of the natural disaster turn on each other.

The Somoza regime controlled all of the incoming donations but misappropriated them for self-enrichment. In the months after the quake, high amounts of international aid poured into the country: FAO, for example, approved more than $450,000 for emergency food aid. In addition, the World Food Programme (WFP) planned three Food for Work projects with food distributions worth nearly three million dollars.[48] President Somoza Debayle himself led the National Emergency Committee. Somoza's son Julio was in charge of food distribution, which was conducted by the National Guard. Nonetheless, it was quickly revealed that the donated food had failed to reach the Nicaraguan people. There was a high prevalence of corruption, and army members had sold donated goods instead of distributing them to the needy.[49] The storage facilities near the airport soon became known as the "black hole" or "Tacho's supermarket," referring to the misappropriation of relief supplies by government officials and the military, as witnessed by several foreign observers.[50] The international community soon realized their donations were not reaching the suffering population. The misappropriation of donations eroded trust and support both within Nicaraguan society and among some international donors.[51] Despite the post-earthquake scandals, foreign aid remained at a high level during the subsequent years. Between 1972 and 1976, the United States contributed $246 million of economic aid.[52] CARE activities increased substantially, converting Nicaragua from one of the smallest into one of the organization's largest missions.[53]

International aid also favored a reconstruction of Managua that led to greater economic and social inequality within the city. After the disaster, the central area of Managua remained abandoned. Following the suggestions of US aid planners, politicians agreed on a decentralized urban development plan. Somoza named himself the head of the reconstruction committee, directing it toward a reconstruction based on US suburbanization models with suburbs and shopping centers. The reconstruction process was another prominent example of the Somozas using their positions for self-enrichment. In the following years, many construction enterprises belonging to the clan benefited from the reconstruction process and foreign funding.[54]

A 1973 newspaper advertisement shows the wide divide between local realities and the elite's visions for reconstruction. Only seven months after the quake, *La Prensa* published an announcement for investments in the shopping center project called San Francisco, depicted in front of a skyline similar to that of a large North American city.[55] In reality, large parts of Managua were still destroyed, and spontaneous settlements had expanded along the lakeshores. Since the poor districts lacked access to urban infrastructure, bad water quality affected food quality and people's health. Furthermore, the inhabitants had to cover long distances to get to the markets and had to rely on insufficient urban transport. Hence, reconstruction created more physical and social distance between different groups of consumers in Nicaragua. The gaps that had been developing since the 1950s had turned into a chasm.

POLITICAL DEBATES OVER US INFLUENCES AND CONSUMPTION

The reconstruction process after the earthquake generated a new debate over globalization and US influences in Nicaraguan society. Both theories of cultural imperialism and research on urban marginality provided the opponents of the Somoza regime with important arguments to criticize the urban development of Managua. Their critiques focused on social inequality, mass advertising, and shopping spaces. Theories on cultural imperialism arising from Marxist debates since the 1960s had shaped the negative perception of US influences all over the continent.[56] In the vision of cultural imperialism theorists, transnational enterprise in cooperation with local elites undermined Latin American culture by making consumers yearn for imported merchandise. The large firms sold their expensive products to vulnerable and inexperienced local consumers who lacked agency against such as powerful enemy.[57] In Nicaragua, these cultural imperialism theories reflected in 1970s social sciences analysis but also influenced the Sandinista discourse on commercial advertising and US cultural influences in the 1980s.

While the regime's elites advanced their reconstruction plans, international observers and Nicaraguan opposition members were concerned about the situation of the urban poor. After the earthquake, research by social scientists generated new knowledge on the living standards and consumption practices in poor Managuan districts. This research was inspired by investigations on urban marginality in other Latin American countries. Managua's popular districts were a sort of labyrinth, especially in the quickly growing areas at the margins of the city. In contrast to other Latin American cities, however, the Managuan slums were less separated from other districts. The so-called *cuarterías*, the improvised housing of the poor, were located nearly everywhere in the city and made up more than 45 percent of all housing in 1960.[58] The Nicaraguan sociologist Reinaldo Antonio Téfel described the marginalized zones of the city after the earthquake:

> Managua has a belt of misery that brings to light the ugliness, sadness, filth, ignorance, apathy, abandonment, darkness, dust clouds, shanties and garbage heaps of marginalization. It's the crown of thorns of a crucified country, dislocated, exploited and tortured. . . . The poor of Managua live there. The marginalized. Those who are on the edge of three square meals a day and of the minimum calories necessary to live, of the schools with all the latest advances in teaching and architecture, of the lovely and comfortable churches. . . . Those are Managua's poor. The marginalized. Fodder for elections, platforms for presidential propaganda, crowds in demonstrations, but always forgotten when it's time to feast and share the benefits.[59]

Téfel characterized the situation in Managua's marginal districts as the most powerful expression of poverty in Nicaragua by using the metaphor of a "crown of thorns." In terms of food, the inhabitants failed to reach minimum caloric intakes or even consume three regular meals a day. Although the political elites clearly exploited the low-income sectors for their political purposes, these sectors had never received any material compensation.

Téfel introduced his research as engaged sociology, which meant sociology with a political emphasis. This approach attracted Latin American intellectuals during the early 1970s when the level of political mobilization and anti-imperialist protests were particularly high. Téfel's objective with his survey was to lay the groundwork for development projects and to promote social change in Nicaragua. Téfel's research fits into a general trend for studies on the urban poor in Latin America that were inspired by Oscar Lewis's research on Mexico City from 1959.[60] For Nicaragua the survey was the first to document living conditions in Managua's poor districts and hence constitutes one of the few sources for shopping and consumption habits of low-income sectors during the 1970s.

Téfel's research team conducted fieldwork in four different areas of the capital, interviewing the household leaders with a questionnaire of 148 questions. His research revealed that more than 47 percent of the inhabitants shopped in local pulperías. Although more expensive, these small shops were located closer to people's homes, and they granted credit. As more than 60 percent of people surveyed claimed to shop daily, this was a significant advantage. Daily shopping was necessary because only few people could afford a refrigerator, and in the hot Managuan climate fresh food perished quickly. In addition, people frequented the Managuan markets on a weekly basis.[61] Overall, the survey examined housing, family structures, education, work, and political participation, and nutrition played only a marginal role. We do not know which foods were the most common and most valued by local inhabitants.

DIVIDED WORLDS OF FOOD CONSUMPTION

Along with the 1970s food crisis, advertising for modern shopping and eating increased. While students and workers mobilized in the cities for affordable milk and meat, food companies intensified their marketing campaigns. Their products responded to urban people's need to save time in preparing meals. People frequently viewed commercials on billboards in public spaces and in the newspapers.

In the oppositional newspaper *La Prensa*, advertisements for supermarkets, soft drinks, and the local fast food chain Pollo Tip Top dominated in the early 1970s.[62] Frequently, advertisements highlighted processed imported foods, such as Maggi soups, ketchup, margarine, and precooked rice. The tomato sauce Sharp explicitly addressed exclusive clients with the slogan "For Discriminating Tastes, the Exquisite and Refined Flavor of Spicy Sauce."[63] These advertisements indicate that more Nicaraguan households were starting to consume processed foods not only in order to accelerate cooking time but also because middle-class households considered them

TABLE 2.1. Share of Products Advertised in *La Prensa*, 1971.

Product	Share (in percent)
Pollo Tip Top	21
Coca Cola	12
Supermercado La Colonia	12
Restaurante Continental	7
Café Caracol	6
Supermercado Más x Menos	5
Flor de Caña	4
Cheez-Trix	3
Supermercado Criolla	2
Tor Trix Tostaditas de	2
Rest	26

Source: The chart is based on an evaluation of 879 *La Prensa* advertisements of food, beverages, restaurants, and supermarkets.

prestigious items. Simultaneously, the presence of the national food industry grew with products such as "Mostaza Indio Moctezuma" or "Alimentos Nacionales Doña Ana," which were probably cheaper than the imported brand products and hence affordable for other social groups. Supermarket chains, Pollo Tip Top, alcoholic beverages, and soft drinks dominated the publicity for food products in 1971 (see table 2.1). These examples show that supermarkets, fast food restaurants, and soft drink producers invested considerable amounts of advertising dollars in attracting Nicaraguan consumers. The increased visibility in advertising influenced the desires of Nicaraguan consumers, even if only the elite minorities had access to the supermarkets or could afford a meal in a fast food restaurant. In the reconstructed city advertisements for expensive imported products and names imitating US models became more prevalent in public spaces.[64]

The prominence of English language advertisements in Nicaragua, however, prompted critiques. In 1973 Dr. Roger Quant Pallavicini got to the heart of the debate when he raised the issue of *gringorización*. He defined it as "the excessive absorption of gringo culture," which had reached new heights after the earthquake.[65] Téfel claimed that advertising effects were significant even if the majority of Nicaraguans could not afford what was being sold: "With its 'go-go' rhythm, propaganda permanently 'hammers' in the need to buy, to a population that cannot. If it does buy, it can't pay and, if it pays, can only afford to do so for a short time. Only a still small emerging middle class can respond to the accelerated rhythm of commercial propaganda. The great majority is frustrated and gazes at that minority who can respond."[66] Téfel observed a deep frustration among low-income families about their limited consumer options.

The conspicuous consumption of the regime's elite also provoked fierce criticism. During the last period of the Somoza regime, rich Nicaraguans consumed more imported foods, consumer goods, and luxury items than in the early period of the regime. Historically, Nicaraguan elites were strongly attached to US consumer ideals. The Somoza clan reinforced this trend with their strong personal and commercial ties to the United States.[67] President Anastasio Somoza Debayle had been educated in the United States and returned to Nicaragua afterward. Consequently, he maintained close links to the United States and promoted US models of consumption and urban development. The US ambassador Lawrence Pezullo remembered how Somoza Debayle proudly claimed during their first meeting in 1979 that "he had modeled his country after the United States."[68] Although political opportunism possibly played a role here, as they met shortly before Somoza Debayle's fall from grace, the remark sheds light on Somoza Debayle's vision. In their social events and public ceremonies, the Somozas influenced not only their immediate social circle but also wider groups of Nicaraguans. For example, exclusive food was flown in by an express plane from Miami for the inauguration of a new airport terminal.[69] The consumption of expensive imported goods served as a means for social distinction, but the regime's decadence also nurtured opposition.

The gap between opulent elite dinners and the precarious food security of the rest of the population came increasingly under fire as another Nicasio comic strip shows. The dictator sits at his table waiting for a luxury dinner to be served, and Nicasio is watching him from the picture on the wall. Finally, the dictator covers the picture with his jacket to clear his conscience. Publicly, he claims that his diet was limited to rice, beans, a piece of meat, and a glass of milk. Nonetheless, the characterization of his meals as luxurious was impossible to miss, and consequently, the protagonist changed the menu to *canard à l'orange*, caviar, smoked salmon, and champagne. As a contrast to the luxury displayed by the Somoza elites, the FSLN developed an ethic based on an austere lifestyle and the rejection of personal belongings.[70] While the caricaturist Alberto Mora Olivares used cartoons about opulent meals to attack social inequality, nutrition experts worked on statistical surveys for the whole country to provide evidence on malnutrition.

Four years after the 1972 earthquake, USAID published a new report that declared: "malnutrition is one of the most serious and widespread socio-economic problems of Nicaragua."[71] Prepared by two external consultants, the account was a summary of several studies completed at the beginning of the 1970s, among them small community surveys. In general, the report confirmed the results of the 1965–1967 INCAP survey and demonstrated that the nutritional situation was at best stagnating. The large amount of aid that poured into the country after the earthquake had not alleviated the dire nutritional situation. Tragically, 56.6 percent of Nicaraguan children under the age of five were still suffering from malnutrition. But the authors also improved on the INCAP study: they criticized the lack of data from communities with less than five hundred inhabitants, which was important as approximately one-third of all Nicaraguans lived in these small communities. The authors pointed out that reliable health data was scarce and that an underreporting of children's deaths, especially in rural areas, should be taken into account. Two surveys in health centers and hospitals showed in 1973 and 1974 that 54.5 percent of all infant diseases were related to nutrition problems.[72] The authors condensed and compared the quantitative evaluations of Nicaraguan diets, but they did not reflect on different food cultures within the country. This would have been relevant, especially for the Caribbean, as local people consumed different basic staples and different meat (such as turtle). Also, the food intake in turtle fishing communities experienced strong seasonal varieties, which is why averages could lead to misleading conclusions.[73]

Building on previous nutrition surveys, the discussion in the USAID report evaluated per capita caloric consumption in relation to income levels. In 1970 the Grupo Asesor de la FAO para la Integración Económica Centroamericana (GAFICA), the FAO advisory group on Central American economic integration, had conducted a survey and estimated consumption for different income groups. GAFICA calculated that the poorest 50 percent of Nicaraguans earned only ninety-one dollars per year, which meant that they could spend only twenty-five cents on food per day. For the recommended caloric intake levels, this was far from enough. The INCAP standards required daily food expenditures of eighty-seven cents a day for one person based on 1976 retail prices.[74] For a family of six people, this would have meant more than five dollars per day or around eighteen hundred dollars per year.

The earthquake and alienation of foreign aid reinforced the opposition while peasants' land occupations escalated in the countryside. Opposition surged from two other sectors as well: the progressive Catholic Church and conservative forces around Pedro Joaquín Chamorro. After a spectacular FSLN coup in 1974 that liberated several political prisoners, Daniel Ortega among them, the government declared martial law and censorship; both remained in effect until September 1977. In the same year the US government under President Jimmy Carter temporarily cancelled military aid to Nicaragua. In July 1977 the Group of Twelve was formed and was willing to take over the provisional government after the fall of the dictatorship. This group included entrepreneurs, intellectuals, church representatives, and FSLN members. With the assassination of Pedro Joaquín Chamorro in January 1978, the bell sounded for the last round of the dictatorship. Outrage over the murder led to a wave of protests with a general strike followed by a local revolt in Monimbó in February 1978. Entrepreneurial groups distanced themselves more clearly from the regime. When the FSLN temporarily took over the National Palace in August, the weakness of the regime became obvious. At the same time Somoza was becoming increasingly isolated on the international level.[75]

Once the dictatorship was already weakened, international donors observed the situation carefully and intervened with large amounts of food aid to influence Nicaragua's future political course. Many countries and international organizations provided food aid during the political transition period. Humanitarian concerns played a role, but also there was the desire to influence the future political development of the country. Both Cold War opponents hoped to redirect Sandinista policy either toward state socialist models or toward representative democracy.

During the insurrectionary period, the number of refugees in Nicaragua increased significantly. International organizations and NGOs distributed food aid and vegetable seeds. From June to August 1979 the International Red Cross handed out survival rations for an average of eight hundred thousand people a week, which was 25.3 percent of the Nicaraguan population.[76] In June 1979 Ray Rigall, the CARE country director in Nicaragua, reported that Red Cross stores were already exhausted. People could only meet around 40 percent of their nutritional requirements with the daily rations.[77] The FAO representative for Central America and Panama, Juan Galecio Gómez, estimated in July 1979 that nearly no sowing of basic grains had taken place during the agricultural year 1979–1980. War had especially affected the rice production zones, but corn production, the meat sector, and the food-processing industry had also suffered.[78] Foreign observers, arriving in Managua during that period highlighted continuous looting and improvised markets while the traditional markets and supermarkets remained closed.[79] Hence, when the Sandinistas marched into the capital in July 1979, they first had to resolve a chaotic food supply situation.

Access to food became an ever-increasing problem in 1970s Nicaragua. Although the Somoza regime had introduced some nutritional institutions because of international pressure, powerful politicians' disregard for widespread malnutrition continued. Responding to international pressure, the regime created some alibi institutions, but these lacked resources and trained staff. In general the regime welcomed external aid only if this promised a gain in prestige and did not include demands for social change. This collaboration worked out, as the first generation of development cooperation staff perceived Somoza to be a capable politician with ambitious aims.

Food aid had temporarily alleviated social tensions in the 1960s. For the United States, food aid was another means to extend political influence during the Cold War. Food donations conveyed a symbolic message of superiority. At the same time donations strengthened popular consumption of imported grains, hence increasing foreign dependence. The use of donated foods in areas without refrigerators and clean water caused additional health problems. The 1970s nutrition surveys demonstrated that small rural communities, especially in the newly colonized zones of the Caribbean, were most affected by undernourishment. In 1976 more than 50 percent of Nicaraguan children suffered from malnutrition and average caloric intakes hovered around 1,900 kcal. However, the surveys failed to cover the impact of regional food cultures and food aid on the nutritional situation.

The Nicaraguan food system was increasingly under pressure as it had to supply a larger urban population while yields decreased. The high prices for basic foods sparked major controversies in the early 1970s. People questioned the government's focus on the agro-export economy and criticized corruption within the basic grain agency INCEI. Rising food prices and the earthquake in 1972 accelerated tensions in both urban and rural areas. Student groups joined the protest in popular districts, to which the regime reacted with repression, as in the countryside. Confrontations with the National Guard radicalized sectors of the Nicaraguan peasantry as well as students and opened up spaces for cooperation with the FSLN. The combination of drought and earthquake caused a severe food crisis in 1972. The misappropriations of aid convinced larger sectors of the elites and middle classes that the Somoza regime was unacceptable.

Along with the food crisis, mass advertising and use of the English language advanced in public spaces. The consumption of processed foods spread because of a stronger national food-processing industry, urbanization, and increased mass advertising. While elites displayed luxury meals and status goods in public, low-income Nicaraguans struggled with high food prices. This gap increased feelings of discontent and encouraged opposition to the regime. In addition, critical intellectuals attacked the spread of US consumption habits, a critique that was taken up by the FSLN.

After the earthquake both members of the regime and the elites encouraged a reconstruction plan based on US models that did not fit the social realities of the majority of the Nicaraguan population. Social gaps became more visible in Managua during the reconstruction process. However, the trope of a popular consumer with rights was already firmly established in 1970s contemporary political debates. By contrast, the FSLN guerrilla fighters distanced themselves from luxury consumption and promoted strict personal austerity. These different visions of consumption would later provoke conflicts throughout the 1980s. During the insurrectionary period, food production came to a halt in many places and distribution structures broke down. This represented a serious burden for the revolutionary government as its aim was to end malnutrition and provide a daily plate of rice and beans for all Nicaraguans.

CHAPTER THREE

THE ENTHUSIASTIC FOUNDING STAGE

EARLY REVOLUTIONARY FOOD POLICY, 1979–1982

"It may be concluded that the theme of FOOD and especially that of National Food Self-Sufficiency and Food Security is considered to have a very high political priority in contemporary Nicaragua."[1] This was how Otto van Teutem, FAO representative in Nicaragua, ended his 1982 report on World Food Day. Not surprisingly, Nicaragua's World Food Day in 1982 had emphasized self-sufficiency. Since the revolution, the Sandinistas had declared self-sufficiency as an important political aim to reverse decades of export dependency under the Somoza regime. The Sandinistas strongly promoted the event with a multimedia campaign that utilized television, radio, and the press. The government's slogan, "Nicaragua in the Fight for Food Self-Sufficiency," depicted a group of Nicaraguans carrying fruits, vegetables, and maize on their heads (see figure 3.1).

To inform the Nicaraguan public about their food policy, government institutions also organized several expositions on revolutionary projects such as the new popular stores and school gardens. Several ministers and members of the revolutionary government junta participated in these demonstrations. Revolutionary food policy aimed at reversing the negative developments of the prior decades, which had led to greater food insecurity and had created separate shopping worlds for the Nicaraguan rich and the Nicaraguan poor. The early campaigns for self-sufficiency mobilized thousands of Nicaraguans for gardening projects, price control campaigns, cooking competitions, and the consumption of local grains. The international nutrition community welcomed Nicaraguans' efforts to take their food supply seriously, as van Teutem's account of the 1982 World Food Day shows. The FAO used Nicaragua in the following years as a testing ground for food security projects.

Figure 3.1. World Food Day, 1982. Source: *Barricada*, October 16, 1982, 9.

How did early Sandinista food policy evolve in exchange with foreign actors during the enthusiastic founding stage between 1979 and 1982? The Sandinista revolution generated enormous hopes both inside and outside of Nicaragua. The revolutionaries had defeated one of Latin America's lon-

gest-lasting dictatorships. People around the globe hoped for a third, democratic way, in between socialism and capitalism. Nicaraguans hoped for an
end of repression and more opportunities for political participation. They
hoped as well for social equality and for equal access to food, land, health,
and education. Soon after the revolution the Sandinistas declared that the
"logic of the majority" would shape their policies. In consequence, food
policy had to assure basic food at accessible prices for all Nicaraguans. This
meant rolling back the trend of the previous two decades under the Somoza
regime toward greater reliance on food imports. Instead, the Sandinistas
worked to strengthen local production.[2]

Nonetheless, Sandinista food policy faced enormous challenges. First,
insurgency had brought food production to a halt in many places. Second, exports of coffee, cotton, and meat generated badly needed foreign
exchange. The resulting dilemma was whether to use land and resources
for exports or for basic grains production. Third, the new government institutions lacked sufficient knowledge about the Nicaraguan food system
because of the previous administration's neglect of food policy. From the
beginning, agricultural planning was limited by the deficit of statistical information. For example, immediately after the revolution, the Sandinistas
confiscated landholdings, and at first they believed that the land confiscated was 60 percent of all agriculturally productive land. After three months
of more thorough research, however, it was revealed they had only confiscated 20 percent, which illustrates how deficient information impeded
thorough planning immediately after the revolution.[3] Finally, US aggression challenged the new food policy from 1981 onward. The cancellation
of US economic aid deprived the Sandinistas of financial resources while
Contra military aggression also affected food production.

The Sandinistas addressed these challenges with both idealism and
pragmatism. On the one hand, by the end of 1982 they had formulated
ambitious aims such as self-sufficiency. On the other hand, they were aware
that the country's economic structure limited their capacity to achieve
these aims. Hence, they followed a strategy of "diversified dependency,"
which meant attracting foreign support from a multitude of different sources.[4] Given the global popularity of the Sandinista revolution, this strategy was highly successful in the early revolutionary years. The Sandinistas
asked for development assistance and support from three groups: bilateral
development aid institutions, international organizations, and relief agencies. In addition, they consulted foreign food experts on land reform, food
distribution, and planning.

In the aftermath of the World Food Crisis, new solutions for global
food problems were badly needed. A small revolutionary country with se-

vere nutrition problems—in the process of overthrowing a dictatorship and giving food a high priority—raised hope and interest. Several international organizations and NGOs started or intensified their work in the country and established relationships with the Sandinistas who were equally eager to work with them. The new government officials were inexperienced and lacked a consistent strategy as well as important data on the country's food situation. They used the presence of international actors as a means to spread revolutionary ideas and the Nicaraguan approach to food policy.

Nicaraguan food policy was broad enough to offer something for each donor: those willing to support agrarian reform, those interested in research, and those active in food donations. This was not an entirely new policy, but it combined initiatives that had already been applied in other contexts such as Mexico, Chile, and Cuba.[5] Members of the FSLN as well as foreign experts disagreed on whether to prioritize large-scale agriculture or small-scale peasant production, so Nicaraguan food policy remained sometimes contradictory. Nevertheless, the government's willingness to make food a political priority impressed foreign experts.

When Ronald Reagan came to power in 1981, US aggression increased, and the food policy entered into a new period. The external threat of the United States made self-sufficiency more urgent as supply could be easily cut off. Hence, the Sandinistas created the Nicaraguan Food Program, rationed scarce goods, and appealed to the international community for diplomatic, material, and military support. But economic problems increasingly thwarted the revolutionary government's ambitious food policy.

SANDINISTA FOOD POLICY IN THE EARLY 1980S

In the early 1980s Sandinista food policy concentrated on reassigning land for basic grains production, controlling food prices, democratizing the distribution system, and establishing food subsidies. Sandinista food policy operated within a broader framework of revolutionary economic policy—a pragmatic policy that adapted to the country's situation instead of following strict models. In contrast to other revolutionary governments, the FSLN never opted for a complete nationalization of the Nicaraguan economy. Instead, a "mixed economy" developed with three main sectors: private enterprise, state enterprise, and mixed enterprise. Immediately after the revolution, the former Somoza holdings were converted into state enterprise. Balancing the three sectors' role in food supply, however, proved to be a difficult task.

Throughout the 1980s food policy was an area that involved many different government organizations, which complicated coordination. Among the ministries dealing with food policy were the Ministries of

Planning, Agriculture, the Interior, and Exterior Commerce. Next, the institutions for coordinating external aid and a new research center at the Ministry of Agriculture influenced food policy. To improve coordination among these actors, the government created the Comisiones Consultivas de Política Agropecuaria (Consultative Commissions for Agricultural Policy) in February 1980 and the Programa Alimentario Nicaragüense (PAN, the Nicaraguan Food Program) in May 1981.[6] As existing institutional archives do not provide a full record of internal discussions and decision-making, I rely on published accounts, correspondence from international actors, and grey literature from Nicaraguan government institutions to fill the gaps.

Generally, the new government designed a program that was acceptable to a broad range of actors. The Junta de Gobierno de Reconstrucción Nacional (Junta of the Government of National Reconstruction) had a pluralist character and included members from opposition parties as well as entrepreneurs. The junta represented the government's executive branch and shared legislative power with the State Council.[7] However, the FSLN National Directorate made the major political decisions, and the junta then implemented these guidelines. As the coordinator of the governing junta, Daniel Ortega was the personal link between the two political bodies.

The revolutionary junta assigned mass organizations an important role in food policy. These organizations, partially founded during insurrection, were created to ensure the participation of workers, small farmers, women, and urban neighbors. In addition, they would constitute a space of exchange between political leadership and the masses.[8] During the revolutionary uprising, Civil Defense Committees had taken over supply of food and medicine in the neighborhoods. During the political transition, the committees continued to fulfill these roles until new government bodies were formed. Up to January 1980, the Comités de Defensa Sandinista, or CDSs, organized vigilance against speculation and provided census data for food aid distributions.

The fair distribution of food for affordable prices was an important goal for revolutionary food policy. In early 1980 the government created supply commissions all over Nicaragua whose task was to define local needs for food distribution.[9] In February 1980 the government also established a price control for basic products with the Ley de Defensa de los Consumidores (the Law on Consumer Defense). From then on, the Ministerio de Comercio Interior (MICOIN) set up price lists for sugar, rice, corn, salt, detergent, and vegetable oil that all shops had to post. The government reacted to speculation with severe punishments for merchants who charged more than the official prices. It also restricted media coverage on the scarci-

FIGURE 3.2. Expendio popular in Managua, 1980. Source: *Barricada*, September 26, 1980, 7.

ty of foods and other products; journalists were required to check all information with the government junta or MICOIN prior to publication.[10] At the same time, official publications distributed information on food prices of the new state distribution system.

To guarantee equal access to food, the government subsidized food prices and expanded distribution to rural areas and low-income districts. By 1980 the government had already spent more than 350 million Córdobas on food subsidies.[11] Subsidized foods in the early revolutionary years included corn, beans, rice, milk, sugar, and vegetable oil. The policy favored locally produced basic grains but eliminated subsidies for meat and eggs. Throughout the early 1980s government spending on food subsidies represented budget shares between 3.7 and 5.5 percent.[12]

At the same time, several channels of the new distribution system opened their doors, such as the popular supermarkets or *expendios populares* (see figure 3.2). These supply chains offered low-income consumers new shopping alternatives that were close to their homes and workplaces. By doing so the revolutionaries reversed the city's socially divided shopping spaces that had emerged during the reconstruction after the 1972 earthquake. To supply these new shopping spaces adequately, the government set up further incentives for peasant producers.

To stimulate basic grains production, in 1980 the government established a new credit program with low interest rates for small- and medium-sized food producers. Compared to 1978, the sum available for these producers had increased sevenfold to one million Córdobas, which signaled the unbridled optimism of early Sandinista food policy. However, the unprecedented expansion of credit showed mixed results. First, peasants considered the official prices of the new state basic grain agency Empresa Nacional de Alimentos Básicos (ENABAS), the National Enterprise of Basic Foods, to be too low, and so they did not expand production. Second, there were problems with obtaining agricultural supplies. When these were not available, peasants spent the money for other purposes. Last, peasants in isolated areas lacked transport facilities to bring their harvest to the markets. In consequence, many producers were unable to repay the debt, which added to governmental budget problems. In 1981 the Sandinistas reduced the program and established new lending criteria. Overall, the program had mostly benefited medium-sized producers. The well-intended initiative in providing more credit was an outcome of initial enthusiasm but ended up proving disadvantageous in practice.[13]

The structure of the agro-export economy created challenges for Sandinista food policy makers. During the early 1980s, export production failed to reach its pre–civil war levels and world market prices for Nicaragua's export products declined. Since the agro-export sector was the country's primary source of income, steady and reliable coffee, cotton, and sugar production was crucial. This dilemma persisted throughout the 1980s and led to conflicts over resource allocation. From early on it became clear that reversing the strong export dependency was not an easy task. Throughout 1980 and 1981 the government hotly debated whether exports or local production should gain priority.[14] As production of important foods decreased in 1978 and 1979, the year 1980 bore witness to widespread speculation and supply problems.

Another challenge for Sandinista food policy was the threat of US intervention against the revolution. Historically, the United States had dominated foreign aid and had continuously intervened in Nicaraguan politics. Would the US government tolerate a revolutionary government in a region relatively close to its borders and the Panama Canal? Thus, the revolutionaries developed a strategy for mobilizing international backing beyond the United States.

INTERNATIONAL SUPPORT FOR THE SANDINISTA REVOLUTION AND ITS FOOD POLICY

During the enthusiastic founding stages of the revolution, the revolutionaries won over numerous international donors who were willing to fund their food policy. Before the insurrection, the Sandinistas had built up an international network to obtain support for the revolution. By presenting the revolution as a pluralist project, the Sandinistas managed to attract aid across the Cold War blocs. For their food policy, they also approached international organizations and NGOs. The result was a heterogenous group of advisers recommending diverging—sometimes even contradictory—strategies for ensuring a more stable food supply.

Prior to the revolution the Sandinistas had created a transnational communication structure to mobilize assistance abroad. The network they had built up in late 1977 included Nicaraguan immigrants in the United States and Nicaraguan students in Europe as well as solidarity organizations abroad. After the revolution the Sandinistas utilized these links to promote their cause among foreign countries. Recent research on the solidarity movements has shown that personal visits of Sandinista leaders, cultural programs, media campaigns, and international visits successfully created support for the revolution.[15] Within these campaigns Nicaraguan actors portrayed a revolution relying on pluralism, social reforms, and a mixed economy. To address international audiences, the Sandinistas organized two communication channels—the news agency and then multilingual publications such as the international edition of the Sandinista newspaper. For material support, the Sandinistas circulated project lists among solidarity networks and development assistance.[16] Initially, mainly Western European and Latin American nations provided support.

Shortly after the revolution, Nicaragua declared itself a nonaligning nation, which made support possible from both Cold War fronts. Between July 1979 and 1981, bilateral support from Western Europe was strongest with 44.4 percent of total foreign grants, followed by Latin America with

30.9 percent, and Western multilateral organizations with 21.4 percent. At that time the United States still contributed 10.5 percent, and the Eastern bloc countries only provided 2.6 percent.[17] Western European governments still hoped for a moderate outcome of the Nicaraguan revolution and hence offered material support. With similar intentions, the United States continued economic aid but with strings attached.

Despite fears of further revolutions in the region, the US government decided to recognize the revolutionary junta. The Sandinistas clearly rejected imperialist interference but were aware that the revolution would survive only if they managed to avoid US intervention. They tried to establish cordial relations and arranged a first meeting with President Jimmy Carter in September 1979. Afterward, the Carter administration offered a seventy-five-million-dollar aid package, which the US Congress approved in May 1980. In all, 60 percent of this aid would benefit private sector organizations. In fact, the United States linked economic aid to the survival of a private sector and the omission of aid for the guerilla forces in El Salvador. At the same time, the US government also provided one million dollars to anti-Sandinista organizations and the oppositional press.[18] In contrast, Mexico and Cuba fully supported the Sandinista government as part of a revolutionary alliance.

Mexico shared the Sandinista political agenda for food self-sufficiency and hence provided capital for food-producing firms. Its support for the Sandinistas dated back years before the revolution, when the Mexican embassy in Managua became a sanctuary for the opposition leaders. In May 1979 Mexico broke off official relations with the Somoza regime—a step that motivated several Latin American countries to follow suit. The Mexican president López Portillo presented himself publicly as the paternal supporter for Sandinista revolutionaries. In the following years, leading Sandinistas frequently traveled to Mexico City to solicit support for revolutionary projects. López Portillo received them on several occasions with the welcoming "Well, boys, what do you need?" Mexican aid to Nicaragua was estimated at more than five hundred million dollars by 1981.[19] For the Sandinistas, it was a very beneficial relationship as Mexico was not associated with either of the Cold War blocs and maintained cordial relations with the United States in the early 1980s.

Beyond looking for bilateral support, Nicaragua also contacted international organizations, NGOs, and development agencies. Their support provided the revolutionaries with financial resources, legitimacy, and know-how in the early 1980s, and a new, more heterogenous group of foreign advisers joined the revolutionaries in their effort to increase food production. Their presence reinforced diverging approaches in Nicaraguan food policy. Beyond the mission assigned to each group of advisers by the Sandinistas, all foreign actors followed their institutional agenda, which further added to contradictions in food policy.

In August 1979 Joseph Collins, cofounder of the initiative Food First, received a phone call from Managua in his office in San Francisco.[20] An official from the Nicaraguan Ministry of Planning asked if he was willing to come to Nicaragua as an external advisor for the Sandinista government. Collins, who had been doing research on food policy in the Global South since the 1970s, agreed immediately and during the following three years traveled ten times to the small country. His 1982 book on his experiences was titled *Nicaragua: What Difference Could a Revolution Make?* In it, Collins invited his readers to study the Nicaraguan transformation through "food glasses."[21]

Collins argued that small farmers should play an important role for stabilizing the Nicaraguan food supply. In his view Nicaragua was a country where the principle of "Food First" had become a basis for government policy. The revolutionaries' main successes, in his opinion, were increased basic grains production, the redistribution of land, and higher food consumption levels. Clearly, Collins perceived Nicaragua as a model for other countries in the Global South that lacked abundant resources in their budgets for food policy. In his book he argued that small farmers were important for increasing basic grains production, but this view contradicted the vision of some of the Sandinista leaders who favored large-scale agriculture.[22] We do not know how the revolutionaries evaluated Collins's suggestions because of a lack of sources. Although Collins was ultimately disappointed with the implementation of the Nicaraguan Food Program, his writings undoubtedly contributed to the global diffusion of the Sandinista approach as his book was widely distributed and translated into Spanish and German.

Similar to Collins, some international organizations and relief agencies promoted the Nicaraguan government as a positive example for other countries to emulate. Several organizations such as CARE valued cooperation with the Sandinistas and expanded their work in Nicaragua. CARE supported Nicaraguan food policy through training measures, food aid, and the distribution of seeds. In contrast to other organizations that had recently entered the country, CARE could still rely on its contacts in the Nicaraguan ministries as there was a high degree of personal continuity in the lower hierarchies.[23] Only five days after the revolution, CARE Nicaragua sent its congratulations to the new government and was officially recognized as one of the first voluntary agencies working in Sandinista Nicaragua.[24] At that time, a new generation of CARE representatives had come to Nicaragua who sympathized with the Sandinistas' aims. In their initial reports these staff members emphasized the new government's openness and positive evaluation of CARE's work. For example, a delegation received a warm welcome at the Ministry of Education in October 1979, where the minister expressed his satisfaction with the new CARE school feeding program. The delegation also discussed cooperation projects with the minister of agriculture and agrarian reform, Jaime Wheelock, whom one delegation member characterized in his report as "thoughtful and cooperative."[25] In the early 1980s CARE distributed basic grains and vegetable seeds to stimulate food production. Planning for the future, the organization also established agricultural schools and projects for school feeding and potato cultivation. By April 1980 CARE's emergency assistance and projects had surpassed the four-million-dollar level.[26] Hence, CARE support expanded knowledge on food production but also contributed with agricultural supplies to the self-sufficiency project.

Nonetheless, the CARE team quickly realized how difficult it was to make long-term plans in a revolutionary setting. The newly created ministries were only at the beginning stages of organization, so the staff frequently had to improvise and adapt to sudden changes. The uncertainty of project planning in a revolutionary country sometimes led to tensions with the CARE offices in New York, where the headquarters followed its ordinary routines. In June 1982 Timothy Lavelle, CARE director for Nicaragua, commented to the central office: "As you probably gleaned from the above referenced, writing multi-year plans in a revolutionary milieu is no easy matter. There are (thank you again T. S. Eliot) 'visions and revisions which a moment will reverse.'"[27] Despite these uncertainties, the revolutionary vision for a new food policy attracted other international actors to support Sandinista projects.

Between 1979 and 1982, the Sandinistas consulted experts from a broad geographical and political spectrum. In some policy areas Eastern bloc representatives became dominant, in others a culture of diversity developed, including former advisers from the Chilean Allende government as well as postcolonial African nations. Many of these foreign experts also contributed to research on Nicaraguan food policy.[28] One of them was the UN Research Institute for Social Development (UNRISD) director Solon Barraclough who had worked during the 1960s and 1970s with FAO and the Chilean government on agrarian reform in Latin America.[29] After the military coup in 1973, he was expelled by the Chilean government and was appointed UNRISD director in 1977. He published an early account of Nicaraguan food policy in 1982. In his analysis, Barraclough judged the first two years of Nicaraguan food policy as generally positive. Specifically, he viewed the improved access to food in urban and rural areas as a success although the new distribution system still did not cover all rural zones. The main challenges for the local food system were economic recovery, institutional reforms, and the need for greater investment in agriculture.[30]

With the exception of Joseph Collins, these experts generally did not reflect in their publication on their role as advisers and on knowledge exchanges in food policy. Collins's account demonstrates that the Sandinistas carefully evaluated different options, but other testimonies indicate they blindly followed other revolutionary models. Collins was particularly impressed that the Sandinista politicians never asked experts to provide rigid guidelines. Instead, the government presented political options to the informal advisory group of foreign experts and asked them about the probable outcome of different solutions. Collins also appreciated the political pragmatism of the Sandinistas, and he rebuffed the notion of a doctrinaire influence of Cuban and Soviet advisers on Nicaraguan food policy.[31]

Nonetheless, former Sandinista government members contested this vision. As a member of the revolutionary government junta and Nicaraguan vice president between 1985 and 1990, Sergio Ramírez, remembered: "Many wanted to adopt the Cuban model in its entirety, even in the most banal matters. It was a question of blind faith." In his 1999 memoirs Ramírez accused part of the Sandinista political leadership of a lack of critical reflection. As a consequence, Ramírez argued, the adoption of a Cuban style became a matter of prestige.[32]

Each group of foreign advisers influenced distinct areas of policy. For example, German Democratic Republic (GDR) influence was strong in the Ministry of Planning, and Cubans were omnipresent in the health sector. The Cuban model also influenced the role of mass organizations in food distribution. In other institutions working on food policy, Cuban advisers were less visible, which most likely explains the different perspectives of Collins and Ramírez.[33]

By 1981 Sandinista food policy had developed through the foundation of new institutions, strategic debates with foreign experts, and the activities of revolutionary mass organizations. Nicaraguan and international agricultural expertise favored industrial farming to increase food production. Both low production at state farms as well as the revolution's inconsistent relationship with peasants undermined the self-sufficiency strategy.

INDUSTRIAL FARMING, AGRICULTURAL EXPERTS, AND THE REVOLUTION'S PROBLEMS WITH PEASANT PRODUCERS

To become more self-sufficient Nicaragua needed to increase food production significantly. The impending war as well as the Sandinista leaders' elite family backgrounds made industrial farming an appealing solution. This

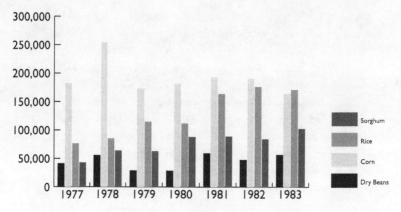

FIGURE 3.3. Basic grains production in Nicaragua, 1977–1983 (in tons). Source: FAO-STAT.

turn matched with the interests of FAO and the Mexican advisers in food policy. Despite this international support, food production on state farms in Nicaragua soon suffered problems, which weakened the self-sufficiency policy significantly. At the same time, the slow agrarian reform and the food pricing alienated peasants from revolutionary food policy.

Despite some improvement in 1982 the Sandinista government's efforts to raise basic grains production remained insufficient to feed the growing urban population. Immediately after the revolution, the consequences of civil war still affected the food supply. In particular, corn production had declined significantly after 1978. Although it recovered with the 1980–1981 harvest, prewar levels were not reached again until the late 1980s.[34] Overall, Nicaragua was far from self-sufficient in the early 1980s (see figure 3.3). The government still had to import basic grains as well as meat, vegetable oil, and sugar during the post-revolutionary period. The efforts to strengthen local production showed some success in 1982 when Nicaragua was able to reduce imports of rice, beans, and maize significantly. With increasing soy and potato production, Nicaraguans could also enrich their diet with new basic staples.

It was clear by 1982, however, that despite these advancements food production would still need to increase significantly. There were three reasons for this: (1) the growing Nicaraguan population, (2) the continued migration to cities, and (3) with the beginning of the Contra War the Sandinistas needed to supply their army. Consequently, some of the Sandinista leaders considered industrial agriculture to be the best way to rapidly increase food production. A significant part of Nicaraguan food production—such as the production of sugar, milk, and meat—already took place on large state farms. The Sandinista government leaders believed in large-scale agricultural production and the use of modern technology. In consequence, they invested in large production complexes such as the milk project in Chiltepe, rice production projects on the Pacific Coast, and vegetable oil production at Kukra Hill.[35] This was in line with a global trend to rely on industrial farming.

Agricultural experts across the Cold War blocs supported the global spread of large-scale farming and Green Revolution technologies. Around the globe, the belief of politicians, planners, and scientists in industrialized agriculture had originated in the early twentieth century. They were convinced that specialized private firms or state enterprise using large-scale machinery as well as chemical fertilizers and pesticides would increase yields and improve food quality. In Nicaragua, large-scale agriculture first expanded on large banana and coffee plantations in the early twentieth century. On a global scale, these strategies advanced further between the 1930s and the 1950s. Both the United States and the Soviet Union had supported large-scale farming projects since the 1930s as a strategy for agricultural development. Agronomic experts did not comply with the strict Cold War division, however, and shared knowledge across the blocs instead. Experts from both countries shared intense exchanges about these new models and exported them to other world regions in the second half of the twentieth century.[36] In particular, US experts moved into development aid and international organizations after the Second World War. In Nicaragua they had supported the Somoza regime's strategy to expand agro exports on large-scale farms. The Somoza dictatorship promoted monocultures and the Green Revolution in the 1960s as part of the Alliance for Progress, a period that the Sandinista agricultural experts had experienced in their youth.

In terms of policy the Sandinistas favored large-scale agriculture over small independent farms. Many of the revolution's agricultural experts came from elite families and had studied at the Instituto Centroamericano de Administración de Empresas (Central American Institute of Business Administration, INCAE, a Nicaraguan business school), the Pan-American Agricultural School in Zamorano (Honduras), or in the United States.[37] In the 1980s when they started working for the Ministry of Agriculture, they brought with them these schools' agricultural methods and the methods used on plantations belonging to their families prior to the revolution. These experiences favored cooperation with FAO and Mexican agricultural advisers who promoted large-scale projects as well.

Soon after the revolution, the Sandinistas approached the FAO to support their food policy and found sympathetic listeners within the organization. FAO only had a weak presence in Nicaragua at the outbreak of the revolution, but its activities increased significantly during the Sandinista period. In April 1980 the Nicaraguan government requested that FAO open a local office. Jaime Wheelock argued that the Sandinistas' new focus on social justice and better living conditions for the Nicaraguan population required FAO's special attention. Collins had advocated that revolutionary food policy should empower small farmers, but FAO promoted the opposite approach—that is, agro-industrial production on large farms. This was also the position of leading Sandinistas within the Ministry of Agrarian Reform.

The first FAO projects promoted ambitious increases in food production based on Green Revolution technologies. The members of the first FAO delegation to Sandinista Nicaragua, in October 1980, considered milk and meat production as deficient; therefore, the first postrevolutionary FAO project aimed at strengthening the Nicaraguan milk sector.[38] The second priority was assigned to projects supporting agro-industrial development in Nicaragua. A 1983 project report identified the optimistic goal of raising agricultural production by 35–50 percent.[39] To meet these ambitious production goals, FAO projects promoted the systematic use of fertilizers. Cooperation projects with PAN focused heavily on technical development and relied on Green Revolution technologies.

Throughout the 1980s FAO completed forty-two projects in Nicaragua with a budget of more than four million dollars.[40] Since the FAO typically archived project reports without correspondence, it is still unclear exactly how the high-ranking FAO officials perceived Sandinista food policy. The final projects, however, demonstrate their mutual focus on basic grains production, food security, and agricultural development. The Sandinista government's vision for food production in the form of large state complexes and the application of modern technology also created common ground for cooperation with the Mexican government.

The Sandinistas shared with Mexico also the political aims of self-sufficiency and state intervention in food prices. In July 1981 PAN signed a two-year agreement with the Mexican food program Sistema Alimentario Mexicano (SAM), which established cooperation between the two entities in agricultural development, irrigation techniques, and improved seeds.[41] The Mexican SAM also promoted self-reliance in corn and beans in the early 1980s. State intervention in food distribution and pricing in Mexico dated back to 1938, when President Lázaro Cárdenas had reacted to inflation and consumer protests with the establishment of a state basic grain agency and price controls. The 1970s witnessed a strong expansion of the food state agency and its distribution networks in Mexico. Within a decade, more than ten thousand rural and urban stores offered food at lower prices than in private retail distribution. This strategy resembled the Sandinistas' plans for democratizing the food supply. The common approach to provide cheap food through state networks provided the basis for close cooperation between the Mexican and the Nicaraguan food programs.[42]

The Sandinistas' attempts to provide Nicaraguan consumers with alternatives to important export products also relied on large-scale state firms. For example, Mexican experts recommended soy production, and the government implemented several projects to promote soy as a cheap alternative to meat. The first project started in the Rivas region in 1982 with three hundred volunteers and expanded gradually to the whole country.[43] After an agreement between Jaime Wheelock and the Compañia Nacional de Semillas de México S.A., the mixed enterprise "Soya-Nica" was founded in February 1982. The vision was ambitious and reflected the initial enthusiasm for large-scale planning: Soya-Nica would become the largest soy producer in Central America. Soybean production increased significantly in the following years. From 1980 to 1982 it tripled to three thousand tons; in the late 1980s Nicaragua produced between fifteen and seventeen thousand tons of soybeans annually.[44] The soy project demonstrates the ambitious vision in early Sandinista food policy as well as the will to increase self-sufficiency through the introduction of new staples. In spite of substantial investments, however, the productivity of state enterprises across the board remained below expectations.

Labor instability on state farms was a major problem in the first years after the revolution. Some workers believed the time had come for a "historic vacation" after years of strict control and repression. They perceived the revolution as a chance to work less, which Sandinista bureaucracy criticized as a "Revolution is *piñata*" attitude. On many state farms, working hours went down to three or five hours per day.[45] In other cases, the limitations of the administrators hindered productivity. New administrators lacked experience but also enthusiasm for administrative tasks. After years of political activism, managing a state enterprise, checking accounts, and keeping statistics seemed a boring endeavor. Finally, the generous credit policy after the revolution fostered an administrative culture that ignored real production costs and tended to blame inefficiency on external reasons. Ministers felt responsible for only certain enterprises and sectors and nearly always managed to obtain further credit, even if the margins for state investments were shrinking.[46]

These disappointing results of large-scale production vindicated the arguments of those experts who perceived small farmers to be the solution to food supply problems. Parallel to the large-scale projects, the government had already supported basic grains producers through a new procurement

system as well as better access to credit. But from the beginning, the Sandinistas' relationship to peasants suffered from problems.

A key issue for food production was land distribution. Immediately
after the revolution, the Sandinistas had expropriated the landholdings of
the Somoza clan and National Guard officers, a total area of more than 1.6
million manzanas that was assigned to state firms. Although peasants clam-
ored for additional land distribution, the Sandinistas did not enact the first
agrarian reform law until nearly two years after the revolution. The delay
had its origins in the Sandinistas' contradictory attitudes toward peasants
and in their political alliances with rural elites. The FSLN leadership viewed
peasants as unimportant for the success of revolutionary transformation,
and they developed only short-term strategies for rural problems. The party leaders also feared that a more radical land distribution policy would
endanger landowners' willingness to cooperate, which was important for
maintaining agro exports.[47] Pressure from landless workers and peasants for
land distribution continued, until finally the law was passed in May 1981.

However, land distribution after the enactment of the reform law proceeded slowly: only 14 percent of all land distributions in the revolutionary
period were completed between 1981 and 1983. By December 1984 the
government had distributed more than 465,000 manzanas of land under
the auspices of the Ley de Reforma Agraria (Agrarian Reform Law). The
main criteria for confiscation was inadequate or non-use of land rather than
the size of a property.[48] During the first period of redistributions, it was
mainly organized cooperatives that benefited. Between 1981 and 1984 cooperatives received more than 80 percent of distributed land. For peasants
who had dreamed for a long time of possessing their own land, this was interpreted as a betrayal.[49] However, individual peasants' social backgrounds
as well as regional differences tended to influence their perceptions of agrarian reform.

The Sandinistas' food price and distribution policy also alienated peasants. ENABAS, the new state agency for basic grains distribution, had been
established in September 1979 and was responsible for both food procurement from producers and distribution within the country. Its aim was to
improve the food supply throughout the country. Initially, ENABAS took
over agricultural storage facilities from its Somoza-era predecessor. Out-
dated technology and a deficient transport network hindered the logistical
reorganization. By the 1979–1980 harvest, the Sandinistas introduced a
new system of guaranteed prices for basic grains, which were calculated by
adding a margin of between 5 and 20 percent to production costs.[50] Peasants considered prices for basic grains to be too low, however, as inflation
was on the rise.

ENABAS's relationship with food producers suffered from two problems. First, trading with ENABAS had disadvantages for peasants as the agency paid by check and not cash. Since local banks could not always cash checks, this payment method required additional travel. As a consequence, the agency in 1980 only procured 12 percent of the total corn harvest and 24 percent of the beans harvest, which weakened the state distribution system. In the following years ENABAS improved its storage system and paid better prices, which led to higher procurement rates, around 60 percent in 1983. Second, the agency was not able to substitute the role of intermediary merchants completely. Prior to the revolution these merchants had fulfilled several social roles; they bought basic grains from the peasants, supplied them with consumer goods, and sometimes provided credit. Over the years an extensive social network had developed that could not easily be substituted.[51] The revolution disrupted established social relations in the countryside. Overall, the problems between peasant producers and ENABAS weakened the Sandinistas' self-sufficiency project.

NEW CONCEPTS IN SANDINISTA FOOD POLICY

The Sandinistas highlighted self-sufficiency in their political discourse, and FAO introduced the concept of food security to Nicaragua. As an outcome the 1987 constitution asserted the right of Nicaraguans to be protected against hunger. Throughout the 1980s FAO supported strategic projects for long-term planning and policy definition. As of September 1981, FAO assisted the definition of a national food security policy.[52] At this point FAO was also participating directly in the development of Nicaraguan food policy with a food security project financed by the Norwegian government. Although the project descriptions strongly emphasized self-sufficiency, the project itself concentrated on technical support through external consultants.[53] Unfortunately, sources do not provide evidence of whether the concepts of food security and self-sufficiency had practical importance during project implementation. Concerning food security, FAO considered Nicaragua an interesting testing ground, and FAO projects aimed at planning its food policy and food security strategies.

A new research center, cooperating closely with the UNRISD research institute, also intervened in the strategic debates on food policy in Nicaragua. In 1980 there was still a lack of knowledge about food consumption as well as production and land distribution, so the revolutionary government created a specialized research institute, the Centro de Investigaciones y Estudios de la Reforma Agraria (CIERA), the Center for Research and Studies on the Agrarian Reform. The Argentine researcher Carlos M. Vilas characterized CIERA as "the most dynamic social science research centre in Nicaragua."[54] From the outset its research was closely entangled with UNRISD, which had introduced the food system approach in Nicaragua, and its approach was based on two pillars: it had to address the interaction of local food subsystems with global markets, and it had to explore social interactions and power asymmetries around food chains.[55] UNRISD research projects were initially located in India, Mexico, China, and Senegal.

Following an invitation from the Nicaraguan government, UNRISD connected with CIERA in 1980 and started research on the Nicaraguan food system. From this point forward the UNRISD research methodology and interests strongly influenced CIERA's research, and CIERA's publications documented the evolution of the new strategies, research on food consumption habits, and the supply situation. Many CIERA publications relied on the food system approach. For example, they provided a detailed historical analysis of the Nicaraguan food system, or they discussed Managua's role in Nicaraguan food production. In general, CIERA promoted peasant-centered strategies, which sometimes led to conflicts with huge investment projects for large-scale agriculture. In advising Nicaraguan government institutions, the institute influenced political decisions over food distribution and production.[56]

Many of the contentious issues from the early period between 1979 and 1981 continued throughout the decade, for example, the recurring lack of basic foods or the role of peasants in food production. In the two first years after the revolution, the rough course for food policy was set. A high level of mobilization and popular participation facilitated the implementation of reforms. However, competing visions and institutions still impeded a coherent strategy, and external aggression complicated planning. After 1981 food policy had to proceed increasingly with economic difficulties, supply problems, and Contra attacks.

US AGGRESSION, INTERNATIONAL AID, AND THE NICARAGUAN FOOD PROGRAM

US president Ronald Reagan perceived Nicaragua as a totalitarian regime that had to be brought down through military attacks and economic warfare. At first US aggression intensified international solidarity with the Sandinistas and led to new loans, food donations, and cooperation projects. Meanwhile, the revolutionaries strengthened food policy through PAN. But eventually important donors caved to US pressure and reduced their support, and US aggression challenged both access to financial resources and food production.

When Ronald Reagan won the November 1980 US elections, it was clear that he would follow a hardline course regarding the Sandinista revolution. Throughout the electoral campaign the Republican Party Platform had characterized the Sandinista revolution as part of a Marxist offensive in Central America and had opposed the maintenance of aid programs.[57] During this period tensions with the United States had increased and led to temporary aid cancellation in early 1980 after the US Central Intelligence Agency (CIA) had discovered that Nicaragua had resumed arms shipments to El Salvador. Shortly afterward, in January 1981, Ronald Reagan came into office.

External events triggered the next phase of Nicaraguan food policy. In February 1981 the US government announced the cancellation of credit for wheat imports to revolutionary Nicaragua. The cancellation precipitated an international campaign for solidarity and the foundation of the Nicaraguan food program PAN. In early 1981 the cancellation of US credit created an atmosphere of urgency and menace. The scarcity of bread soon made Nicaraguans feel the consequences of the new US policy in their daily lives; national wheat reserves were only expected to last for another month. In March 1981 the government decided to freeze the wheat supply and reduce distribution by one-third.[58] Many people were worried about their daily bread supply. To address this problem, the government started an international solidarity campaign with the motto "Bread for Nicaragua." Soon Canada, Argentina, the Soviet Union, and East Germany announced initial donations. At the same time Sandinista propaganda emphasized that these donations were part of the international fight against US imperialism rather than acts of "charity."[59]

In May 1981 PAN set to work. Although it promoted the production of local grains, its acronym stands for *pan*, the Spanish word for bread, but whose production required imported ingredients. The organization focused on coordinating the work of different institutions that were active in food policy. PAN director Pedro Antonio Blandón explained the aims of the program to the Nicaraguan public. In the short term, PAN would extend the areas for basic grains production as well as improve the credit system and food storage facilities. In the long run, Nicaragua would reach self-sufficiency in basic grains and then convert into a food exporting country. Moreover, the country would reach an equilibrium between the needs of the agro-export economy and internal consumption.[60] External aggression complicated the task of balancing these two areas.

In November 1981 a group of right-wing advisers convinced Reagan to support armed resistance against the Sandinista revolution.[61] Between 1981 and 1990 the US government provided $322 million to contrarevolutionary forces organizing in Honduras and Costa Rica, the so-called Contras, whose forces attacked Nicaragua from their bases at the Nicaraguan borders. Over the course of 1982 the Contra War seriously affected food policy. The Sandinistas estimated that the material destruction and production losses in 1982 alone stood at $32.1 million.[62] The Contra war demanded resources that could have otherwise been spent on social projects. In addition, US pressure weakened the international support for the Sandinistas' food policy around 1982, as the examples of CARE and Mexican cooperation demonstrate.

With increasing US aggression, CARE's activities faced greater challenges despite the initial enthusiasm of local CARE staff. Soon, Cold War conflicts increasingly overshadowed the agency's work. Rumors were already circulating in March 1981 that the US government would ask CARE to stop its work in Nicaragua. From July 1982 onward, conflicts over USAID assistance for CARE projects intensified. In one case, USAID informed CARE that it could not give support to the Agricultural School project, to which Timothy Lavelle commented in his letter: "The cold war goes on and on." The US ambassador and the USAID director in Nicaragua pressured the CARE executive committee to review their work in Nicaragua and maintain relations with oppositional organizations. In defiance, CARE Nicaragua cancelled cooperation with oppositional groups in July 1982 and insisted on remaining neutral and apolitical.[63]

In practice, many of the local CARE staff members sympathized with the revolutionary project and attempted to maintain good relations with the Sandinistas. In the context of the Contra War and increasing political pressure from the US government, the CARE Nicaragua mission was torn between multiple fronts. Finally, in July 1986, CARE Canada took over the responsibility for the Nicaragua mission so as to avoid further conflicts.[64] Apart from military aggression, the United States also increased pressure on other countries and international organizations to withdraw support from Sandinista Nicaragua.

After Mexico's initially strong support for the revolution, Mexican aid declined after 1982, because of growing US pressure, the change in presidency, and the Mexican financial crisis. The new Mexican president, Miguel de la Madrid (1982–1988), maintained more distance from the Sandinista government and reduced economic aid considerably. Finally, in 1984, Mexico ceded to US pressure and stopped all its credit programs for its small revolutionary ally.[65]

Although CARE and Mexico reduced their support for revolutionary food policy, FAO was an exception: the organization intensified its work Nicaragua throughout the 1980s. In fact, FAO opened its offices in the country in 1982 amid a tense political situation when other organizations had already left Nicaragua or cancelled support because of US pressure. The same year, the decision to choose Nicaragua to host FAO's seventeenth regional conference for Latin America offered the Sandinistas new opportunities to promote their strategies for improving food supply in Nicaragua. For Sandinista public diplomacy this was an opportunity to promote Nicaraguan solutions to global food problems, including self-sufficiency and regional food security alliances. That same year, CIERA published the brochure *El hambre en los países del tercer mundo* (Hunger in Third World countries). The report recommended the implementation of national development plans promoting food self-sufficiency and argued that "Third World" countries should seek multilateral food aid to avoid political dependence on any single donor country.[66]

At the 1982 conference in Nicaragua, the Sandinistas promoted a common Latin American food supply strategy and argued for stronger South–South cooperation to secure the food supply in Third World countries. Jaime Wheelock introduced the idea of a council on food security, which would provide credit for food to member countries. He emphasized the need for stronger interregional trade to reduce dependency on industrialized countries. Mexico, Venezuela, Costa Rica, Guatemala, and Granada approved the Nicaraguan proposal. The official conference report described stronger Latin American cooperation as a promising strategy, but it lacked any FAO commitment to support the implementation of stronger Latin American cooperation. Instead, the authors delegated the follow-up to staff at remote FAO headquarters and the regional governments.

Nevertheless, the resolutions approved by the conference bore a strong mark of Nicaraguan influence. For example, Resolution 8 expressed support for the design of a regional food security system and further plans for food self-sufficiency projects.[67] Archival evidence provides no answer to the question as to what happened to the proposal after the conference, but in any case, the Sandinistas had taken the opportunity to diffuse their vision among the Latin American delegates. Not surprisingly, *Barricada* portrayed Nicaragua's relationship with the FAO as a success story. It presented Wheelock as a triumphant campaigner for Nicaraguan social reforms who won the audience at international conferences for the revolution.[68] Despite the rhetoric, however, the outcome of the Nicaraguan initiative for regional cooperation remains unclear.

Nicaragua was not an exceptional case in its promoting of food self-sufficiency during the second half of the twentieth century. Similar food policies emerged within wide-ranging political contexts in other Global South countries. Similar to Nicaragua, they also reassessed the value of locally produced consumer goods over imports between the 1950s and the 1980s. For example, India's first post-independence government launched a self-sufficiency campaign in the 1950s. Similar trends, but under a populist government, were apparent in Perón's Argentina, where wheat and beef became the icons of self-sufficiency.[69] There, the debate over self-sufficiency was closely related to the strategy of import substitution still in vogue on the Latin American continent through the 1960s. Smaller countries such as Nicaragua faced even more difficulties in following a self-sufficiency strategy as they depended on agro-export products and therefore on the capitalist world economy. Despite this, the Dominican Republic, Jamaica under the Michael Manley government (1972–1980), and Burkina Faso under President Thomas Sankara (1984–1987) all championed the cause of self-sufficiency.[70] Research on these self-sufficiency projects has not yet been completed, so it is unknown if or how experts from the international nutrition community were involved in these efforts, but the evidence for Nicaragua indicates that international organizations and bilateral support influenced strategic decisions about food policy beginning in the early 1980s.

Nicaraguan food policy faced enormous challenges after the revolution; food production was very unstable and the country's finances depended on agro exports. Hence, the Sandinistas declared self-sufficiency to be an important political aim. The efforts to increase local food production were successful with rice and beans but failed for vegetables, meat, and milk. The contradictory approach to peasant production as well as inefficiencies in large state complexes were the main reasons for this. The Sandinistas' relationship with individual peasant producers was problematic from the outset. Throughout the decade it was struggle to find a balance in food policy between internal consumption and agro exports.

Sandinista food policy combined overly ambitious visions and realism. The revolutionaries promised equal access to food for all Nicaraguans and hoped to convert Nicaragua into a food-exporting country. At the same time they actively sought new alliances with Western Europe, Latin America, and socialist countries as well as international organizations and relief agencies. To do so they created a sophisticated transnational communication network and a strategy for public diplomacy. Part of this strategy was to launch alternative proposals for food policy in Global South countries, such as regional food security systems.

In the initial period the revolutionaries tried enthusiastically to reverse inequalities in the Nicaraguan food system. They democratized food distribution, established price control, and reassigned land for basic grains production. At that time the government could rely on strong political mobilization and the support of mass organizations for food policy in Pacific Nicaragua. Nevertheless, some initial experiments had counteractive effects. Initial euphoria led to overly ambitious production goals. Political transformation, fluctuating world market prices, lack of knowledge, and tensions with the United States made planning almost impossible. In addition, the large number of institutions resulted in a fragmented food policy during the early years.

Although leading revolutionaries favored large-scale agriculture, other institutions favored strategies concentrating on small farmers. Conflicts and fragmentation resulted in a broad, sometimes contradictory, food policy. This favored the involvement of international actors, as each actor found an element to support and identify with. In the 1980s a more heterogeneous set of actors moved into the nutrition sector than in the 1960s and 1970s. Members of small NGOs mixed with Eastern bloc advisers, and development cooperation staff negotiated with guerrilla commanders as well as with former Somoza bureaucrats in low-ranking positions.

Nicaraguan food policy during the revolutionary period attracted a wide range of international experts and organizations to the small country. For the Sandinista government this meant credibility, an inflow of resources, and technical know-how on food production. All of the organizations pursued their own agendas, however, which sometimes created conflicts, especially when the United States was involved. Even Mexico decided in the end to reduce its support for Nicaragua.

In general, the organizations already working before the revolution in Nicaragua adapted rapidly to political change. In many cases contacts at the lower-level institutions remained the same while networks to the FSLN leaders had to be established. At CARE, a new generation of staff members had come to the country, perceiving revolutionary change as an opportunity for their work. At FAO, it was also a common belief in technology-based approaches that provided a basis for cooperation in food production. In addition, FAO perceived the revolutionary country as a testing ground for new approaches for food policy. Sandinista politicians relied heavily on this support, but they also used it for political initiatives and internal campaigns. FAO's approaches influenced project work and food policy strategies in Sandinista Nicaragua. At the same time UNRISD had an important influence on the research agenda of CIERA. As government institutions consulted CIERA before decision-making, UNRISD also influenced policymaking on food and consumer issues.

As the Nicaraguan government records on food policy are now lost, it is difficult to analyze the impact of these different advisers. Actors with more financial resources, such as FAO and Mexico early on, received the most coverage in the Sandinista press. However, individual experts such as Joseph Collins and Solon Barraclough might have had a stronger impact through their participation in expert commissions and the shaping of CIERA's research agenda. The archival records consulted demonstrate that each donor focused on their own activities, and cooperation with other international organizations had low priority.

After the rough general course for food policy was set, after 1981 economic problems and US aggression increasingly affected Nicaragua. The Sandinistas reinforced campaigns for self-sufficiency and strengthened state control over food distribution. Financial resources for social policies became more limited as US pressure also provoked other donors to limit or end their support for Nicaragua. The Contra War seriously affected food production, but at the same time it also strengthened international solidarity and motivated some donors to increase their presence. The ambitious projects, however, faced serious economic limitations: the nation's dependency on agro exports generated resource conflicts, basic grains production did not expand sufficiently, and tensions weakened the relationship between Sandinistas and peasants. Hence, the initial enthusiasm had faded away by the mid-1980s.

CHAPTER FOUR

THE REVOLUTIONARY CONSUMER

FOOD CONSUMPTION, NATIONAL SELF-SUFFICIENCY, AND EXTERNAL AGGRESSION IN THE EARLY 1980S

"There was everything, there was everything." This was how Rina Méndez Osorno, one of my interviewees, closed her story about her backyard garden, which she cultivated in León during the 1980s. The garden included thirty-one different plant varieties, including oranges, papaya, green beans, tomatoes, and radishes. Around the fruits and vegetables Rina Méndez also planted achiote, producing a harvest of three quintals every six months. Enthusiastically, she remembered her participation in a local garden competition where she won first prize in the 1980s.[1] The Sandinistas regularly organized these types of competitions in neighborhoods and schools to stimulate food production in Nicaragua.

Early on, Sandinista planners identified urban gardening as a possible solution to the problems of both supply and foreign cultural influences. Urban gardening would induce a social transformation of urban consumers into food producers. Historically, the cultivation of fruits, vegetables, and herbs in patio and backyard gardens had been crucial for food supply in times of scarcity, especially for low-income families. Sometimes large extended families even shared a plot and exchanged food.[2] These traditions were never lost, but the Sandinistas wanted to expand them.

Beginning in 1982, because of a new sense of urgency prompted by the Contra War, the Sandinistas designed a program to establish gardens in factories, schools, prisons, and hospitals. These gardens would make vegetables available to workers, prisoners, students, and patients throughout the year and help to mediate transportation problems in regions affected by the war. The urban gardening campaign was one of several government efforts to mobilize consumers for self-sufficiency and to promote the consumption of locally produced food.

How did the Sandinista government develop its food policy for Nicaraguan consumers in the early 1980s? During this period consumers became an important focus for Sandinista food policy although political actors disagreed about their role. To explain the different meanings of the term "consumer," historian Frank Trentmann has suggested the distinction between "the consumer as social identity and as a category of knowledge and ascription in the making."[3] After the revolution, the consumer represented new attributes.

The aim of self-sufficiency required a change in consumption habits, from imported to locally produced foods. To introduce new foods successfully, the government had to convince people of their advantages, such as high nutritional value, lower prices, or good taste. Hence, the government created several campaigns around the ideal of responsible, revolutionary consumers who subordinated their individual preferences to revolutionary needs. The broadest campaigns including material incentives and cultural activities took place in 1981 and 1982 when people's enthusiasm for the revolution was still high.

The revolutionary mass organizations played a leading role in implementing campaigns. For example, the CDS took on important tasks in food distribution and price control at the district level. Nicaraguans participated enthusiastically in some activities, but other campaigns prompted mixed responses. Sometimes food production did not advance fast enough to supply all consumers; sometimes the campaign strategists used the wrong language. In particular, the campaigns' promoters failed to address gender inequalities in food supply and the needs of rural consumers, which weakened their impact among these groups.

Nicaraguan consumers' reactions to rationing, the introduction of new staples, and the efforts to reform the state distribution network strongly influenced food policy outcomes. For example, the first initiative for sugar rationing came from a local Sandinista committee and was then incorporated into national policy. In other cases, consumers refused to adapt their habits according to revolutionaries' instructions and continued buying on the black market. With worsening access to food after 1983, Nicaraguans needed survival strategies beyond the formal supply channels. Despite limitations because of the war and rationing, they carved out in-between spaces to maintain their preferred food habits.

The Contra War severely affected the Nicaraguan food system and undermined the Sandinistas' ambitious reforms in food policy. Indeed, food production in the war zones declined despite the need to supply food to the growing population and the military. Contra attacks on infrastructure hampered national food distribution. Especially in Northern Nicaragua

Todo buen Revolucionario
gasta
menos azucar a diario
MICOIN

FIGURE 4.1. MICOIN advertisement for the sugar campaign. Source: *Barricada*, September 9, 1980, 4.

and the Caribbean, the war made a stable food supply impossible and led to conflicts between soldiers and peasants.

Because of external aggression and natural disaster, maintaining a stable food supply became increasingly difficult in 1983 and 1984. In particular, poor Nicaraguans suffered from the lack of basic staples as they could not afford to pay the high prices on the black market. By 1984 Nicaragua had declined into a "shortage economy," in which consumers experienced a constant lack of important goods. To administer the limited resources the Sandinistas redefined supply priorities and expanded rationing, which exacerbated tensions within society. The government blamed speculators as enemies of the revolution and established heavier sentences for illegal price hikes. Mass organizations played an important role in enforcing the new sanctions, but district leaders themselves sometimes committed abuses. Despite these difficulties the Sandinistas still obtained a comfortable majority in the 1984 elections. People were still willing to accept a reduced food supply, but they maintained hope that the situation would eventually improve.

THE IDEAL OF A NEW REVOLUTIONARY CONSUMER

The campaign to reduce sugar intake was the first broad campaign to change consumption habits. In 1980 Nicaragua was among the five highest consumers of sugar in the world with 96 pounds per capita annually. The high demand for sugar conflicted with economic interests as sugar was an important Nicaraguan export. Initially, the government had made its calculation for sugar supply based on a monthly level of 216,000 quintals, but sugar consumption surpassed the 300,000-quintal level in April 1980. Yet, production did not keep up with local or foreign demand. Raw sugar did not recover to prewar levels until 1982. The government, however, decided to continue exports so as to generate foreign income. By August 1980 the government declared that a reduction of consumption was necessary and initially announced five pounds of sugar per month as the acceptable need for individuals. This meant a reduction of roughly 30 percent.[4] To communicate its decision to Nicaraguan consumers, the government started a political campaign to reduce sugar consumption in autumn 1980. "Every Good Revolutionary Uses Less Sugar Each Day" was one of the key slogans of the government's campaign, equating restricted consumption to revolutionary dedication (see figure 4.1). Self-restriction would help the Nicaraguan economy to recover and hence benefit the revolution. This was the first campaign where the idea of the revolutionary, frugal consumer became clearly visible.

Apart from moral arguments, the authorities soon established material incentives as well. In 1980 the government decided to reward sugar-saving departments with investments equaling the earned income from sugar exports.[5] Estelí and Managua proved most successful in the reduction of their sugar consumption. By January 1981 Nicaragua had saved more than fifteen million dollars through the reduction of monthly consumption by around 30,000 quintals.[6] Data on per capita sugar consumption in the early revolutionary years is contradictory but generally indicates a decline of consumption between 1980 and 1982. CIERA's calculations revealed an average consumption of 90 pounds of sugar per person per year, but a survey for urban Managua only found a level of 56.4 pounds in 1982.[7] Given the ongoing scarcity of sugar, mass organizations attempted to improve distribution.

Sugar became the first item to be rationed in revolutionary Nicaragua. A solution to unstable sugar supply came along from a local CDS initiative in Estelí. After completing a census to secure adequate distribution within the city, the CDS successfully introduced a card distribution system in early 1982. All cardholders received five pounds of sugar per month. Soon afterward the government implemented a similar system on the national level, which marked the beginning of rationing. The plan proved successful, although abuses did occur—for example, some CDS workers based the distribution on political support such as assistance at its assemblies.[8] The Sandinistas announced publicly that the new supply mechanism was a great success achieved by mass mobilization.

Nevertheless, the Nicaraguan people were continuously worried about the lack of sugar. Frances Moore Lappé and Joseph Collins observed the anger of people in Managuan popular districts over the lack of sugar at the beginning of the 1980s. One woman told them: "Everyone's talking about the sugar shortage. Everyone's upset. When you go to the movie, you can't even hear the movie because everyone's talking about sugar!"[9] Although the situation calmed down in early 1983, concerns over the sugar supply continued throughout the 1980s.

It was not only the availability of sugar that was being questioned but also its quality. Occasionally, the distribution system supplied Nicaraguans with brown sugar, which provoked resistance from consumers. In this case the FSLN failed to find the right language to convince the Nicaraguan people. Cultural anthropologist Richard Wilk has argued that the dialogue of goods has no common codes. Sender and receiver sometimes interpret the consumption of certain goods in totally different ways depending on the individual significance they assign them.[10] The FSLN assigned health benefits to brown sugar, but Nicaraguan consumers considered it of inferior quality. In León and Chinandega, people were afraid that the dark sugar had caused illness among their children, as local delegates reported to MICOIN in September 1981. The authorities hence declared that brown sugar had higher nutritional qualities and contained more vitamins. Beyond fears of illness, aesthetic issues also mattered in the debates over sugar. As one interviewee related, *frescos* prepared with dark sugar did look less attractive. Consequently, brown sugar remained on the shelves of many Managuan supermarkets. In addition, inhabitants of the capital perceived a social gap in sugar distribution. People from Nueva Libia, a poor Managuan neighborhood, suspected that they received higher quantities of brown sugar while the supermarkets in well-off neighborhoods received more white sugar.[11] People increasingly insisted on an equal supply as promised by the revolutionaries. The controversies continued over two years and show that fears, rumors, and aesthetics all influenced food choices. Nicaraguans perceived brown sugar as a second-class food.

The Sandinistas publicly promoted sober, self-disciplined consumption despite their own personal preferences for imported luxuries. Revolutionary propaganda depicted the ideal revolutionary consumer as frugal, responsible, and rational, someone who subordinated their personal needs under revolutionary needs. Therefore, austerity was established as a guiding principle, both on the state and on the individual level. While there were efforts to stop the nepotism from the Somoza era, testimonies also indicate a growing gap between some leading Sandinistas and the ordinary people. The leaders increasingly displayed a wealthy lifestyle: they drove through the capital in new vehicles, went abroad for shopping trips, and organized receptions of the FSLN National Directorate in elite clubs. They also frequently visited the dollar shops that sold imported goods for foreign exchange.[12]

For ordinary consumers, the Sandinistas established different rules. As imports were a burden for the national budget, the ideal revolutionary consumer would prefer Nicaraguan products. To promote this new initiative the government started Buy National campaigns. For instance, a writer for the Sandinista women's organization magazine *Somos* tried to convince Nicaraguan women to buy local products: "It seems incredible that, when it's time to do something so common and ordinary as buy some soap, sham-poo, food for our children or some makeup, we can put our patriotism into play. And that's what we're really doing. We'd have to ask ourselves how many women take the time to see whether a product is made in Nicaragua, and how many of us are concerned with choosing it."[13] According to the revolutionaries, the consumption of local products became a patriotic act for the defense of the revolution by converting daily consumption into an arena of revolutionary struggle.

Although *Barricada* had announced by December 1981 that a "new period in the life of national consumers" had started, characterized by the preference for national products, the ongoing demand for imported foods revealed a different reality.[14] The symbolic value of imported foods such as Gerber baby foods or Maggi soups survived the revolution.

A 1982 survey in Managua highlighted the consumption of soft drinks, cookies, sauces, and Maggi soups. Maggi soups, in particular, had gained a high status in popular households, which the authors explained by the high significance of soups in the Nicaraguan diet. Unfortunately, the sur-vey contained no information about whether it was the quality, prestige, or flavor that influenced consumers' choices. Instead, authors denounced the "manipulative power" of international companies that persuaded Nic-araguans to buy expensive products with poor nutritional value.[15] Despite the campaigns against imported products, the poorest urban households continued to consume a limited number of foreign processed foods. By blaming mass advertising for this trend, the researchers failed to examine people's motivations for consuming imported products, which could have inspired new ideas for Sandinista campaign strategists. While the Sand-inistas frequently criticized conspicuous consumption, they nevertheless assigned consumption a new political importance.

THE SANDINISTA CAMPAIGN TO PROMOTE CORN CONSUMPTION

External events triggered the next large campaign to change consumption habits. Soon after the United States had announced the cancellation of wheat credits, the minister of culture Ernesto Cardenal introduced a cam-paign to increase corn consumption in Nicaragua. This formed a part of the Sandinistas' efforts to reduce dependency on imports and improve the basic grains supply. As part of the campaign, festivals throughout the country promoted corn as a revolutionary alternative to wheat. The festivals bore the name of the Nahuatl princess Xilonem. In a special issue the magazine of the Ministry of Culture explained: "In answer to the imperialist aggression that denies us wheat, the people of Nicaragua held a magnificent 'Corn Festival.' . . . This festival was named 'XILONEM' for a Nahuatl princess.

According to our ancestral myth, she was sacrificed to the gods in a time of drought and, with her death, she produced corn for her people. . . . At XILONEM, we also recognized everyone in our Revolution, who sacrificed their lives for the people."[16] The article linked the Nahuatl past with the heroic sacrifice of Nicaraguan guerrilla fighters. Furthermore, the magazine contained other references to Mesoamerican history such as legends and imagery. The Sandinistas also promoted corn consumption through popular music. In 1982 the government released an album entitled *Somos Hijos del Maíz*. Luis Enrique Mejía Godoy contributed the title song, which promoted a return to traditional survival methods and introduced corn also as a food of resistance. In this sense, seeding corn and cooking corn dishes contributed to the revolutionary transformation of Nicaraguan society. To stimulate corn consumption, the Sandinistas also published a cookbook and organized corn festivals.[17]

The first national festival took place in Masaya and was attended by two hundred thousand people including Sandinista leaders such as the government junta members Daniel Ortega, Jaime Wheelock, Sergio Ramírez, and Ernesto Cardenal. The high number of participants proves that the subject of food security mobilized people in the early years of the revolution. During the festivals a cooking competition for corn dishes offered a trip to Corn Islands as the top prize. Throughout the country fourteen hundred people participated with dishes such as indio viejo, nacatamales, and *tistes*. Interviewees remembered the corn campaigns as a positive experience, especially the songs and the festivals. A woman from León brought a self-made recipe for corn flour to distribute it among the participants. Prior to the event she had convinced a local mill owner to grind a quintal of corn very finely, which she then used for cake making. Even if the consistency was a little different, her clients hardly noticed the change. This was confirmed at the festival where she presented pastry in the form of a corncob and sold all her baked goods. She remembered that Daniel Ortega tried her pastry and doubted it could be made out of cornstarch.[18]

As the example of corn flour indicates, people's ingenuity surpassed the revival of traditional corn recipes. *Barricada* highlighted people's creativity in inventing new recipes as well as the resurgence of old culinary traditions as the campaign's most important successes. However, foreign culinary influences also remained visible. A local fast food restaurant participated with a *tortiburguesa* where tortillas substituted for bread; this transcultural fusion demonstrates that fast food was already entrenched in Nicaraguan consumption habits by the early 1980s. At the Caribbean Coast the festivals had a distinct character and promoted recipes based on coconut, breadfruit, and cassava. Although the campaign stimulated a general rediscovery of food traditions, it did not promote the regional diversity of Nicaraguan cultures.[19]

The corn campaign mobilized tens of thousands of people, but it was still difficult to change individuals' consumption habits. A 1982 study revealed that people in popular Managuan districts consumed an average of seventy-three bread rolls and thirty tortillas monthly.[20] Interestingly, the average consumption of wheat flour actually increased in the first two years after the revolution. Bread and pastry were deeply entrenched in urban food culture as consumption surveys had already demonstrated in the 1950s. After 1981 the cancellation of the import credits, however, reduced the availability of wheat and hence its per capita consumption declined throughout the rest of the 1980s.[21] Despite the campaign for corn consumption, people in Nicaraguan cities still demanded wheat products. They had become used to wheat bread over the decades, and not all consumers changed their habits immediately.

Although wheat was scarce because of budget problems and the US sanctions, peasants also harvested less maize between 1981 and 1983. Corn production did not increase sufficiently to satisfy consumer demand. After per capita corn consumption reached its height in 1983 with 188.8 pounds yearly, it decreased in 1984 and 1985 to a level of around 155 pounds. Production problems and natural disasters limited corn availability beginning in 1983. The political campaign had lost importance by the mid-1980s, and only irregular local activities took place—for example, the 1983 festival in Totogalpa, Las Segovias.[22] Nonetheless, the corn campaign demonstrated the Sandinistas' use of mass media to mobilize people and spread their political messages. The revolutionary media also included new formats for political dialogue.

Mass media and assemblies were important mechanisms for communicating and debating the Sandinistas' food policy. When the Sandinistas came to power in 1979 they founded their own official daily newspaper, *Barricada*, which produced at its height up to one hundred thousand issues daily. *La Prensa* continued its role as an oppositional newspaper and entered into a continuous antagonism with *Barricada*. In general, newspapers remained a relatively expensive medium during the revolutionary period; thus, they were more easily accessible for middle- and upper-class readers.[23] Nonetheless, individual issues were probably read by several people and sometimes used in popular education activities. Through these activities the newspaper reached other social groups such as workers or street vendors.

Indeed, *Barricada* was meant to be a "medium of communication between the masses and the FSLN," and all Sandinista media was meant to promote dialogue among government officials, experts, and Nicaraguan

FIGURE 4.2. "Buzón popular" section. Source: *Barricada*, July 18, 1982, 24.

citizens.[24] Consequently, a "Buzón popular" section was established (see figure 4.2). People could call or send their concerns to the newspaper and then a team researched the origins of the problems. According to the motto: "In Difficult Situations, the Mailbox Will Give You the Answer," reporters tried to come up with a convincing explanation or a possible solution. They visited neighborhoods and shops and interviewed ordinary citizens as well as representatives of state institutions and mass organizations. In the end, journalists generally made suggestions for improvement. By 1985 "Buzón popular" had grown from a small section to a two-page contribution.[25]

The "Buzón popular" section reflected the most popular concerns expressed by Nicaraguan urban consumers, such as speculation, food distribution, and prices. Frequently people complained about limited opening hours and abuses in the expendios populares. *Barricada* published fewer voices from rural communities, hence its readers were unaware of rural people's supply problems. When the section was suspended, readers successfully demanded its return, which shows that people valued "Buzón popular" as a forum for them to express their concerns and anxieties.[26]

The Sandinistas applied new political criteria to the evaluation of Nicaraguan diets that went beyond protein and caloric averages. They valued locally produced food as a contribution to anti-imperialist resistance and paid close attention to food prices. Political, economic, and health arguments intersected in Sandinista campaigns depending on the envisaged audience and political purposes of each campaign. The evaluation of the diet changed significantly in comparison to prior decades, but health institutions did not challenge established nutritional recommendations. They relied on the standards established by nutritional research between the 1950s and 1970s. Setbacks in food production continuously undermined the campaigns to change consumption habits, as promoted foods were temporarily unavailable. This was shown in the first revolutionary surveys on food consumption in the early 1980s.

RESULTS FROM THE FIRST REVOLUTIONARY CONSUMER SURVEYS SHOW CONCERNS ABOUT HIGH PRICES

The government had a real desire to find out more about consumers' needs, especially in the early years of the revolution. Hence, CIERA carried out investigations into the supply situation and food consumption in different parts of the country. In 1982 CIERA conducted a study on consumption in ten Managuan popular districts. The researchers concluded that average caloric and protein intakes had not worsened compared to 1966, but that the composition of food had changed. By 1982 people consumed less meat but more eggs and beans.[27] People experienced the decrease of meat consumption as a decline in quality. Eggs and beans also provided protein but were less valued by low-income consumers.

When the researchers asked participants for their perception of the supply situation, the results were discouraging: around 40 percent stated that their nutritional situation had worsened after the revolution, and only 50 percent reported a stable food supply for their households. Indeed, only eight out of one hundred interviewees perceived an improvement. Furthermore, the CIERA team determined that the general public perceived the lack of access to meat—prompted by its 300 percent price increase between 1979 and 1982—as a bad sign of the overall food supply situation. As meat was a traditional indicator for good nutrition and its average consumption had decreased by 50 percent compared to 1966, people tended to judge the nutritional situation in a negative way.[28] In a similar way, sugar rationing had reduced average per capita consumption by one-third. Although average caloric intakes had not worsened, Nicaraguans perceived reduced meat and sugar availability as a sign of deterioration. These findings confirm that average food consumption statistics fail to cover people's complex evaluations of a diet's quality.

The majority of interviewees perceived high prices as being their main problem, which indicates that the food subsidies introduced in 1980 had not sufficiently alleviated the situation. According to the survey, Managuans living in the popular districts still spent an average of 74 percent of their annual income on food. Although CIERA researchers observed increasing consumption of milk, cheese, fish, bread, and vegetable oil in all income groups, the poorest sectors still did not reach contemporary nutritional requirements.[29] In consequence, in the report the authors recommended maintaining the subsidies. Instead of a general food subsidy, how-

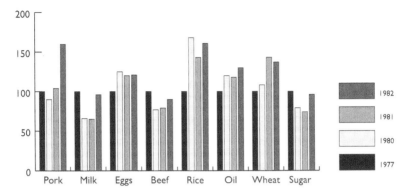

FIGURE 4.3. Evolution of basic food per capita consumption, 1977–1982. The index (1977=100) is based on MIDINRA and MICOIN data. Source: *Barricada*, November 21, 1983, 3.

ever, researchers advocated a special subsidy limited to the poorest sectors. The Sandinistas did not follow this advice and continued general subsidies for corn, beans, rice, milk, sugar, and vegetable oil until mid-1984. Hence, the subsidies benefited all social sectors instead of supporting the low-income consumers specifically. Although the survey's results showed that the Sandinistas still were far from establishing an equitable food supply for all Nicaraguans, the government remained transparent and even released unfavorable data (unlike the Somoza regime).

In the first half of the 1980s, the Sandinistas widely published data on food supply in the general media and government publications. The chart above shows a recovery of per capita consumption for important foods (see figure 4.3). Only for sugar, milk, and beef were prerevolutionary levels not achieved. However, the averages hide differences according to social strata and region. *Barricada* published this data in November 1983 when the supply situation was worsening. The surrounding articles introduced consumption as an important area to evaluate the revolutionary transformation of a society. Per capita consumption of some basic foods had improved, but still the distribution system could not adequately satisfy demand for all foods. At that time, US aggression had already aggravated the inadequate supply situation and authors warned of further declines in food access.[30]

In 1982 natural disasters threw back all the efforts that had been made to revive food production. In early 1982 droughts persisted over several months, and they were followed by intensive rains after Hurricane Alleta in May. The disasters destroyed 22.2 percent of the planned corn harvest, 48.0 percent of the sorghum harvest, and 34.9 percent of the rice harvest. Finally, the subsequent floods damaged 40 percent of asphalted roads, which complicated food distribution. Relief organizations estimated the total economic damage at $356 million, which was 40 percent of Nicaragua's export earnings at that time.[31] The Sandinistas had to deal with a severe crisis: food production suffered a setback while damaged infrastructure impeded supply and the marketing of basic grains. In poor urban areas, food access declined, food prices increased, and speculators tried to take advantage of the food crisis.

In addition, population growth remained a challenge for food policy and planning. Throughout the 1980s Managua attracted rural migrants. Between 1982 and 1984, there were 50,000 Nicaraguans who moved to the Nicaraguan capital every year, partially to escape the war zones. The city's total population increased from roughly 614,000 in 1980 to more than 754,000 in 1983.[32] In consequence, more food had to be produced for the urban centers, which was a problem for the Sandinista planners. The supply problems worsened in 1983 when the Contra War demanded more resources.

WAR, ECONOMIC AGGRESSION, AND THE RADICALIZATION OF FOOD CAMPAIGNS

In November 1981 Ronald Reagan authorized the CIA to train and organize the military forces assembled at the Nicaraguan borders. In his view, the Nicaraguan revolution would lead to a new global communist offensive. Initially, he justified support for the Contras on the pretext of impeding arms trade to the Frente Farabundo Martí para la Liberación Nacional (FMLN) guerrillas in El Salvador. Publicly, he praised the Contras as "freedom fighters" for democracy and human rights. However, these groups were mostly led by former National Guard officials who brought with them the heritage of brutality and nepotism from the Somoza era. The CIA and the US Army's Special Forces started military training including instructions for sabotage acts in spring 1982. At that time, leading military and intelligence circles revived the strategy of low-intensity conflict. These counterinsurgency tactics went beyond traditional warfare and included covert operations, psychological interventions, and intelligence work.[33] As brutality was a "constitutive element" of these actions, the Contras regularly murdered, tortured, and raped Nicaraguan civilians during their attacks.[34]

Alongside the Contra War, the United States followed a strategy of economic aggression toward Nicaragua in the hopes of destabilizing the country through food shortages, unemployment, and lack of foreign exchange. In the minds of the US military strategists, this would encourage internal opposition and lead to the defeat of the revolution. Economic warfare started with the cancellation of US economic aid on April 1, 1981.

Next, the United States used its influence within international financial bodies to obstruct further credit. For example, the United States impeded several Inter-American Development Bank (IADB) loans for assistance to Nicaraguan farmers. The CIA also organized sabotage activities in early 1984 to destabilize foreign trade. Mercenaries contracted by the CIA and US Special Operation Forces set up mines at important Nicaraguan harbors during the main export season, which resulted in damage to more than ten vessels. Finally, the United States established a complete trade embargo in May 1985.[35]

All of these measures as well as the spread of fighting severely affected basic grains supply and agro exports in Nicaragua. The war regions were often important areas for food production and agro exports, mainly cattle and coffee. In 1982, for example, the Contras began attacking northern Nicaraguan villages. During these attacks, they burned crops and warehouses, which immediately affected the local food supply. The fact that local peasants stopped agricultural work and fled the war zones also weakened the national project for self-sufficiency.

The Contras carried out sabotage operations on infrastructure, including destruction of bridges and disrupting the electricity supply. Consequently, communication and transport were affected, which significantly complicated food distribution and access to agricultural supplies. They assaulted people working for Sandinista projects, such as health workers and agronomists. In 1984 alone, 270 agricultural technicians died.[36] By 1985 one-third of the local population had left the war zones. This meant labor shortages for basic grains production and agro exports. In addition, the government had to provide food for soldiers and displaced persons. In 1985 the Nicaraguan government estimated that the war had reduced basic grains and coffee production by one-third.[37]

Ultimately, the war led to the radicalization of the Sandinistas' self-sufficiency campaigns. By 1985, for example, the government promoted urban gardening through militant propaganda, which portrayed urban gardening as an answer to "imperialist aggression." *Barricada* described the gardens as "trenches against hunger."[38] By cultivating maize, beans, and vegetables locally, urban and rural people could ensure their own food supply and hence contribute to revolutionary victory. Also, the shrinking state budget would benefit from less food imports.

Urban gardens played an important role in the country's food supply during the 1980s. On the national scale, PAN estimated in June 1985 that there were 16 regional gardens, 608 institutional gardens, and 2,440 private gardens. These numbers include only gardens established within the Ministry of Agriculture's programs. However, most Nicaraguans supplied themselves from their own backyard gardens.[39] Urban gardens contributed to more food diversity and higher caloric intake as they provided fruits, vegetables, and herbs. It is impossible to assess their quantitative contribution to national supply as the gardens were located in private homes, institutions, and public spaces. The Nicaraguan Food Program was only aware of those gardens established during the Sandinista campaign but collecting data on the food produced was beyond its logistical capacities.[40]

Similar to the mixed responses for other self-sufficiency campaigns, not all Nicaraguans supported urban gardening efforts. A 1982 survey clearly documented resistance: out of seventy interviewees, only thirty-five people supported the urban gardening project. The opponents referred to problems with landholding rights, theft, and insufficient knowledge of gardening.[41] Lukewarm attitudes toward urban gardening most likely changed when supply problems became more drastic between 1985 and 1990, but household gardens could not fully solve the problem of Nicaragua's inadequate food supply, especially as ongoing migration into cities reduced available spaces for cultivation. In general, the possibilities for designing an ambitious food policy had become far more limited by 1985.

Overall, the war undermined the self-sufficiency efforts. Nicaragua had to import more food while income from exports and access to credit dwindled. In addition, the Sandinistas had to allocate larger portions of the state budget to military expenditures. In the end the Contra War left an economic disaster and a legacy of violence. The Nicaraguan government estimated the total economic cost of war between 1980 and 1988 at $9 billion.[42] By 1985 the Contras had executed more than thirty-six hundred civilians and kidnapped more than five thousand people.[43] Although they gained support among peasant communities over the years, the Contras were far from occupying large territories in Nicaragua.

By spring 1982 the Sandinistas had declared a state of emergency, which led to new forms of censorship. The main areas of censorship were food supply, war, and the mismanagement of government institutions.[44] Censorship authorities prohibited *La Prensa* from publishing stories about the long lines at shops—in particular, photos showing the queues. The Ministry of the Interior suppressed news about the protests against food deficits and high prices.[45] Nevertheless, *Barricada* covered the supply situation throughout the 1980s and also communicated critical voices. We do not know how many critical statements were sent to *Barricada* and how the journalists made their choices about which to publish, but the war against speculation became ever more important in the newspaper's coverage while the crisis advanced.

FOOD SHORTAGES AND THE RISE OF THE BLACK MARKET
BETWEEN 1982 AND 1984

Food shortages provoked public debates during which Nicaraguans expressed their dissatisfaction with state distribution and demanded their rights as consumers. These debates represented continuity with the struggles of the 1970s when popular social movements demanded rights for consumers. When the state supply system failed to provide basic grains or powdered milk in the early 1980s, people went to the black market which was both an alternative supply chain and an alternative source of income when wages started to decline. The Sandinistas harshly denounced speculators, but without differentiating between survival activities and large-scale speculation, and since government agencies also provided goods to the black market, this hypocrisy undermined the Sandinistas' credibility.

Between 1982 and 1984 the supply situation worsened. *Barricada* reported on the scarcity of salt, chicken, and rice, and soap, potatoes, eggs, and bread disappeared temporarily from store shelves. The paper's "Buzón popular" section filled with complaints about unavailable products and distribution problems. Long lines outside of stores became a common phenomenon, and people had to invest more time in shopping. In 1984 *Barricada* interviewed a woman from Villa Fraternidad district shopping at Roberto Huembes market. As the official vegetable oil quota assigned to her family was insufficient, she came to the market to search for alternatives. She concluded "Look, I am enthusiastic about the revolution, but now it affects our stomach."[46]

Market women reported that consumers frequently complained about high vegetable prices. Since people could no longer afford to buy many vegetables, the traditional Nicaraguan beef soup became thinner and thinner.[47] However, Sandinista supporters were still willing to hold out and even evaluated their experiences with scarcity as positive. For example, the *Barricada* journalist Gabriela Selser remembered these periods as strengthening the collective spirit. She described the experience of sharing a plate of spaghetti or exchanging a can of sardines for a glass of jam as moments of joy. In her social circle, people were convinced that the revolution would soon overcome all difficulties.[48]

The black market witnessed an unprecedented rise after 1983. The number of vendors in the largest Managuan market, the Managuan Oriental market, soared from between 3,000 and 4,500 in 1983 to 27,000 by 1985. This boom was a result of rising unemployment, declining wages in the formal sector, and the introduction of multiple exchange rates in 1982. In particular, different exchange rates created new business opportunities for speculation with high profit rates. Consequently, the *New York Times* correspondent Stephen Kinzer concluded that a new class had emerged in Nicaraguan society with a name that was "a wonderful transliteration from English: bisnes."[49]

In countries with a planned or partially planned economy such as Nicaragua, the rise of secondary economies was widespread, including small trade, black markets, and smuggling. One common practice in the 1980s was the so-called *negocio de fila*, which referred to people who took the time to wait in line for small quantities of food and then resold them at higher prices to those who did not have the time to spare. Another widespread custom was the resale on the black market of food rations originally distributed at workplaces.[50] These practices occurred throughout Nicaraguan society but in relatively small numbers. Larger speculators paid people from the poor Managuan districts to buy large quantities of basic products at the official prices and to resell them later on the black market. The authorities were aware of these practices but found it difficult to control them.

In the Sandinistas' eyes, the Oriental Market represented the expansion of speculation in Nicaraguan society. In September 1984 the government estimated that 10 percent of the Managuan population were working at the markets throughout the city.[51] The government's displeasure with these developments represented more than concerns about chaos and speculation. The Oriental Market was also a source of political opposition, as market women soon opposed state intervention in their business affairs. They wanted the liberty to buy and sell as they had previously done. Vendors attacked Sandinista police and government inspectors on several occasions when in the mid-1980s they tried to intervene against speculation.[52]

As people became angrier about the high prices on the black market, the government reacted with campaigns against speculation. In fact, speculators became the new enemies of revolution. Government propaganda characterized them as "leeches" or "lizards."[53] In Róger Sánchez Flores's caricatures for *Barricada*, he depicted speculators either as crocodiles or snakes—dangerous animals considered as sneaky and aggressive. Apart from the campaigns, CDS and Sandinista police intensified control. Inspectors performed daily inspections that provoked social conflicts within the districts. For example, they increasingly made accusations against highly respected local shop owners. In retrospect, some Nicaraguans judged the control measures as excessive.[54]

As speculators turned into the new enemies of revolution, Sandinista publications rarely acknowledged corruption by government representatives.[55] When the government promulgated the new consumer law, it changed the structure of MICOIN. During the process it laid off some corrupt employees, which illustrates that by 1984 corruption cases already existed. This is confirmed by testimonies of former female Sandinista supporters interviewed in 2014. These women identified corruption among medium-level officials as a serious problem, and they referred to abuses of Nicaraguan embassy staff managing incoming donations.[56] Corruption most likely increased hand in hand with the shortage economy as desperate people were willing to pay higher prices for limited foodstuffs.

FEMALE CONSUMERS AND GENDER INEQUALITIES IN NICARAGUA

Throughout the revolution, food preparation and shopping were important areas for the negotiation of gender relations in Nicaragua. In many cases, women bore the burden of procuring food. Traditionally, women were responsible for food preparation. Although the Sandinista revolution advanced legislation for female rights, the male revolutionary leaders did not address gender inequalities in household work and child education. To a greater degree than men, women had to overcome the hardships of cooking with increasingly scarce ingredients along with completing the daily shopping and generating additional income through food sales. Unlike other Latin American governments, however, general revolutionary propaganda dealing with food and consumption in Nicaragua seldom addressed women directly.[57]

Instead, the Sandinistas included specific advice for women only in publications directed exclusively to a female audience. Other campaigns materials sometimes showed women in traditional female roles such as secretaries or housewives. Male FSLN leaders, who were responsible for designing most campaign strategies, continued to uphold these gender stereotypes. Thus, the highly moral and political discourse on food typically ignored the real-life challenges faced by Nicaraguan women. The magazine of the revolutionary women's organization Asociación de Mujeres Nicaragüenses Luisa Amanda Espinoza (AMNLAE, the Luisa Amanda Espinoza Association of Nicaraguan Women) only partially filled this gap. The magazine, *Somos*, combined practical advice for times of scarcity with general reflections on women's consumerism. It failed, however, to discuss conflicts between men and women over decisions such as how much money to spend on food and for which food items.

By and large AMNLAE magazine articles called on Nicaraguan women to try vegetarian recipes in times of meat scarcity. The magazine's authors offered practical suggestions for recycling food packages and inventing homemade presents. This advice might have been more useful to women facing scarcity than the political call for bringing down sugar and meat consumption. However, we lack sources on the reception of these proposals among Nicaraguan women.

In terms of nutrition, recommendations for a healthy diet outweighed the political arguments to consume certain foods. *Somos* recommended boiling vegetables in such a way as to preserve the vitamins and explained the significance of vitamins to the readers. Breastfeeding or pregnant women as well as children should consume fruits and vegetables on a daily basis, explained the authors. Many recipes published in the magazine were vegetarian, such as yogurt with different fruits.[58] During the 1980s the magazine often promoted creative solutions for other difficult situations that women were facing, such as the need to improvise cheap presents based on available food or to make household supplies such as soap. In 1982 *Somos* presented suggestions for homemade Christmas presents, among them a recipe for carrots in oil or mixed vegetables in vinegar. It also showed women how to produce homemade washing powder out of old bar soap.[59] In this sense *Somos* responded to women's concerns about new strategies in times of scarcity.

Somos also published some strong political articles on the role of female consumers. A common argument was that the United States had spread a model of female consumerism around the world that linked women's fulfillment with consumption.[60] Although *Somos* writers discussed the political role of female consumers, the magazine's authors never addressed gender inequalities in food supply nor conflicts between men and women over decision-making about purchases. These omissions reflect the limitations of the Sandinistas' efforts to change established gender relations.

Overall, the revolutionaries were more successful in advancing practical gender issues in their food campaigns.[61] In 1985 the sociologist Maxine Molyneux introduced the distinction between practical and strategic gender issues. Practical gender issues emerge out of the daily experiences of gender inequalities such as lacking access to health services, food, or education. The demands cover specific measures for improvement. Strategic gender issues, by contrast, include aims to overcome gender inequalities through fundamental political changes.[62]

Although the Sandinistas established important rights for women in the first years of the revolution, they failed to bring about a change in gender relations in the long run. In food policy, for example, the Sandinistas neglected strategic issues such as the debate about gender inequalities and failed to include these in their food campaigns. One reason was the absence of pressure from the Sandinista women's organization. In general, AMNLAE's approach to gender relations suffered from internal contradictions and from submission to the Sandinista party's priorities. Even though the organization was successful in mobilizing women in the early 1980s, hierarchical structures led to a decline in female participation afterward.

During the Contra War AMNLAE subordinated women's demands to the war effort.[63]

EXPANDED RATIONING, NEW SUPPLY PRIORITIES, AND THE "WAR AGAINST SPECULATION"

At the same time as the intense debates over the supply situation in 1983 and 1984, the government introduced three reform projects: (1) the establishment of supply priorities, (2) the extended control exercised by the CDS as well as state authorities, and (3) an expansion of rationing. As the war demanded more resources from the state budget, the Sandinistas also decided to reduce food price subsidies by 50 percent in June 1984. Only sugar and milk remained subsidized.[64] Consumers had to pay higher prices for basic grains and vegetable oil. From one day to another, the cost for preparing a daily gallo pinto surged. As privation became a central concern of Nicaraguans by 1984, the Sandinistas decided to reorganize the supply priorities.

First, the government responded to the lack of food by introducing supply priorities for different social groups and regions. Hence, the year 1984 witnessed an intense debate over supply priorities at all levels of the distribution system. The debate over what was necessary and what should be guaranteed by the state distribution network prompted contentious discussions concerning the relative importance of urban versus rural or army supply versus the needs of malnourished children, which caused feelings to run high. Faced with the scarcity of important goods, the revolutionary authorities had to make difficult decisions. What could authorities do if supply was insufficient for all regions? Whose supply would strengthen the revolution, and which products were essential?

In 1984 a CIERA report recommended making rural consumption a higher priority, but this was subject to intense debate.[65] For example, at the third Sandinista Assembly, some delegates criticized the lack of attention paid to rural zones; however, in the end, the assembly decided to prioritize urban workers.[66] In contrast MICOIN agreed to provide the war zones in northern Nicaraguan regions and at the Caribbean Coast with much-needed food in August 1984. However, the MICOIN was aware of the decision's limitations, and the ministry acknowledged that the consequences of war affected all regions in different ways.[67] Defining supply priorities and quotas was a delicate task.

The example of the municipality Matiguás in Northern Nicaragua demonstrates how difficult it was to maintain a secure food supply during the war. The municipality had more than thirty-seven thousand inhabitants but only four expendios and forty-eight small state distribution points in the countryside. The monthly supply deficit in June 1984 was estimated

FIGURE 4.4. Map of Nicaraguan departments and regions in the 1970s and 1980s. The Sandinistas introduced a new regional division in 1982 consisting of six regions (I–VI) and three special zones (1–3).

at 600 quintals of sugar, 451 liters of vegetable oil, and 226 milk packages. For a month there had been rice shortages, and at many stalls food staples were either unavailable or imported from Honduras and sold at very high prices. The whole region V (see figure 4.4), covering Boaco, Chontales, and Nueva Guinea, was also affected by insufficient roads and a general lack of transportation. People from rural places sometimes had to walk six hours or travel four hours by boat to reach the next supply point.[68]

Apart from regional criteria MICOIN also established priorities for social groups and goods, which generated controversies, especially over supplies for soldiers and essential foods. War led to the prioritization of army supply and war zones, but the lack of sources on distribution quota impedes an analysis of the implementation. MICOIN's plans to include the military in self-supply activities might indicate some discontent about high supply quotas for soldiers. In fact, there is evidence of conflicts between the military and peasants. Officially, soldiers should have paid for the food they commandeered; however, as soldiers lacked money, many peasants received no payment. The government defined basic foods such as rice, beans, sugar, and vegetable oil as necessities. Lower priority goods included animal protein sources, hygienic articles, radios, and tools. Even foods from the first category were frequently scarce, however, as production stagnated and urban demand increased.[69]

By 1984 the Nicaraguan economy bore all of the characteristics of a "shortage economy."[70] The insufficiency of foreign exchange, food, consumer goods, and services had become a universal phenomenon and substantially affected consumer behavior. A few months prior to the elections, in June 1984 the government reformed the Law on Consumer Defense. The law expanded MICOIN's control over food distribution, transport, and price definition. MICOIN gained exclusive right to distribute and define the prices for eight basic products: rice, beans, salt, sugar, corn, oil, soap, and matches. The distribution of food with a rationing card had started with sugar and extended then to rice, vegetable oil, and soap. Finally, in 1984, consumers could obtain eight products with the card. The law established heavy penalties, including jail sentences, for selling basic products at higher prices.[71] State control expanded through price definitions and extended sanction mechanisms. At the same time, the law's name shows again that the Sandinistas viewed consumers' rights as a high priority. At this point the government wanted to protect consumers from high prices, but legislation still failed to address product quality. Legislators chose not to establish an institution to deal with consumers' concerns, as the government assumed people would utilize the different revolutionary mass organizations and media forums to express their demands.

Public debates reveal that the government's explanations for the poor supply situation—concentrating on speculation—did not mitigate people's concerns about their low purchasing power. During the months surrounding the passage of the reforms *Barricada* explained the new measures to the Nicaraguan population. Sandinista leaders justified the new supply priorities as an outcome of the war. They attributed responsibility for supply problems to speculation, which they characterized as antisocial and counter to good revolutionary practices.[72] In contrast, workers highlighted their concern about the poor supply of *comisariatos*, which had become an important additional income source as many people sold their cheese or butter on the black market.

The government's attempt to improve access to food through providing workers with payment in kind only temporarily alleviated their situation. By 1984 workers often received part of their salary paid in merchandise. For example, workers of a shoe factory received twelve pairs of shoes monthly, which mostly ended up on the black market.[73] At the same time wages in the formal sectors lost purchasing power. According to calculations based on the consumer price index and the Managuan minimum industrial wage, workers' purchasing power for food declined by 74 percent between 1972 and 1984 with general purchasing power down by 56.2 percent.[74] Hence, the revolution had failed to provide workers with an improved standard of living. Over the years, workers' despair increased, which eroded their confidence in the revolution. With the looming crisis, tensions over food supply increased and were expressed in occasional violent outbreaks.

In August 1984 the Bello Horizonte supermarket announced powdered milk distribution for all consumers with a vaccination certificate. At that time Bello Horizonte district lacked sufficient state distribution points for basic foods. There was only one supermarket and one expendio for the nine thousand inhabitants of the district. In particular, there were regular shortages of chicken, sugar, powdered milk, and eggs.[75] In a short time, three thousand people showed up at the doors, but the frightened employees decided to keep the entry closed. As the entrance was blocked, disappointed consumers destroyed the doors. For the first time since the revolution had begun, consumers resorted to violence to gain access to a state supermarket. As this incident shows, the tense supply situation provoked occasional violent outbreaks during the mid-1980s. More common were daily tensions at the district level. In October 1984, several Managuan expendio owners resigned as they could not stand the complaints from consumers over unavailable products any more.[76]

Also, the mass organizations felt the growing pressure in their daily work at the district level. After the role of the CDS in food distribution increased in 1983, control and abuses intensified social tensions about food supply. At that time the local Comité de Defensa Sandinista responsible for economic defense monitored prices and distribution. The CDS provided twelve hundred voluntary popular inspectors to monitor for potential speculation. Some CDS coordinators, however, abused their position: for example, they gave food rations to friends and family members. In other cases, food merchants stood as candidates for CDS posts in order to be in a position to ignore official price regulations. People in Managuan districts reacted with indignation as they disliked watching CDS members pursue their own business interests.[77]

In February 1984 the FSLN commandant Leticia Herrera argued that some CDS coordinators had transformed into "little dictators" who were abusing their power.[78] The satirical weekly *Semana Cómica* also attacked the moral doggedness of the CDS committees. In one drawing CDS members appear with a giant stick saying, "We are the highest authority." The legend says that a CDS member is a citizen like every other Nicaraguan citizen, thus they must not behave arrogantly. The public and revolutionary leaders criticized CDS members for viewing themselves as being above ordinary citizens and for abusing their positions.[79] As these examples illustrate, the general public's confidence eroded as a result of CDS members' behavior as well as the public's suspicions that CDS workers were misappropriating food distributions. However, the government proceeded with its "war against speculation" and argued that every citizen should convert into a popular inspector.[80]

By 1984 some Nicaraguans lacked enthusiasm for the antispeculation campaign and hence participated less at CDS assemblies. For example, in August 1984 *Barricada* criticized public apathy and overreliance on the CDS leadership. The CDS experienced a crisis of confidence among the urban population; people perceived the committees as taking over state functions instead of representing the people's interests. On the other hand CDS members also experienced difficult situations; people held them accountable for the poor supply situation and attacked them verbally, sometimes even physically.[81] Eventually, the influence of the CDS on food policy declined because of the lack of public confidence and insufficient participation from community members. The 1984 elections considerably reduced the overall influence of mass organizations on food policy.

Despite growing tensions over food supply, the Sandinistas won the 1984 elections with a safe majority. The revolutionary junta had promised in 1979 to hold free elections. After rescheduling the date several times, the Sandinistas finally announced elections for November 1984. Seven parties participated while the Contras and *La Prensa* made calls to abstain. After a relatively calm electoral campaign, the Sandinistas won 63 percent of the votes, and the six opposition parties received 33 percent. The new government, led by Daniel Ortega, replaced the revolutionary junta and took over power in January 1985. At that time the State Council was dissolved, and mass organizations' participation in Nicaraguan legislation came to an end. Daniel Ortega maintained the state of emergency and gained considerable power in national politics.[82]

NICARAGUAN CONSUMERS' STRATEGIES AGAINST FOOD SHORTAGES

During the Nicaraguan supply crisis, people depended on traditional methods of food supply such as urban gardens and food exchanges as well as seeds from the government. Although the government worked to reform the distribution system many Nicaraguans developed their own survival strategies to counter food scarcity. As practiced in poor families for decades beforehand, improvisation in daily cooking was important. What was available had to be combined sometimes in unexpected and original ways. Even a small ingredient could change the monotonous diet and give it a special flavor, especially for children. One of my interviewees remembered how her mother enriched simple dishes with small details. For example, she added mint from the patio to a chicken soup or added a little chorizo to a *pipián* sauce.[83] Another strategy, adopted mainly by women, was to sell food in their neighborhood or on the street. By doing so they contributed to the family income, which was important when inflation undermined their purchasing power. Sales of food that had become unavailable such as cookies and pastries were particularly flourishing.[84]

In inventing new recipes based on available ingredients these women successfully convinced consumers with their substitutes, but many other food substitutes for unavailable products were rejected because of their taste. Cooking was even more difficult if several staples became scarce at the same time. Vegetable oil, for example, had to be substituted either with beef tallow or whale oil. Food fried with beef tallow was only edible up to fifteen minutes after preparation, and the flavor of whale oil could make people "lose their appetite," as one interviewee expressed it. People also started to cook rice with coconut milk instead of adding vegetable oil, an adaptation of a culinary practice from the Caribbean.[85] However, improvisation had its limits, as the flavors of plantains, *chayotes*, and Nicaraguan cheeses were difficult to substitute.[86]

Sometimes substitutes met cultural resistance as in the case of imported beans. Nicaraguans preferred red beans to all other types. As the large beans that ENABAS distributed did not meet consumers' expectations for quality, consumers bought beans on the Managuan markets for prices up to 50 percent higher.[87] To compensate for the lack of beans, the government imported a large bean variety that Nicaraguans consumers disliked and nicknamed "Viterra," after a nutritional supplement packaged in capsules. One interviewee contrasted the "horrifying" Viterra beans with "our beans" and described them as "a giant grain, huge but without flavor."[88] People even avoided mentioning their dishes contained Viterra beans, and rumors circulated regarding the origins of their "vitaminized taste." For example, people attributed this flavor to the use of Viterra beans as medicine against anemia. They also suspected that the beans included substances that could sterilize poor Nicaraguan and Latin American people as a way to limit demographic explosion (which was perceived as being in the interest of the US government).[89]

People also negotiated food insecurity by maintaining relations to people in the countryside, by crossing the border, or by producing their own food. Sometimes people traveled to rural zones to buy basic grains;

sometimes rural families distributed their products in the cities. Other people crossed the borders to buy scarce goods in neighboring countries, but this required sufficient resources for travel expenses. Beginning in August 1984 governmental roadblocks hampered these practices. Peasants felt the limits on transporting food as an unwelcome state intervention in their autonomy.[90]

Urban gardening was also important for improving food supply. Many Nicaraguans could only rely on their own patio production to grow vegetables, herbs, and fruits. More people started to keep animals such as cows or pigs in the cities. Informal meat exchange already had a tradition in low-income households, especially for beef, but consumers faced new difficulties in the 1980s. As the Sandinistas aimed at eradicating informal exchange processes, they promulgated a decree forbidding slaughter without official permission. Animals had to be brought to authorized slaughterhouses, where the meat was sold at the official prices. In consequence, cattle smuggling to Costa Rica and Honduras increased substantially and worsened beef supply problems. In addition, informal slaughtering in inadequate installations posed serious hygienic threats.[91]

The years between 1982 and 1985 were critical years for Sandinista food policy as the Nicaraguan economy turned into a shortage economy. The Contra War, natural disasters, and the lack of financial resources made it increasingly difficult to fulfill the revolutionary promise of ensuring equal access to food for all Nicaraguans. In this setting the consumer was an important but ambiguous political figure. Sandinista campaigns designed a vision of austere consumers buying locally produced food, who limited their desires for the sake of revolution. Self-sufficiency required a change in consumption habits from imported to local foods. Accordingly, the Sandinistas started large-scale education campaigns to convince people to buy corn and to plant vegetables. They applied new political criteria to the Nicaraguan diet, denouncing the consumption of imported food as antipatriotic.

These campaigns mobilized large numbers of Nicaraguans in the early years of revolution in Pacific Nicaragua, and the campaigns that included cultural activities or established material incentives were particularly successful. However, the national campaigns fell short in addressing rural people, the Caribbean communities, or gender inequalities in food supply. Despite their research on consumption habits, the Sandinistas sometimes failed to understand people's desires and accused consumers of being manipulated by mass advertising.

At the same time real consumers demanded improved access to sugar, meat, or milk at reasonable prices. Real consumers also shopped on the growing black market although the Sandinistas depicted speculators as main enemies of the revolution. Finally, ordinary consumers observed that part of the Sandinista leadership abandoned their ideals and publicly displayed expensive imported goods.

War and natural disaster challenged the Sandinistas' efforts to increase self-sufficiency. Food production in war zones was especially difficult, as routes were interrupted, people were on the move, and the Contras attacked storage facilities. The economic blockade orchestrated by the United States limited the government's possibilities for importing and subsidizing food. Step by step the Sandinistas expanded rationing to ensure the supply of basic products, but distribution problems continued. This contributed to growing tensions in Nicaraguan society: between shop owners and consumers and between mass organizations and inhabitants as well as between rural producers and the state. Occasionally these conflicts became violent, but nevertheless the Sandinistas won the 1984 election with a comfortable majority.

On the one hand, Sandinista supporters still believed the supply situation would improve again. They valued improvisation and sharing food as strengthening solidarity and social cohesion. On the other hand, even sympathizers of the revolution were increasingly concerned about food insecurity. High food prices were a major concern for workers as well as for people in low-income districts. The official media addressed these issues but always tried to emphasize the role of external aggression in supply problems.

During the crises Nicaraguan activated old survival mechanisms of self-supply, such as food exchanges, the invention of substitutes, and urban gardening. Women carried a heavy burden during periods of shortage as traditional gender divisions persisted. Frequently, they also contributed to family income through informal activities. Some food substitutes entered collective memory for their dreaded taste; others enriched daily diets. In inventing new recipes based on scarce ingredients Nicaraguans created in-between spaces of food consumption. Taste as well as aesthetics and health concerns motivated consumers to reject certain foods.

After years of supply problems enthusiasm for the revolution faded away and turned into anxiety and discontent. Dissatisfaction increased when the Sandinistas changed their economic policy in 1985. Food insecurity in addition to the conspicuous consumption and corruption of some revolutionary leaders undermined the political authority of the Sandinista government.

CHAPTER FIVE

FOOD POLICY DETERIORATES INTO CRISIS MANAGEMENT

ECONOMIC CUTS, INDUSTRIAL AGRICULTURE, AND FOOD AID IN THE MID-1980S

In May 1986 *Barricada* reported that nineteen thousand pounds of meat had been lost in the storage facilities of the national slaughtering enterprise. Given the tense supply situation the news generated a scandal that forced Jaime Wheelock to set up a fact-finding commission with representatives of different ministries and the FSLN. After the commission published its report the slaughterhouse director was fired immediately. The scandal included all of the main problems affecting food production by 1986—lack of foreign exchange and storage facilities, the economic blockade by the United States, bureaucratic negligence, and the lack of workplace discipline. The scandal also illustrates how food policy deteriorated into crisis management by the mid-1980s.

In January 1986 the government had prohibited unauthorized slaughtering because it needed to increase meat exports and generate more foreign exchange. The promulgation of the meat law led to an increased supply available for legal slaughtering. At the same time higher meat prices reduced consumption; hence, storage facilities soon reached their limits. As a result, five million pounds of meat were stored in short-term storage facilities. In addition, the government assigned one hundred thousand dollars for suitable packaging material, but too late, and workers were forced to use plastic bags instead. As workers had no experience with this material, hygienic problems occurred. In April 1986 technicians discovered that nineteen thousand pounds of meat had spoiled in storage. If this was not enough, the commission's report also revealed internal conflicts within the enterprise, including tensions between management and the unions, a lack of workplace discipline, and frequent meat robberies.[1] Given the difficult supply situation, people were angry about food that spoiled as a result of neglect. As meat

had always been a highly valued food, consumers experienced the decline
in per capita consumption as another sign of the government's failure to
provide sufficient food for every Nicaraguan. Consequently, informal meat
exchanges and sales were maintained whenever possible. People slaughtered
their own cattle, bypassing official slaughterhouses, and exchanged the meat
with friends or family members or sold it to urban consumers.

Early in the 1980s the Sandinista reforms had gained broad support
from international organizations and nutrition experts. With external financing the Sandinistas had started many new projects to increase basic
grains production and improve the supply situation. The new distribution
structure democratized access to food, although periodic scarcity of sugar
or meat prompted discontent, but by 1984 the situation had worsened significantly. The economic crisis accelerated and the Contra War demanded
more financial resources. Basic products were frequently unavailable in the
official channels, and prices on the black market soared. Sandinista food
policy lost its allure and turned more into crisis management. External advisers' initial euphoria changed to disillusionment: they criticized the low
priority of food policy, the overreliance on large-scale agricultural production, and the dependency on donated and imported food. Nonetheless, the
Sandinistas won a comfortable majority during the 1984 elections, indicating that people still hoped for improvement.

With the ongoing war and the 1985 US trade embargo, however, the
economic situation worsened considerably. In response to the crisis the Sandinistas radically changed their economic policy in 1985, including the
elimination of food subsidies. Eroding purchasing power as well as spoilage
and misappropriations of donated food provoked widespread disillusionment among Nicaraguans.

Sandinista food policy up to 1985 had mainly benefited urban consumers, and rural peasants had experienced greater hardships. In particular, low
prices for basic grains and a lack of access to agricultural supplies as well as
clothes and shoes plagued rural Nicaraguans. Peasants in the Nicaraguan
interior had opposed state intervention in food distribution and farming,
along with the military service introduced in September 1983. Peasants
rejected collective landholding as well as the military draft, which made
it difficult to maintain their farms. The Contras and the Sandinistas increasingly pressured local people to take sides. From 1984 onward, more
and more peasants joined the Contras. Cultural gaps between urban party
leaders and the peasantry contributed to this worsening situation. Between
1984 and 1986 the Sandinistas changed their policy and paid more attention to the Nicaraguan countryside. They conducted surveys on rural consumption and built up a network of rural stores, financed by development

cooperation with Sweden. However, this was insufficient to overcome the urban-rural gap in food supply.

The first sign of the Sandinista food policy's deterioration into crisis management was when the Sandinistas radically changed their economic policy from reform and redistribution to adjustment measures. Through budget cuts, tax increases, and a currency devaluation they adapted the economy to the ongoing war effort and the shrinking government revenues. Economic pragmatism had clearly won out over the revolutionary government's initial idealism. Not surprisingly, the shift contributed to the disillusionment of both urban and rural consumers who suffered from shortages and prohibitive food prices during these years. Second, the government intensified agrarian reform, but this came too late to prevent peasants from supporting the Contras. Third, food aid filled the supply gaps but undermined the revolution's self-sufficiency project. The ongoing Contra War reinforced dependency on foreign donors, but international circumstances resulted in serious declines in aid during the second half of the 1980s. The government's new economic course, its contradictory and ultimately unsuccessful government campaigns, and the general stagnation in food production prompted widespread disillusionment in the revolutionary project.

FROM REFORM AND REDISTRIBUTION TO ADJUSTMENT POLICY

The Contra War and US economic sanctions had strongly affected the Nicaraguan economy and resource allocation by the mid-1980s. In 1985 military expenditures already made up 50 percent of the national budget. Then the United States imposed a trade embargo against Nicaragua. The embargo blocked $58 million of Nicaraguan agricultural exports planned in 1985, which strongly affected the state budget. At the same time it impeded imports from the United States worth $110 million, consisting in large part of agricultural supplies. The Sandinistas' main economic problems originated from the loss of US imports and the blocked access to spare parts for machinery.[2] These problems affected both the food industry and agriculture.

The Sandinistas had been prepared for this step and had diversified their trade relations beginning in the early 1980s. Nicaragua still transacted 30.4 percent of their foreign trade with the United States in 1980, but by 1984 the Sandinistas had managed to bring down this share to 14.9 percent. However, the United States was still Nicaragua's major bilateral trading partner.[3] The embargo forced Nicaragua to further diversify trade links and to search for new sources for financial aid.

With spreading news reports of Contra violence, the Sandinistas intensified their public diplomacy campaigns. They had some important successes in denouncing US aggression internationally, which eased their requests for external support. In April 1984 the Sandinistas submitted a complaint against US aggression to the International Court of Justice at The Hague and won the suit in 1986. The court ordered the US government to stop financing the Contras and to compensate Nicaragua for the damages. Although the United States ignored these requests, the suit added to international condemnation of the Contra War. At the same time the Sandinistas successfully mobilized opposition against the war in the United States: they established good relations with US journalists as well as congressional leaders (Daniel Ortega even published an editorial in the *New York Times* in 1985). As a result, Congress limited funding for the Contras beginning in 1983. However, the Reagan administration then created illegal networks for continuing support. The most controversial action was the illegal arms sale to Iran, whose revenues were used to finance the Contras. When discovered in late 1986, this became publicly known as the Iran-Contra scandal. From then on, Congress approved no further military aid for the Contras.[4]

At first, international opposition to US aggression helped the Sandinistas to find new assistance abroad and export markets, but after 1985 external assistance declined. As a reaction to the trade embargo Nicaragua exported more bananas to Western Europe, more beef to Canada, and more seafood to Japan, Western Europe, and Latin America. Nevertheless, the combination of the US embargo, blocked loans, and production problems severely affected the Nicaraguan economy. Two months after the United States implemented the embargo, Daniel Ortega embarked on a trip to Europe and the Soviet Union. During his journey, he acquired $190 million in loans from Western Europe and $202 million in aid from Eastern bloc countries.[5]

Although the amount of economic support remained stable until 1985, the composition of donors had changed considerably. The share of Eastern bloc aid in medium- and long-term loans increased significantly from 33 percent in 1983 to 60 percent in 1984 and 84 percent in 1985. The total share of the socialist bloc aid reached two-thirds between 1984 and 1986 while Western Europe, Canada, and the European Economic Community (EEC) contributed only 22.2 percent.[6] Eastern bloc support reached its peak in 1985 and declined thereafter because of economic crises and the Perestroika reforms in the Soviet Union.[7]

At the same time some Western European governments, the solidarity movement, trade unions, and NGOs all criticized the lack of internal democracy within Nicaraguan politics and also reduced their support.[8] After 1985 the total amount of foreign aid declined significantly, and this accel-

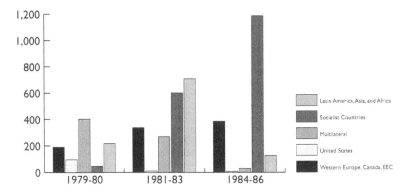

FIGURE 5.1. Sources of medium- and long-term loans and credits and multilateral, bilateral, and NGO grants, 1979–1986. Source: Barraclough, van Buren, Garriazzo, Sunderam, and Utting, *Aid that Counts*, 73.

erated Nicaragua's economic crisis. The strategy of diversified dependency reached its limits. Overall, Nicaragua had become more dependent on financial support from the Eastern bloc countries. As in Sandinista food policy, the diverse economic alliances of revolutionary Nicaragua created contradictory approaches.

The economic crisis Nicaragua was facing by the mid-1980s had both external and internal origins. It happened at a time when all Central American nations were experiencing an economic crisis because of falling prices for their exports and high interest rates on foreign debt. In Nicaragua, the Contra War and the US economic blockade exacerbated the crisis. But internal factors also mattered: a new exchange rate policy and new expenditures in large state investments weighed down the national finances and access to credit became more difficult. Nicaragua's external debt exploded during the 1980s, from $1.3 billion in 1979 up to $6.0 million dollars in 1986.[9] The government established the first adjustment measures in 1985. This decision coincided with a broader trend toward adjustment policies throughout Latin American countries. After the serious debt crisis in the early 1980s, the United States and multilateral lending organizations established economic stabilization and structural adjustment as new conditions for loans. These programs generally shared several characteristics, such as currency devaluations, austerity policies, trade liberalization, and privatizations.

By 1985 the exchange rate policy had become a liability for the Nicaraguan economy. In 1982 the government had introduced a multiple exchange rates regime, which offered favorable rates to export producers in order to stimulate production. The Nicaraguan Central Bank printed more money to cover the rate difference, which prompted inflation. These measures affected the economy in several ways: they put a serious strain on the state budget, and they boosted the growth of a parallel economy, as different prices offered opportunities for speculation. Although Sandinista leaders were aware of these problems, they opted against reform, as they feared losing agro-export producers' political and economic support.[10] The Nicaraguan GDP began to fall in 1984.

After 1983 the Sandinistas were divided over future economic policy and consulted a broad group of foreign advisers. Finally, the government declared the first austerity program in February 1985. External advisers from both the Cold War blocs and from international organizations influenced the decision-making, though sources do not allow us to reconstruct how the Sandinistas framed their proposals.[11]

Heavily debated in the 1980s, the adjustment program meant a fundamental shift of economic policy: the government froze spending, reduced social expenditures by 30 percent, eliminated most food subsidies, increased taxes, and devalued the Córdoba.[12] As several observers pointed out, the economic program shared the characteristics of a classical structural adjustment program without the benefits of further credits by international financial institutions.[13] The program led to higher food prices and affected the revolution's social welfare projects. Nevertheless, basic elements of food policy remained in place, such as the state distribution system and price control.

Given the devastating conditions of the war, the economic blockade, and sagging external aid, adjustment could not alleviate the crisis. The Sandinistas tried to ameliorate the social impact with wage increases, but inflation undermined this effort immediately. Inflation reached new heights with 334 percent in 1985 and 778 percent in 1986. The crisis caused growing unemployment and an 85 percent erosion of real wages between 1985 and 1987. By 1985 an average wage covered only 53 percent of a minimum consumption basket.[14] Hence, Nicaraguans struggled continuously to gain access to food and basic supplies such as soap or toilet paper.

EXPLAINING THE NEW ECONOMIC COURSE AND LIMITS OF THE 1985 INFORMATION CAMPAIGN

Since the shift from expansive spending to austerity programs was radical, the government rolled out a broad information campaign including assemblies and the distribution of educational materials. They published comic books on economic topics and ran cartoons in *Barricada* intended to educate citizens about the new economic policy, which shows that government propaganda relied mainly on repetitive moral appeals. However, this

Figure 5.2. Comic on economic policy. Source: *Barricada*, March 1, 1985, 4.

communication strategy fell short of reaching the illiterate poor, and it also reproduced gender stereotypes. This failure to reach those who suffered the most from the desperate economic situation contributed to the demise of the revolution.

Sandinista leaders traveled the country, gave interviews, and launched a new popular education campaign on economics. In February 1985 five ministers took on the task of addressing the public to explain the impact of the new economic policy on consumption, salaries, and food distribution. The government organized a wave of assemblies with around ninety thousand workers throughout the whole year. In March the FSLN periodical *Barricada* published a cartoon strip series entitled "What Is the Economic Policy in 1985?"[15] The series introduced the new economic measures, described economic concepts, and tried to explain supply problems. Male characters clearly dominated in all the cartoons of the series. When women did appear they adopted traditional female roles such as secretaries, market women, and shoppers.

Throughout 1985 the cartoon series called for stimulating production, saving resources, and stopping speculation. They attributed the country's

FIGURE 5.3. Comic on economic policy. Source: *Barricada,* March 6, 1985.

supply problems primarily to the Contra War and the economic blockade, but the writers also acknowledged internal difficulties (see figure 5.2).[16] The scarcity of foreign exchange impeded the import of packaging material, which affected the production of everyday goods. Human and nonhuman actors guide the readers through the story.

For example, the cartoon depicted a tube of toothpaste with a human face saying, "I'm disappearing because of the lack of packaging material." But the cartoon also referred to internal problems. One panel shows a bureaucrat in a comfortable armchair with his feet up on the desk. He is insisting to someone on the phone that there is still sufficient time for seeding. A peasant wearing a straw hat comments that the time for seeding has already passed. Among other things, the cartoon illustrates the state bureaucracy's limited understanding of peasants' needs. Some Sandinista elites perceived the peasantry as unprogressive.

The success of these cartoons in state campaigns on economic policy was persuasive up to a point as the government used some advantages of the genre effectively. For instance, the artists included graphic examples based on readers' daily experiences. One cartoon strip illustrated inflation with the growing number of banknotes necessary to buy one tortilla (see figure 5.3).[17] However, the full explanation remained dependent on someone being able to read the text. Several cartoons on economic policy lacked a visible dramaturgy: the few illustrations with human characters had no relation to the text and speech balloons dominated the panels. Hence, only literate audiences could understand explanations of economic terms such as "inflation" and "exchange policy."[18]

In general, the cartoons about economics and supply had a strong moral subtext that urged people to increase production, stay away from the black market, and reduce their personal consumption in support of the revolution. According to the government campaigns, people were expected to change their lifestyles to help achieve the revolutionary aim of austerity. Many of the cartoons ended with radical exhortations for consumers to

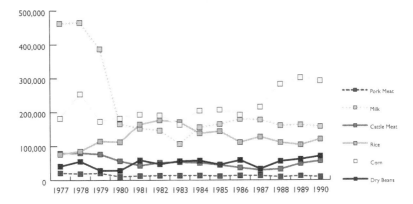

FIGURE 5.4. Food production in Nicaragua, 1977–1990 (in tons). Source: FAO-STAT.

hold out until revolutionary victory against the Contras, such as "Fight and produce to survive. We will win!"[19] It is difficult to determine whether these slogans convinced people or were perceived merely as platitudes. In 1985 the head of the national advertising system and renowned writer Gioconda Belli criticized most advertisements for having too many slogans and repeating the same rhetorical elements, which audiences found boring. Once the Nicaraguan people became used to the political messages, Belli argued, they no longer paid attention.[20]

Even if the educational cartoons were meant to address large sectors of the population, their content and visual repertoire were largely limited to the experiences of men from Central Nicaragua. Once again, the Sandinistas failed to cover the diversity of Nicaraguan society. The comic strips frequently depicted farmers and workers, but women and members of other ethnic groups were almost completely absent.[21] As in other political campaigns intended to influence consumers, the writers failed to depict the lived experiences of women as well as people on the Caribbean Coast.

STAGNATING FOOD PRODUCTION WORSENS THE SUPPLY SITUATION

Despite continuous external support between 1979 and 1985, food production in the mid-1980s remained insufficient to feed the Nicaraguan population, which contributed to the revolution's eventual demise. As the chart above illustrates, food production stagnated by the mid-1980s (see figure 5.4). The scarcity of milk and meat, in particular, prompted widespread discontent as people considered these foods essential for a healthy diet. Furthermore, the population grew by an average rate of 2.64 percent in the first half of the 1980s, from 3.25 million in 1980 to 3.71 million in 1985. Hence, a stagnating system of production had to feed nearly 500,000 additional people.[22]

The food industries most affected were rice, meat, and milk production. In many cases it was a combination of different factors that led to the downturn. Especially in the case of milk and irrigated rice, the low productivity of state farms contributed significantly to the problem of supply. The Sandinistas tried to fill the gaps with imports, which further affected the state budget. Overall, imports of basic grains and milk increased between 1984 and 1986. In total the government spent $159 million on imports of food and agricultural supplies, which was one-third of the country's commercial deficit in the mid-1980s, but it was insufficient to compensate for stagnating production.[23]

Nicaraguans considered milk as essential for child nutrition, and they experienced the decline of fresh milk consumption as a serious disruption. Throughout the 1980s production remained more than 50 percent below prerevolutionary levels while demand increased, which created a tense situation.[24] Food aid and nutrition education during the 1960s and 1970s had established that milk was a necessity for young children. Since then, powdered milk gained importance through distribution to Nicaraguan children in food aid projects, commercial propaganda of child formula producers, and a decline in breastfeeding. As people were convinced that milk scarcity endangered their children's health, the debate in the mid-1980s soon became fraught with emotions. In addition, milk scarcity also endangered the availability of by-products such as *cuajada* or cheese. As fluid milk was scarce, the state milk producer Empresa Nacional de Industria Láctea (ENILAC) depended on powdered milk donations to produce recombined milk from 1982 onward.

The supply of milk powder started to decline, and its unequal distribution caused feelings to run high. The emotional debates over the lack of powdered milk in the mid-1980s prove that many Nicaraguan consumers already considered it to be essential for good nutrition. In May 1986 consumers flooded the "Buzón popular" section of *Barricada* with letters complaining about the shortage of powdered milk available through official distribution channels. Given the frequent deficiencies the government finally limited distribution to children under the age of two. People looked for alternatives but found the prices unaffordable. The price for five pounds of powdered milk on the black market exceeded fifty thousand Córdobas, which was the equivalent of a month's minimum salary.[25]

Barricada blamed the scarcity on Nestlé, as the multinational owned the only powdered milk production plant in Nicaragua. At that time Nestlé sold 70 percent of its production to private distributors, which put the state distribution system at a substantial disadvantage. In March 1987 the Central Sandinista de Trabajadores (CST), Sandinista Workers' Central, announced a demonstration at Nestlé's headquarters where two thousand workers showed up demanding the distribution of powdered milk through the official channels. The protest was successful: only a month later a new agreement guaranteed MICOIN 60 percent of Nestlé's powdered milk production for sale at subsidized prices. The case was a welcome opportunity to channel popular anger against a multinational enemy. When state enterprises' activities caused a similar scarcity, "Buzón popular" reported on these cases but failed to launch a sufficient examination into the crisis. Exorbitant prices and the lack of critical foods increased disillusionment with the state supply system.

The Contra War had also affected meat production in several ways, most notably because of the increasing difficulty of importing agricultural supplies and because of cattle smuggling across the border. In the course of 1986, for example, around four thousand head of cattle disappeared from the war zones; most were stolen or brought by their owners to neighboring countries. About 60 percent of all slaughtering took place in the war zones, as the North was the traditional center of the Nicaraguan cattle sector. Hence, the Sandinistas tried to reduce per capita meat consumption from twenty-seven pounds to twelve pounds per year, a more than 55 percent decrease.[26] According to CIERA data, the government reached this goal: per capita beef consumption decreased from 26.1 pounds per year in 1984 to 17.1 pounds in 1986 and finally to 10.9 pounds in 1988.[27] A reduction of more than 58 percent within two years was a dramatic shift. Beans per capita consumption experienced a similar decline. Although people experienced the scarcity of meat as the more radical change, since meat was traditionally an indicator for good nutrition, the combination of scarce meat and scarce beans nurtured the feelings of crisis. Throughout the first half of the 1980s some of the Sandinista leadership considered industrial farming as the best way to increase food production. With continuing war and scarce financial resources, however, it became obvious that large-scale technological systems were difficult to maintain.

THE CRISIS OF INDUSTRIAL AGRICULTURE

The Sandinista government believed in state-run, large-scale agricultural production and the use of modern technology such as automatic milking machines, tractors, and irrigation systems. Beginning in 1983 government plans focused increasingly on agroindustry and technology as a means to increase yields. Despite scarce financial resources, the Sandinistas initiated several large-scale investment projects that same year.[28] The multiple exchange rates policy favored the spread of technology in rural areas between 1982 and 1985. At that time the overvalued Córdoba cheapened imports, so it became more profitable to buy new equipment than to repair the old. Tractors, threshers, irrigation facilities, and harvesters spread throughout the Nicaraguan countryside. A CARE staff member, for example, reported in 1985 that 55 percent of all tractors and 80 percent of all harvesters in Nicaragua were less than five years old.[29]

The economic crisis affected technology-based solutions for food production after 1984, when the state budget had fewer resources to pay for costly investments, and the trade embargo made it difficult to import spare parts for maintaining production. Occasionally, foreign development aid filled these gaps and provided the necessary foreign exchange. Once again, external support proved critical for Nicaraguan food production.[30] Given the financial problems and low productivity, however, the government abandoned a number of large investment projects in 1984. The debates continued between those who favored small-scale agricultural production and those who believed in industrial agricultural practices. The disconnect between the government's vision and day-to-day rural realities transcended the problems associated with diminished revenue and the continuing war.[31]

The increased use of technology in agriculture sparked fierce debates. Both Sandinista elites and foreign advisers were divided over the matter. Initially there was a strong faction within each group arguing for technological fixes. Sergio Ramírez remembered that at a certain point it was considered "blasphemy" to criticize the use of technological solutions, even if the negative consequences were obvious:

> The revolution could not proceed step by step, phase by phase; it had to skip all the stages and fulfill its claim to modernity. Every statement . . . that four thousand tractors required a maintenance network that exceeded our abilities, or that every liter of milk from the "high-performance" cows was ten times as expensive as one from local cows, was akin to blasphemy. Nobody was allowed to claim that, in our country, farmers had to evolve from planting with a stick—a pre-Colombian system in which the corn was planted in the soil grain by grain—to plowing with a team of oxen, and that that alone would double their harvest.[32]

This code of behavior—the suppression of any concerns or doubts about large-scale development projects—impeded critical discussions and the search for viable alternatives. At lower levels, however, the efforts of development assistance focused on improving small-scale food production within peasant communities.

By the mid-1980s foreign experts increasingly questioned the focus on technology in Nicaraguan food production. After several decades of increased investment in agricultural technology, the experts were forced to consider other solutions. My findings on Nicaragua in the mid-1980s contradict those authors of development literature who have argued for a continuous spread of development discourse and models into Global South countries.[33] Several authors have argued that the idea to modernize local agricultures through technology persisted in development aid up to the 1980s. Experts across the Cold War blocs perceived modern industrial farming as the way to transform Global South countries into developed economies. This trend was also visible in Nicaragua, but the economic downturn shook the experts' belief in technology around 1985. During the Nicaraguan crisis, development experts started to voice criticism as technology-based solutions did not fit with local realities at all. For example, a Swiss development assistance project in Northern Nicaragua focused explicitly on small-scale production, after the introduction of some machinery intended for large-scale farming such as milking parlors, pumps, and liquid manor tanks for the milk industry had failed.[34] The project manager concluded on another donation that it was a "classic example of too rapid mechanization through outside agents."[35]

Since the mid-1980s, FAO project reports warned about the negative effects of a technology-based strategy. For example, the reports argued that the corn irrigation programs had generated low yields. For them to continue would require technicians who were unavailable in Nicaragua.[36] Even East German advisers questioned the technology strategy in the late 1980s and argued for developing intermediate technologies that would be adapted to Nicaragua's capacities. They suggested a reduction of mechanization and the introduction of alternative methods to exterminate weeds.[37] Hence, doubts about technological fixes for food production afflicted external advisers across East–West divisions and different organizations. These doubts contributed to their disillusionment with those Sandinista leaders who continued to promote large-scale industrial agriculture.

THE SANDINISTAS' CONTENTIOUS RELATIONSHIP WITH NICARAGUAN PEASANTS

The combination of the war and the economic blockade required new solutions for improving the revolutionaries' relationship with basic grains producers. In particular, the government needed to prevent peasants from joining the ranks of the Contras. Beginning in 1985 the government established a new focus on small-scale farm production. These new policies deemphasized the focus on large-scale agricultural solutions and accelerated land distribution and efforts to improve the food supply situation for peasants in rural areas.

Peasants had been joining the Contras for several reasons. The most important was that they were disillusioned with the revolutionary state because it could not resolve important problems of agricultural production such as land distribution and the supply of agricultural tools. State intervention in the forms of agricultural production, trade, and consumption prompted further resentment among the peasants. Village people criticized the long lines at stores and the lack of available clothes and shoes of adequate sizes. They rejected the obligation to buy supplies at shops defined by Sandinista authorities. In hindsight some women interviewed even credited frustrations with rationing as being an important reason that local people joined the Contras.[38] The cultural gap between urban FSLN representatives and the peasants in the northern and central highlands contributed to these tensions. The party representatives lacked knowledge of local customs as well as agricultural production. Finally, peasants resisted the introduction of obligatory military service in late 1983 because conscription disrupted their agricultural activities.[39] Hence, by the mid-1980s, the Contras had a stronger peasant basis than before, especially in Boaco, Chontales, Nueva Guinea, Matagalpa, and Jinotega, where they established permanent bases.

It would be inaccurate to generalize about peasants' attitudes, however, as conditions varied according to local circumstances and social stratification within the peasantry. People in the war zones experienced serious disruptions in their lives. Sometimes they were forced to leave and abandon their land. People in rural villages suffered military invasions and abuses from both sides. Contra atrocities were well documented and formed part of Sandinista public diplomacy campaigns abroad. Sandinista soldiers and state security also committed serious—but less violent—abuses. For example, in a settlement in the interior mountains, Sandinista troops threw away peasants' food supplies, destroyed their clothes, and took away their cattle.[40] Over the years the villages in war zones were abandoned by state institutions, party members, and businesses. Recent testimonies from women who lived in the war zones indicate that the food supply deteriorated drastically. In times of food scarcity, they and their children survived on a diet of salted bananas exclusively.[41]

The Sandinista government's ignorance of peasants' needs and preferences largely contributed to its declining support in the countryside, a deterioration of support that was part of a broader question about the role of peasants in revolutionary Nicaragua. The political scientist Salvador Martí i Puig has argued that the peasants were the Sandinistas' Achilles' heel.[42] The educational backgrounds of pro-Sandinista rural elites contributed to their misunderstanding of peasants' lives. Elites were frequently liberal professionals who had been educated in the United States or political activists with an Eastern bloc education.[43] Political elites in Nicaragua romanticized the preconquest indigenous past while interpreting contemporary indigenous culture as an obstacle to modernization. Jaime Wheelock, for example, publicly denounced peasants' backwardness. There was a tradition of idealizing the lives of peasants in the past while the realities of life for modern-day peasants were not taken into account.[44]

In spite of these limitations the Sandinistas did try to learn more about the situation in rural communities, especially within those institutions that favored small-scale food production. For example, CIERA researchers regularly went out to talk to farmers after the government had introduced new policies.[45] Ultimately, a combination of rural people's demands for land redistribution and external pressure made the government change its course around 1985 so as to weaken peasant support for the Contras and to stimulate local food production. First, the state agency for basic grains, ENABAS, started to pay higher prices starting with the 1984–1985 harvest.[46] Second, the government prioritized the countryside in economic planning and supply. Third, the government gave up its exclusive focus on cooperatives, which was also visible in the acceleration of agrarian reform assigning land titles to individual peasants. The government changed agrarian reform law in January 1986 to allow for the expropriation of landholdings under five hundred manzanas. In contrast to previous years, land was redistributed mainly from large state enterprises to small- and medium-scale producers. The war regions in interior Nicaragua in particular benefited from the new wave of land distribution. Finally, in 1985 the government also started to liberalize the corn and beans trades. It abrogated the ENABAS exclusive monopoly and allowed other actors to participate in basic grains marketing.[47]

Whether the new Sandinista focus on the countryside improved rural food supply is difficult to determine conclusively as no systematic surveys exist for rural consumption in the late 1980s. Nonetheless, what scarce evidence there is indicates that Sandinista food policy provided cooperative members with better access to consumer goods and foods than peasants had. CIERA researchers argued that the situation improved for cooperative members after the revolution. In their eyes, rural people's improved access to new products was a result of state distribution channels reaching the countryside. CIERA also concluded that cooperative members' higher incomes permitted them to buy more goods than before the revolution, but rural workers and other peasants benefited less from revolutionary food policy.[48]

Regarding agricultural laborers, the available evidence provides ambiguous findings. Surveys revealed that the situation for agricultural laborers in Managua's surroundings worsened, as they had less access to goods than before the revolution. Later on, the Sandinistas established material

incentives, however, including a reward system for highly productive workers based on Cuban models. The Sandinistas reestablished country fairs
during harvest times where trucks sold basic goods to agricultural workers
at official prices. These measures most likely improved laborers' access to
consumer goods.[49]

Overall, food policy favored workers in state enterprise and cooperatives whereas independent small farmers received few benefits. The deficiencies in rural supply are confirmed by other contemporary testimonies
and reports. The *New York Times* correspondent Stephen Kinzer reported
on food scarcity after visiting a rural community in Jinotega in 1983. He
spent some time in the local food store, observing consumers, and remembered: "Half the shelves were empty. Women from the outlying hills came
looking for all manners of goods, and almost all left disappointed. Nearly
every one of the fifty or so customers who passed through the store had
something nasty to say about the Sandinistas. Most were from farm families themselves, and talked of how they had stopped growing food or raising animals because government-imposed controls were too onerous. As a
result, in stores like this one there was no cooking oil, no chicken, no beef,
no rice, no eggs."[50]

Kinzer's report shows that rural people in Northern Nicaragua faced
problems in acquiring goods and rejected state control over food distribution. One of my interviewees recalled how rural people traveled to the cities
to acquire processed foods such as canned sardines or spaghetti but found
these products far too expensive. He added, "but no peasant will die if
these products were unavailable," indicating that processed foods were not
considered essential for local diets. More than by the scarcity of processed
foods, rural people were affected by the scarcity of vegetable oil as it impeded the ability to fry foods.[51]

During wartime the availability of food varied considerably according
to time period and region. A 1985 special report on the situation of poor
peasants confirmed the negative effects of increasing food prices. This survey diagnosed an increased consumption of vegetable oil, rice, beans, chick-
en, and pork, while the consumption of corn, milk, and beef had dropped.[52]
Given that corn was the most important staple in the countryside, a reduction of corn consumption worsened the nutritional situation considerably.

Stark imbalances in food consumption separated urban areas from rural regions by 1985. This imbalance made rural people feel that their supply
was of secondary priority for the revolutionary authorities. The data shown
in the chart below is based on two CIERA studies completed in 1982 and
1985 in Managua and the rural areas of Estelí in Northern Nicaragua (see
figure 5.5).[53] On average rural people consumed considerably less rice, veg-

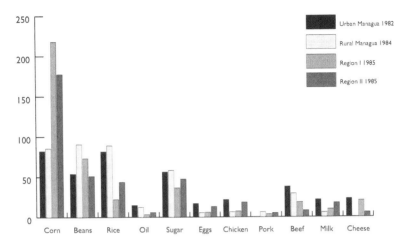

FIGURE 5.5. Food consumption in four Nicaraguan regions, 1982–1985. Source: CIERA, *La reforma agraria*, 207. All products are measured in pounds, except milk (gallons), vegetable oil (liters), and eggs (dozens).

etable oil, sugar, and beef although it is very likely that the supply situation in Managua in 1985 was worse than in 1982. Because of the local cattle industry, people in the northern regions still had access to meat and milk products. The chart also demonstrates that people in the north relied heavily on corn and beans for their nutrition. Comparative data from other zones is not available. The war made the food supply unstable, so surveys made in any one month or region can only provide an idea of community supply at this precise moment and location but not on the situation throughout war.

Several different reports addressed the general neglect of rural consumers in Sandinista supply policy. For example, the Sandinistas did not take important agricultural supplies such as rubber boots and tools into consideration when making decisions about imports. A 1985 report described the peasants' arduous and frequently unsuccessful efforts to acquire grinding files or trousers. Peasants approached different state institutions without success, and low prices for basic grains limited their purchasing power. Calculations on the purchasing power of one quintal of corn revealed that the ability to afford clothes had declined by more than 70 percent between 1978 and 1985.[54]

Unequal access to food and consumer goods combined with the general rejection of their needs in the state distribution networks made peasants increasingly oppose the revolution. However, the Sandinistas also made efforts to level the rural-urban gap in food consumption. With its new focus on peasants, the government strived to address rural food insecurity and

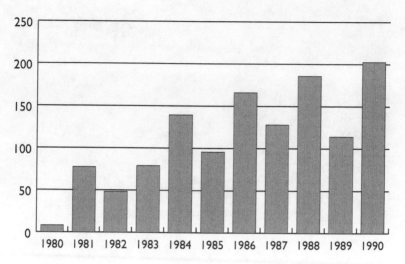

FIGURE 5.6. Food aid in Nicaragua, 1980–1990 (in 1,000 tons). Source: Garst, *La ayuda alimentaria*, cuadro 15.

the lack of agricultural supplies. In 1985 the government launched a new rural supply network. The main pressure group behind the initiative was the Unión Nacional de Agricultores y Ganaderos (UNAG, the National Union of Farmers and Ranchers), the mass organization of agricultural producers that had established initial contacts with Swedish development aid in 1984. In 1985 UNAG's influence on Sandinista food policy increased.[55] A trip by Daniel Ortega to Sweden in 1985 resulted in a large amount of emergency aid to mitigate the effects of the economic blockade. The Sandinistas used part of this aid for building up a network of rural cooperative stores in the war zones. The number of stores increased from 55 in 1985–1986 to 197 in 1988 with a total membership of around sixty thousand people. These stores sold nine essential agricultural supplies as well as a limited number of consumer goods and basic food. Although subsidies in general were on the wane, the financial support from development aid enabled the government to subsidize the products with around eight million dollars until 1989.[56] The political scientist Ilja A. Luciak has interpreted the initiative as strengthening grassroots democracy in Nicaragua. However, he also admitted some weaknesses, such as the absence of educational programs, abuses by store administrators, and a lack of clarity among the members about the cooperative structure. In the end the new network suffered a downturn after the 1988 economic adjustment.[57] The economic crisis, war, and natural disaster undermined Nicaragua's capacity to feed its own population. As a result, international food aid to Nicaragua increased by 48.5 percent between 1985 and 1988.[58]

INCREASING DEPENDENCY ON FOOD AID

By 1985 Nicaragua's increasing dependence on food aid had undermined the aim of revolutionary self-sufficiency. At the same time economic crisis affected the country's capacity to store and distribute aid adequately. Beyond this, misappropriations of donations caused people to lose confidence in the state distribution network. A 1991 study concluded that food aid had formed a "key piece" for the national food supply during the previous decade. Food worth more than $375 million comprised as much as 25 percent of the total Nicaraguan food supply.[59] From 1983 food aid increased, although fluctuations occurred regularly, as the chart shows (see figure 5.6). This instability made it difficult for the Nicaraguan government to predict the amount of aid that would arrive and to plan accordingly. In 1988 Nicaragua received the most food aid, almost certainly in response to Hurricane Joan.[60]

What were the sources and composition of food aid? As in trade, credit relations, and development cooperation, the Sandinista strategy of diversified dependency worked out well in the area of food donations. As the crisis worsened, dependency on external food sources increased. But the Sandinista government's attitude to these donations throughout the decade was contradictory. On the one hand, they were aware that food aid could weaken local food production, increase the demand for imported foods, and hence undermine their goal of converting Nicaragua to a self-sufficient country. On the other hand, they welcomed all donations as international support for the revolution, and they organized public ceremonies to welcome those donations. With food policy turning into crisis management after 1985, the government's capacity to distribute donations declined and corruption increased. Donated food surfaced on the black market, which undermined Nicaraguans' confidence in the revolution and its government.

FAO statistical data reveals that throughout the 1980s Nicaragua depended heavily on imported and donated foods. In the case of corn, the peak was reached in 1983 with 39.5 percent of the national supply; in the case of beans and rice it was 40.2 percent and 54.8 percent respectively in 1988.[61] Throughout the 1980s imports and donations composed shares of more than 20 percent for rice, corn, beans, and milk, although these fluctuated significantly. In 1985 and 1986 rice and corn donations particularly increased. Unfortunately, the FAO did not break down imports and donations by year, and data from Nicaraguan institutions has some inconsistencies.[62] Nevertheless, the evidence indicates clearly that the Sandinista government failed in reaching food self-sufficiency for important basic foods even with food aid.

Although the composition of donors changed significantly throughout the 1980s, they all used food distributions to communicate their political messages to the Nicaraguan public. Food donations from socialist countries by 1983 had increased significantly and by 1984 had become the most important aid. Over the whole decade their share in food aid for Nicaragua was slightly more than 50 percent. Bilateral aid reached a share of nearly 30 percent, with the largest contributions coming from European countries.[63] This dependency implied the need to remain in close contact with donors, win their sympathies again and again, and accept their political agendas. One expression of this relationship was the organization of public ceremonies when new donations arrived. At these ceremonies, the Sandinistas generally gave foreign diplomats a platform to address the crowd. *Barricada* commemorated the ceremonies with articles such as "Bread That Nicaragua Receives with Dignity."[64] Sandinista leaders used "dignity" as a key term at the public ceremonies so as to distance Nicaragua from the image of a poor, dependent recipient country.

The Sandinista attitude toward food aid was contradictory from the beginning and oscillated between fundamental criticism and enthusiastic acceptance enacted through public ceremonies. One of the earliest negative statements on food aid can be traced to *Barricada* in January 1980 when the newspaper published a caricature showing a mousetrap with a piece of cheese inside, identified by a sign as "food for poor countries." The mousetrap had a sharp knife labeled "birth control." The caricature established a relationship between the conditioning of aid to political reforms promoted by US development cooperation.[65]

However, the Sandinistas also received aid with open arms, even donations from the United States. *Barricada* regularly reported on new donations and celebrated them as support for the revolution.[66] As food production had declined in the insurrectional period, the Sandinistas urgently needed food donations to improve the supply situation. In the first six months after the revolution, Nicaragua received thirty-two thousand tons of food aid. Sources included a broad range of countries and organizations: USAID, CARE, both German states, Brazil, Cuba, China, Canada, and the Soviet Union.[67] As in development cooperation and trade relations, the strategy of diversified dependency proved initially successful for attracting food donations. Nonetheless, after the United States canceled their wheat credits in 1981, Sandinista political propaganda denounced food aid as a political weapon of imperialism.

In general, the Sandinistas argued that food aid was not adequate to alleviate world hunger. CIERA analyzed the role of food aid more systematically in its publication *El hambre en los países del tercer mundo* (Hunger

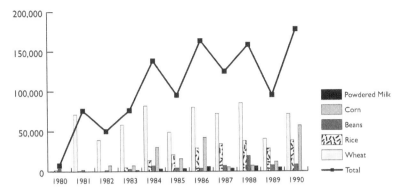

FIGURE 5.7. Composition of Nicaraguan food aid, 1980–1990 (in tons). Source: Hernández, "La ayuda alimentaria," 35.

in Third World countries). After explaining the advantages of food aid for the donor countries, the pamphlet questioned the ability of food aid to end global hunger, whose roots, as the authors argued, resided in the dependency of peripheral countries on the capitalist center. This analysis was strongly influenced by dependency theory; it focused on the principal division between the center and the periphery, identifying Nicaragua as part of the dependent periphery. The publication criticized the negative influence of food aid on local grain production. Hence, the report recommended the implementation of national development plans promoting food self-sufficiency.[68]

The Sandinistas also recognized that food aid could make Nicaraguan people dependent on donations. After the 1982 floods the magazine *Envío* argued for temporary limits on food aid, as dependence on donations would affect people's dignity. Instead, the authors suggested the implementation of food-for-work programs in the affected communities.[69] Again, in 1985, a *Barricada* article on economic policy reminded its readers: "We cannot expect that during our whole life we will receive donations and donations, instead we should understand the collaboration of other countries as a supplement to our own efforts."[70] The newspaper did not reject foreign aid completely but argued for considering it only as additional support instead of relying entirely on donations. However, during this period Nicaragua's reliance on external food sources increased. Reports from the Ministry of Health established a moderate position: food aid was viewed as a temporary answer to nutritional problems rather than as a long-term solution. The reports included rather vague references to the principle of self-supply while focusing on the implementation of technical projects.[71] As in other aspects of economic policy, pragmatism won out over the idealist rejection of food aid.

The continuous influx of donated food between the 1960s and the 1980s influenced Nicaraguan consumption habits. In the long run, food aid increased Nicaragua's reliance on imported food, particularly on canned food, wheat, powdered milk, and food for children. Most food aid rations contained both wheat flour and powdered milk, whereas corn was only seldom included, as for example in the WFP rations for a Nicaraguan hospital in the mid-1980s. Recipients of WFP donations considered skim milk, canned meat, and vegetable oil as high prestige foods, and they had very high acceptance rates. Wheat by far surpassed all other donations as the previous chart demonstrates (see figure 5.7). Corn donations had two peaks in 1984 and 1986. After that they decreased significantly; instead, rice became more dominant, and donations of rice increased continuously from 1983 onward. Powdered milk donations had also increased significantly by 1983, ranging in quantity roughly at the same level as beans.[72]

Nonetheless, some food aid products never gained acceptance in the Nicaraguan population, as they did not appeal to local food preferences. Sometimes nutritional education could resolve doubts, sometimes not. East European products provide an interesting example for the acceptance (or not) of food aid and its influence on local consumption habits. The debate concentrated on fish, food for children, and different canned products such as the infamous Bulgarian cans. The US researcher Forest Colburn observed: "Relatively quickly, supermarkets became rather curious places. They are usually bereft of necessities. . . . What the supermarkets really excel in, though, is imported goods, which appear and disappear. For a time, there were tins of tasty Soviet sardines. But there were also cans of strange meats and sausages from somewhere in Eastern Europe. These cans remained on the shelves until the bourgeoisie discovered they made excellent pet food."[73] It is not surprising that Western observers highlighted the presence of East European products in their descriptions, but how did Nicaraguans react to these products? Occasional press reports indicate that in fact there were acceptance problems, for mainly three reasons: when the East European food items did not adapt well to local consumption habits, when hygienic problems occurred because of storage limitations, or when instructions were inadequate. In 1984 *Barricada* reported that donated Soviet mackerel was not well received on Managuan markets. People were so hesitant to buy mackerel that market vendors even reduced the official price from twelve Córdobas to nine Córdobas. Mackerel was unknown to most Nicaraguans, and consumers generally preferred other fish such as sea bass, for instance.[74] It has to be added that fish, in general, was not widely accepted, as meat was considered more prestigious.

With the economic decline, the ability of government institutions to distribute donated foods had waned by the mid-1980s. In particular, storage and transport facilities were increasingly scarce during the economic crisis. Inadequate storage led to food spoilage and the loss of donated food, which added to Nicaraguans' loss of confidence in the revolution. In March 1985, for example, canned meat donated by Hungary and Czechoslovakia was stored too long in the heat and spoiled. In most cases the authorities disposed of the spoiled food, but on the local level merchants sometimes continued to sell it, either because they were uninformed or because they wanted to make a profit. The hygienic conditions at the markets were also not favorable for selling fresh fish as it spoiled quickly under the sun. Hence, consumers became increasingly worried about the quality of donated food.[75]

Nicaraguans were mostly unfamiliar with East European foods, which sometimes led to their being rejected. In particular, the unpleasant flavor of canned foods entered the collective memory of crisis years. For example, in 1984, a distribution of Soviet baby food raised concerns among Nicaraguan consumers. Packages with Cyrillic letters were distributed without any Spanish-language instructions, which led to rumors that the donations had already spoiled.

Oppositional newspapers such as *La Prensa* took up these consumer issues and lamented the poor quality of food donations. Concerned consumers bombarded *Barricada* reporters with phone calls asking for clarification or expressing their worries about the quality of donated Eastern bloc products. To respond to these concerns, *Barricada* reported that all food had passed quality control testing based on World Health Organization standards.[76] Government institutions learned from this incident and accompanied the distribution of canned meat donations from Hungary and Czechoslovakia with information on how to store and prepare the food.[77] In particular, Bulgarian canned products were widely present in the daily diets of Nicaraguans and entered collective memory for their unfamiliar flavors. One interviewee reported that he regularly consumed canned tuna with sauces or vegetables and got fed up. He suspected that Bulgaria was flooding the Nicaraguan market with canned goods. When these foods were included in state rations, by 1988 they were soon appearing in local markets because the recipients did not eat them.[78] Overall, unfamiliar foods often received a less than enthusiastic response from Nicaraguan consumers.

Nonetheless, the widespread popularity of most donated foods led to a higher demand for imported food, which fundamentally contradicted the government's goal of food self-sufficiency. Although FAO had long been in favor of milk and wheat distribution, in a 1990 report the international organization criticized the distribution of wheat products at subsidized prices. According to FAO authors, wheat distribution lowered the consumption of locally produced foods and favored higher income groups who were the main consumers of bread.[79] Between 1977 and 1990, wheat products made up an average of 66.1 percent of all food aid in Central America, compared to 3.3 percent of milk powder, 5.9 percent of rice, and 10.4 percent of secondary grains.[80] Hence, food aid strengthened the preference for wheat at the cost of local grains throughout the region.

CORRUPTION AND FOREIGN EXPERTS' DISILLUSIONMENT WITH SANDINISTA FOOD POLICY

In the midst of the economic crisis and decreasing wages, state employees sometimes sold food donations for their own benefit. The Sandinistas rarely reported publicly on such cases, but people became aware through rumors and through the presence of donated foods at markets or shops where they were previously unavailable. The gap between the crusade against self-enrichment through speculation and the silencing of similar practices among state employees undermined the credibility of the revolutionary government.

Corruption most likely increased hand in hand with the shortage economy, as desperate people were willing to pay higher prices for limited foodstuffs. In 1985 Róger Sánchez Flores published a telling caricature that openly attacked government employees' corruption. The drawing shows an office desk whose surface is empty but whose open drawers are filled with cans of donated food. Besides pencils, some blank papers, and a telephone, the desk is bare and signals inactivity. On the opposite wall a sign reveals the bureaucrat's motto: "If you have nothing to do, don't do it here."[81] This caricature criticized state bureaucrats for being absent from work while food aid was not being distributed. Even worse and beyond this particular caricature, bureaucrats were sometimes perceived, fairly or unfairly, to be withholding food donations in exchange for monetary bribes from external buyers. These accusations are supported by evidence that indicates a general increase of corruption in food distributing state agencies.

By the mid-1980s mass organizations, trade unions, and shop owners publicly denounced corruption within the Ministry of Internal Commerce (MICOIN). After speculation had reached unprecedented levels, MICOIN announced it would withdraw the licenses of the corrupt merchants. Immediately, UNAG responded that this was insufficient as illegal networks had already infiltrated the ministry and its local offices. This case shows that formal and informal economies were closely interrelated as government officials passed on goods to speculators.[82]

Nonetheless, government media in Nicaragua during the revolution typically silenced corruption for two reasons. First, the Sandinistas had fiercely attacked corruption in the Somoza regime, which is why corruption in their own ranks would damage their public image. News that food donations were disappearing through state channels would have reminded people of the misappropriation of aid after the 1972 earthquake. Second, corruption contradicted the ethics promoted by the revolution—namely, austere consumption and the rejection of prodigality. By the mid-1980s, however, some of the Sandinista leadership had already abandoned these values and assigned privileges to government functionaries. Political corruption and greed as well as the mid-1980s adjustment policy contributed to widespread disillusionment as the economic crisis deepened.

External advisers also became disillusioned with the Sandinistas' insufficient efforts to move toward self-sufficiency. By the mid-1980s external advisers' initial enthusiasm regarding Nicaraguan food policy turned into a feeling of deception. Nutrition experts in the mid-1980s observed with increasing concern the high levels of basic grains imports. Solon Barraclough and Peter Utting analyzed the nutritional situation of several Latin American countries in 1986 and presented a pessimistic report. Comparing Mexico, Chile, Bolivia, and Nicaragua, they concluded that rice, beans, and corn imports amounted to as much as one-third and one-fourth of total grains consumed. In the end the authors argued for political mobilization—food rationing, restrictions on luxury consumption, and an alliance between workers, rural poor, and small farmers.[83]

Joseph Collins, formerly a strong advocate of the revolutionary food policy and adviser from the US nonprofit organization Food First, also criticized the lack of attention given to peasants' needs and the declining importance of the Nicaraguan Food Program in a third, extended version of his book in 1986. In the new chapters, he described how his disappointment with the Nicaraguan Food Program eventually replaced his initial enthusiasm. Collins argued that food policy never gained the same importance as other political projects such as the literacy campaign. In Collins's opinion, technological help for small producers had been neglected and land distribution had been accomplished too slowly to increase food production. PAN never managed to liberate itself from bureaucratic obstacles and institutional competition, which Collins blamed for the lack of adequate leadership for the program. He also admitted that external advisers had underestimated the degree of Nicaragua's external dependence.[84] As in the case of Barraclough and Utting, experts expressed greater skepticism in their evaluations of the revolutionary transformation that had taken place by the mid-1980s. The initial enthusiasm to promote Nicaragua as a model for Global South countries faded away.

By 1985 Nicaragua was on its way into a deep economic decline and a widespread supply crisis. Food policy turned more and more into crisis management, and the Sandinistas' original ambitious aims faded away. They argued that this crisis had two main causes: the US economic blockade and the Contra War. The origins of the crisis, however, were more complex. First, it was not only the blockade that caused economic crisis. Exchange-rate policy, large state investments, and decreasing prices for Nicaraguan export products caused a deep financial crisis that accelerated after the 1985 US trade embargo. The second factor, the Contra War, clearly affected food production because of the scarcity of resources and the declining workforce. As cattle farming was concentrated in the war zones, meat supply was reduced considerably. In the end the government sought a 55 percent reduction of individual meat consumption, which was a blow for Nicaraguan consumers who perceived meat as the most important indicator of good nutrition.

Finally, Nicaragua's high dependence on imports weakened the economy further. Because of war and economic crisis, Nicaragua became more dependent on external aid in general and on aid from the socialist countries in particular. Loans and external advice were important in the areas of economic policy; development cooperation provided resources for agricultural supplies and food policy projects. Although the strategy of diversified dependence was initially successful against US aggression, external support could not compensate for the damages brought on by war and economic aggression. Foreign aid declined after 1985, which worsened the economic crisis during the late 1980s. With less financial resources, food aid became more important. Although it was badly needed, food aid undermined the self-sufficiency project by strengthening popular demand for powdered milk, canned foods, and wheat products. The Sandinistas' attitude to food aid remained contradictory, however, varying between enthusiasm and criticism. Storage problems and corruption within the state distribution network further undermined peoples' confidence in the revolution.

The adjustment policy was a victory for economic pragmatism, but it ultimately failed to alleviate the crisis. With the new economic measures the Sandinistas became less committed to ensuring equal access to food for all Nicaraguans. The economic crisis provoked a dramatic loss in purchasing power for both rural and urban consumers. Rural people had access to basic grains but lacked agricultural supplies and vegetable oil; urban consumers struggled with high prices on the black market and the periodic lack of important basic foods. The lack of milk and powdered milk caused feelings to run high, as people considered milk fundamental for children's good health. At the height of crisis the government tried to redirect consumers' anger with a campaign against multinationals.

Overall, government propaganda was too repetitive and failed to reach certain audiences, such as people from the Caribbean and rural peasants. Hence, revolutionary food policy failed in valuing the diversity of food cultures as well as restoring a balance of food distribution. There were sharp differences in food supply in urban and rural areas, among different regions, within the family, or among different social groups. Rural people in the Nicaraguan interior rejected state intervention in land distribution and food supply. Communities in the war regions suffered from military interventions, confiscations, and abandonment. By the mid-1980s the Contras had gained a significant peasant base.

Given the Sandinista leadership's contradictory perception of peasants, food policy could not resolve the conflicts arising from demands for land and equal access to resources for rural communities. The promises of modernization and technology-based solutions for food production impeded political measures favoring individual access to land and small farmers' autonomy. By the mid-1980s, however, the gap had widened between local realities and the vision of large-scale food production on state farms utilizing the latest agricultural technology. Qualified technicians, spare parts, and imported agricultural tools were in limited supply, which resulted in daily emergencies and standstills. The debate over large state farms and the use of industrial agriculture versus small farms run by peasants gained importance in the mid-1980s. Accelerated land distributions had a favorable impact on corn and sorghum production, but this was insufficient to combat food insecurity.

Some experts had criticized the reliance on industrial farming at state enterprises from the outset. By the mid-1980s some former advocates of the large-scale approach criticized planning failures and the waste of resources on state farms. This contradicts the development literature by scholars between 1998 and 2010 who describe the monolithic spread of industrial agriculture and dependence on technology as the basis for development throughout the Global South. By the mid-1980s crisis management in revolutionary food policy had disenchanted several consultants of the Nicaraguan government. Foreign observers argued that food policy was no longer a priority, that the agrarian reform had been too fainthearted, and that the unquestioned faith in large-scale enterprise was misplaced. Nicaraguan consumers' dissatisfaction over food insecurity turned into an overall disillusionment with the revolutionary project in 1988.

CHAPTER SIX

FOOD POLICY IN TATTERS

THE RETURN OF HUNGER DURING ECONOMIC TRANSITION, 1988-1993

"The hurricane turned everything on its head, and the pre-hurricane crisis, serious as it was, is looked on with something approaching nostalgia given the current state of affairs."[1] This was how the magazine *Envío* characterized the situation in Nicaragua after Hurricane Joan hit the country in October 1988. By that time, however, revolutionary food policy had already deteriorated into crisis management: leading up to the hurricane Nicaraguans had already experienced drought, hyperinflation, and two adjustment programs, which all seriously hurt Nicaraguans' living standards. Although the Sandinistas were aware that Nicaraguans were once again suffering from hunger, they only acknowledged the severity of the situation in the foreign press.

On October 22, 1988, Hurricane Joan hit the Nicaraguan Caribbean and almost completely destroyed the city of Bluefields. Only 148 people died because of the timely evacuation, but the economic consequences were disastrous. CEPAL estimated the total damage at $839 million. The hurricane especially affected natural resources and food production. Cattle, seeds, and machinery were lost, and floods eroded more than ten thousand hectares of arable land. The small farmers at the Caribbean Coast were the most affected. Many people became dependent on food aid or moved to the capital despite the difficult economic situation there. The government rationed access to electricity and water: electricity was turned off for up to eight hours a day and water was unavailable twice a week. People had to wait on line for hours to buy basic food items. The effects of Hurricane Joan intensified the sense of crisis that already pervaded Nicaraguan society.[2]

By 1988 the revolutionary promise of food security for all Nicaraguans had clearly failed.[3] By December 1987 the caloric average intake had fallen below 1950s levels, and the government declared a national food emergency. Sandinista supporters, however, were challenging the government's explanation for the crisis and demanded changes in food policy. To many Nicaraguans the government had lost control over the economy, as the country experienced hyperinflation, lack of foreign exchange, natural disaster, and rapidly expanding scarcity. At the height of the crisis, in February and June 1988, the government implemented two new stabilization packages that were far more radical than their 1985 predecessor. At this point the Sandinistas abandoned important aims of their revolutionary food policy, in practice and in rhetoric. Both the ideal of self-sufficiency and the political militancy of food campaigns waned. These economic reforms marked the beginning of Nicaragua's move toward the market side of its mixed economy.

In 1988 and 1989 new market mechanisms—such as the liberalization of basic grains prices, the elimination of food subsidies, and the end of attempts to democratize the food supply—undermined the remnants of revolutionary food policy. The limited food distribution still in existence mostly favored state employees and ignored more vulnerable groups. These adjustment measures and the widespread deterioration of living standards for many Nicaraguans, including supporters of the revolution, provoked a crisis of confidence in the FSLN and threw the revolution's future into question. After years of sacrifice, people felt betrayed, especially when they compared their poor supply situation with the luxurious lifestyle of some of the Sandinista leaders. Even if no massive wave of protest took place, Nicaraguans expressed their discontent through public criticism, strikes, and low participation in mass organizations. This discontent and the reappearance of hunger in Nicaraguan society contributed to the Sandinista government's electoral loss in 1990. The defeat shocked and disillusioned remaining FSLN supporters, but it was perceived by others as emblematic of the broader social crisis. PAN also experienced a severe institutional crisis during the late 1980s from which it never recovered, and it was dissolved in 1994.

How did food policy erode during the transition period between 1988 and 1993? In my work I challenge that of other scholars who have argued that food security only waned with neoliberal economic policy after 1990.[4] The transition period represented both continuity with and change from earlier periods. The intensifying social crisis as well as the coexistence of market mechanisms and state intervention represented continuities. In national politics there were significant changes, such as the transformation of the FSLN into an opposition party and the reestablishment of political and economic relations with the United States. By 1993 Nicaraguan politics and economics had transformed significantly: most state enterprises had been privatized, hyperinflation had come to an end, and the new government had stabilized, although the social crisis continued.

The Nicaraguan transition between 1988 and 1993 also occurred within a context of global change, most notably the policy reforms associated with Perestroika, which transformed many Eastern bloc countries. For Nicaragua this meant the loss of economic support at a critical moment of the Sandinista revolution. The economic elements of Perestroika favored the intensification of adjustment policy. By 1987 market mechanisms had gained strength in the centralized Soviet economy, which accelerated trends from the "late socialism" period, such as the development of more autonomous consumers with improved access to goods.[5] Beyond the European borders, Eastern bloc advisers abroad insisted less on state-led economic solutions. In the Nicaraguan mixed economy, politicians reinforced adjustment policy and strengthened market mechanisms. Other socialist Global South countries experienced similar transformations, such as Cuba, Mozambique, and Vietnam. However, their economies, historically shaped by colonialism, depended on agro exports and were far more vulnerable than those in their Eastern European counterparts.

The crises in Nicaragua, Vietnam, and Mozambique were crises of states that were unable to fulfill their populations' basic needs.[6] Hence, the reintroduction of market mechanisms and the promotion of a commercial consumer occurred in a context where people were struggling with hunger. Accordingly, these transitions provoked controversial debates about the role of the consumer in society. In Nicaragua the vulnerable consumer suffering from scarcity and price shocks was joined by the resurgent commercial consumer who was eager to explore the new shopping options after 1990. However, commercial consumerism had survived in niche spaces, such as the dollar shops of the 1980s where revolutionary elites, foreigners, and businesspeople could buy imported goods using foreign currency. During the late 1980s the Sandinistas were already facilitating the availability of imported goods in supermarkets and strengthening market influences in shopping, such as commercial advertising.

THE NATIONAL FOOD EMERGENCY AND CRITICISM OF SANDINISTA POLICY

Production problems and natural disasters led to a lack of basic grains that prompted the government to declare a food emergency in December 1987. Unlike earlier years when consumers had complained about the lack of milk and meat, the late 1980s food shortages affected basic grains supply, and shortages persisted over longer time periods. As a result, criticism of Sandinista economic policy intensified, even from people who had formerly sympathized with the revolution, and this marked a significant change in public attitudes.

In December 1987 a drought significantly affected basic grains production. The government expected major losses, including 75 percent of bean production, 25 percent of maize production, and 10 percent of rice production. Rice production had already decreased beginning in 1984 because of the lack of laborers, problems with the machinery, and transport bottle-necks. Consequently, the per capita quota assigned with the rationing card decreased from four pounds per month in 1986 to three pounds in 1987. Since beans were also scarce from time to time, people had difficulties in preparing gallo pinto, one of the most important dishes in Nicaraguan cuisine. Hence, the crisis seriously disrupted daily food practices. The government combined the national food emergency with a call for more external aid.[7]

Skyrocketing food prices prompted debates over the origin of Nicaragua's economic problems. Since 1985 inflation had exploded, going from 334 percent to as high as 1,347 percent in 1987. Low purchasing power worsened the social situation and generated widespread discontent. Workers interviewed in the Centros de Abastecimiento para los Trabajadores (CATs), the worker supply centers, reported that their wages were only enough to buy food and nothing else. In June and July 1987 prices for basic foods increased considerably. For example, the cost of a loaf of bread went up from 180 to 300 Córdobas and the cost of a liter of milk went up from 250 to 600 Córdobas.[8] Controversy quickly arose over whether it was the war or political mistakes that should be blamed for the country's severe economic problems. For the first time *Barricada* demanded a change of attitude among Nicaraguans and an open discussion of the government's mistakes. Researchers and external advisers emphasized that the war served too frequently as an excuse.[9]

Critical voices within the Sandinista camp also questioned the focus on speculators as the main enemy and the government's explanations for the supply crisis. In 1987 *Barricada* published for the first time demands to change economic policy and reintroduce food subsidies instead of fighting speculation. This shift shows that the revolution had lost support from within, as the FSLN newspaper now occasionally turned against government measures. It also indicates that similar criticisms had become more widespread in Nicaraguan society. Initially, *Barricada* had followed the FSLN's instructions to promote the new economic policy implemented after 1985, but journalists struggled to defend policies they did not believe in. By the late 1980s there was a trend toward autonomy from the party; hence, the newspaper published voices that were more critical about the government's supply policy and campaign against speculation.[10]

For the February 25, 1987 issue, *Barricada* published Nicaraguan poet Gioconda Belli's questioning of the government's emphasis on speculation as a root cause for the crisis. Reality was more complex than was suggested by government propaganda about exploitative merchants, she argued, as workers had become increasingly involved in informal activities to make ends meet. In her opinion, two steps would be necessary: the reintroduction of subsidies and a tax reduction, which would have meant a reversal of the 1985 economic reforms.[11]

Only ten days later a *Barricada* journalist stated openly that the black market was necessary for daily food supply. Daniel Martínez explained his thoughts about the role of speculation in coping with the everyday realities of the nation's supply problems. He began by admitting his own involvement as a client on the black market. Like Martínez many people, including state employees, shopped on the black market. After years during which *Barricada* had fiercely criticized shopping at the black markets, Martínez's article marked a turning point, because he characterized the black market as the only alternative for consumers to acquire basic foods. Criticism had never before been expressed so openly in the FSLN newspaper, which was a sign of Sandinista supporters' eroding confidence.[12]

By contrast, high party functionaries expressed their concerns about the poor economic situation only at internal meetings, and they censored surveys on popular discontent. GDR advisor Theodor Bothe reported in May 1987 that FSLN functionaries characterized the situation as the most complicated since the revolution. They kept strictly secret about a survey of the party's propaganda department that revealed declining confidence in the FSLN's capacity to resolve the crisis.[13] This shows that the party leaders were aware of growing criticism but feared a public debate in which oppositional voices could question the government's legitimacy. These fears increased with structural adjustment programs in 1988.

THE INTENSIFICATION OF ADJUSTMENT IN 1988

In the late 1980s the combination of war, decreasing external support, and misguided economic strategies brought Nicaragua to the brink of catastrophe. The years of economic crisis were years of perpetual improvisation for both government and consumers. As foreign exchange funds were extremely scarce, the government conducted expenditure planning on a weekly basis.[14] Hyperinflation as well as advances in peace negations sparked a new debate over future strategies in 1987. By then, Central American presidents had developed a regional peace plan, which raised hopes for an end to the violence and encouraged politicians to implement economic changes.[15]

After substantial debate, the Sandinistas decided to implement stricter economic adjustment policies in 1988. The 1985 economic reforms had been an important shift but failed to alleviate the crisis. Since then, differences over economic policy prevailed among leading politicians. One group favored further adjustment programs, but opponents feared the social consequences. Before making the decision the FSLN leadership again consulted external advisers from both Cold War blocs.[16]

In the end they chose two additional adjustment programs that were put into place in 1988. The 1988 adjustment policies were far more radical than their 1985 predecessor in terms of budget cuts, layoffs, the elimination of subsidies, and price increases for public services. The first adjustment package in 1988 relied on the introduction of a new currency, the adaptation of different exchange rates, and budget cuts. Next, the government merged state institutions and dismissed eight thousand public employees, which seriously affected the capacities of various government entities, among them the Nicaraguan Food Program. As in 1985 the government also implemented a wage increase to alleviate the social effects, but the increase was quickly undermined by inflation. The concurrent adjustments of exchange rates, prices, and wages had generated further economic chaos and sparked a new inflationary cycle.[17]

Only four months later the government designed a second package. The June 1988 package liberalized wages in the private sector and established higher prices for public services. It eliminated rationing cards and the last food subsidy for milk, which made consumers more vulnerable to price shock. These additional measures, in particular, had a powerful effect on food consumption and purchasing power. Inflation from January 1988 to January 1989 reached 43,000 percent, one of the highest rates ever reached in Latin America.[18] The price fluctuations for food and consumer goods during this period were severe. Once workers and state employees received their wages, they had to make their purchases immediately to avoid their money losing value. Hyperinflation together with the unstable water and electricity supply prompted widespread uncertainty among Nicaraguans.

The 1988 adjustment policies marked a turning point. The adjustment was the beginning of a transition back to a capitalist market economy with credit, commercial advertising, and the state retiring from nationalized firms. Market influences gained in strength—in basic grains trade and food distribution, for example. The combination of economic crisis, hunger, failed dialogue with the public, and the public display of luxury by some revolutionary leaders provoked disillusionment. The year 1988 is an important moment for understanding the reasons that the revolution lost support.

Aware of the people's eroding confidence Sandinista politicians fervently insisted that their economic strategy did not resemble neoliberal policy, but their plans included elements of neoliberal adjustment. After the debt crisis in the 1980s, most adjustment programs in the rest of Latin America were introduced by a new generation of politicians who had turned from state intervention to market liberalism. In doing so these leaders were following the suggestions of neoliberal economists who advocated deregulation and austerity. The Sandinistas argued that their adjustment had a different orientation, but in fact it incorporated many classical adjustment measures.

At the same time, the official discourse on food and economics became more contradictory. *Barricada* journalists filled its pages with appeals for cost effectiveness and productivity. In September 1988, for example, *Barricada* declared "efficiency, profitability, productivity and savings" as the primary economic goals. Only one day later, *Barricada* announced that "egalitarianism" had to be sacrificed to ensure the survival of the revolutionary project.[19] The Sandinistas had moved away from their initial aim of equal access to food and social services for all Nicaraguans. They liberalized basic grains trade, lifted price control, eliminated food subsidies, and maintained separate shopping worlds in the dollar shops. Similar to the unsuccessful education campaigns that had accompanied the 1985 adjustment, the Sandinistas ultimately failed to reach their audiences in 1988 as well. Even *Barricada* had to admit that information on economic problems remained far too abstract for the Nicaraguan consumers: "Our functionaries don't speak the people's language."[20] Although adjustment logic had entered political discourse and practice, for the Sandinista leaders it was important to defend the revolutionary project as being different from conventional economic policy. This message targeted both internal supporters of the revolution and foreign donors, whose economic support was bitterly needed. Hence, the official discourse remained contradictory as it attempted to defend adjustment policies in a revolutionary setting.

The 1988 adjustments also prevented the Sandinistas from continuing their ambitious reforms of the early 1980s, as in the case of the state basic grain agency ENABAS. After the revolution ENABAS had played an important role in democratizing access to food supply in Nicaragua and building up a new network for basic grains procurement. With shrinking state finances and the decision to liberalize the Nicaraguan economy in the late 1980s, however, ENABAS lost its capacity to benefit marginal groups. The transformation started in 1987, when the Sandinista government further liberalized the corn and beans trades. Simultaneously, the government adapted ENABAS to the new economic policy. The state enterprise, for example, was no longer limited to official prices and competed with private basic grains traders to buy peasants' harvests. ENABAS encountered serious difficulties when the state's financial crisis meant that it lacked the ability to pay higher prices. The agency's basic grain procurement levels eventually decreased and financial problems limited its capacity to pay producers immediately. Thus, procurement levels for corn, rice, and sorghum declined significantly. Whereas in the mid-1980s ENABAS procured, for example, more than 20 percent of corn harvests, in 1988–1989 it procured only 13.2 percent.[21] The state channels had even less access to basic grains than before, which made Nicaraguans lose even more confidence in the government and to consider other shopping options.

THE SOCIAL CONSEQUENCES OF ADJUSTMENT AND HYPERINFLATION

The adjustment programs accelerated the social crisis in Nicaragua. By 1988 it was becoming clear that the Sandinistas could not guarantee stable access to basic foods. After years of scarcity people now suffered from hunger. Social crisis brought back widespread malnutrition, the spread of illnesses, higher levels of infant mortality, and illiteracy. Wage liberalization increased the social gaps within Nicaraguan society. In February 1988 the basic food basket's cost of 2,320.6 Córdobas nearly equaled the average wage levels, estimated at 2,400 Córdobas. The lowest salary covered only one-fifth of the cost of the basic food basket.[22] Newspaper headlines such as "Crazy Prices at Managuan Markets," "Milk Prices and Quality: Where Is the Logic?" and "How Bitter Will the Cost of Sugar Grow?" illustrate that the price of food was one of the key problems for Nicaraguan consumers during the late 1980s.[23] People suffered from price shocks and experienced the situation as getting out of control.

Things got worse by August 1988, with urban wages only covering between 20 and 30 percent of basic food needs. The anthropologist Roger Lancaster observed during his fieldwork in Managua that there was a short rise in purchasing power after the reform, then it declined again and reached preform levels in May 1988, which made people feel that adjustment had been useless.[24] Despite the two adjustment packages, workers in Managuan CATs reported that it had become difficult to live on a normal wage. A survey among workers in one hundred firms revealed in August 1988 that industrial workers' wages covered only 19 percent of the basic basket, the wages of state administration employees 21 percent, and the wages of mid-rank professionals 28 percent.[25] Hence, the food crisis was increasingly affecting the middle class. Widespread disillusionment with economic policy by the late 1980s would play a central role in the Sandinista government's electoral defeat in 1990.

After several years of difficult living conditions, the 1988 adjustments introduced new economic threats such as job insecurity. Reactions included feelings of insecurity, disillusionment, indignation, and resistance. The journal *Envío* argued that the main difference between the two packages was popular support. As late as February 1988 large sectors of the population still maintained hope for improvement. When people realized that their living standards had deteriorated further, a sense of betrayal spread throughout Nicaraguan society. The June package followed a top-down approach as the government involved neither mass organizations nor its own institutions in the decision-making process; some measures even surprised government functionaries. By June the unions had organized several marches to protest the deterioration of workers' living standards. Anger also exploded. There was a series of wildcat strikes that introduced a new period of labor conflicts in Nicaragua. These developments marked a dramatic shift from workers' longtime support for the Sandinistas.[26]

Social scientists have debated the extent to which the mood of Nicaraguans worsened during the crisis. For example, sociologists from the Universidad Centroamericana (UCA), the Central American University, contended that people might have become more critical between 1985 and 1987 but they continued to support the Sandinistas. Other social scientists published more negative evaluations based on their research in 1989 when the crisis had further deepened.[27] At that time, direct criticism of the Sandinistas was more common in urban areas; in rural zones, the majority continued to blame external aggression for economic problems. By contrast, most Managuan interviewees held the government responsible for the crisis, and only 25 percent believed US aggression to be the main reason for the crisis. These findings indicate a clear difference between rural communities and Managua; however, the survey had a limited scope and the situation in rural zones could vary considerably between different regions. The research institute ITZANI interviewed more than one thousand people in five Managuan districts during spring 1989. Two-thirds perceived their personal economic situation as worse than a year before. This survey based on a larger sample of interviews demonstrates that a majority of urban Nicaraguans experienced a decline in their living standards.[28]

Throughout the transition from 1988 to 1993, hunger affected many Nicaraguans while the state's capacity to provide assistance declined. Numerous surveys from Nicaraguan institutions and international organizations documented the nutritional consequences of the economic crisis during the transition years. Between 1976 and 1986, the average per capita caloric intake in Nicaragua had ranged between 2,000 and nearly 2,400 kcal. By 1986 it had started to fall: first to 1,932 kcal in 1987, then to 1,610 kcal in 1988, and finally to 1,591 kcal in 1989, which meant a 22.5 percent decline.[29] These averages were lower than those documented by the nutritional surveys between the 1950s and the 1970s. Hence, the living standard had fallen below the levels of the Somoza dictatorship period although regional variations probably existed. As the following chart demonstrates (see figure 6.1), the decline was particularly serious in terms of per capita maize, flour, sugar, beef, and milk consumption. Whenever several important foods considered as essential for good nutrition became scarce simultaneously, people became more desperate. In 1989 poor Managuan

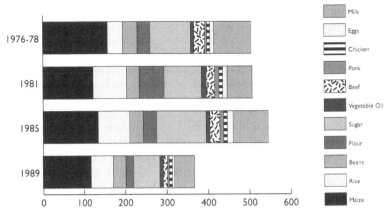

FIGURE 6.1. Per capita consumption of selected foods, 1976–1989 (in pounds). For milk and vegetable oil, the measurement is liters, for eggs dozens. PAN provided the data for the statistics. Source: Utting, *Economic Adjustment*, 45.

families spent 80 percent of their income on food, and the average caloric intake of the poorest sectors fell below the 1,200 kcal line.[30] Consequently, hunger was back on the political agenda.

Although the nutritional situation of many Nicaraguans had become dire by the late 1980s, the term "hunger" remained completely absent from public debates. I argue that this was due to political reasons: for the Sandinistas, and even more so during the electoral campaign, it was not opportune to admit that people were suffering from hunger. Only in the foreign press did Sandinista politicians acknowledge the existence of hunger. For example, the former mayor of Managua Moisés Hassan commented to a *Washington Post* journalist in October 1988 that for the first time since the revolution people were suffering from hunger.[31] This statement shows that the political leaders were aware that the nutritional situation had deteriorated by the late 1980s. Although Nicaraguans experienced this in their everyday life, the Sandinistas did not respond to people's concerns by admitting the problem. Instead, they continued to promote cheap, local foods as opposed to imported goods. By contrast to the early 1980s, however, Sandinista political propaganda no longer equated the consumption of local food to the success of the revolution. Instead, they promoted these food items for being cheap and healthy.

During the transition between 1988 and 1993 emphasis on local foods lost its political militancy. By 1988 the Sandinistas had abandoned the discourse on maize as a revolutionary grain. With rising rates of malnutrition, state institutions, nutritionists, and civil organizations intensified their promotion of cheap, local alternatives to meat, milk, and wheat. Government programs and development projects presented potatoes, fish, and soy products as the best alternatives for daily consumption. After Nicaragua had received donations of potatoes, the Health Ministry recommended potatoes for the preparation of traditional dishes and fast food, such as nacatamales and pommes frites. One woman contributed a potato pizza recipe to the national campaign to promote potato consumption. She instructed cooks to puree the potatoes and then add grated cheese and tomato sauce with oregano with the option of salami or chicken. At the end of the recipe she praised the virtue of creative cooking in times of food scarcity. According to *Barricada*, consumers accepted the vegetable as a cheap alternative to bread and tortillas.[32]

There is only scarce evidence, however, to know whether these recipes and campaign materials successfully spread new consumption habits. For example, potatoes were not included in many consumption surveys published in the 1980s. In 1991 a consumption survey revealed that only 13.3 of the interviewees habitually consumed potatoes.[33]

The education campaigns were most successful when accompanied by cooking activities at the local level, as the soy promotion campaign demonstrates. Efforts to promote soy as a cheaper alternative to meat intensified during the transition years, and the most effective were local grassroots initiatives sponsored by the Nicaraguan Food Program, UNICEF, and the Sandinista women's organization AMNLAE.[34] In Estelí local soy consumption was widespread, as UNICEF had supported a community health project in the region since 1986. Each Saturday AMNLAE members first produced soy flour and milk and then prepared different recipes based on those soy products, integrating them as meat substitutes into traditional Nicaraguan dishes. Although soymilk gained higher acceptance than soy meat among locals, soy meatballs convinced some skeptical consumers. A 1991 survey revealed that 23 percent of Nicaraguan households already had become familiar with the new staple, which had been introduced to Nicaraguan consumers only a decade earlier.[35] The NGO Soynica continued soy promotion into the early 1990s and founded sixty communal kitchens in Nicaragua where people met to prepare soy dishes.

Beginning in the late 1980s the gap widened between development plans and the institutional realities of food policy. This was also a result of adjustment policy that had established budget cuts in many state initiatives. Official reports of the Nicaraguan Food Program recommended ambitious plans for nutrition education to be funded with support from PAHO and UNICEF.[36]

A German development cooperation agency supported this effort by sending the cartoonist Harald Juch to Nicaragua in early 1987 to support PAN's campaigns as a media specialist. However, feelings of disillusionment and frustration characterized his experience as the Nicaraguan Food

Program entered into a severe institutional crisis. After the program struggled with a corruption scandal, employees divided into different factions.
Trained workers for food production were lacking. Out of 196 employees,
there were only 10 specialists for plant cultivation. Workplace morale was
low. Most employees showed up for only three hours a day; because of low
wages, they spent the rest of the day on private matters, survival activities,
or other jobs. Owing to structural adjustment in 1988, the government
also reduced personnel from 196 to 65, which further limited PAN's op-
erational capacities.[37] In Juch's opinion PAN had become a façade to win
over international donors: "The only one at PAN who understands me and
my futile mission is my trainee. . . . In fact, he is responsible for the graph-
ical adornment of daily life at the office, Sandinista ceremonial acts and
campaigns at PAN, and for everything related to the design of presentation
boards, statistics, and organizational charts, which are meant to convince
numerous foreign delegations of how much PAN has already achieved, so
that they are willing to flip open their checkbook and make financial or
material donations."[38] As Juch perceived no serious interest in his work at
PAN, he left the country, frustrated, in 1989. His reports fit with Joseph
Collins's observations in the mid-1980s. Collins had also claimed that food
policy was no longer a political priority and that PAN suffered from lack of
personnel and from ineffective bureaucratic structures.

HUNGER, EMERGENCY ACTIONS, AND SURVIVAL STRATEGIES

During the transition, hunger occurred in several regions throughout
Nicaragua, particularly in the North as well as in Managua and on the
Caribbean Coast. Emergency actions supplanted long-term strategic programs although these still existed on paper, and Sandinista food policy
eroded into crisis management. Government attempts at emergency help
focused on state employees whom the Sandinistas needed to implement
their policies and whom they considered their supporters. From July 1988
the government distributed rice, sugar, and beans to state employees;
the whole package became known as AFA (for *arroz, frijoles, azúcar*, the
Spanish words for rice, beans, and sugar). State employees received ten
pounds of rice, ten pounds of beans, and five pounds of sugar per month.
The rations provided an average of 483 kcal per day or around 10 percent
of caloric intake for a family of six people. Therefore, AFA improved basic
food supply considerably, especially when several household members had
access to the package.[39] Because of supply problems, however, packages
sometimes only included rice. Most likely, the Sandinistas perceived the
AFA also as an effort to stabilize government institutions whose working capacities had been seriously eroded as employees used their working
hours for survival activities. During the transition years AFA's contri-

bution to workers' nutrition was important. Other sectors received no support, however.[40]

In the late 1980s people were desperately trying to make ends meet and developed a wide range of survival strategies. Some families benefited from state food distributions; others survived on remittances from family members abroad. In Managuan working-class neighborhoods, kinship and friendship networks were crucial. People exchanged food and other scarce goods against favors such as household repairs or child care.[41] Anthropologists observed the existence of "silent solidarity networks" in the Managuan settlement called Pablo Ubeda. For example, tortilla vendors sold at lower prices within their own neighborhood. Other people paid neighbors for small services such as washing whenever they could afford to do so. It became common for cows, pigs, or chickens to wander through Managuan streets as more people kept animals for their personal supply. The cities' garbage dumps filled with people digging for food.[42] Many Nicaraguans were forced to make desperate efforts to locate food wherever possible.

Food scarcity during transition increased the pressures on women as they faced a higher workload related to survival activities. At the same time, emotional pressure intensified when women had to explain the lack of food to other family members. The crisis powerfully affected unemployed urban women in particular. Urban women often engaged in informal survival activities, reduced consumption, and accepted help from their families. About 50 percent of women interviewed for a poverty research project in 1991–1992 received help from family members not belonging to their household.[43] Long-term dependence on extended family, however, could also embitter family relations. After losing their jobs many urban women looked for work in domestic service or street commerce or decided to set up small household businesses.

In terms of strategies many women also reduced the number of family meals per day or eliminated milk and meat from their household's diet. In general, they prioritized children's nutrition over their own needs; one woman acknowledged, "I am the last to eat." The women were particularly concerned about acquiring milk for their small children and to avoid family members' complaints about a monotonous diet.[44] In general, Nicaraguans combined several survival strategies during the transition period. External support from emigrated family members or food aid distributions were important, but many people also cultivated their own food or took up additional wage labor.

SOCIAL GAPS IN SHOPPING AND SUPPLY

The financial crisis and economic liberalization ultimately reversed the democratization of the food distribution network that had been accomplished

in the revolution's earlier years. After 1979 the Sandinistas had improved
the supply network in poor neighborhoods and opened supermarkets for
a broader clientele. Although this new network struggled with difficulties
throughout the first half of the 1980s, it established the ideal of equal access to food for all social groups. But this policy suffered from internal
contradictions once the Sandinistas established exclusive dollar shops in
the early 1980s. By 1988 the Sandinistas abandoned the political ideal of
equal access. For example, the state network dried up as ENABAS cut credit for popular stores. Only those stores with their own financial resources
survived. Supermarkets turned again to a middle-class clientele by offering
imported goods and more expensive foods. In general, low-income consumers turned from popular stores and supermarkets to traditional forms
of shopping at markets or in pulperías as these sold very small quantities
of food and reintroduced credit.[45] Finally, the state distribution and grain
procurement networks gave up the aim of equal service to all Nicaraguans
during transition.

In the late 1980s social crisis entered the supermarkets in spite of the
Sandinistas' efforts to improve workers' access to basic supplies. At the beginning of 1987 the Sandinistas introduced additional CATs to provide
workers with more flexible shopping options, which consumers approved.
Nevertheless, all *Barricada* interviewees insisted on the need to improve
the centers' inventories, otherwise the increased number would make no
difference.[46] Apart from the availability of products, people worried about
the high prices. One worker even characterized the rising prices as "brutal." As a result, shoplifting in Managua increased. For example, the Plaza
España supermarket reported losses of about twenty thousand Córdobas
in mid-1988. Shoplifting by women who hid their loot in their underwear
received special attention. After the second adjustment package, the social
crisis became even more visible. In July 1988 sales at supermarkets declined
by 50 percent in one week.[47] Despite growing social inequalities in food
supply, the Sandinistas stocked supermarkets with more expensive imported products.

The aim of self-sufficiency—namely, reliance on locally produced
goods—had lost its importance by the late 1980s. Supermarkets were eager
to reestablish commercial relations to imported products such as instant coffee, vegetable oil, and textiles. The chain called Supermercados del Pubelo
hoped to attract customers by offering quality brand products, mainly
Nestlé, Gerber, and Lipton Tea. The aim was to achieve an inventory of
80 percent imported products and 20 percent national products.[48] Consequently, in October 1988, one supermarket published advertisements with
the slogan: "It Has It All . . . It's Super!"[49] Although supermarket shelves

filled with products again, the long lines disappeared, as people were unable to afford the new imported items.

While Nicaraguans survived on small food rations, Sandinista leaders continued to display exclusive goods. During the adjustment period criticism of political leaders' lifestyle proliferated. *New York Times* correspondent Stephen Kinzer observed that the Nicaraguan people were incensed by political leaders who exhibited their Mercedes Benz cars in public while large sectors of the population could not satisfy their most basic needs.[50] In the course of the 1980s political leaders had abandoned the early ethic of a modest lifestyle, as Sergio Ramírez recalled:

> Power was the enemy of that code, and it created offensive contrasts in an immensely poor country, where even the middle class was hit by the rigors of the war. . . . The leadership's houses had to be spacious because that was also where you worked and where you received official visitors. They were surrounded by walls for security reasons, and more than a few had pools, saunas, billiard rooms, gyms, and tennis courts, because the leadership could not frequent public places like other people. The size of the military escort, which required facilities and vehicles, was part of the prestige.[51]

Political leaders' rhetoric of individual sacrifice and revolutionary austerity contradicted their reliance on prestige items, and this undermined their credibility.

Public criticism of the exclusive dollar shops exploded at the height of the economic crisis in 1987. For the more affluent clientele and foreigners, the Nicaraguan government had created a special shopping space, the *diplotiendas* or dollar shops, probably designed according to the Cuban model.[52] The diplotiendas sold imported goods for foreign currency. In Nicaragua the minister of tourism, Herty Lewites, initiated the project after conducting a study on the market for luxury goods in the early 1980s. The shops were one measure to generate foreign exchange. During the economic crisis *Barricada* writers raised strong criticisms of diplotiendas: "Is it proper that in Sandinista Nicaragua there's a 'diplotienda' or international store in which products are sold in dollars? By allowing Nicaraguans with access to dollars to buy there, aren't we stimulating more or less parasitic sectors of society?"[53]

It did not make sense to many Nicaraguans that the government maintained a shop for luxury consumption in the face of widespread economic problems and food scarcity. The longer the social crisis unfolded, the more people disapproved of the lifestyle of Sandinista leaders. One woman, interviewed by the anthropologist Inger Lundgren for her research on Sandinista professionals in the early 1990s, argued: "They [the Sandinistas] talked about how one had to accept poverty and scarcity. I am sure no comandante went to a distribution center [expendio] to get half a bar of washing soap a week. This became more obvious when they started the Diplotienda. Who were the most frequent customers there? They were! Why was it only the people who had to put up with hunger and shortages? The same inequality as always! . . . The leaders never deprived themselves of anything. We, the people, had to go through very difficult times."[54] In the late 1980s, only a small segment of militants still justified the leaders' luxury consumption, arguing that it was compensation for the hardships leaders had experienced during guerilla fighting and as prisoners.[55]

In February 1988, shortly after the first adjustment program, Daniel Ortega defended the dollar shops and the practice of allowing only distinguished party members the privilege to shop there. He accused Nicaraguans of buying products from speculators at higher prices than the official prices set by the government. As basic products at official prices had been scarce for years, his criticism illustrates the distance between leading Sandinistas and the concerns of the general public. As in Cuba the existence of stores with limited access divided urban society into first- and second-class consumers.[56] These increasing social gaps eroded confidence in the Sandinista revolution among Nicaraguans by the late 1980s. Hurricane Joan worsened the supply situation, which led to further disillusionment.

FROM HURRICANE JOAN TO THE 1990S ELECTIONS

Soon after the second adjustment package, Hurricane Joan hit the country in October 1988. The hyperinflation that followed was a major blow to the government's revolutionary projects. With inflation levels surpassing 40,000 percent, the country remains an exceptional case in Latin American history. Simultaneously, the government had to organize care for disaster victims and reconstruction. The price of the basic food basket soared from 21,714 Córdobas in August to around 60,000 Córdobas by November 1988. From November 1988 to January 1989 consumer prices doubled every month. Finally, the government drastically reduced government expenditures by 44 percent with a third austerity package in 1989.[57] Although this package did put an end to hyperinflation, it generated even more social tensions. GDR advisers reported that adjustment policies strongly affected the social basis of the revolution: for workers and urban poor, basic foods were no longer accessible. These groups and also the middle class partially held the FSLN responsible for the problems.[58]

The deep economic crisis, disillusionment with the revolutionary project, and a strong desire for an end of the war meant that the FSLN lost the 1990 elections. Shortly after the third adjustment package, during Central American peace negotiations the Sandinistas promised to advance the next elections from November to February 1990. In June 1989 the Nicaraguan opposition organized and gathered fourteen parties to form the Unión Nacional Opositora (UNO), the National Opposition Party coalition for the 1990s election. Owing to her wide popular support, UNO named Violeta Chamorro—the widow of former *La Prensa* editor Pedro Joaquín Chamorro who had been assassinated in 1978—as their presidential candidate.

Surprisingly to many observers, the 1990 elections ended with the triumph of UNO, with 54.7 percent of the votes whereas the FSLN mobilized only 40.8 percent of the voters. Two weeks prior to the elections Chamorro had already gained higher competence assessment ratings in important areas. Voters perceived her to be the most capable to end the war, address the economic crisis, and obtain foreign aid. Frustration with the unreliable food supply and high food prices were important reasons for the Sandinista government's defeat as well as the widespread disillusionment prompted by some Sandinista leaders' luxurious lifestyles.[59] Although in shock, the FSLN agreed immediately to hand over power to the winning party. Both Daniel Ortega and Violeta Chamorro appealed for the demobilization of the Contras. Although the 1990 electoral defeat was undoubtedly a turning point in Nicaraguan political culture, it did not substantially change the daily food insecurity and the hunger experienced by many Nicaraguans throughout this period.

CONTINUITY AND CHANGE DURING THE TRANSITION

The transition years from 1988 to 1993 represented elements of continuity and change. Despite the Chamorro government being far more radical in promoting trade liberalization and privatizations, I argue that many developments in the early 1990s had precursors in the late 1980s. Instead of the sudden break from revolution to neoliberal policies that many historical accounts assume, market mechanisms and state interventions coincided until 1993. High levels of inflation and unemployment continued during the early 1990s along with state intervention in food price setting. The new government, however, could count on large sums of foreign aid from the United States and international financial organizations, and it utilized these resources mainly for debt payment, economic policy, and imports while social policy received less attention.

In terms of economic policy, the UNO government opted for a neoliberal agenda and reestablished relations with international financial institutions. According to this agenda, the government would significantly limit its role in the economy. Instead of designing social policy to help the victims of crisis, government officials viewed Nicaraguans as responsible for their own economic situation, their health, and their daily nutritional intake. Thus, all of the common features of neoliberal adjustment policy can be found in Nicaragua in the early 1990s: (1) currency devaluation, (2) trade liberalization, (3) austerity measures, and (4) privatization. These measures had profound effects on Nicaraguans' food situation. After devaluation, people could acquire fewer goods with their salaries. In particular, the prices for imported foods increased significantly. Austerity programs and privatizations led to growing unemployment in Nicaragua. Thousands of people struggled for survival. The move away from state nutritional programs also affected people suffering from malnutrition. By the late 1980s the work of health organizations and other social services had already eroded. The further dismantling of these institutions in the 1990s represented both continuity with the past and the new government's shift from assistance to self-responsibility.

As in the late 1980s, currency devaluations also provoked resistance from workers and the urban poor. Indeed, these groups built on their protest experiences from the late 1980s to resist the continued deterioration in their living standards in the early 1990s. Initially, the UNO government established the optimistic goal of eliminating inflation within the first one hundred days. It introduced a new currency connected to the US dollar: the gold Córdoba. The gradual changeover to the new currency further harmed workers' already diminished living standards. A wave of protests and strikes finally accomplished some policy changes. As state deficit spending increased and protests continued, in October 1990 the president dismissed the Central Bank president responsible for the new economic policy.[60] This short-lived plan shows that the government had underestimated the difficulties in bringing inflation under control. The next plan to bring down inflation also relied on neoliberal solutions but offered some measures to help the victims of the crisis, such as a temporary freeze of water and electricity prices. Backed by the renewed financial support of the IMF, the plan reduced inflation significantly between March and June 1991. After a 400 percent devaluation of the Córdoba, inflation decreased from 865.6 percent in 1991 to 3.5 percent in 1992.[61] Despite its neoliberal agenda, the government still intervened occasionally against price shocks so as to ameliorate their effects and to avoid further protests. ENABAS intervened at least four times in price assignments by June 1993, which shows that the UNO government still relied occasionally on state interventions. Nonetheless, the period of state intervention in food prices had ended by June 1993.[62] While Nicaraguans experienced economic insecurity amid extreme price changes, several members of the Sandinista leadership ascended as a new economic elite.

The FSLN reorganized as opposition party in the early 1990s. It maintained its political influence but lost supporters when leading members took over former state properties. While ordinary Nicaraguans were struggling for survival, some of the Sandinista leaders enriched themselves shortly before the transfer of power. Adapting to their new role as the opposition party, FSLN leaders moved from radical opposition to cooperation between 1990 and 1991. Hence, the party maintained considerable political influence. However, its moral authority suffered from party leaders' self-enrichment, which was a continuation of FSLN leaders' abandonment of revolutionary ethics since the late 1980s. Shortly before Chamorro took power, the FSLN's credibility fell apart when the government validated all property transfers from the 1980s including the expropriations of the Somoza clan and land distributions after agrarian reform.[63] Like children who dive for the sweets falling out of a piñata, leading party members started a run on valuable estates, businesses, and luxury homes. This property transfer laid the groundwork for the rise of a new economic elite and damaged the FSLN's image considerably.[64]

After the 1990 elections the FSLN also entered a process of internal reorganization and reflection while at the same time confronting the new government by supporting strikes and roadblocks.[65] After a year of confrontations Daniel Ortega veered to a more pragmatic approach and agreed to enter negotiations on social and economic policy, a process that became known as Concertación. During the talks one main conflict was the question of privatization, which the unions initially rejected but then agreed to during the second round of negotiations from May to August 1991. The UNO government converted state firms into the National Corporation of State Enterprise and had sold 80 percent of the 351 firms by the end of 1993. As of 1991 Chamorro mainly worked with moderate UNO members and Sandinistas to implement reforms as she had entered into open conflict with liberal politicians from the Partido Liberal Independiente.[66] The fact that former Sandinista leaders still influenced the political course reinforces my interpretation of the 1990s transition as a period of continuity rather than a sharp break. The nutritional surveys during transition also indicate a continuing social crisis.

HUNGER AND MALNUTRITION IN THE EARLY 1990S

Hunger persisted, especially among poor urban people and in rural zones. Contrary to the late 1980s, however, it received broad coverage in the Nicaraguan press during the early 1990s. The first nutritional surveys after the elections showed a slight recovery of caloric intake compared to the late 1980s as the surveys were conducted in areas less affected by malnutrition. Whether state institutions chose those regions for practical or political reasons is unclear. The average caloric intake increased from around 1,600 kcal to 1,808 kcal. However, the survey in region III also demonstrates that poor people still suffered from hunger. People living in extreme poverty, around 19 percent of the Nicaraguan population in the early 1990s, were only consuming an average of 977 kcal per day.[67] Even if it is a valuable source for the nutritional situation in the early 1990s, the survey only reflected the situation in Managua and Central Nicaragua. In the surveyed rural communities situated around the capital, the supply situation was probably better than in the rest of the country. A FAO/WHO report from 1992 states that the highest malnutrition levels existed in rural zones around Matagalpa and Jinotega while Managua had the lowest levels.[68] These quantitative evaluations, however, fail to capture people's limited diets in the early 1990s. Whereas nutrition experts and politicians referred to the statistical averages to diagnose hunger, Nicaraguans measured their nutritional situation in other terms. These included the ability to have three meals a day or the availability of a plate of rice and beans.

Press reports give more detailed insight into the deterioration of daily meals during transition. In the second half of 1990, *Barricada* reported regularly on hunger in different regions of the country, among them Bello Amanecer district in Managua, the Masaya region, and the Caribbean. In August 1990 the first notice appeared on *Barricada*'s title page drawing attention to hunger and malnutrition in Madriz department. After a drought had destroyed the local harvest, the newspaper reported, approximately 5,000 children were suffering from malnutrition. In July and August 1990 approximately 350 children died from malnutrition, mainly the children of single mothers, the most vulnerable group during periods of economic crisis.[69] In the countryside people stopped lighting their stoves as food was unaffordable. In times of crisis people viewed even basic foods such as gallo pinto as a luxury. People omitted the simplest ingredients, including the use of vegetable oil to fry tortillas or the addition of salt to give some flavor. Coffee, a traditional means of relieving feelings of hunger, had become too expensive. In Matagalpa and Jinotepe, people organized demonstrations to demand aid and to protest against the high prices for agricultural supplies. The *Barricada* articles formed part of the FSLN's broader attack on the new government. The newspaper frequently quoted disappointed people who had voted for the Chamorro government.[70]

With political confrontation decreasing between FSLN and the UNO government, *La Prensa* also covered the deteriorating nutritional situation. While *Barricada* initially used the nutrition crisis to attack the UNO government, *La Prensa* did not devote much attention to the topic but, rather, highlighted the new freedom for Nicaraguan consumers. In a 1993 series, however, the newspaper focused on Chinandega department where the situation of communities surrounding the banana plantations had become desperate. In all, 80 percent of the local population was unemployed and surviving only on cooked bananas or hunted reptiles such as iguanas. Even these desperate food choices had their limits. Owners of the banana plantations introduced armed vigilance and established punishments such as unpaid work in the form of cutting firewood for men or peeling fruits for women. Iguanas were about to disappear by June 1993.[71] In the early 1990s the economic and political circumstances severely limited people's food choices, making it impossible to defend in-between spaces. The UNO government improved conditions for well-funded consumers but neglected ordinary Nicaraguans' needs.

FOOD POLICY IN TATTERS

Unlike the Sandinistas in the first half of the 1980s, the new government lacked any coherent strategy and political will for addressing malnutrition. As UNO had not seriously expected to win the elections, its policy planning was insufficient.[72] Consequently, the government only managed to continue a few food distribution projects from the 1980s. For example, the government carried on the AFA program until 1991 but reduced the number of beneficiaries.[73] Although the measure contradicted its neoliberal approach, the UNO government maintained the program, probably for the same reasons as the Sandinistas had introduced it, to maintain the working capacity of state institutions. In 1992 the government founded the National Commission for Nutrition, whose tasks, however, remained rather vague in official government documents.

In early 1993 a World Bank Report evaluated the government's nutrition policy and declared it a disaster. Donors such as the WFP became discouraged because of the low interest among government officials. FAO reports supported this critique. The organization criticized that its projects' impact was limited as the Nicaraguan government had not taken the necessary measures. In its final report on the Nicaraguan Food Program, the FAO diagnosed its failure. After severe budget cuts, the number of employees decreased from twenty-two (1989) to seven (1994). Yet food insecurity in Nicaragua remained high with more than 60 percent of the population being unable to afford the basic food basket.[74]

One main reason for this was stagnating grain production. Food production was still affected by the long-term consequences of war, natural disaster, and land conflicts in the early 1990s. Abandoned or damaged land needed care to prepare it for cultivation again. Hence, the harvests of several basic gains stagnated or declined at the beginning of the decade. Corn production suffered a decline in 1991 but recovered afterward, and bean

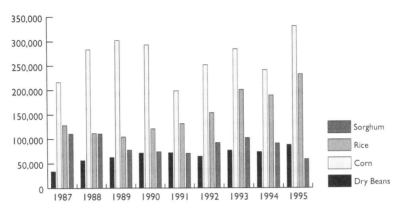

FIGURE 6.2. Basic grains production during transition, 1987–1995 (in tons). Source: FAO-STAT.

production stagnated and recovered around 1995. Only rice production increased significantly. The recovery of food production occurred in the second half of the 1990s, but the increase was insufficient to keep up with population growth.[75]

Land conflicts and reduced state support for peasants provoked the stagnation in basic grains production in the early 1990s. During the transition FSLN and UNO had negotiated a protocol for the transfer of landholdings to the beneficiaries of the agrarian reform. However, this was met with fierce resistance by former landowners and UNO supporters. By interfering through decrees in the transitional legislation the UNO government created a chaotic situation. Many properties were registered to two owners, which has left a legacy of land conflicts that continues today. In addition, the end of state banking limited the ability of peasants with small landholdings to acquire credit. Many peasants became indebted, as subsidies for pesticides and fertilizers had been eliminated.[76]

These uncertainties of transition affected basic grains production, so Nicaragua continued to depend on imports or donations from abroad. During the first years following the 1990 elections, the need for food aid was still overwhelming as the social crisis deepened. Soon after the UNO government came into office, it signed an agreement with the United States that allocated $12.5 million for food aid as part of the "Food for Progress" program. In 1990 every Nicaraguan received a daily average of 355 kcal of food aid, which was 23 percent of the average daily caloric intake.[77] Total food aid reached its peak with more than 200,000 tons in 1990. From then on, the amount decreased by half until 1993. In 1991 the United States was by far the largest donor with more than 123,000 tons of foods and maintained its dominant position in the following years.[78]

Although these donations alleviated the situation for vulnerable groups, most Nicaraguans still struggled to make ends meet. Nutritional surveys demonstrated how high prices limited peoples' food choices. This was one important factor in what anthropologist Sidney Mintz has called the "outer sphere" of consumption. This sphere of economic, political, or social circumstances limited people's food choices.[79] In Nicaragua, high food prices, an erosion of food policy, and stagnating production restricted poor people to a very limited diet in the late 1980s and early 1990s.

This was still visible in a 1991 survey conducted by the Nicaraguan Food Program that comprised twelve hundred households in Managua department. On average people spent 68 percent of their income on food. Hence, it is fair to assume that the poorest sectors of Nicaraguan society spent almost their entire income on daily supplies. The survey documented that high prices limited the consumption of meat, dairy products, and vegetables. For instance, only 4.7 percent of all households consumed meat on a daily basis. In the poorest three income groups, it was less than 1 percent of all households. Urban people consumed a larger variety of food than rural inhabitants. In the cities, 50–70 percent of all households consumed bread, chicken, dried cheese, and beef on a daily basis. In rural areas the variety was far more limited and consisted of tortillas, eggs, and coffee.[80] Hence, the urban-rural gap in food consumption existing in the 1980s persisted until the early 1990s.

To vary the limited diets nutrition experts started education campaigns. Throughout the late 1980s and early 1990s Nicaraguan and international organizations promoted herbs, leafy greens, and local vegetables as resources for cheap and healthy diets. The education materials show that the campaigns lost the political militancy that had been prevalent in the early 1980s. At the same time, they indicate that government agencies and aid workers were more receptive to diverse food cultures. For example, one guide edited by INCAP and the Nicaraguan Ministry of Health introduced the following vision for good nutrition: "So that adults can live healthfully and in condition to work, and so that children grow up normally, they must all nourish themselves in a complete, varied and balanced way. This should always be the bottom line of community resources. That is, we must plant more fruits and vegetables to make beneficial foods more available. . . . To have a good diet is to consume meals that are sufficient, varied, balanced and sanitary. It does not necessarily imply rare or expensive foods with foreign names, or those prepared with complex recipes."[81] NGOs and international organizations promoted healthy nutrition based on local sources and vegetable protein sources. This vision perceived the community as the basis for local nutrition, which left more room for regional diversity. Each village could contribute with different food resources. By contrast, the Sandinistas had argued with the nation, characterizing for example corn as a national resource. By doing so, they ignored that Caribbean food culture relied on other staples. The authors of the 1990s guide quoted health and working capacity as key aims that a balanced diet should guarantee. Their proposals lost the political militancy that nutrition campaigns had acquired in the 1980s and remained at the margin of public debates. The nutritional guidelines do not reveal what dishes and desires became popular during transition. But the promotion of US dietary models by government officials and economic elites triggered a trend in fast food consumption among different social sectors.

THE AMBIGUOUS RENEWAL OF US MODELS FOR CONSUMPTION

In early 1990s Managua, traditional street food faced competition from the new fast foods offered by multinational chains and local enterprise. Most of this food remained unaffordable for poor people, except for the hot dogs and burgers sold by street vendors. In 1991 *Barricada* attacked the growing presence of fast food firms and convenience store chains such as Domino's Pizza and Seven Eleven. Managuan bakeries also tried to compete with the growing fast food industry; local bakeries started selling pizzas, candy, and popcorn to their upper-class clientele.[82] In the early 1990s the hot dog conquered Managuan streets. Hot-dog vendors appeared in front of office buildings, supermarkets, and public gathering places in the Nicaraguan capital. Consumers interviewed by *La Prensa* emphasized the cheap prices and good hygienic conditions of the hot-dog stalls. In February 1991 *Barricada* warned that traditional *carne asada* had lost ground against hamburgers at the food stands. The younger generation, in particular, increasingly preferred North American fast food sold at cheaper prices and under better hygienic conditions. However, fast food sold in restaurants remained unaffordable for many Nicaraguans. Reviews in *La Prensa* criticized the high prices and bad service at McDonalds and Sandy's.[83] During the economic crisis of the early 1990s only very cheap fast food gained popularity, much of which was sold on Managuan streets. In 1990, eleven thousand street vendors were selling their products in the capital. At that time Nicaragua had the highest percentage of street food vendors in all of Central America.[84]

The Managuan mayor's vision for urban change attempted to provide business opportunities to those former elites returning from exile in the United States. One of his prestige projects was the Shopping Center Metrocentro, relaunched in 1998.[85] The return of exiled Nicaraguans from Miami also facilitated the distribution of US luxury items for consumption in Managua. To meet the demands of these elites, the government illegitimately authorized the use of foreign aid for luxury imports. *La Prensa* introduced its readers to the new consumer environment in a special section for new consumer opportunities entitled "Lo nuevo en Managua (The new in Managua). In 1991 the section described a video rental store, a beauty products store, and a shop specializing in macrobiotic products. In some articles *La Prensa* depicted the new Nicaragua as a shopping paradise, criticizing, wherever possible, former Sandinista limitations on free commerce.

But even market advocates had to admit that the growing social gaps affected Nicaraguan society and only a small minority could participate in this wonderful new shopping world. The reintroduction of credit enlarged the clientele but led to growing indebtedness. *La Prensa* published a caricature in October 1991 showing a poor woman with a headscarf saying "Justice" looking at a splendid shop window displaying a dummy wearing an elegant dress. Frequently, people entered the shopping centers only to walk through the lines asking for prices or just to look at the merchandise, as *La Prensa* observed at the Metrocentro in December 1991.[86] The new commercial establishments survived only because of the reintroduction of credit in May 1991. Until economic liberalization started, only cash payment was permitted, but in the late 1980s, for example, pulperías had reintroduced credit. In light of the economic crisis, more clients needed short-term credit than pulpería owners could provide, especially to people from the neighborhood. According to a survey conducted in the San Luis and Altagracia districts in Managua, between 55 percent and 66 percent of clients bought on credit.[87] Overall, food supply in the capital became more unequal. The new authorities promoted similar ideas as the Somoza regime in the 1970s including US models for urban renewal and stores catering to an upper-class clientele.

In the transition period from 1988 to 1993, the Nicaraguan public debated animatedly the role of the consumer. Fundamental changes in the shopping environment and economic organization made people reflect on consumer behavior and the dangers of manipulation through advertising. Some voices described a critical consumer with high expectations, and others feared gullible consumers believing in catchy advertising slogans. Frank Trentmann's argument for understanding the consumer as "ascription in the making" proves important again.[88] During the late 1980s the public debates were dominated by the vulnerable consumer suffering from speculation and high prices, but this person was soon joined in the early 1990s by the figure of the newborn commercial consumer. The influx of imported goods and the rise of mass advertising triggered a new debate over consumerism in Nicaraguan society. In a comment in *La Prensa*, Leopoldo

Barrianuevo characterized the new consumer in 1991 as "more careful, less manipulatable and firmly demanding." At the same time, he admitted that consumers initially analyzed the price and then the prestige of a product.[89] In the early 1990s *Barricada* focused instead on the vulnerable consumer. Alarmed by the growing amount of advertising, the *Barricada* author saw the danger that it could become the new "sovereign influencing the behavior of Nicaraguans," showing the influence of cultural imperialism theory on Sandinista political thought. The author overemphasized the power of mass advertising that appeared as "sovereign" with absolute authority over Nicaraguans' consumer habits.[90]

The year 1988 was a turning point for the Nicaraguan revolution. The economy had entered an impasse. The government was unable to stop hyperinflation and assure basic food supply to all Nicaraguans while the global transformation of the Eastern bloc first started and then reduced outside support for the Sandinistas. When Hurricane Joan hit the country this reinforced the overall feelings of crisis. People lost confidence in the revolution as part of the Sandinista leadership continued to display luxury goods in public while calling on people to practice austerity.

Already in 1987 voices within the Sandinista-controlled media had contested the interpretation that speculators were the national enemies, instead arguing that social crisis forced people into informal activities. At the end of 1987, the supply situation deteriorated so fast that the government declared a national food emergency. At this point the government was divided over economic strategy. Eventually, the possibility of peace and the economic advisers' recommendations reinforced the course toward adjustment policy.

The 1988 adjustments marked the beginning of transition back to a capitalist market economy with credit, commercial advertising, and the state's retiring from nationalized firms. Market influences gained strength, in basic grains trade and food distribution, for example. The government declared the end of egalitarianism and said goodbye to ambitious social reform programs. Suddenly, *Barricada* writers were defending market mechanisms. Adjustment also led to the massive dismissal of state employees, which undermined the work capacities of some state institutions. Take the case of the Nicaraguan Food Program, where the gap between ambitious development plans on paper and institutional realities was enormous.

In the late 1980s Sandinista food policy eroded completely. Although PAN still developed ambitious plans for external cooperation, scarce resources and internal conflicts weakened its capacity. Campaigns for alternative nutrition based on local resources lost political militancy. Global attention to Nicaraguan food policy faded away. Wage liberalization increased social gaps in Nicaraguan society. For instance, urban workers earned only enough to buy 20 percent of the basic basket. Reactions to adjustment included disillusionment, deception, indignation, and resistance. Given the disastrous supply situation, people reactivated old survival strategies, but meals became ever scarcer. Even if Sandinista leaders did not publicly admit the existence of hunger, people were aware that it existed. After years of war and scarcity the majority of Nicaraguans voted for the opposition.

Hunger persisted after the 1990 elections as the Chamorro administration failed to establish a coherent food policy, and food production stagnated. Low government interest disillusioned several donors who had planned to extend their Nicaraguan projects. Relying on neoliberal ideology, politicians and health staff promoted the idea of self-responsibility for a good diet. Despite nutritional surveys indicating a slight recovery in Central Nicaragua, poor Managuans and people in northern rural communities suffered from malnutrition. Peasants suffered, in addition, from the insecurity of land titles and reduced state support, which affected basic grains production. Hence, Nicaraguans still depended heavily on food aid, in these years mainly from the United States.

Despite widespread scarcity, the political and economic elites promoted a return to US models for consumer culture and urban development. The new Managua mayor, Arnoldo Alemán, vigorously promoted shopping centers and the consumption of imported goods, bringing the old solutions from the Somoza period back to the forefront. Nevertheless, most Nicaraguans could only afford very cheap imported products and relied on credit to make their daily purchases. During the transition years state intervention and market mechanism coexisted, and the government dismantled enterprises and institutions involved in food policy from the Sandinista period. After a period of confrontation the FSLN cooperated with President Violeta Chamorro. Once again, the corruption of its leadership disillusioned some of their followers.

CHAPTER SEVEN

CARIBBEAN TRANSITIONS

AGRICULTURAL COLONIZATION, NOSTALGIA, AND FOOD CULTURES, 1960S–1990S

"Bluefields is becoming one big market" the sociologist Ronnie Vernooy wrote in his fieldnotes in September 1990.[1] In the late 1980s Bluefields was one of the main cities at the Caribbean Coast with around forty thousand inhabitants. In 1988 Hurricane Joan destroyed more than 90 percent of the city. During the early 1990s market stands appeared all over the city: on sidewalks, in parks, outside public buildings and even private houses. Vendors tried to survive by selling bread, meat, fish, sweets, cigarettes, and liquor. Women offered regional dishes such as Johnny cakes or homemade chicken soup, tortillas, or nacatamales. Vendors with more capital also sold shoes, perfumes, or portable sound systems. The boom in street trade was the result of the war and the economic crisis, which had forced many peasant families to move to the city. Many people lost their jobs in the lumber and fishing companies and the state administration during the transition years between 1988 and 1993. International organizations estimated that between 70 and 80 percent of the local population were living in poverty. Numerous children were begging on the city streets; the number of robberies and assaults increased.

At the same time the Caribbean Commercial Corporation opened a new supermarket in Bluefields, which offered a large variety of imported products including condensed milk, cornflakes, whiskey, instant coffee, and makeup. These were products many local people had longed for during the years of revolution when international trade relations were disrupted. Other merchants started to sell electronic devices such as televisions, microwaves, and radios. Middle-class and elite consumers filled these shops to acquire the latest imports and replace equipment destroyed during the hurricane. This was facilitated through access to US dollars through relatives abroad. Bluefields soon became known as "the dollar paradise in the country."[2]

The situation in Bluefields in the early 1990s shows that street trade had become an important survival strategy during the social and economic crisis. The trend also occurred in Managua but manifested more dramatically in the Caribbean. The city of Bluefields had been the epicenter of the crisis since Hurricane Joan hit the Coast in October 1988. When the Sandinistas lost power in 1990 the city was still in the process of reconstruction. The opening of new shops and the active street trade of imported products represented the local population's strong attachment to US consumer goods, which had caused numerous conflicts during the revolutionary period. People eagerly consumed these imported products when they reappeared in shops in the early 1990s.

Food and its scarcity shaped the negative reception of the Sandinista revolution on the Coast. For Caribbean people the revolution meant a radical change in what anthropologist Sidney Mintz has called the "outer sphere" of consumption, setting limits to consumers' individual decisions. During the 1980s Nicaraguans' opportunities to consume were limited by trade restrictions, food rationing, and limited mobility because of the war.[3]

Although the region occupies 56 percent of the nation's territory, the Caribbean Coast has remained at the margins of mestizo Nicaragua long before and after its incorporation in the national territory in 1894. The reasons for this marginality lie partially in geography but primarily in the region's history, in particular its distinct development of foreign contacts and the colonization attempts by both the British and the Spanish. The Caribbean lowlands have a hot, humid climate with nine months of rainy season. Several large rivers cross the region flowing into lagoons, swamps, or deltas. The only fertile land is situated in the floodplains and on the riverbanks. Vegetation is dominated in the northern Caribbean by pine and palm savannas and in the southern Caribbean by wet tropical rainforest and mangroves. Climate and the large humid areas have impeded road construction for a long time. The main cities are the coastal towns Bluefields and Puerto Cabezas as well as the northern mining towns Siuna, Bonanza, and La Rosita.[4]

The Nicaraguan Caribbean is a region with a very heterogeneous population: different indigenous groups (Miskito, Mayangna, and Rama), black Creoles, Chinese merchants, and English-speaking Garífunas, as well as mestizos from Central Nicaragua, whose number started increasing significantly in the 1950s. Each of these groups had its own consumption habits and traditions. Hence, Richard Wilk's description of Belizean consumption patterns as a "mosaic" seems to be true also for the Nicaraguan Caribbean. Because of globalization and local political changes, pieces changed place and were reformed into new configurations during the course of the twentieth century.[5]

Historically, people on the Coast have referred to the rest of the country as Spanish Nicaragua, and they felt more attached to a cosmopolitan

Caribbean culture, strongly influenced by the Anglo-American presence in the region. In contrast, the mestizo population in Central Nicaragua viewed the Caribbean for a long period as a "wild" and "undeveloped" area. These prejudices about the Coast were also reflected in the discourses on Nicaraguan cuisine. José Coronel Urtecho remarked in his famous essay "Elogio de la cocina nicaragüense" (In praise of Nicaraguan cuisine) that mestizo cuisine "even" included African antecedents along with Hispanic and indigenous ones. Among the dishes he listed, there was not one mention of Caribbean cooking except a short paragraph on turtle meat.[6] Hence, although Coronel Urtecho acknowledged historical Afro-Caribbean influences on the food culture, he did not consider them as forming part of national cuisine.

Still, in 2007, the Nicaraguan writer Sergio Ramírez claimed in his book *Tambor olvidado* that African influences in Central Nicaraguan cuisine had been ignored. To refute the myth of a mestizo cuisine based exclusively on indigenous and Spanish food traditions he argued that black populations had contributed to the change of culinary cultures throughout the country. Black immigrants had introduced new methods of preparation and spices into the Coast's food culture, and in Central Nicaragua black slaves and their descendants had worked frequently as cooks in elite households. As Ramírez concluded, the culinary influences from the Pacific had more strongly influenced the Caribbean than vice versa, which remains true up to today, even if the last years have witnessed some efforts to save Caribbean culinary traditions.[7] The Sandinistas initially made some limited efforts to promote Caribbean food in Pacific Nicaragua in the 1980s, but the Somoza regime treated the Coast mainly as a space for resource extraction.

The agro-export economy promoted by the Somoza regime also affected the Caribbean Coast's food system. On the one hand, local seafood resources were exported, which meant that local people had to substitute these items with other foods. On the other hand, the expansion of cotton and cattle in Pacific Nicaragua pushed more peasants to the agricultural frontier in the interior of the Caribbean departments. These people had to adapt their agricultural methods and consumption habits to the local climate, but they also brought with them their own food traditions, so the local demand for rice, corn, and beans increased.

Contrary to the rest of Nicaragua, these new tensions in the Coast's food system did not result in social protest. While part of the peasantry in Pacific Nicaragua fought for their landholdings and better living conditions, no similar movement took place at the agricultural frontier. There were no confrontations with large landowners or the National Guard, and the FSLN failed to gain any strong foothold in these dispersed settlements. People living on the Coast did not attribute rising food prices to the Somoza regime's economic policy. As a result, no social basis for the revolution ever arose in the Coast's countryside or its cities. At first, local people considered the revolution a distant event, but they soon felt its effects on the food supply, land distribution, and local enterprise.

In general, revolutionary food policy for the Coast followed the same approach as in the rest of the country. However, it lacked the support provided by the mass organizations in Pacific Nicaragua, which had facilitated revolutionary policy in the early 1980s. The Sandinistas failed to consider the region's distinctive history, which had resulted in different food and consumer cultures from the rest of the country. The failure of the Sandinistas to react adequately to regional diversity contributed to the demise of revolution, and this was particularly visible in the Caribbean.

Since the late nineteenth century, people living on the Caribbean Coast had welcomed the arrival of imported foods from the United States. Whenever economic crisis or political change cut off trade links to the United States and the wider Caribbean, a feeling of crisis spread throughout the Coast. This is what occurred after the Sandinista revolution, which local people mostly rejected. Among different ethnic groups, people feared the nationalization of industries, restrictions on trade, and increasing state intervention. When the Sandinistas implemented their economic and food policy, people perceived some reforms as unwanted interventions into local affairs. Similar to Northern Nicaragua, peasants on the agricultural frontier aspired to personal landholding and reacted negatively to the creation of cooperatives. Supply problems affected the Caribbean more dramatically than Pacific Nicaragua as it was one of the main areas where the war was being fought, and the revolutionaries cut off trade links to the wider Caribbean. Insufficient transport infrastructure contributed to higher increases in food prices than elsewhere in the country.

During the transition years between 1988 and 1993, uncertainty and economic crisis hit the Caribbean harder than the rest of the country. This was because of natural disaster, higher food prices, return migration, and a new wave of agricultural colonization. Entire cities had to be reconstructed, and food production took a longer time to recover from the severe destruction. At the same time, the regional autonomy project generated hope but also political uncertainties. The strong desire for autonomy has long-term historical roots.

Twentieth-century food and consumption at the Coast can only be understood by looking at the region's history of colonization efforts, migration, and boom-and-bust economic cycles since the seventeenth century.

For the 1960s and 1970s developments during the Somoza period can be seen by analyzing CARE records for the newly colonized agricultural communities and US anthropologists' publications on Miskito communities. For the 1980s *Barricada* and the Sandinista's publication for the Coast entitled *Sunrise* provide important sources about the supply situation. Finally, regional autonomy of the Caribbean departments and tourism have generated more interest in Caribbean food cultures since the 1990s.

A SHORT HISTORY OF THE NICARAGUAN CARIBBEAN AND ITS FOOD CULTURES

Central and coastal food cultures have differed in terms of basic staples. While cassava and plantains were dominant on the Coast, the interior relied on maize. Rice is the shared basic grain, though at the Coast it is cooked with coconut milk. In general, basic grains cultivation was more difficult at the Coast given the hot, humid climate and intense rainfalls. Consequently, the Coast communities relied much more on hunting and seafood. Trade mainly concentrated in Bluefields and Puerto Cabezas; these cities supplied networks of small stores in communities throughout the region. The Caribbean's different history of colonization and foreign contact has left a legacy of fragmentation in political, economic, and culinary Nicaragua.

The strong influences of the British date back to the seventeenth century, when English settlements were first established in the Central American Caribbean to stem Spanish expansion. Formally, British influence ended in the aftermath of the 1783 Treaty of Versailles, when, after long negotiations with Spain, the British agreed to leave the Coast in 1786. While the British were retreating from the region, a new wave of immigrants arrived from Jamaica and other parts of the Caribbean. These new immigrants were merchants as well as freed slaves of African descent who were attached to British values and the English language. This group came to be known as Creoles, a term that was also used by immigrants and their descendants to identify themselves.[8]

Black immigrants contributed new spices and herbs to a common Caribbean food culture of roots, tubers, and seafood, and British culinary influences introduced wheat, sugarcane, and some spices to the Coast.[9] Even after Nicaraguan independence in 1838, British interests in the region persisted through the nineteenth century. By the 1860s Creoles had emerged as the new elites and had consolidated a hegemonic position in Coast society. They perceived themselves as British subjects predestined to assume leadership in the absence of direct colonial rule. As the new elite the Creoles promoted consumption habits and a lifestyle related to British traditions. Nevertheless, ethnic identifications remained contradictory, incorporating both Anglo and black cultural influences. Anglo influences included the widespread practice of Protestant Christianity and the predominance of the English language; black influences included an identification with a black diaspora as well as the social memory of slavery.[10] Although anthropological research has focused on the important role of ethnicity in the continuation of culinary traditions, I argue that food cultures at the Coast were in a state of continuous exchange that cannot be attributed to ethnicity alone. Instead, economic organization and regional interactions have played crucial roles in changing food practices beyond the nineteenth century.

In the second half of the nineteenth century, US influences in the Nicaraguan Caribbean increased. In 1860 a new period of Coast history began when Britain renounced all claims to the Nicaraguan Coast in the first Treaty of Managua. Britain's retreat paved the way for the ascendancy of US companies in the late nineteenth century. Throughout this period the Coast experienced a period of limited autonomy with self-government opportunities for the Miskito and Creole populations. Nicaragua incorporated the Coast into its national territory in 1894, which provoked a short Creole revolt that the government quelled with US support. Miskito authorities signed a declaration of reincorporation that converted the Nicaraguan Caribbean into Zelaya department. Shortly afterward US influences infiltrated Coast daily life through religion. New US missionaries from the Protestant Moravian Church arrived in the region; the church simultaneously started education and health projects that were strongly impacted by North American models and concepts. These activities also contributed to a growing demand for US consumer goods within the region.[11] In the late nineteenth century, increasing economic penetration by US firms coincided with stronger US influences through religious and community organizations.

The Coast's culinary mosaic was also shaped by the economic boom-and-bust cycles of its export products during the late nineteenth and twentieth century. A short period of rubber extraction in the 1870s was followed by the banana boom, which peaked in the 1920s. After US banana companies settled at the Coast, Puerto Cabezas port grew quickly.

Local people established the term "company time" for this period, which throughout the twentieth century they associated with the broad availability of foreign goods. With the advent of "company time," the employees of US firms replaced Creole elites, who were forced into mid-range jobs in the enclave economy. This position still allowed Creoles to consume imported goods, which they considered an important symbol of middle-class status. When the US banana company Standard Fruit hired black workers from the West Indies and the United States, ethnic hierarchies became more complicated and conflicts arose between different groups of workers.[12] Nonetheless, the nostalgia surrounding the period of "company time" has removed these tensions from collective memory.

Large-scale production in mining and on plantations also prompted new consumption habits among workers through the establishment of company stores ("commissaries"), which offered US products for sale. At Standard Fruit, the largest employer in the region, workers received part of their wages in company scripts that they had to spend in the commissary. On the one hand, workers objected to the high prices and the lack of variety in the commissaries. On the other hand, inhabitants of Puerto Cabezas identified the availability of US products, cultural exchange, and mobility between port cities as indicators of their city's cosmopolitanism. In many mining and plantation companies, workers received standardized food rations for their daily diets. In the work camps, rice and beans was the most common dish. In addition, wheat bread, condensed milk, and canned food gained popularity during this period.[13] Thus, large numbers of workers became familiar with imported and canned foods; they brought them back to their communities and spread their consumption.

The presence of thousands of workers also increased the need for locally produced basic grains. Because of their climate, the communities at Río Coco on the border of Honduras had fulfilled this task since the 1920s, but the Contra War and political conflicts disrupted this tradition in the early 1980s.[14] The presence of mining firms and plantations significantly changed the local culture of food production. By the late 1920s a new bust cycle affected the plantation economy and caused severe political disruptions, most notably through the Sandino uprising, which contributed to the negative reception of the 1979 revolution at the Coast.

The worldwide economic crisis of 1929 hit the export sector hard in Central America. The Nicaraguan real GDP contracted by 43 percent between 1928 and 1936.[15] Local newspapers reported on widespread poverty and "the calamity of hunger." Regional farmers' diets were limited to bananas. They even lacked money to buy salt to flavor their food.[16] It was a period of significant political instability. In 1926 the United States intervened in the civil war between conservatives and liberals, which provoked the resistance of Sandino and his armed movement in 1927. The liberation struggle endured seven years and caused a wave of solidarity in many Latin American countries; it was the "first modern, networked anti-imperialism campaign" on the continent.[17]

At the Coast, however, reactions were mixed. The liberation movement of Augusto César Sandino in the late 1920s occurred in a period of economic decline, inspiring resistance against US imperialism throughout Latin America, but people at the Caribbean mostly rejected his activities.

In 1928 he arrived at the Coast and took over La Luz Mine near Siuna. Some Miskito communities from the upper Río Coco actively supported the movement, but others opposed it because of its attacks on Moravian missionaries and the banana companies. Many locals did not perceive these entities as foreign or exploitative. Local narratives portrayed the period of Sandino's presence as a period of loss and chaos; they characterized Sandino as a "bandit," terrorizing Miskito communities to the point that people temporarily moved out of their villages. This historical legacy contributed to the negative reception of the 1979 revolution at the Coast. Historians and anthropologists observed that the memory of violent conflicts in the 1920s were still very salient between the 1960s and the 1980s.[18]

When historical events interrupted trade connections to the United States and the Caribbean, the region had to depend on food from Central Nicaragua. Given the high transport costs, food prices at the Coast increased. Economic crisis and plant diseases had caused the departure of all banana companies by the early 1940s. Occasional food shortages occurred, and because of their low wages workers throughout the region were often unable to feed their families. In the 1940s to 1980s, the region relied on the importation of many food and goods, mainly from Managua, which resulted in many transport problems and higher prices. These problems continued until the 1980s and were related to the region's isolation. As a result of geography and history, the region has traditionally been cut off from Central Nicaragua. It was not until 1961 that the first paved road to the southern Caribbean was opened when the Somoza regime showed interest in seafood and metal extraction. The first all-weather road to the northern Caribbean was opened in 1981 but frequently remained closed.[19]

The difficulties with the food supply after the banana boom led to nostalgic memories of "company time," which survived from the 1960s through the 1990s. For the Miskito in Asang, the banana period represented a "golden age" that was used as a reference point to measure contemporary crises.[20] Participants in an oral history project in Bluefields during the 1990s characterized this period as a time of abundance. "This is what they say about those days," Hugo Sujo Wilson reported. "There was plenty of work, therefore a lot of money, there were banana ships, mahogany ships, plenty of big and well supplied stores, etc. You could buy anything you wanted in the line of food, clothing, and luxuries. Everything was cheap. . . . They never used to consume Nicaraguan products. Everything was 'from out' as they say."[21]

Caribbean people often rejected food and consumer goods produced within Nicaragua itself. To consume products "from out" was a symbol of prestige. Urban Coast people in Puerto Cabezas, for example, perceived themselves as "cosmopolitan" for their contacts to the United States and the wider Caribbean and their access to imported goods.[22]

Nostalgia for an enclave economy among people living on the Coast originated in their access to imported goods, and it persisted over decades. The term "enclave economy" originated from dependency theory. Generally, it refers to a distinct economic sector focusing on exports and controlled by foreign capital, such as the Chilean mines or the Central American banana plantations. The sociologists Fernando Henrique Cardoso and Enzo Faletto distinguished between a foreign controlled enclave and a nationally controlled economy.[23] This concept was in line with the Sandinista interpretation of Coast history. The revolutionaries accordingly nationalized enterprise at the Coast and established state control of foreign trade. In contrast, people living in the Nicaraguan Caribbean remembered the strong presence of foreign enterprise as a positive period.[24] Even in the 1980s the absence of imported goods still served as an indicator for crisis in the region. Nonetheless, the Sandinistas tried to invalidate feelings of nostalgia by offering a different interpretation of Coast history through propaganda, but they were not successful.

Nostalgia for "company time" did not focus on special brand products but on the general availability of imported goods that formed part of a local social memory. Although imported goods were mostly available between 1890 and 1960, ethnic and social hierarchies limited access. The glossing over of contradictory elements such as ethnic conflicts or high food prices at the company stores represent a case of "restorative nostalgia."[25]

THE LOCAL FOOD SYSTEM UNDER THE SOMOZA REGIME

Under the Somoza regime, new economic boom-and-bust cycles continued to shape regional food consumption. The Somoza regime perceived the Coast as a vast source of valuable resources. Copper production and commercial seafood exploitation became new sources of revenue during the 1950s. US firms extracted resources and made considerable profits while the region suffered from basic problems. Many social indicators such as rates of literacy and nutrition were far below national averages. Nutritional surveys conducted by INCAP neglected Caribbean communities. A 1976 US AID report referred to an average per capita consumption of 1,069 kcal, which was far below national averages, but the source for this statement remains unclear.[26]

After the Second World War the Somoza regime's vision for the Coast followed a "modernizing approach" influenced by development initiatives from abroad such as the Alliance for Progress. During the 1960s the government started to integrate the region into its national infrastructure.

However, the modernizing approach implied "hispanizing" the local population so as to convert them into suitable citizens for a mestizo nation. Although few plans were successfully implemented, these efforts illustrate the "bureaucratic fantasies" of a government interested in attracting foreign aid for development projects that primarily benefited elites.[27]

The Somoza regime's interest in the Coast was pragmatic—plentiful natural resources and space to resettle people from Central Nicaragua—but it is more difficult to assess how the Coast communities perceived the Somoza regime. People responded to some aspects of the regime positively, such as Somoza's ties to the United States and his anticommunism. Contrary to Central Nicaragua and the interior regions of the Caribbean department, National Guard repression was absent at the Coast. Nevertheless, foreign observers concluded that Somoza's popularity was limited.[28] This might have been a consequence of the hispanization policy in the school system, disdain from mestizo state bureaucrats, and concerns about the ecological consequences of intense resource extraction. Soil degradation and polluted rivers affected local food resources, which, together with increasing immigration, contributed to inequalities in the local food system.

Development cooperation and resettlement projects led to an increased mestizo influence at the Coast that affected local food production and consumption habits. The regime followed a pragmatic development approach and accepted foreign aid willingly when it served the regime's needs. Although local institutions were involved, mestizos generally occupied the leading positions in state development projects. Also, for merchants from Managua, it was far easier to sell their products at the Coast, but merchants from the Caribbean experienced limitations when trying to sell in the capital.[29]

One of the most important projects that led to a stronger mestizo presence was the colonization program, which provided a new home to peasants forced out of the Pacific regions by expanding export agriculture. Peasants from Central Nicaragua relocated independently to the Coast, either to work in the mines or to settle in one of the interior's new communities. Between 1945 and 1975 around one hundred thousand people moved into the Coast region, which led to several conflicts over land and maritime resources. The settlers perceived their migration as a "civilizing mission" that would modernize the region through hard work in agricultural production. They also perceived themselves to be superior to the local Afro-Caribbean and indigenous population. Not surprisingly, they often ignored the land rights of these communities.[30] In many regions, migrants introduced slash-and-burn agriculture, which permitted the use of larger land plots but also accelerated deforestation and soil erosion. Rapid population growth increased the need for basic grains production in the region as the mestizo immigrants demanded food based on Central Nicaraguan staples. While they produced corn, beans, and rice wherever possible, the Miskito communities at Río Coco River also expanded rice and beans cultivation. For the migrants from inner Nicaragua, however, the adaptation to the new climate and vegetation proved difficult.

Reports from the nongovernmental organization CARE document settlers' harsh living conditions as well as their deficient nutritional situation. CARE started to work with some of the new mestizo settlements in 1970.[31] In their early reports staff members described the Caribbean Coast as "almost completely undeveloped" and the Nueva Guinea region as a "semi-wilderness."[32] The community Nueva Guinea, founded in 1965, belonged to the Rigoberto Cabezas settlement project of the Agrarian Institute of Nicaragua (IAN). The whole settlement project included thirteen colonies with around ninety-nine hundred inhabitants, of which 83 percent were illiterate, and only two doctors and three nurses worked in the area. After the 1972 earthquake, the local population increased to twenty thousand as a new wave of urban migrants arrived.[33]

The disaster also challenged food supply far away from the capital. Two years later, several surveys by local CARE staff members revealed the disastrous nutritional situation. The pediatrician Ralph Foulke diagnosed "widespread protein caloric malnutrition," especially among young children. Glenn Porter reported that in the communities Jerusalem and El Corocito 86 percent of all children were suffering from different degrees of malnutrition. According to Cam McIntyre in a 1974 report, the average family earned $444 a year and were $570 in debt. Consequently, most people could only afford basic grains. Their most frequently consumed food was beans, followed by rice, tortillas, cuajada, cassava, and eggs. Hence, the settlers maintained the most important elements of their diet but incorporated cassava as a new basic staple. Among the highly desired but unavailable or unaffordable foods, meat ranked first, followed by vegetables and milk.[34] The case of the Nueva Guinea communities demonstrates that settlers had an extremely limited diet. Although they readapted to their new environment, food aid and nutrition education also influenced their consumption habits.

CARE staff concentrated on activities with the settler peasants, but academic researchers from the United States focused their attention on the Miskito communities. The work of three US researchers demonstrates that the seafood export boom affected local nutrition and created conflicts over the distribution of turtle meat in the Miskito communities. They studied food habits in the Coast communities Tasbapauni and Little Sandy Bay as well as in the Asang community located at Río Coco. The three communities varied in size, ranging from 370 to 1,000 people. The researchers' fieldwork shows that the commercialization of turtle meat had affected local subsistence economies in these communities. Large-scale commercial seafood had experienced rapid growth during the 1960s and 1970s. By 1975, eight firms operated in the region employing more than 860 people. These firms benefited from the absence of state protection measures for seafood resources.[35] The export boom reduced local shrimp, lobster, and turtle populations considerably, which negatively affected the nutrition of local people and led to conflicts within the Miskito communities. Miskito people neglected local agricultural production for turtle fishing, as turtle sales provided a higher income. As most turtle meat was sold on commercial markets, it became scarce in local communities, which provoked conflicts over distribution. Because of the scarcity of meat, local Tasbapauni women once attacked commercial turtle fishers. Instead of traditional sources of protein such as seafood, people consumed more carbohydrates, such as sugar and wheat flour.[36]

The researchers' work also provided insights into other aspects of Miskito food culture. Although the US researchers extensively documented "traditional" Miskito food, they only occasionally mentioned how people prepared the food bought at the local stores. According to these references people in Asang, Tasbapauni, and Sandy Bay used wheat, sugar, and baking powder for flour tortillas, bread, and other baked products. For example, Bernard Nietschmann identified oatmeal, candies, soda crackers, and margarine as being among the most commonly sold foods, but none of these products appears in his descriptions of families' actual meals. For the Tasbapauni community he described a typical dish as a piece of fish or meat, cooked cassava, *duswa*, and *wabul*. In addition, sweet coffee and bread were served. In Sandy Bay and Asang, people remembered early commercial contacts and foreign presence positively. Both Mary Helms and Dorothy Cattle concluded that imported goods had become "cultural necessities."[37] At the time, these scholars did their fieldwork in the 1960s and 1970s, social organization in Miskito communities had advanced significantly.

Owing to the economic crisis and the dissolution of traditional social and cultural networks, the Miskito organized in the late 1960s. In 1973 they founded the organization Alianza para el progreso del Pueblo Miskito y Sumu (ALPROMISU), the Alliance for the Progress of the Miskito and Sumu People, a "grassroots organization with origins in Miskito social activism along the Río Coco."[38] The leaders, mainly Moravian pastors and teachers, promoted the Coast's integration into the Nicaraguan nation as the path to development. In general, they perceived the new, modernizing development projects as an opportunity to demand equal access to state services for the Coast population.[39] Hence, local political leaders were willing to embrace the development promise of modernization. Although social activism at the Coast increased throughout the 1970s, no fundamental opposition to the Somoza regime evolved as with the FSLN in Central Nicaragua.

THE REVOLUTION AT THE COAST

Before the revolution there had been few contacts between the Sandinistas and the Coast population. In the FSLN historical program of 1969, the chapter on the Coast bore the title "Reincorporation of the Atlantic Coast," which meant integration into the mestizo nation. The aim of the program was to end the influence of foreign monopolies, to develop local production, and to end discrimination against indigenous groups. At the outbreak of the revolution approximately 70,000 Miskitos and 30,000 Creoles faced a majority of 182,000 mestizos. The smaller indigenous groups accounted for less than 10,000 people while the number of Garífunas was estimated at 1,500 people. The party's understanding of the Coast's social realities, however, was simplistic. For example, the FSLN perceived Miskitos as proletarian workers because of their work on plantations and in the mines, but their economic activities were in fact far more complex and included fishing, craftwork, and hunting.[40]

At first local people perceived the revolution as a "distant drama," as anthropologist Charles Hale has pointed out.[41] The main events of the Sandinista revolution happened in Central Nicaragua. Local people did not identify with the revolution's demands; large sectors of the Caribbean population did not perceive the capitalist economy and the presence of foreign companies to be exploitation or imperialistic dominance. Peasants in the colonized areas valued private landholdings and individual agricultural work highly. Soon it turned out that the "distant drama" would have significant consequences for the Coast's economy and daily life. When the Sandinistas nationalized nearly every important enterprise on the Coast, local inhabitants perceived this as a threat. The presence of foreign firms had always been associated with economic prosperity, and nationalization seemed to indicate economic downturn.[42]

In fact, the local economy did decline after the revolution. The revolution interrupted contact with the wider Caribbean, the United States, and Costa Rica.[43] Although smuggling activities developed, ingredients for some traditional Caribbean dishes suddenly became unavailable. Food scarcity contributed to local people's rejection of Sandinista economic policy.

Although the Sandinistas started social reforms at the Coast and invested in local infrastructure, Coast people perceived state intervention in the local economy as both insufficient and disturbing. For example, on Corn Island, the state enterprise paid fixed monthly wages, but local people would have preferred a payment according to the amount of fish handed in.[44] The Sandinista development program remained, as the researcher Carlos M. Vilas has argued, a "development strategy for the Coast, but not with the Coast." This was also visible in the ethnic composition of local state institutions. In 1983, for example, 80 percent of local state employees were mestizos, which led to protest among the Miskito inhabitants.[45]

The Miskito community's demand for fairer representation in local development efforts soon brought them into conflict with the FSLN. Already, in November 1979, a group of young Coast students had founded a new organization for Miskito interests called MISURASATA (Miskito, Sumo, Rama, Sandinista, Asla Takanka). In February 1981, after the organization proposed a Miskito territory at the Coast, the government detained the organization's leadership. After an armed confrontation with Sandinista soldiers, three thousand young Miskitos fled to Honduras and joined the Contras.[46] In the following years the Coast remained one of the main war zones.

The Sandinista government's efforts to strengthen local food production faced a special challenge at the Coast. Agricultural production had historically been weak, and the beginning of the Contra War soon affected local grain production. The Sandinistas further weakened local rice and beans production by resettling communities from the Río Coco region close to the Honduran border. In December 1981 armed Miskito groups attacked people who were cooperating with the Sandinistas in Río Coco communities, killing more than sixty people. The government reacted with a large resettlement project to move civilians out of the conflict zone to the Tasba Pri area, seventy miles south, but the communities resisted. More than half the population of the resettled communities fled to Honduras.[47]

The resettlement project cut communities off from their sources of food supply. The affected families, around nine thousand people, were forced to organize agricultural production in cooperatives. However, in the first two years, the communities depended almost completely on external food aid. Although local production initially showed positive results, food resources were less diverse than in the Río Coco environment. Fruit trees, fish, and affordable meat were unavailable. In retrospect, it can be seen that the project was a complete failure. Most people wanted to return to Río Coco, and many local inhabitants moved on to Honduras. The period of open conflict lasted until 1984. After negotiations between the FSLN and MISURASATA, autonomy plans moved forward, and in May 1985 the government authorized the return of the communities to Río Coco. Military confrontations had nearly ceased by 1986, but conflicts over state intervention and the supply situation continued throughout the 1980s.[48]

The state distribution system was an additional source of discontent, although government propaganda was eager to depict it as a success story. During the early years of the revolution *Barricada* regularly published articles on the new system at the Coast. In 1980 the newspaper reported on the ambitious plan to install thirty-one popular stores and four popular supermarkets. At that time three new shops were operating in Bluefields, El Bluff, and on Corn Island.[49] Another article emphasized the high food prices before the new distribution system was established and concluded: "We draw attention to the fact that our brothers from the Atlantic Coast are benefiting for the first time with a continuous supply and reasonable prices."[50]

Whether the government accomplished these ambitious plans is unclear, as *Barricada* coverage on the Coast's food supply became scarce after 1981. Regardless, many sources point out that the Coast population reacted very negatively to state intervention into supply issues. In Miskito communities, for example, the state distribution quota for families challenged the traditional practice of food sharing. The departure of most Chinese merchants left a significant gap in the region, which suggests that the state supply network did not expand as fast as initially reported.[51] The discontent over the supply situation was also expressed in *Sunrise*, the FSLN's magazine for the Coast.

In general, the supply problems at the Coast were similar to those in the rest of the country, but they were exacerbated by the difficult transport situation and even higher food prices. In addition, nostalgia for "company time," the significance assigned to imported goods, and broken connections to the wider Caribbean prompted local dissatisfaction, as *Sunrise* reports show. The periodical, printed in Spanish and English, published six thousand copies monthly.[52] Its creation in 1983 was prompted by the FSLN's attempts to revise food policy for the Caribbean and negotiate issues of autonomy. From the periodical's beginning, supply problems were a central concern. The high prices for fruits and vegetables prompted some of the biggest discussions. In reaction to the higher food prices and the growing unrest at the Coast, the government maintained food subsidies for rice, sugar, flour, and oil longer than in the rest of the country. In addition, MICOIN subsidized transport prices. Nevertheless, food prices in Bluefields were still 25 percent higher than in the rest of the country.[53]

In December 1983 *Sunrise* reported that the scarcity of imported goods was considered one of the most frustrating factors resulting from the revolution. It is interesting to observe that *Sunrise* published critical voices earlier and more frequently than *Barricada*, which mainly dealt with supply problems in Central Nicaragua. In January 1984, when a local MICOIN representative attributed the supply problems to the war and the lack of foreign exchange, *Sunrise* offered an alternative interpretation, suggesting the lack of coordination among state institutions.[54] In November 1986 *Sunrise* attacked MICOIN's empty promises and concluded: "It's not surprising that people are suggesting that MICOIN take note of that old saying that 'Actions speak louder than words.'"[55] Most likely, *Sunrise* criticized state institutions more openly than *Barricada* for three reasons: (1) supply issues had a higher importance at the Coast; (2) Coast people were more critical of the state supply system, and (3) food prices were higher at the Coast than in Central Nicaragua.

Although *Sunrise* gave broad coverage to supply problems, it also criticized excessive consumer demands and people's aspirations to the North American lifestyle. In an attempt to counter widespread nostalgia for "company time," the newspaper offered its own historical interpretation of the former US presence. In December 1983 one author stated:

> Supposedly, one of the most "irritating" facts of the Sandinistas' People's Revolution, is that we can't find special fruits . . . and other foods with the distinctive, magic label "Made in the USA." With little effort, the people of Bluefields close their eyes to the real problems that the revolution faces, those caused by the United States. They childishly complain because they can't have their "Kellogg's Corn Flakes" for breakfast. . . . Very effectively, the Yankees have made us covet the "American Lifestyle" (living the American way), while assuring that none of us has the means to satisfy our greed. All of that is part of a larger campaign spurred by American imperialism, in its eagerness to convince Latin Americans that the Anglo-Saxon U.S. culture is supreme.[56]

Here, the Coast population is accused of ignoring US aggression while still desiring imported products. Another article, in 1985, was about the "gringo mentality" in Bluefields, where people were still measuring prices in dollars. The author concluded: "It looks like they are all family to rich Uncle Mac Duck because they too have the greenback sign in their eyes."[57] Most likely, these depictions of the Coast by writers for *Sunrise* were not a winning strategy for gaining new supporters among a local population who were already skeptical toward the revolution while suffering from ongoing supply problems. However, *Sunrise* writers wanted to establish a different interpretation of Coast history. They explained that the presence of North American firms had divorced the local peasants from their land, thus regional food production had declined.[58] *Sunrise* interpreted the history of foreign presence as a history of exploitation and manipulation. As the author of an article claimed, in 1984: "With the goods that the Yankees brought, they bought our dignity and our natural resources."[59]

Sunrise writers' attempts to adapt Sandinista campaigns to local situations and to offer solutions to local supply problems were probably more successful strategies for gaining support for the revolution. This is a parallel to the Nicaraguan women's organization magazine *Somos*. *Sunrise* adapted national campaigns for local food consumption to Caribbean habits, for example. In December 1983 the periodical argued that the campaign slogan for strengthening local food consumption should be changed on the Coast: "The 'Pinolera' response [to the US cancellation of credits for wheat imports] was, corn tortillas in place of bread. However, while this reflects the Pacific reality, for us on the Atlantic Coast, the answer should be, YUCA BAMI IN PLACE OF BREAD."[60] At the national level, the Sandinistas called for substituting bread with corn tortillas after the United States cancelled credits for wheat imports. At the Coast, *Sunrise* authors suggested Bami instead, a Caribbean flatbread based on cassava flour, which was a basic staple of Caribbean food culture. Hence, *Sunrise* authors insisted that the promotion of Caribbean alternatives for imported foods were necessary for local food consumption campaigns to be successful.

To strengthen awareness of the local culinary abundance, *Sunrise* provided its readers with reports on Caribbean food culture and many locally inspired recipes. For instance, the magazine promoted local alternatives such as fruit frescos and guava jelly as substitutes for soft drinks and peanut butter.[61] It also published recipes and articles on local food traditions. Recipes included medicinal teas, breadfruit cake, Chinese noodle soup, turtle meat dishes, and some Garífuna recipes. Writers promoted seafood consumption and published recipes for fish dishes, which was a parallel to similar campaigns in Pacific Nicaragua. For example, in October 1986, one *Sunrise* article argued for consuming smaller fishes that fishers normally throw back into the sea: "Fish is cheap, nutritious and delicious so let's all be more adventurous and demand the full wealth of our oceans from our fishermen!"[62] When campaigns to promote local food production encountered difficulties at the Coast because of unsuitable soils or climatic conditions for products common in Central Nicaragua, *Sunrise* writers promoted a project to increase dasheen production in 1987.[63]

While *Sunrise* better represented the local population because it was produced at the Coast, *Barricada* expressed disdain for the loss of national culinary traditions, ignoring the fact that Coast food cultures did not share the same culinary past as the rest of the country. For example, the Nic-

FigURE 7.1. Recipe for fish rondón. Source: *Barricada*, May 29, 1987, 6.

araguan writer Carlos Alemán Ocampo worried that wheat imports had substituted for corn during the banana boom in the early twentieth century—but the Coast population relied on other staples such as cassava or plantains. "The dependence was created," he concluded and then remarked disappointedly that the campaign to increase maize consumption lacked enthusiastic responses.[64]

Barricada also criticized how Caribbean people circumvented trade restrictions, through lobster smuggling, for example. Fishers often sold their catches to Costa Rican and Colombian boats for payment in dollars or in consumer goods such as Nike shoes or jeans. Foreign vendors in speedboats also offered basic foods such as rice or vegetable oil in exchange, which again points to the serious supply problems at the Coast. A *Barricada* article in June 1987 compared Corn Island to a maritime dollar shop.[65]

Barricada's efforts to introduce Caribbean recipes to the general Nicaraguan public were limited. However, they constitute the beginning of promoting Caribbean food in Pacific Nicaragua and mark the start of a trend that accelerated with autonomy. Only once between 1979 and 1990 did *Barricada* publish a Caribbean recipe, the particular dish being fish *rondón* (see figure 7.1). The newspaper published one report on a Caribbean food festival, which took place in Managua in 1986, where rondón and rice and beans with shrimp were served.[66] In 1988, however, Hurricane Joan put the Caribbean on *Barricada*'s front page.

NATURAL DISASTER, AUTONOMY, AND FOOD SCARCITY DURING THE TRANSITION YEARS, 1988–1993

With Hurricane Joan, the Caribbean became the epicenter of the 1988 crisis. The food crisis was much more serious at the Coast than in Central Nicaragua. As local food production was severely affected, people depended for longer periods on external food aid. The reconstruction of housing, roads, and power supply lines affected food distribution, storage, and trade throughout the transition. Reconstruction also delayed the autonomy process that had advanced between 1984 and 1987.

When Hurricane Joan hit the Caribbean Coast in October 1988, this severely affected local agricultural production and food delivery to the region. The winds eroded the soil and the heavy rains flooded farmlands. The hurricane destroyed the city of Bluefields almost completely, which affected seventy-one thousand people; it demolished roads, schools, farms, companies, and health centers throughout the region. Numerous families lost their houses and all of their crops. Comparing the disaster to the 1972 earthquake, local inhabitants concluded that Joan was as if twenty earthquakes had happened at the same time. The CEPAL diagnosed "a serious food shortage" at the Caribbean Coast and estimated that agricultural production in the whole country would decline by 17 percent. In January 1989 still more than thirty thousand quintals of bean seeds and more than eight thousand quintals of corn seeds were needed, as well as significant amounts of food aid, to help local people until the next harvest.[67]

The economic and social crises tore large holes in the Coast's food supply during the transition period. By the early 1990s local food production had still not recovered from the war and Hurricane Joan. When food aid

from Cuba stopped in March 1990 because of Cuba's own economic problems, a supply crisis developed in the northern Caribbean. The erosion of
Sandinista food policy led to the closure of the local MICOIN office in
March 1989. Basic foods such as rice, beans, and vegetable oil disappeared
temporarily from the local markets. Food brought in from the Pacific Coast
failed to alleviate the situation as the prices were too high. In October 1990
the situation worsened and provoked fourteen hundred people to attack a
food storage center owned by the Moravian Church.[68] At the same time,
Bluefields witnessed a dramatic increase in informal commerce, especially undertaken by female vendors whose number had increased to several hundred. In November 1990 returning Contras blocked the road from
El Rama, which caused a temporary supply crisis in the city. Only a few
months later, in April 1991, *Barricada* reported on hunger in Puerto Cabezas. People were desperate, and hysteria erupted in the city because of food
scarcity and the lack of water and electricity. While food shortages and
high prices were prevalent throughout the country, the Caribbean was particularly affected because of its precarious economic and social conditions
during the early 1990s.[69]

When the central government introduced a new currency in March
1991 as part of its economic reforms, price increases provoked strong discontent in Bluefields. In particular, the rise of meat prices made local people
angry. As a response, the local authorities established a regional price commission that defined maximum prices for thirty-eight products. Twenty
price inspectors were appointed to enforce the commission's regulations.
However, these measures soon turned out to be ineffective. Complaints
about prices were widely reported on local radio stations throughout April
and May 1991. Reporters and consumers denounced the price hikes for
foods such as cassava, tomato, onions, rice, sugar, and tortillas. Local prices
increased by nearly 100 percent from April to May. At that point, the regional commission had to publicly admit its failure. From the beginning, it
had only half-heartedly designed the project. For example, only five out of
the twenty inspectors received a salary for their work. Accordingly, inspectors often did not show up for work or failed to enforce the sanctions; some
also accepted bribes from merchants. With expanding street sales throughout the city, it was impossible to enforce maximum prices. Food prices in
Bluefields remained between 25 and 50 percent higher than in the rest of
the country during the early 1990s.[70]

Given the high rate of unemployment, the land conflicts, and internal
migration, high prices remained a contentious area in local politics. The
end of the war and the 1990 elections prompted major political changes
at the Coast. The elections at the Coast were also elections for the new

regional councils and marked an important step for the passage of the 1987 autonomy statute. In the northern autonomous zone, the Región Autónoma del Atlántico Norte (RAAN), a Miskito organization known as YATA-MA (Yapti Tasbaya Maraska Nani Asla Takanka, meaning "Descendants of Mother Earth") and composed of ex-combatants won twenty-three out of forty-eight seats in the regional autonomous council and was successful in other regional elections. In the southern autonomous zone (RAAS) the UNO won twenty-three seats, the FSLN nineteen, and YATAMA five from a total of forty-seven seats. Nonetheless, conflicting visions of autonomy still existed. The vision based on ethnic and territorial autonomy was represented by YATAMA. By contrast, the FSLN argued for a multiethnic model of autonomy. Over the years a coexistence of both models has developed, but nevertheless, conflicts over indigenous land rights and resource extraction still persist.[71]

At the same time as the formation of regional political authorities, the region experienced an influx of migrants during the transition years. On the one hand, many Contra members and refugees returned from Honduras. Many of the former Contra combatants were still armed, and violent conflicts between different armed groups persisted throughout the 1990s.[72] On the other hand, people from Central Nicaragua once again moved to the agricultural frontier. There was a high uncertainty of land titles in the early 1990s. Demobilized Sandinista soldiers, former Contras, and returning refugees urgently needed land to settle on. Most migrants either moved to the Río San Juan in the southern Caribbean or the region around Siuna in the northern Caribbean. Some migrants dedicated themselves to cattle farming, which further affected soil quality in the region. Given the absence of state support for small food producers, however, many peasants had to sell their land. They often moved further into the agricultural frontier, or emigrated to the cities, or left Nicaragua altogether.[73] By 2005 migration to the Caribbean had resulted in a 60 percent mestizo majority in the autonomous regions. Simultaneously mestizos increased their influence in local politics.[74] The new wave of agricultural colonization intensified land conflicts and advanced the ecological degradation of soils, which continues to affect basic grains production in the twenty-first century.

The autonomy process continued throughout the 1990s with some important legal improvements for the Caribbean. The framework was considered one of the most advanced Latin American autonomy projects at that time, as it included communal land rights and regional authority on social, economic, and cultural policy. However, the different Nicaraguan national governments, mainly interested in resource extraction, gave concessions to international firms without consulting regional institutions. The

Nicaraguan government protracted land titling and assigned few resources for social policy to the Coast. Therefore, high expectations turned into disillusionment for many Coast people.[75] Resource extraction continued to weaken local food production. Nevertheless, the autonomous institutions made some important advances in documenting and valorizing local cultural heritage.

Autonomy and new regional institutions promoted research on Coast history and traditions. The two new regional universities—Universidad de las Regiones Autónomas de la Costa Caribe Nicaragüense (URACCAN) and Bluefields Indian and Caribbean University (BICU)—became important actors in this process. Several oral history projects collected the memories of the older generations in Bluefields and Puerto Cabezas. Several publications documented Caribbean recipes during the 1990s, mostly small collections in newspapers and booklets. Recently, tourism has become an important catalyst for change, as the demand for "authentic" Caribbean food has increased.[76]

In 2004 the RAAN government published *Bluefields Creole Kitchen* in cooperation with the Tourism Faculty at BICU. Participants recorded more than 120 recipes from elderly people in Bluefields. The recipes are published in English and Spanish, and the book includes descriptions of Caribbean spices and demonstrates the importance of coconut milk in local food traditions. The introduction portrays the cultural fusion of European, Asian, and African influences as a harmonious history: "The nearly magical sound of Bluefields' recipes, with their throb of ancient Africa, is translated in a harmonious concert that outlines how to cook 'Rice and beans, Rondón, Patí, Bon, Jhonycake, Cococake, Pinetart, Gingerbeer y Totó,' among others."[77]

This vision of an uncontested culinary mosaic, however, reflects what Western academics have recently criticized as "happy hybridity." Researchers have extolled certain dishes as examples of transculturation, but they have excluded power asymmetries in food cultures from their analysis.[78] In spite of efforts to promote Caribbean food since the 1990s, Caribbean recipes in Nicaraguan cookbooks have remained at the margins. Two books published around 2005 contain only a small section of Caribbean recipes, among them rice and beans, rondón, and ginger beer.[79] The latest project on Caribbean food documented Caribbean recipes from 2012 and presented Caribbean culinary knowledge as a contribution to a "multinational and intercultural Nicaraguan society."[80]

Although autonomy legislation had established an ambitious framework, different national governments since the 1990s have continued to violate local authorities' rights at the Coast. In addition, many of the region's autonomous institutions such as the local universities lack sufficient financial resources. Persistent ignorance for the Coast's problems in Central Nicaragua still impedes an intercultural society with equal rights for all of its inhabitants.

Throughout its history, resource extraction, migration, and trade has transformed food and consumption habits at the Coast. With expanding mining, banana, and lumber businesses the region quickly became incorporated into the world economy. During this process of globalization in the late nineteenth century the region developed particularly strong links to the United States and the wider Caribbean. The separation of the Caribbean from the Nicaraguan nation ended formally in 1894 when President Zelaya intervened with the military in Bluefields to bring the Caribbean Coast under the control of the Nicaraguan nation. However, the social and cultural gap between Pacific and Caribbean Nicaragua persisted throughout the whole twentieth century and has influenced the region's movement for autonomy.

Historically, Nicaraguan Caribbean consumption patterns have been in constant motion. Different waves of foreign influence and migration as well as racial and class identifications have shaped and reshaped food practices. Since the seventeenth century, British settlers have been present at the Coast; waves of Caribbean migrations followed. In the late nineteenth century an enclave economy dominated by US enterprise developed. These external influences encountered a heterogeneous society of different indigenous and Afro-Caribbean cultures.

Historically, the regional food system at the Coast has relied on trade links to the wider Caribbean and the United States. People in Caribbean communities typically consume cassava, plantains, and rice as basic staples, adding imported products such as wheat flour, condensed milk, or margarine. Seafood has been an important source of protein. The boom-and-bust cycles of plantation economy and resource extraction over time as well as political developments contributed to a constantly changing local food system. To feed the large number of workers, from the 1920s onward producers expanded rice and beans cultivation in the Miskito communities along the Río Coco river. Through food rations and company stores, workers were exposed to imported processed foods. Although there were concerns about high prices and unequal access to these goods, people over the years idealized the abundance of imported foods during economic booms. Whenever economic or political circumstance disrupted regional food supply, people interpreted the unavailability of imported goods as a degradation. Nostalgia for the "golden age" of "company time" between the 1890s and the

1960s survived over decades. Revolutionary propaganda, however, attempted to depict those years as a period of foreign dependence and exploitation.

After this intense period of boom-and-bust cycles, the interest of the Somoza regime in resource extraction and the migration from Central Nicaragua led to increased interaction with the Nicaraguan nation. The Somoza regime's policy to expand resource extraction put the local food system once again under pressure. In Coast communities people increasingly sold seafood instead of consuming it and substituted this protein source with carbohydrates. Although national surveys rarely included the Caribbean, the limited evidence indicates higher malnutrition levels than in the rest of the country for the 1960s and 1970s. This was also true for the new peasant settler communities from Central Nicaragua that underwent a difficult process of adaptation to the new environment. The stronger presence of mestizo groups influenced local food culture and basic grains production, for example, by strengthening the production and consumption of corn and beans. The earthquake in 1972 provoked further migration to the agricultural frontier and hence increased pressure on local food resources.

Contrary to Pacific Nicaragua, however, the FSLN failed to gain a strong foothold at the Coast. People had ambivalent feelings toward the Somoza regime. Attachments to the United States were perceived by some people as a positive of the Somoza government while others criticized its exploitation of natural resources and hispanization efforts. Since the 1960s Miskito organizations demanded equal access to the (limited) social state services. Mobilization along ethnic lines increased throughout the Coast in the 1970s, which facilitated resistance against the Sandinistas in the 1980s.

At the Coast, people responded to Sandinista food policy more negatively than in most of Nicaragua. Caribbean communities as well as settlers in the interior rejected state intervention in food production and distribution. From early on, political conflicts and the Contra War affected local food production, which undermined efforts to strengthen local self-sufficiency. Only when the negotiations on autonomy advanced did the Sandinistas adapt their food campaigns to local circumstances. How people received these efforts in Coast communities would benefit from further research. Nevertheless, letters to the regional Sandinista newspaper suggest that people were highly dissatisfied with high prices and the scarcity of certain products.

Early on, the Sandinistas drafted a development project "for the Coast" that failed to meet local expectations and hence became unpopular in the region. Many people considered nationalization an inappropriate and risky attempt by the government to intervene in food distribution. Furthermore, the Contra War and resettlement of communities quickly weakened local food production. People in these settlements were cut off from traditional supply sources and mostly depended on food aid. As the Coast was one of the war zones, the government decided to maintain food subsidies longer than in the rest of the country. However, complaints about supply and food prices were expressed openly in the local Sandinista publication, revealing higher discontent but also a more difficult supply situation than in other parts of the country.

The conditions at the Coast in the 1980s also provided in-between space for consumers to assert their autonomy. FSLN propaganda continuously attacked conspicuous consumption, but Caribbean people insisted on their right to sell seafood to their traditional export markets and engaged in smuggling to assure their access to foreign currency. Nevertheless, traditional trade links to the United States and other Caribbean areas had been weakened significantly, which also limited access to important ingredients for Caribbean dishes.

Hurricane Joan cast a dark shadow over the transition years at the Coast. Transition was a period of reconstruction, dependency on external aid, returning refugees, and the movement toward autonomy. Enthusiasm for autonomy soon converted into disillusionment as the national government ignored the needs of people at the Coast and violated the rights of the regional governments. Again, resource extraction seriously affected local food production. Nonetheless, the autonomy process and tourism generated interest in the documentation of Caribbean food cultures. Although US anthropologists in the 1960s perceived Miskito diets as stable, more recent research has focused on creolization and culinary change. These trends carry the risk of idealizing cultural fusions and ignoring power asymmetries, however. The massive migration of Central Nicaraguan mestizos to the Coast influenced food consumption in the second half of the twentieth century while Caribbean food only seldom found its way to the Pacific.

NICARAGUA'S ROLE IN THE DEBATES ON FOOD SECURITY AND FOOD SOVEREIGNTY, 1980S–2019

"There is hunger in the 'Zero Hunger' country." This was the title of a 2017 piece in the oppositional paper *Confidencial* analyzing the latest FAO report on food security in Latin America. In Nicaragua still, more than one million people (17 percent of the population) were undernourished despite the Ortega government's Zero Hunger program. The author claimed that the Nicaraguan diet had become more limited, consisting mainly of rice, maize, plantains, sugar, milk, and beans. By comparison to average meat and milk consumption in neighboring countries, Nicaragua had fallen behind. The author concluded that thousands of families in Nicaragua faced the daily drama of hunger, empty stomachs, and hardship.[1] By contrast, government officials publicly highlighted Nicaragua as a showcase for its successful food policy, most notably the Zero Hunger program, a food sovereignty law, and decreasing malnutrition.[2]

How did the Nicaraguan revolution contribute to understanding food security as a basic right and to the rise of a global peasant movement for food sovereignty? The debates over food security and food sovereignty were closely intertwined in Nicaragua between the 1980s and the 2010s. Although peasant activists did not establish "food sovereignty" as a term until the 1990s, Sandinista food policy and peasants' activism foreshadowed some of the important aims of the food sovereignty movement. Despite the setbacks of the 1980s the revolutionary experience laid the foundation for an approach to food policy that is, in some ways, distinctive. The Sandinista revolution left a legacy of peasant networks who reorganized in the 1990s and mobilized to improve the social situation in the Nicaraguan countryside, for example, in access to land, health service, and education.

These networks contributed to the foundation of the global peasant movement La Vía Campesina and the campaign for a food sovereignty law in Nicaragua.[3]

Because of the close cooperation between the Sandinistas and FAO, food security entered the political debates in Nicaragua in the early 1980s. In 1987 the Nicaraguan constitution included food security—as the right of Nicaraguans to be protected against hunger—with a state guarantee for adequate availability and equitable distribution. At that time, however, the Sandinistas were unable to ensure access to basic grains, milk, and meat. During the late 1980s widespread food insecurity reappeared in Nicaragua because of the economic crisis, natural disasters, and the decline of support from Eastern bloc countries. And the Sandinistas lost the 1990 elections as a result.

Food sovereignty supporters aimed at politicizing the international debate over food production and consumption. Food security is concerned with the general availability of food, but for the food sovereignty movement it also matters where and how food is produced. In 1980s Nicaraguan political discourse, the term "food sovereignty" did not appear, but some elements of Sandinista food policy anticipated demands subsequently raised by the food sovereignty movement. These demands were the result of emphasis on local consumption and production, on agrarian reform, and on the right to define the local food system autonomously. Peasant activists continued to use food security in their practical work into the early twenty-first century. Field research in Honduras and Nicaragua has demonstrated that peasant leaders found sovereignty more difficult to pronounce and explain. Hence, peasant activists transformed the political messages of the concept into an easier language and still used the concept of food security.[4]

In Nicaragua food insecurity remained an important problem throughout the 1990s. International donors, among them FAO, were deterred by the Chamorro government's lack of interest in food policy despite the disastrous situation in Nicaragua. During the early 1990s basic grains production stagnated, and hunger continued to affect Nicaraguan people, especially in the rural north. Around 1995 food production recovered but still was insufficient to feed the growing population of 4.65 million inhabitants.[5] Given the difficult situation of small producers in the early 1990s, peasant organizations started to mobilize for a different food policy inspired by peasants' needs.

PEASANT ACTIVISM FOR FOOD SOVEREIGNTY AS REVOLUTIONARY HERITAGE

The revolution left a strong heritage of peasant activism and education programs in Nicaragua. This history made Nicaragua an important place for the global and regional food sovereignty movement, which intensified in the 1990s. Some researchers have even characterized Nicaragua as the movement's "birthplace," but other Central American peasant organizations also contributed to the movement's rise.[6] Through improved access to university education and political activism, beginning in the 1970s a new generation of peasant leaders arose in Central America, including Nicaragua. The anthropologist Marc Edelman has characterized these leaders as "a type of peasant intellectual" and underscores their practical knowledge of agricultural production combined with their university education.[7]

The Programa de Campesino a Campesino (From peasant to peasant), the popular education initiative, was also influential. The basic idea of this movement was that local community members would teach their fellows and promote their knowledge in other peasant communities. This movement extended from 1970s Guatemala throughout Central America and Mexico. In 1986 Mexican promoters came to Nicaragua and founded the first de Campesino a Campesino program in Nicaragua, with support from organizations such as UNAG, Oxfam, and the Ford Foundation. Given the organizational support by UNAG and the revolutionary context, the network grew quickly and inspired international visitors from Latin America and Europe to promote similar initiatives. The international networks strengthened at a time when global support for Nicaraguan food policy waned. At the local level, peasant networks in the late 1980s continued to grow as a result of the economic crisis and the erosion of state support, which included the end to state programs providing agricultural supplies to communities. By 1991 Nicaraguan activists had already organized more than five hundred workshops for around three thousand peasants.[8]

These peasant initiatives in Nicaragua and Central America more generally were the catalyst for the food sovereignty movement. In 1992 UNAG organized its second congress in Managua, and it was attended by members of numerous farmer organizations from Europe, the Caribbean, Latin America, and North America. The meeting's final resolutions denounced neoliberalism as intolerable, given that increasing competition through imports and the preference for large-scale agriculture endangered the very existence of small peasants. Instead, the delegates called for a new vision for food policy, a vision from below, developed by the peasants themselves and oriented toward the needs of rural communities.[9]

The 1992 meeting of peasants in Nicaragua was an important predecessor to the 1993 meeting of peasant activist groups in Mons, Belgium, where the transnational peasant organization La Vía Campesina (the peasant way) was founded, with Asociación de Trabajadores en el Campo (ATC, the Association of Farm Workers) and UNAG, two Nicaraguan organizations, among the founding members. This shows again the impact of Nicaraguan peasant networks. In subsequent years, the movement maintained its strong focus on education and close links to rural communities. The borders between NGOs, peasant organizations, and researchers are sometimes difficult to identify.[10] Since 1996, when La Vía Campesina started its global campaign for food sovereignty, the concept increasingly influenced political debates in Nicaragua.[11] At the same time, however, the political environment became less favorable to peasant activism.

By the late 1990s the FSLN had already abandoned the aim of revolutionary change and entered a political pact with the governing Partido Liberal Constitucionalista (PLC), the Constitutionalist Liberal Party. Under President Arnoldo Alemán (1997–2002), Nicaraguan food policy focused on fighting the consequences of Hurricane Mitch, which hit the country in 1998, and the resulting food crisis. Corruption scandals discredited ENABAS, and President Alemán exploited food aid for electoral purposes. In this setting, peasant organizations became less influential in national politics and turned their attention to regional and local issues.[12]

LEGAL INITIATIVES FOR FOOD SECURITY AND FOOD SOVEREIGNTY

Nevertheless, the Sandinista deputy Dora Zeledón launched the first initiative for a food security law in 1997. The proposal rejected the perception of food as merchandise and suggested that 50 percent of Nicaragua's food supply should be provided by national production. Food aid distribution that the law considered as "unfair competition" to local production would be limited to exceptional supply crises resulting from natural disasters and other unforeseen events.[13] In the years after 1997 the initial proposal was modified several times, but the government of President Enrique Bolaños (2002–2007) still remained unwilling to pass the legislation.

In Nicaragua the concept of food sovereignty gained influence after the 2001 World Forum on Food Sovereignty. After that, the Nicaraguan delegates promoted food sovereignty in peasant organizations and civil society initiatives such as Soynica. As a result, La Vía Campesina member organizations began to discuss a new initiative for a food sovereignty law. In 2004 forty organizations from Nicaraguan civil society founded the Grupo de Interés Soberanía y Seguridad Alimentaria y Nutricional (GISSAN), the Food and Nutrition Sovereignty and Security Interest Group, which promoted the law. As the name of the group indicates, the debate over concepts continued among supporters of the initiative, because the term "food security" seemed more familiar and concrete to many of them. In 2005 GISSAN member organizations worked out a new draft for a law that Deputy Wálmaro Gutiérrez (FSLN) introduced to the National Assembly in 2006.[14] In 2006, thanks to electoral reforms established during the pact period, Daniel Ortega won the elections with 38 percent of the vote and became president again. When the National Assembly discussed the law in June 2007, the new Ortega government was already in power.

Researchers have characterized Daniel Ortega's second presidency as a new *caudillismo* or a "populist left regime with hybrid economic features."[15] Contrary to other left-wing Latin American governments, he maintained more institutional continuity and refrained from a strong redistributive policy, eschewing nationalizations, land reform, and price controls. He built up a strong alliance with large enterprise, partially consisting of those FSLN members who had enriched themselves in 1990. As between 1990 and 2006, agro exports have remained concentrated among a few large players under the Ortega government.[16] This political climate explains why the final food sovereignty law assigned a leading role to the state and sought a compromise with entrepreneurs.

The legislation prompted contentious debates in 2007, and deputies of the National Assembly rejected the law during its second reading. The private sector was particularly opposed to Article 5 of the law, which prohibited imports of genetically modified food. The business community feared that the law would also affect the implementation of the Central America Free Trade Agreement (CAFTA) and hence convinced PLC members to oppose the project. After the first initiative failed in 2007, FAO joined the effort, which deradicalized the law project. Those articles permitting the creation of grain reserves and price regulations were eliminated from the draft legislation. In addition, Article 9 of the law clearly established that state policies should not touch free enterprise and commerce, which meant a surrender to market mechanisms.[17] Contrary to the original intentions of the food sovereignty project, Article 9 envisioned food policies where the state takes a leading role.[18] The deradicalization of the law reflected the government's interest in avoiding further conflicts with the private sector and the IMF. While discussions about the legislation continued, the government launched the Zero Hunger program as a core element of its antipoverty policy. The basis for this policy was the new alliance among Latin American countries with left-wing governments, with the Alianza Bolivariana para los Pueblos de Nuestra América—Tratado de Comercio de los Pueblos (ALBA-TCP), the Bolivarian Alliance for the Peoples of Our America—Peoples' Trade Treaty, whose funding permitted expansive social policy initiatives (until Venezuela entered a deep economic crisis in 2013).[19] Nonetheless, Venezuelan support and the new social programs improved the nutritional situation in Nicaragua between 2007 and 2015.

NICARAGUAN FOOD POLICY BETWEEN 2007 AND 2019

The Zero Hunger program aimed at improving the food security of peasant families through material support. Its name was inspired by the Brazilian *Fome Zero* program. Launched in 2003 by President Luiz Inácio Lula da Silva, Fome Zero included cash transfers to poor families, favorable interest rates to family farmers, and a school meals program. Whether the focus on peasant farmers was the result of lessons learned in the 1980s or simply an attempt to jump on the bandwagon of the Brazilian initiative remains subject to further research.[20] The Nicaraguan project, however, had a narrower focus than the Brazilian program, mainly providing peasants with the necessary supplies for food production. Initially, it distributed animals, seeds, and construction material to seventy-five thousand peasant families. The government included women with access to some land who would participate in education programs and would promise to pay back 20 percent to a rural development fund.

The focus on individual beneficiaries had its weaknesses. At the micro level the program improved beneficiaries' access to food. At the macro level, however, it was not incorporated into a broader strategy against malnutrition and failed to address problems such as access to land, education, and health in rural areas. Critics bemoaned the program's lack of transparency with regard to the selection of beneficiaries and accused the Sandinistas of political favoritism. A 2007–2008 evaluation suggests that the selection criteria for the program were too vague and allowed political considerations to play a role.[21] In a 2014 survey in Matagalpa department researchers observed that, with reduced funding, state technical assistance for beneficiaries had declined. In several communities women expressed feelings of abandonment, which led to lower participation in Zero Hunger activities.[22]

Beyond the Zero Hunger program, the Ortega administration also relaunched urban gardening projects and cooking competitions and strengthened the tradition of corn festivals. This revived some initiatives of the 1980s Sandinista food policy.[23] Although similar in names and rhetoric, the framework for the Ortega government's food policy in the early twenty-first century differs from the framework of the 1980s. The Sandinistas based their policy on the idea of the mixed economy, but the Ortega government and the new Sandinista economic elites have accepted capitalism and adapted their policies accordingly, taking care not to endanger agreements with the IMF or to violate CAFTA rules. Unlike other Latin American left-wing governments, the Ortega government has not embarked on profound changes in economic structures or land distribution. Instead, it refers rhetorically to projects from the 1980s and relates them to food sovereignty as in the case of the corn festivals.

After 2007 Sandinista leaders frequently referred to maize as the basis for food sovereignty. Corn festivals had continued uninterrupted at the regional level since the Sandinista defeat in 1990, and they gained a more touristic character. Especially in Jalapa and Matagalpa the tradition remained strong. In the early twenty-first century, their mottos emphasized Nicaragua's role as a significant corn producer, for example with "The Large Cornfield of Nicaragua" (2008) or "Jalapa with Its Corn . . . The Pride of My Country!" (2009).[24] At the 2011 corn festival in Matagalpa, the local FSLN mayor specifically discussed the food sovereignty movement. He argued that it was necessary to rescue Nicaraguan culinary practices for future generations; according to him, food was a cultural heritage and its protection was part of Nicaraguan food sovereignty.[25] Nonetheless, government officials were using food sovereignty in their political discourse while they were simultaneously strengthening the agro-export sector. Coffee, cattle, and sugar exports increased significantly between 2006 and 2014. As in earlier decades, these projects occupied large plots of lands and were commercialized by a small group of elites.[26]

Although the Zero Hunger program showed some favorable results in rural communities, malnutrition remains an important problem in Nicaragua. Between 2007 and 2015 the economic upsurge, foreign aid, and the government's social policy led to a reduction in malnutrition. According to FAO data malnutrition has reduced from 22.3 percent in 2007 to 16.6 percent in 2015. Since then, however, the rate stagnated at around 17 percent between 2016 and 2018. Nicaragua is one of the countries with the highest rates of malnutrition in Latin America.[27] Undernourishment still affects more than one million Nicaraguans. More detailed data on child malnutrition or food availability for the years 2017–2019 is difficult to obtain under the current political administration in Nicaragua.[28] However, it is likely that people clearly perceive the growing gap between the government's success stories of food sovereignty and the growing food insecurity.

Overall, the Sandinista revolution of the 1980s has left an ambivalent heritage for food security and food sovereignty. On the one hand it empowered peasants to organize in their struggle for land and access to resources. The education initiatives created in the 1980s survived the Sandinista electoral defeat and contributed to the rise of a global peasant movement. Faced with adverse conditions in the late 1980s, these peasants also utilized traditional methods of farming without relying on high-yielding seeds.

However, the revolution's relationship to peasants was tense and contradictory. The perception of the peasantry as backward survived among

FSLN leaders. Some of these leaders also became active in food policy after 2007, bringing with them a focus on large-scale agriculture. It is no surprise that FSLN politicians, in cooperation with FAO, deradicalized the suggestions from the food sovereignty movement and instead created a law that assigned the state a key role in food security. The law also tried to avoid conflicts with agrobusiness and international financial organizations. Although the Ortega government revived some initiatives from the 1980s, the FSLN's food policy after 2007 never proposed a radical turning toward equal food supply, giving priority to basic grains, or making changes in economic structures. With the Ortega regime's repression of independent social movements during recent years, the possibilities for peasant activism have been far more limited.

The history of food security and food sovereignty are closely intertwined in Nicaragua. Food security for all Nicaraguans was a promise of the 1979 revolution. The concept came to Nicaragua with growing FAO presence and was widely used in international cooperation. In 1987 the idea entered the Nicaraguan constitution, paradoxically at a time when the revolution was far from guaranteeing access to basic food to Nicaraguan people. Food security was also an important aim of the international development cooperation after the World Food Crisis of the early 1970s. Initially, members of the international nutrition community perceived revolutionary Nicaragua as a country that took food policy seriously and hence supported many projects for basic grains production, rural education, and food processing. By the late 1980s, however, international nutrition experts had become disillusioned with a food policy eroded by war, scarce resources, and poor administration. This disillusionment continued during the early 1990s when the Nicaraguan government neglected food policy despite widespread malnutrition.

Although the Nicaraguan governments in the 1990s produced vague documents on food policy, peasants increasingly mobilized both for access to land and against cheap food imports that endangered their existence. They criticized the apolitical discourse of development cooperation on food security and introduced food sovereignty as an alternative project to advance their demands. Food sovereignty would not only establish a priority for local food production and consumption but also promote peasants' land rights and autonomy. However, food security survived as a political promise and as a legal framework. Accordingly, the Nicaraguan law included both food security and food sovereignty as political aims. This broad approach allowed diverse actors to identify with and support the project. The Ortega administration appropriated food sovereignty as a political project, but in fact it has pursued a contradictory food policy, supporting free trade agreements and agro exports.

NOTES

INTRODUCTION

1. The FSLN was founded in 1961 as a guerrilla organization. Inspired by the successful Cuban revolution, a small group of young Nicaraguans took up the fight against the Somoza dictatorship. At first the group focused on guerrilla activities, but they gained broader support in the second half of the 1970s. The final offensive against the Somoza regime started in June 1979.

2. Translation from Spanish original. Transcription from my sound recording at the event.

3. INIDE and MINSA, "Encuesta Nicaragüense," 39.

4. Close, *Navigating*, 125–55. According to the independent Nicaraguan Fundación Internacional para el Desafío Económico Global (FIDEG), the International Foundation for the Global Economic Challenge, poverty levels in Nicaragua have decreased from 44.7 percent (2009) to 41.2 percent (2017). The FIDEG statistics are based on a poverty definition of daily expenditures of less than $2.40 per day. By contrast, the Instituto Nacional de Información de Desarrollo (INIDE), the Nicaraguan Institute of Development Information, works with a poverty definition of less than $1.71 per day and hence reported lower poverty rates of 24.9 percent in 2016. FIDEG, "Encuesta," 9; INIDE, "Reporte," 7; CEPAL, "Preliminary Overview."

5. FAO-STAT refers to an average of 1.0 million undernourished people between 2015 and 2017 and 1.1 million people between 2016 and 2018. The prevalence of undernourishment was on average 16.9 percent between 2015 and 2017 and 17 percent between 2016 and 2018. This data, however, does not provide information by individual year. FAO, "Food and Agriculture"; Olivares, "Hambre y pobreza."

6. FAO, IFAD, UNICEF, WFP, and WHO, *State of Food Security*, 182.

7. Inter-American Commission on Human Rights, "Special Monitoring." The commission estimates 328 victims, but Nicaraguan human rights organizations have estimated more than 650 victims.

8. Banco Central de Nicaragua, *Informe Anual 2018*, xi. Reliable data under the current conditions is difficult to obtain. The latest FAO report lacks the 2018 data for prevalence of severe food insecurity as well as child malnutrition. FAO, OPS, WFP, and UNICEF, *Panorama*, 129.

9. The economist János Kornai who analyzed the historical development of economies in Eastern Europe since the 1950s coined the term "shortage economy." It refers to chronic privation of important goods as a result of the economy's structure. Tomka, *Social History*, 242.

10. On the history of US imperialism, see Gobat, *Confronting the American Dream*; Grandin, *Empire's Workshop*, 22–33.

11. See, for example, Randall, *Todas estamos despiertas*. For an analysis of testimonial writings in Nicaragua, see Mackenbach, *Die unbewohnte Utopie*, 90–104.

12. Gobat, "La Reconstrucción histórica." For autobiographies, see Ramírez, *Adiós muchachos*; Belli, *Country under My Skin*; Cardenal, *La revolución perdida*. In 1995 dissident Sandinistas founded a new party, the Movimiento de Renovación Sandinista. For testimonies, see Bendaña, *Una tragedia campesina*; Ferrero Blanco, *De un lado*; Soto Joya, *Ventanas en la memoria*; Rueda Estrada, "Sandinismo."

13. Ferrero Blanco, *De un lado*; Selser, *Banderas y harapos*; Francis, *Nicaraguan Exceptionalism*; Close, Martí i Puig, and McConnell, *Sandinistas*; Aguilar Antunes, DeGori, and Villacorta, *Nicaragua en crisis*; Gould, "Ambivalent Memories."

14. Francis, "Introduction"; Francis, "Difference the Revolution Made"; Cooper, "Grassroots"; Martí i Puig, "Nicaragua: The Roots."

15. Anderson, "Health Care"; Ommen, "Sandinista Revolution"; Perla, "Heirs of Sandino"; Christiaens, "Between Diplomacy"; Helm, *Botschafter der Revolution*.

16. There are only a few long-term analyses of economic elites and agrarian change. See Spalding, "Los empresarios"; Marti i Puig and Baumeister, "Agrarian Policies."

17. Francis, "Introduction."

18. Siegrist, "Konsum, Kultur," 16; Douglas and Isherwood, *World of Goods*.

19. Ritzer, *McDonaldization of Society*.

20. Emilce María Vega Sandoval, interview by author, León, September 2012. I have changed all the names of all my interviewees.

21. Friedman, "Hybridzation of Roots"; Stewart, "Creolization."

22. Wilk, *Home Cooking*, 10–14; Welsch, "Transculturality"; Ernst and Freitag, "Einleitung." On the possibilities for applying transcultural approaches to historical research, see Herren-Oesch, Rüesch, and Sibille, *Transcultural History*.

23. "Henceforward there is no longer anything absolutely foreign. Everything is within reach." Welsch, "Transculturality," 198. For a critical position arguing that Western academic discourse idealizes hybridity, see Beushausen, Brüske, Commichau, Helber, and Kloß, "Caribbean (on the) Dining Table."

24. Mintz, "Zur Beziehung," 64–66; Wilk, "Consumer Goods," 37.

25. Higman, *Concise History*, 7; Wilk, *Home Cooking*; Beushausen, Brüske, Commichau, Helber, and Kloß, *Caribbean Food*; Higman, *Jamaican Food*.

26. Officially, the Caribbean regions have belonged to the Nicaraguan nation since 1894. Most historical publications focus almost exclusively on Central and Pacific Nicaragua. See, for example, Booth, *The End*; Enríquez, *Harvesting Change*; Gould, *Aquí todos mandamos*; Dore, *Myths of Modernity*; González-Rivera, *Before the Revolution*; Close, *Navigating*. By contrast, anthropological research has focused often exclusively on the Caribbean. See Pineda, *Shipwrecked Identities*; Hale, *Resistance and Contradiction*; Gordon, *Disparate Diasporas*.

27. Pilcher, "Introduction," 6–7.

28. Streeter, "Liberal Developmentalism."

29. Cullather, *Hungry World*, 42–44; Siegel, *Hungry Nation*, 12–13.

30. Barrett and Maxwell, *Food Aid*, 37–39. World Food Programme (WFP) statistical data shows that the value of WFP commitments in Latin America increased significantly between 1966 and 1971. Shaw, *UN World Food Programme*, 255.

31. Pernet, "L'UNICEF," 35; Peña Torres, *Historia de la salud*, 128.

32. Garst and Barry, *Feeding the Crisis*; Brockett, "Right to Food"; Barry and Preusch, *Soft War*.

33. Cullather, *Hungry World*, 7; Harwood, "Peasant Friendly Plant Breeding," 384–410; Sonnenfeld, "Mexico." The Alliance for Progress was a US development initiative for the Latin American region that was launched in 1961 by President John F. Kennedy.

34. For an overview on the debates, see Cullather, "Development?"; Cooper, "Writing the History."

35. Cullather, "Foreign Policy"; Porter, *Trust in Numbers*.

36. Biltekoff, "Critical Nutrition."

37. By 1939 Argentina, Chile, Cuba, Mexico, Peru, Uruguay, and Venezuela had established national nutrition councils. Pernet, "Developing Nutritional Standards." For the debates in 1930s Peru, see Drinot, "Food, Race."

38. Yates-Doerr, "Intervals of Confidence."

39. At that time, the FAO defined food security as "availability at all times of adequate world food supplies of basic foodstuffs to sustain a steady expansion of food consumption and to offset fluctuations in production and prices." United Nations, "World Food Conference." For early FAO history, see Jachertz, "To Keep Food."

40. See Article 63 of the 1987 Nicaraguan Constitution, Asamblea Nacional Constituyente, "Constitución Política de 1987."

41. Ganuza and Vilas, "Nicaragua," 11–13, 54–55.

42. FAO statistics rely mainly on information provided by national governments in their statistical publications or in a special FAO questionnaire. If official

data was missing, FAO also utilized unofficial sources or statistical material from international organizations.

43. Access to archival documents in Nicaragua varies according to political circumstances and the situation of individual archives. The papers of some former Sandinista leaders, such as Sergio Ramírez or Ernesto Cardenal, have been moved to US library collections.

CHAPTER ONE: GROWING TENSIONS

1. Scrimshaw, "Los problemas nutricionales"; Álvarez Montalván, "Requerimientos."

2. Polèse, "Ciudades y empleos," 19.

3. Asamblea Nacional Constituyente, "Constitución Política de Nicaragua," Article 201.

4. Ferrero Blanco, *La Nicaragua de los Somoza*, 617.

5. Walter, *Regime of Anastasio Somoza*, xvii, 116.

6. While fascism spread in Germany and Italy, Franklin D. Roosevelt declared in 1933 a new era of foreign relations with Latin America: the era of the Good Neighbor Policy. He publicly repudiated the right to intervention as established in the 1904 Roosevelt Corollary, withdrew troops and financial advisers from the Caribbean, and intensified trade relations.

7. Friedman, *Nazis*, 182–83.

8. In Guatemala the fall of Jorge Ubico resulted in free elections, which were won by reformers, but the opening in El Salvador remained far more limited and short-term.

9. Gambone, *Eisenhower*, 32–35; Peña Torres, *Historia de la salud*, 112–28.

10. Rabe, *Killing Zone*, 85–96, 149–52; Staten, *History of Nicaragua*, 63–67; Booth, *The End*, 71–95.

11. Ferrero Blanco, *La Nicaragua de los Somoza*, 518, 541–42, 578–98, 615–22; Walker, *Nicaragua: Living*, 86.

12. Growth rates varied from 3 percent to 3.26 percent between 1950 and 1980. United Nations, "Department of Economic," DataQuery.

13. González-Rivera, *Before the Revolution*, 12, 161; Booth, *The End*, 104–14.

14. Gould, *Aquí todos mandamos*.

15. Wünderich, *Sandino*, 31; FIDA, "Informe de la Mision Especial," vi; Barraclough, *Preliminary Analysis*, 29–31; Radell, " Historical Geography," 22–30.

16. Gould, *Aquí todos mandamos*, 27, 45–50, 233.

17. Gould, *Aquí todos mandamos*, 89.

18. Biondi-Morra, *Revolución y política*, 49, 57–59; Booth, *The End*, 60–66.

19. Bulmer-Thomas, *Political Economy*, 162; CIERA, *La reforma agraria*, 26, 52.

20. Vilas, *State, Class and Ethnicity*, 62–66, 72–75; Barraclough, *Preliminary Analysis*, 19–21; Biondi-Morra, *Revolución y política*, 56–59.

21. Bulmer-Thomas, *Political Economy*, 105–10.

22. Laure, "Nicaragua: Salarios mínimos," 45.

23. Bulmer-Thomas, *Political Economy*, 189.

24. The Central American Common Market (CACM) was founded in 1960 and included Guatemala, El Salvador, Nicaragua, Honduras, and from 1962 also Costa Rica. After the initial golden years of the 1960s, the alliance entered into deep crisis in the late 1960s. Bulmer-Thomas, *Political Economy*, 180–205; Antonio Ramírez, "Comercio de alimentos," 73.

25. "No hay tortilla, no sirve." Rina Méndez Osorno, interview by author, León, September 2012.

26. Wilk and Barbosa, "Unique Dish"; Preston-Werner, "Defending National Foodways."

27. Ximena Cubero, interview by author, León, September 2012; Marlen Jimena Guillén Mora, interview by author, Managua, August 2012. For typical meals in 1954, see Flores, Caputti, and Leytón, "Estudios dietéticos," 6–10; Romero, "El inventor de la Kola Shaler," 186.

28. Ximena Cubero, interview by author, León, September 2012. See also Emilce María Vega Sandoval, interview by author, León, September 2012; Rina Méndez Osorno, interview by author, León, September 2012.

29. Gabriel Diego, interview by author, León, September 2012.

30. Rina Méndez Osorno, interview by author, León, September 2012; Emilce María Vega Sandoval, interview by author, León, September 2012.

31. The archiving of culinary literature in Nicaraguan libraries is poor. Some books survive only in US libraries, such as de Pasos, *Cocina nicaragüense*.

32. Ramírez, *Lo que sabe*, 24.

33. Vivas, *Cocina Nica*, 44; Montes Orozco, *Una pizca de amor y sabor*, 40–41.

34. Translation from Spanish originals. Coronel Urtecho, "Elogio de la cocina," 30; Ramírez, *Lo que sabe*, 18. Both writers have expressed their concerns about the potential loss of traditional recipes: Coronel Urtecho in the 1960s and Ramírez in 2014.

35. Ramírez, *Lo que sabe*, 18; Coronel Urtecho, "Elogio de la cocina," 30.

36. Flores, Caputti, and Leytón, "Estudios dietéticos"; Flores, "Estudios dietéticos."

37. Nestle and Nesheim, *Why Calories*, 86–89.

38. Pernet, "FAO."

39. INCAP, "Recomendaciones nutricionales," 119.

40. On FAO standards, see Nestle and Nesheim, *Why Calories*, 121–22. In San Isidro 72 percent of families did not consume the estimated daily need of calories and 58 percent of proteins. In Managua it was 53 percent for calories and 47 percent for proteins. Flores, "Estudios dietéticos," 44; Flores, Caputti, and Leytón, "Estudios dietéticos," 14.

41. Álvarez Montalván, "Requerimientos," 19.

42. This debate already has a long history. For example, in Britain these arguments have been raised since the 1890s and led to social controversies between the conservative government and labor opposition during the 1930s.

43. Álvarez Montalván, "Requerimientos."

44. Ramiro Arcia, "La desnutrición," 16.

45. Translation from Spanish original. Cuadra, *El nicaragüense*, 28, 29.

46. Polèse, "Ciudades y empleos," 19.

47. Tagle, "Cambios en los patrones"; Flores, "Food Patterns."

48. "La Historia de Supermercados," 2–3; Romero, "El inventor de la Kola Shaler," 186.

49. "La Historia de Supermercados," 2–3; Romero, "El inventor de la Kola Shaler," 186; König, *Kleine Geschichte*, 88–95.

50. Translation from Spanish original. Coronel Urtecho, "Elogio de la cocina," 34.

51. Beverley and Zimmerman, *Literature and Politics*, 59–66.

52. Whisnant, *Rascally Signs*, 148; Barrientos Tecún, "Acerca de las concepciones."

53. Colburn, *My Car*, 20–23. The fast food industry surged in the United States during the 1950s. The tendency to consume cheap, rapidly prepared food in simple restaurants, however, was increasing in various industrialized societies from the late nineteenth century on. It was a response to increased mobility and new working environments. König, *Kleine Geschichte*, 111–21.

54. *Nicaragua guía oficial de turismo*, 14.

55. *La Prensa*, November 5, 1971, 6, November 20, 1971, 3.

56. Vogl Baldizón, *Nicaragua con amor*, 133–38.

57. Pérez, *On Becoming Cuban*, 365–69; Rinke, *Begegnungen*, 396.

58. Pilcher, "Industrial Tortillas," 223.

59. Argüello Hüper, "Ciudad de Managua," 53; Gambone, *Capturing the Revolution*, 83–84.

60. Gambone, *Capturing the Revolution*, 27–31; Dosal, "Accelerating Development," 75–77.

61. Dosal, "Accelerating Development," 83.

62. Gambone, *Capturing the Revolution*, 87–88.

63. Whitted, "Analytical Description"; Dosal, "Accelerating Development," 83–89.

64. Gambone, *Capturing the Revolution*, 235–36.

65. INCAP and ICNND, *Nutritional Evaluation*, 1–4.

66. INCAP and ICNND, *Nutritional Evaluation*, v–ix.

67. INCAP, *Evaluación nutricional*, 53.

68. INCAP, *Evaluación nutricional*, 13. The term "protein gap" was used to explain the different nutritional situation of industrialized and poor countries whose

inhabitants had little access to animal proteins. The Protein Advisory Group, an expert body founded in 1955 to guide international organizations working on nutrition, spread this interpretation further. Nalibow Ruxin, "Hunger, Science, and Politics," 276–77.

69. INCAP and ICNND, *Nutritional Evaluation*, 7, 122.

70. INCAP and ICNND, *Nutritional Evaluation*, 16.

71. INCAP, *Evaluación nutricional*, 10–11; INCAP and ICNND, *Nutritional Evaluation*, 29. The calculations were based on requirements of 2,700 kcal for men with a weight of 55 kg and 2,000 kcal for women with a weight of 50 kg. INCAP and ICNND, *Nutritional Evaluation*, 143.

72. The calculation was based on 1965 food production and the INCAP recommendation for basic food intakes. INCAP, *Evaluación nutricional*, 60.

73. USAID, "Memorandum for the Development Assistance Executive Committee, Loan Title: Nutrition Improvement," January 22, 1975.

74. Flores, Menchú, Lara, and Béhar, "Dieta adecuada."

CHAPTER TWO: TENSIONS REVEALED

1. Draft, "Nicaragua: 1972 Earthquake," December 26, 1972, box 401, "Fact Sheet: CARE Nicaragua Earthquake Fund," December 26, 1972, box 22, both in CARE Archives; "Report on the Situation in Nicaragua," January 26, 1973, IODG 8 F 4/4, FAO Archives.

2. Kinzer, *Blood of Brothers*, 33; Diederich, *Somoza*, 96.

3. FSLN, *El programa histórico*.

4. Poyner and Strachan, "Nutrition Sector Assessment," preface.

5. INCAP, "Informe anual, 1968," 20; INCAP, "Informe anual, 1974," 41.

6. FAO, "Food and Agriculture"; INCAP, *Evaluación nutricional*, 60.

7. Translation from Spanish original. "Primer Congreso Nacional de Alimentación," 4, 15–16.

8. Josué de Castro (1908–1973) was a Brazilian physician. In 1951, he published his famous *Geopolítica da Fome*, which was translated into more than twenty languages, published in English as *The Geography of Hunger*.

9. Translation from Spanish original. "Primer Congreso Nacional de Alimentación," 13.

10. Poyner and Strachan, "Nutrition Sector Assessment," 54.

11. Poyner and Strachan, "Nutrition Sector Assessment," 53–55.

12. Friedman, "Political Economy of Food."

13. The law was changed significantly in 1990 and was replaced in 2008 by the Food for Peace Act.

14. Shaw, *World's Largest Humanitarian Agency*, 3–4.

15. Garst and Barry, *Feeding the Crisis*, 6–9.

16. Bobrow-Strain, "Making White Bread."

17. Gambone, *Capturing the Revolution*, 139–41.

18. USAID, "U.S. Overseas Loans."

19. CARE was founded in 1945 as a relief agency to support people in postwar Europe and turned to the distribution of food aid on a global level in the 1950s. The next decade was a period of geographical expansion for the agency. Wieters, *NGO CARE*.

20. Valenze, *Milk*, 253.

21. Flores, "Estudios dietéticos," 50; Patten, "Dairying in Nicaragua"; Sasson, "Milking the Third World?"

22. Catholic Relief Service Nicaragua, FY 1967, box 657, CARE Archives; "Summary of Nutrition Survey Results: Rio Plata," December 1974, box 184, CARE Archives.

23. Fred Anderson to William M. Langdon, March 7, April 5, 1968, box 678, CARE Archives.

24. Elinor Foulke to Mr. Coopold, February 25, 1975, box 1074; Linda Lafoley, End of Tour Report, box 174, CARE Archives.

25. Cam McIntyre, "Community Information and Opinions on Family Planning, Nutrition and Medicine in Proyecto Rigoberto Cabeza, Nicaragua," March 1974, box 184, CARE Archives.

26. Diane Trembly to Jack Cohen, March 22, 1977, box 752, CARE Archives.

27. For rumors, see Fred S. Anderson to Bertran D. Smucker, November 25, 1966, box 657, CARE Archives. For reselling donated food, see Garst and Barry, *Feeding the Crisis*, 68–69.

28. "Discursive Report, Nicaragua," March–May 1967, box 841, CARE Archives.

29. Fred Anderson to Bertran D. Smucker, August 11, 1967, box 80, CARE Archives; Merton F. Cregger, Memorandum to Bertran Smucker, May 16, 1968, box 401, CARE Archives (quote).

30. Ronald Burkard, "Self-Help Evaluation Report," November 21, 1968, box 678, CARE Archives. Ronald Burkard was assistant executive director of the Public and Donor Relations Department from 1979 to 1984.

31. "Discursive Report," Nicaragua, December 1967–February 1968, box 678, CARE Archives; James Puchetti to Peter Reitz, December 13, 1972, box 108, CARE Archives (quote).

32. The data collected by Joseph Laure demonstrates an increase from 100 (in 1972) to 141 in 1973 and 204 in 1977. Data for the period before 1972 was unavailable. Laure, "Nicaragua: Salarios mínimos," 45.

33. Translation from Spanish original. *La Prensa*, August 14, 1970, 10.

34. *La Prensa*, August 7, 1970, 1, 12.

35. Translation from Spanish original. *La Prensa*, May 4, 1972, 1, 8, May 6, 1972, 1, 8, May 8, 1972, 1, 16, May 9, 1972, 1, 8, May 13, 1972, 1, 12.

36. Ferrero Blanco, *La Nicaragua de los Somoza*, 318–33.

37. Nicasio was the protagonist of a comic strip created by Alberto Mora Olivares (1929–1974) that was published in *La Prensa*.

38. *La Prensa*, May 13, 1972, 11B.

39. *La Prensa*, May 21, 1972, 8.

40. *La Prensa*, August 20, 1972, 4, September 27, 1972, 1, 8, October 23, 1972, 1, 16.

41. Gerlach, "Die Welternährungskrise."

42. Translation from Spanish original. *La Prensa*, December 13, 1972, 1, 12.

43. *La Prensa*, December 6, 1972, 1, 10.

44. Ferrero Blanco, *La Nicaragua de los Somoza*, 143–50.

45. Report on Nicaragua, January 26, 1973, IODG 8, F.4.4, FAO Archives.

46. *Süddeutsche Zeitung*, January 2, 1973, PA AA 100678.

47. *La Prensa*, June 3, 1973, 1, 10, August 5, 1973, 15.

48. "Report on Nicaragua," January 26, 1973; "Present Situation of FAO Activities," March 6, 1973, both in IODG 8 F 4/4, FAO Archives.

49. Ferrero Blanco, *La Nicaragua de los Somoza*, 143–50; Diederich, *Somoza*, 96–100; "Botschaft Managua to AA," January 23, 1973, PA AA 100678.

50. Kinzer, *Blood of Brothers*, 33; Ferrero Blanco, *La Nicaragua de los Somoza*, 145. Tacho was a common nickname for Anastasio Somoza García; his son Somoza Debayle had the nickname Tachito.

51. "Director General's Brief, Visit of Dr. A. H. Boerma," August 1974, ODG Old FA 6/1 NIC, FAO Archives.

52. Ferrero Blanco, *La Nicaragua de los Somoza*, 146–50.

53. James J. Puccetti to Peter Reitz, April 5, 1974, box 108, CARE Archives.

54. Lee, "De-centring Managua"; Argüello Hüper, "La ciudad de Managua," 23–26.

55. *La Prensa*, July 24, 1973.

56. Mattelart, *Communicating in Popular Nicaragua*.

57. Tomlinson, *Cultural Imperialism*, 113–20; Rinke, *Begegnungen*, 447–49.

58. Argüello Hüper, "La ciudad de Managua," 21.

59. Translation from Spanish original. Téfel, *El infierno de los pobres*, 10. Téfel was minister for social welfare during the 1980s.

60. Téfel, *El infierno de los pobres*, 15; González de la Rocha, Jelin, Perlman, Roberts, Safa, and Ward, "From the Marginality."

61. Téfel, *El infierno de los pobres*, 86–88.

62. La Prensa, *85 años: Al servicio*, 65.

63. *La Prensa*, August 27, 1970, 19.

64. *La Prensa*, June 15, 1973, 4.

65. *La Prensa*, June 8, 1973, 2.

66. Translation from Spanish original. Téfel, *El infierno de los pobres*, 107.

67. Gobat, *Confronting the American Dream*.

68. Pezzullo and Pezzullo, *At the Fall of Somoza*, 13.

69. Ramírez, *Adiós muchachos*, 28.

70. Mora Olivares, *Nicasio 2*; Ramírez, *Adiós muchachos*, 28–31.

71. Poyner and Strachan, "Nutrition Sector Assessment," preface.

72. Poyner and Strachan, "Nutrition Sector Assessment," 9, 13–14, 20–23.

73. Nietschmann, *Between Land and Water*, 214–19.

74. Poyner and Strachan, "Nutrition Sector Assessment," 25–26, 32–34.

75. Staten, *History of Nicaragua*, 67–90; Rojas Bolaños, "La política," 133–56.

76. League of Red Cross Societies, "Relief Bureau Circular No. 768," September, 24, 1979, OSRO FP 5/3, FAO Archives.

77. Press Release, August 6, 1979, box 880; Ray Rigall, "Report No. 7," June 30, 1979, box 403, CARE Archives.

78. Juan Galecio Gómez to Yriat, July 12, 1979, OSRO FP 5/3, FAO Archives.

79. Kinzer, *Blood of Brothers*, 46.

CHAPTER THREE: THE ENTHUSIASTIC FOUNDING STAGE

1. Otto van Teutem, "Report on World Food Day," November 2, 1982, ESH WFD IN 4/9 NIC, FAO Archives. In 1979 FAO established the tradition of World Food Days as an instrument to raise global consciousness on world food problems.

2. Walker, *Nicaragua: Living*, 92. In the 1970s there were strong fluctuations in food imports with two temporary heights after the 1972 earthquake and in the late 1970s, especially in corn, sorghum, and wheat.

3. Collins, *Nicaragua: Was hat*, 9–10.

4. Prevost and Vanden, *Democracy and Socialism*, 103.

5. For parallels with Chile, see Frens-String, "Communists"; Melo Contreras, "Las Juntas de Abastecimiento," 111–26; for similarities between the Cuban Comités para la Defensa de la Revolución (CDR) and the Nicaraguan Comités de Defensa Sandinista (CDS), see Fagen, *Transformation*, 101–2; Collins, Scott, and Benjamin, *No Free Lunch*.

6. Booth, *The End*, 188–91.

7. The first junta was composed of three Sandinista leaders (Sergio Ramírez Mercado, Moisés Hassan Morales, and Daniel Ortega), Violeta Chamorro, the widow of Pedro Joaquín Chamorro, and businessman Alfonso Robelo Callejas who represented the Nicaraguan Democratic Movement. Because of political differences, Chamorro and Robelo left the junta in the first half of 1980. They were replaced by Arturo Cruz, a former IADB official, and Rafael Córdova from the Partido Conservador Demócrata (PCD), the Democratic Conservative Party. In 1981 the junta size was reduced to three members: Daniel Ortega, Sergio Ramírez, and Córdova. They remained in office until January 1985. The Consejo de Estado (State Council) was founded in May 1980. As an assembly with appointed delegates, it represented

a compromise between representative and participatory democracy. The council included representatives of political parties, mass organizations, unions, and private sector organizations. Prevost and Vanden, *Democracy and Socialism*, 72–74; Booth, *The End*, 186–87.

8. Prevost and Vanden, *Democracy and Socialism*, 51–57.

9. *Barricada*, January 17, 1980, 1, 12, January 23, 1980, 1, 10.

10. Junta de Gobierno de Reconstrucción Nacional de la República de Nicaragua, "Ley de Defensa." For price lists, see *Barricada*, February 10, 1980, 1, 5, February 12, 1981, 1, 7. For journalists reporting, see Junta de Gobierno de Reconstrucción Nacional de la República de Nicaragua, "Ley para Regular Informaciones."

11. *Barricada*, November 10, 1980, 12, October 31, 1980, 1, 14.

12. Stahler-Sholk and Spoor, *La política macroeconómica*, 123.

13. Colburn, *Post-revolutionary Nicaragua*, 90; Collins, *Nicaragua: Was hat sich*, 43–47; Austin, Fox, and Kruger, "Role of the Revolutionary State," 20.

14. Collins, *Nicaragua: Was hat*, 86–87.

15. Helm, *Botschafter der Revolution*, 158–64, 171–77; Perla, *Sandinista Nicaragua*.

16. See, for example, the lists in the folder Fondo Internacional para la Reconstrucción 3.855.1, HEKS J 2 233 1999/248 BO 31, Bundesarchiv Bern.

17. These are my own calculations based on Barraclough, van Buren, Garriazzo, Sunderam, and Utting, *Aid That Counts*, 139–41. This table refers only to the grants and not to the loans.

18. Leogrande, "Making the Economy Scream"; Pastor, *Condemned to Repetition*, 194–210; Rabe, *Killing Zone*, 154–55.

19. Herrera León, "Apoyo de México," 223–26; Vázquez Olivera and Campos Hernández, *México*; Riding, *Vecinos distantes*, 418, quoted in Herrera León, "Apoyo de México," 233 (quote); Herrera León, "Apoyo de México."

20. In 1975 Joseph Collins and Frances Moore Lappé founded Food First (known also as the Institute for Food and Development Policy). One of its first publications argued that social movements in Global South countries should implement local food systems. Lappé and Collins, *World Hunger*.

21. CIERA, PAN, and CIDA, *Informe del Primer Seminario*, 5; Collins, *Nicaragua: What Difference*, 2.

22. Collins, *Nicaragua: Was hat*, 5.

23. The Sandinistas filled the top positions with their political supporters, but the lack of qualified personnel obliged them to compromise. Especially, at the administrative level, there was a continuity favoring corruption.

24. Ray Rigall, "Nicaragua Options," June 20, 1979, box 403, CARE Archives.

25. Ron Burkard, "Visitation Report," October 17–21, 1979, October 1979, box 405, CARE Archives.

26. Art Flanagan and Timothy Lavelle, "Project Proposal, Rural Vocational Agricultural Schools, FY 1981–1983," box 404, and Timothy Lavelle to Harold Northrup, April 26, 1980, box 403, both in CARE Archives.

27. Timothy Lavelle to George Kraus, June 22, 1982, box 1138, CARE Archives.

28. Among them were Jonathan Fox, Michael Zalkin, Joseph Collins, Solon Barraclough, Peter Utting, Peter Marchetti, Elizabeth Dore, Laura J. Enríquez, and María Veronica Frenkel.

29. Kay, "Reflexiones."

30. Barraclough, *Preliminary Analysis*, 107–21.

31. Collins, *Nicaragua: Was hat*, 6–7, 50.

32. Ramírez, *Adiós muchachos*, 78.

33. Philip Ulman, interview by author, Geneva, September 4, 2013.

34. FAO, "Food and Agriculture Data."

35. Solá Montserrat, *Un siglo y medio*, 73–74.

36. Scott, *Seeing like a State*, 193–99.

37. Baumeister, *Estructura y reforma*, 208–10.

38. Jaime Wheelock to Edouard Saouma, April 17, 1980; "Misión del 14 al 23 de octubre, 1980," Yriat Files, Nicaragua 1980–1981, FAO Archives.

39. "Misión a Nicaragua del 14 al 23 de octubre, 1980," Yriat Files, Nicaragua 1980–1981, FAO Archives; Programa cooperativo FAO/Gobiernos, Plan de Operaciones—Proyecto: "Aumento de la Producción Agrícola por medio del Uso de Fertilizantes y otros Insumos (Programa de Fertilizantes)," August 1, 1983, FAO Archives, GCPF/NIC/015/NOR.

40. "List of Completed Projects," ODG New, CO Nicaragua, FAO Archives.

41. *Barricada*, July 7, 1981, 1, 5.

42. Ochoa, *Feeding Mexico*, 177–94.

43. Soynica, "Historia Soynica."

44. *Barricada*, February 6, 1987, 7; FAO, "Food and Agriculture Data."

45. Collins, *Nicaragua: Was hat*, 60; Martínez Cuenca, *Sandinista*, 47–49; Kaimowitz and Stanfield, "Organization of Production," 65–69; Colburn, *Managing the Commanding Heights*, 122–24.

46. Kinzer, *Blood of Brothers*, 76; Colburn, *Managing the Commanding Heights*, 122–24; Biondi-Morra, *Revolución y política*, 22–23; Kaimowitz, "Nicaragua's Experience," 126–27.

47. Kaimowitz and Stanfield, "Organization of Production," 53–54; Zalkin, "Nicaragua: The Peasantry," 74–75; Rocha, "Agrarian Reform."

48. Solá Montserrat, *Un siglo y medio*, 65; Baumeister, "Agrarian Reform"; Enríquez, *Harvesting Change*, 89–91.

49. Baumeister, "Agrarian Reform"; Dore, "Great Grain Dilemma," 102–4, 115–17.

50. Spoor, *Agricultural Markets*, 97.

51. Saulniers, "State Trading Organizations," 119; Martí i Puig, "Origins of the Peasant-Contra Rebellion," 12; Austin, Fox, and Kruger, "Role of the Revolutionary State," 26–27.

52. Edouard Saouma to Jaime Wheelock, September 1, 1981, FA 13/1 FSAS ODG Old, FAO Archives.

53. Programa cooperativo FAO/Gobiernos, Plan de Operaciones—Proyecto: "Aumento de la Producción Agrícola por medio del Uso de Fertilizantes y otros Insumos (Programa de Fertilizantes)," August 1, 1983, FAO Archives, GCPF/NIC/015/NOR.

54. Vilas, *Scientific Research*, 25.

55. Barraclough, *Preliminary Analysis*, 7.

56. Philip Ulman, interview by author, Geneva, September 4, 2013; CIERA and UNRISD, *Managua es Nicaragua*.

57. Perla, *Sandinista Nicaragua*, 28–29.

58. *Barricada*, February 16, 1981, 3, March 8, 1981, 1, 7, March 10, 1981, 1, 5.

59. *Barricada*, March 8, 1981, 1, 7, April 23, 1981, 1, 16, June 8, 1981, 7.

60. *Barricada*, May 3, 1981, 1, 8, May 27, 1981, 8.

61. Pastor, *Condemned to Repetition*, 191, 224–27; Grandin, *Empire's Workshop*, 83–84; Rabe, *Killing Zone*, 154; Soares, "Strategy, Ideology."

62. Brands, *Latin America's Cold War*, 213; Barraclough, van Buren, Garriazzo, Sunderam, and Utting, *Aid That Counts*, 48.

63. Executive Committee Meeting, March 11, 1981, box 1174, Timothy Lavelle to George Kraus, July 22, 1982, box 405, Executive Committee Meeting, December 8, 1982, box 1174, Dale Harrison to Philip Johnston, February 7, 1983, box 405, all in CARE Archives.

64. Minutes, Executive Committee Meeting, July 9, 1986, box 1174, CARE Archives.

65. Barraclough, van Buren, Garriazzo, Sunderam, and Utting, *Aid That Counts*, 17–18.

66. CIERA, *El hambre en los países*.

67. FAO, "Report of the Seventeenth FAO," 3–5, 11–13.

68. *Barricada*, November 12, 1981, 1, 5.

69. Milanesio, "Guardian Angels," 101.

70. Mitchell, "Democratisation, External Exposure"; Harsch, *Thomas Sankara*, 90–96.

CHAPTER FOUR: THE REVOLUTIONARY CONSUMER

1. Rina Méndez Osorno, interview by author, León, September 2012.

2. Ximena Cubero, interview by author, León, September 2012.

3. Trentmann, "Modern Genealogy," 50.

4. *Barricada*, August 8, 1980, 1, 5; CIERA, *La reforma agraria*, 169–74; Collins, *Nicaragua: Was hat*, 104–5; FAO, "Food and Agriculture Data"; *Barricada*, August 10, 1980, 7.

5. *Barricada*, September 9, 1980, 4, April 8, 1981, 4.

6. *Barricada*, October 27, 1980, 14, January 20, 1981, 1, 5.

7. CIERA, *La reforma agraria*, 207, 211.

8. *Barricada*, January 17, 1982, 4, January 19, 1982, 5, January 24, 1982, 1, April 15, 1982, 10, April 23, 1982, 5.

9. Lappé and Collins, *Now We Can Speak*, 55.

10. Wilk, "Consumer Goods."

11. *Barricada*, September 11, 1981, 7, September 14, 1981, 10, November 20, 1983, 7, November 22, 1982, 6; Esther Marina Vanega Saavedra, interview by author, León, September 2012.

12. Carrión, "Austeridad"; Ferrero Blanco, *De un lado*, 69–71, 115, 190, 292. Ferrero Blanco's book contains testimonies of Nicaraguan women based on interviews that she conducted. She has arranged the chronological narrative and made a thematic selection. As the character of each transcribed interview was lost, I do not quote these testimonies individually.

13. *Somos*, no. 3 (July 1982): 2.

14. *Barricada*, December 18, 1981, 3.

15. CIERA, *Distribución y consumo*, 12–13.

16. *nicaráuac* 2, no. 6, 1981, 57. Nahuatl is a language spoken by indigenous people in Central Mexico. In the above-mentioned source, it refers to the Aztec people in preconquest Mexico who spoke Nahuatl languages and whose influence extended to Central America.

17. *Barricada*, May 12, 1981, 3; Tapia Barquero, *Nicaragua*.

18. Rina Méndez Osorno, interview by author, León, September 2012; also Marlen Jimena Guillén Mora, interview by author, Managua, August 2012.

19. *Barricada*, May 7, 1981, 9, May 4, 1981, 1, 5; Collins, *Nicaragua: Was hat*, 91–93. The history of fast food has not been studied in Nicaragua. The first McDonalds opened in 1975, but there is no information on its reception and further development.

20. CIERA, *Distribución y consumo*, 13, 54.

21. Flores, "Estudios dietéticos." Again, there are contradictions in the available statistics: CIERA calculated average annual wheat flour consumption at 31.4 pounds between 1976 and 1978, which increased to 39.9 pounds between 1980 and 1982. Richard Stahler-Sholk quotes for 1981 an average of 58.5 pounds, which decreased to 41.7 pounds in 1982 and 33.9 pounds in 1983. CIERA, *La reforma agraria*, 211; Stahler-Sholk, *La política macroeconómica*, 110.

22. Stahler-Sholk and Spoor, *La política macroeconómica*, 110; FAO, "Food and Agriculture Data"; *Barricada*, September 9, 1983, 9.

23. Jones, *Beyond the Barricades*, 75, 231.

24. Perfil editorial de *Barricada*, quoted in Jones, *Beyond the Barricades*, 9. See also Arnove, *Education and Revolution*, 66.

25. *Barricada*, July 8, 1984, 8, August 31, 1985, 4.

26. *Barricada*, October 6, 1987, 4.

27. CIERA, *Distribución y consumo*, 12–15, 17, 43–47, appendix.

28. CIERA, *Distribución y consumo*, 7–9, 12–13, 17, 78.

29. CIERA, *Distribución y consumo*, 12–13.

30. *Barricada*, November 21, 1983, 3.

31. FAO, "Office for Special Relief," 7; Equipo Envío, "Nicaragua's Floods"; CEPAL, "Nicaragua: The Floods."

32. Argüello Hüper, "La ciudad de Managua," 50.

33. Rabe, *Killing Zone*, 160–62; Voss, *Washingtons Söldner*, 391–93; Grandin, *Empire's Workshop*, 92–94.

34. Grandin, *Empire's Workshop*, 94.

35. Kornbluh, *Nicaragua*, 50–51; Leogrande, "Making the Economy Scream," 341.

36. Frederick Royce, "Program Proposal: The Luis Hernandez Aguilar School of Agricultural Mechanization," November 1985, box 1235, CARE Archives.

37. Fitzgerald, "Una evaluación de los costos económicos"; Kornbluh, *Nicaragua*, 23, 40–41; Equipo Envío, "Economic Costs."

38. Translation from Spanish original. *Barricada*, June 3, 1985, 3.

39. Translation from Spanish original. *Barricada*, June 24, 1985, 3.

40. *Barricada*, June 3, 1985, 3, June 24, 1985, 3.

41. CIERA, *Distribución y consumo*, 82–83.

42. Estimates vary according to the sources and the type of damages included. The total sum of damages presented by the Nicaraguan delegation at The Hague Court was $17.8 billion. Krujit, *Guerrillas*, 73; Close, *Nicaragua: Chamorro*, 122.

43. Kornbluh, *Nicaragua*, 40–41.

44. In September 1980 the government introduced its first censorship measures when it passed amendments to the media law, which allowed the temporary closure of media by the government. Spicer Nichols, "The Media"; Mattelart, "Communication in Nicaragua."

45. These findings are based on a 1989 investigation published in Costa Rica. On the whole 12,291 censored pieces of information were classified by twelve categories. The supply topic fell into the economics section, which made up 15.56 percent of all censored information. Cardenal, *Lo que se quiso*, 86, 240–45.

46. *Barricada*, July 13, 1984, 4 (quote), also April 10, 1983, 7.

47. *Barricada*, August 7, 1984, 7.

48. Selser, *Banderas y harapos*, 160.

49. Solá Montserrat, *Siglo y medio*, 83; Kinzer, *Blood of Brothers*, 154. A system of multiple exchange rates establishes different rates according to the nature of the transaction such as, for example, more favorable rates for export firms.

50. Ricciardi, "Economic Policy," 258; Utting, "Political Economy," 113–14.

51. Kinzer, *Blood of Brothers*, 154.

52. González-Rivera, *Before the Revolution*, 100–101; *Barricada*, December 15, 1985, 3.

53. *Barricada*, January 29, 1985, 3, December 24, 1985, 1.

54. *Barricada*, March 18, 1985, 3; "Participación popular," 87, 96.

55. Salman Rushdie, for example, remembers an awkward silence when he addressed the issue in a conversation with two FSLN members in Matagalpa. He traveled to Nicaragua in July 1986 as an invited guest of the Sandinista Association of Cultural Workers. Rushdie, *Das Lächeln des Jaguars*, 75–76.

56. Collins, *Nicaragua: Was hat*, 179–84; Ferrero Blanco, *De un lado*, 65, 190.

57. Milanesio, "Guardian Angels," 101.

58. *Somos*, no. 9 (January/February 1983): 20, no. 10 (March 1983): 20, no. 11 (April 1983): 20.

59. *Somos* no. 7 (November 1982): 17, no. 8 (December 1982): 16, no. 3 (July 1982): 15, no. 19 (February 1984): 5.

60. *Somos* no. 13 (June 1983): 17, 18.

61. Luciak, *Sandinista Legacy*, 163–66.

62. Molyneux, "Mobilization."

63. Isbester, *Still Fighting*, 19; Kampwirth, *Feminism*, 24–35.

64. *Barricada*, June 1, 1984, 1.

65. CIERA and UNRISD, *Managua es Nicaragua*, 177–80.

66. "Lineamientos para fijar las cuotas regionales para el abastecimiento de productos de consumo," August 1984, EB 028 D33 g2, IHNCA Library. The Sandinista Assembly was a political body appointed by the FSLN National Directorate to advise the party leadership. It met on a yearly basis but had no strong decision-making power.

67. Translation from Spanish original. "Lineamientos para fijar las cuotas regionales para el abastecimiento de productos de consumo," August 1984, EB 028 D33 g2, IHNCA Library.

68. *Barricada*, June 9, 1984, 1, 8, June 18, 1984, 3.

69. Horton, *Peasants in Arms*, 210–11; "Lineamientos para fijar las cuotas regionales para el abastecimiento de productos de consumo," August 1984, EB 028 D33 g2; "Abc del abastecimiento," Managua, [1984?], IHNCA library.

70. Tomka, *Social History*, 242.

71. *Barricada*, July 5, 1984, 7; Collins, *Nicaragua: Was hat*, 181–86.

72. *Barricada*, June 2, 1984, 3.

73. *Barricada*, December 24, 1984, 1, May 20, 1985, 3. The government suspended payment in kind by mid-1985.

74. Laure, "Nicaragua: Salarios mínimos," 45.

75. *Barricada*, August 17, 1984, 10, January 9, 1984, 8.

76. *Barricada*, October 30, 1984, 12.

77. CIERA, *La reforma agraria*, 198–201; Kühn, *Agrarreform*, 91–93; Brenner, "Sie sollen sich immer," 77, 86; Geiser, "Ni del uno ni del otro," 180.

78. Leticia Herrera Sánchez (born 1949) was the national CDS coordinator and (from 1985 to 1990) vice president of the National Assembly. *Barricada*, February 17, 1984, 1.

79. *Semana Cómica*, no. 109, 9.

80. *Barricada*, May 19, 1984, 12.

81. *Barricada*, August 1, 1984, 3; Utting, "Political Economy," 126; Brenner, "Sie sollen sich immer," 87.

82. Prevost and Vanden, *Democracy and Socialism*, 71–88; Walker, *Nicaragua: Living*, 156–59.

83. Emilce María Vega Sandoval, interview by author, León, September 2012. *Pipián* is a special pumpkin variety common in Mexico and Central America.

84. Marlen Jimena Guillén Mora, interview by author, Managua, August 2012; Rina Méndez Osorno, interview by author, León, September 2012.

85. Gabriel Diego, interview by author, León, September 2012.

86. Philip Ulman, interview by author, Geneva, September 4, 2013.

87. Collins, *Nicaragua: Was hat*, 87.

88. Translation from Spanish original. Gabriel Diego, interview by author, León, September 2012.

89. Ayala, "Iguana en amaranto"; Alvarez and Escobar, *Pedazos de historia*, 65.

90. Emilce María Vega Sandoval, interview by author, León, September 2012; Marlen Jimena Guillén Mora, interview by author, Managua, August 2012; Spoor, *Agricultural Markets*, 190; Martí i Puig, "Origins," 12.

91. *Barricada*, June 8, 1984, 10.

CHAPTER FIVE: FOOD POLICY DETERIORATES INTO CRISIS MANAGEMENT

1. *Barricada*, May 29, 1986, 1, 5, May 31, 1986, 1, June 13, 1986, 1, 5.

2. Leogrande, "Making the Economy Scream"; Kornbluh, *Nicaragua*, 101–3.

3. Leogrande, "Making the Economy Scream," 339.

4. Perla, *Sandinista Nicaragua*, 86–88, 111; Rabe, *Killing Zone*, 162–63; Grandin, *Empire's Workshop*, 114–16.

5. Leogrande, "Making the Economy Scream," 337–40.

6. Barraclough, van Buren, Garriazzo, Sunderam, and Utting, *Aid That Counts*, 73.

7. Ricciardi, "Economic Policy"; Ferrero Blanco, "Daniel Ortega y Mijail Gorbachev"; Conroy, "Nicaragua," 8–9.

8. Christiaens, "Between Diplomacy and Solidarity," 625.

9. Conroy, "Nicaragua," 6; Barry and Preusch, *Soft War*, 212–17; Ricciardi, "Economic Policy," 249.

10. Ricciardi, "Economic Policy."

11. Martínez Cuenca, *Sandinista*, 65–66; Ramírez, *Adiós muchachos*, 166. Among the advisers were the British economist Valpy FitzGerald, the Chilean economist Roberto Pizarro, Alban Lataste from UNDP, and several GDR experts.

12. Solá Montserrat, *Un siglo y medio*, 100–101; Ricciardi, "Economic Policy."

13. Close, *Nicaragua: Chamorro Years*, 124.

14. Conroy, "Nicaragua"; Stahler-Sholk, "Structural Adjustment," 80–82; Stahler-Sholk, "Stabilization, Destabilization," 73.

15. *Barricada*, February 9, 1985, 1, 3, June 3, 1985, 3.

16. *Barricada*, March 1, 1985, 4.

17. Translation from Spanish original. *Barricada*, March 1, 1985, 4.

18. *Barricada*, March 19, 1985, 8.

19. Translation from Spanish original. *Barricada*, March 12, 1985, 4.

20. Mattelart, "Communication," 20–21.

21. *Barricada*, January 4, 1984, 8.

22. FAO, "Food and Agriculture Data"; United Nations, "Department of Economic."

23. FAO, "Nicaragua," 19.

24. FAO, "Food and Agriculture Data"; Biondi-Morra, *Revolución y política*, 166–78.

25. By 1987 the monthly minimum salary was 42,126 Córdobas. Stahler-Sholk "Stabilization, Destabilization," 72; *Barricada*, March 31, 1987, 1.

26. *Barricada*, May 12, 1986, 5, November 29, 1986, 2, December 9, 1986, 3, January 25, 1986, 5, August 10, 1986, 6.

27. Stahler-Sholk and Spoor, *La política macroeconómica*, 110.

28. CIERA, PAN, and CIDA, *Informe del Primer Seminario*, 29, 44–46; Ramírez, *Adiós muchachos*, 168; Kaimowitz and Stanfield, "Organization of Production," 65–69.

29. "Program Proposal: The Luis Hernandez Aguilar School of Agricultural Mechanization," November 1985, box 1235, CARE Archives.

30. "Nicaragua: Relance et développement de la production alimentaire dans la Région des Segovias, Phase 5," August 20, 1985, Bundesarchiv Bern, E2025A#1997/200#1505.

31. FAO and Ministerio de Agricultura y Ganadería, *Proyecto FAO*, 103–4; Biondi-Morra, *Revolución y política*, 29; Utting, "Oferta interna," 166.

32. Translation from German. Ramírez, "Ströme von Milch," 161.

33. Mitchell, *Rule of Experts*, 223–25, 242; Ferguson, *Anti-politics Machine*, 257–60; Escobar, *Encountering Development*.

34. "Informe final Proyecto 'Las Segovias' del 6 de agosto 1979 al 22 abril de 1987," E2025A#1997/200#1506; "Relance et développement de la production alimentaire dans la région des Segovias," vol. 3, Bundesarchiv Bern.

35. Translation from German original. Gino Baumann to Ernesto, July 8, 1985, E2025A#1997/200#1505, "Relance et développement de la production alimentaire dans la région des Segovias," vol. 1, Bundesarchiv Bern.

36. FAO, "Proyecto Apoyo a la formulación del plan quinquenal del sector agropecuario y agroindustrial," Rome, 1986, TCP/NIC/4504, FAO Archives.

37. Dr. Bothe, "Standpunkt zum Dokument: Zusammenfassung der Perspektiven und Alternativen für deren Beeinflussung 1988–1990," February 8, 1988, Bundesarchiv Berlin-Lichterfelde (hereafter cited as BArch) DE 1/58122.

38. Luciak, *Sandinista Legacy*, 123–24; Horton, *Peasants in Arms*, 158–60; Ferrero Blanco, *De un lado*, 118, 126, 128, 272.

39. Zalkin, "Nicaragua"; Dore, "Great Grain Dilemma"; Martí i Puig, "Origins."

40. Ferrero Blanco, *De un lado*, 128.

41. Martí i Puig, "Origins," 29; Ferrero Blanco, *De un lado*, 110, 126.

42. Martí i Puig, "Origins," 3.

43. Martí i Puig, "Origins," 17; Baumeister, *Estructura y reforma*, 208–15.

44. Saldaña-Portillo, *Revolutionary Imagination*, 143–44; Soto Joya, *Ventanas en la memoria*, 30–32; Minks, "Reading Nicaraguan Folklore"; Gould, *To Die in This Way*. On peasants' perceptions, see Müller, "Favores, ayuda."

45. Philip Ulman, interview by author, Geneva, September 4, 2013.

46. Spoor, *Agricultural Markets*, 98.

47. Baumeister, "Agrarian Reform," 239–40; Dore, "Great Grain Dilemma," 115; Utting, "Introducción," 6–8.

48. CIERA, *La reforma agraria*, 210–14.

49. Enríquez, *Harvesting Change*, 137, 169; Philip Ulman, interview by author, Geneva, September 4, 2013.

50. Kinzer, *Blood of Brothers*, 121.

51. Gabriel Diego, interview by author, León, September 2012.

52. FAO and CIERA, "Nicaragua," 23.

53. Unfortunately, the report contains no detailed information on the scope and methodologies of the survey. CIERA, *La reforma agraria*, 207.

54. Utting, "Political Economy," 110; "Lineamientos para fijar las cuotas regionales para el abastecimiento de productos de consumo," August 1984, EB 028 D33 g2, IHNCA; Martí i Puig, "Origins," 26; Stahler-Sholk, "Stabilization, Destabilization," 78.

55. Utting, "Political Economy."

56. The financial support for the project from different donors exceeded twenty-two million dollars. Luciak, *Sandinista Legacy*, 124–31.

57. Luciak, *Sandinista Legacy*, 159–60.

58. This calculation is based on the data provided by Garst, *La ayuda alimentaria*, cuadro 15.

59. The estimate only refers to donations of milk, flour, and vegetable oil, which Hernández defined as basic foods. Hernández, "La ayuda alimentaria," 5, 29.

60. Garst, *La ayuda alimentaria*, table 15. The data is based on statistics from the Ministerio de Cooperación Externa (Nicaraguan Ministry of Exterior Cooperation).

61. FAO and WHO, *Conferencia internacional*, 56.

62. For example, the statistics register no donations of wheat flour between 1981 and 1985, although several nations provided wheat in these years. Stahler-Sholk and Spoor, *La política macroeconómica*, 101–8. Despite the fact that all authors rely on data from the Ministry of External Commerce, the data presented by Hernández contradicts these findings. Hernández, "La ayuda alimentaria," 35.

63. Garst, *La ayuda alimentaria*, cuadro 15.

64. Translation from Spanish original. *Barricada*, March 14, 1981, 3.

65. *Barricada*, January 21, 1980, 2.

66. *Barricada*, January 5, 1984, 8, March 29, 1984, 8, May 6, 1986, 1.

67. *Barricada*, January 24, 1980, 1, 5.

68. CIERA, *El hambre en los países*, 33, 36.

69. Equipo Envío, "Nicaragua's Floods."

70. *Barricada*, March 12, 1985, 4.

71. Ministerio de Salud, "Apoyo nutricional," 9; "Avances en el mejoramiento," 6.

72. Programa Mundial de Alimentos, "Informe," 30; Hernández, "La ayuda alimentaria," 35.

73. Colburn, *My Car*, 30–31.

74. *Barricada*, January 4, 1984, 7.

75. *Barricada*, February 22, 1985, 6, March 8, 1985, n.p., April 14, 1986, section B.

76. *Barricada*, June 19, 1984, 8, June 21, 1984, 4.

77. *Barricada*, December 12, 1984, 5.

78. Gabriel Diego, interview by author, León, September 2012.

79. FAO, "Nicaragua," 30.

80. Garst, *La ayuda alimentaria*, 87.

81. Translation from Spanish original. *Barricada*, March 10, 1985.

82. *Barricada*, January 20, 1985, 4; Ferrero Blanco, *De un lado*, 221.

83. Barraclough and Utting, "Ernährungssicherung," 130–32.

84. Collins, *Nicaragua: Was hat*, 148, 154–64.

CHAPTER SIX: FOOD POLICY IN TATTERS

1. Equipo Nitlápan-Envío, "Toll Rises."

2. CEPAL "Damage"; Selser, *Banderas y harapos*, 161.

3. This refers to a statement by Joseph Collins, who argued that many Nicaraguans would measure the success of revolution by a plate of rice and beans. Collins, *Nicaragua: Was hat*, 86.

4. Linkogle, "Soya," 97; Godek, "Institutionalization," 164–65.

5. Chernyshova, *Soviet Consumer Culture*; Weinreb, *Cuba in the Shadow*, 7–8.

6. Henriksen, "People's Republic"; Utting, *Economic Reform*, 1–2.

7. *Barricada*, May 28, 1987, 5, December 20, 1987, 1, 5.

8. Ricciardi, "Economic Policy," 261; Stahler-Sholk, "Structural Adjustment," 80–82; *Barricada*, July 8, 1987, 5, August 22, 1987, 2.

9. *Barricada*, May 18, 1987, 3; Biondi-Morra, *Revolución y política*, 29; Horst Schulz to Dieter Albrecht, August 15, 1988, BArch DE 1/58121.

10. Jones, *Beyond the Barricades*, 48–51. *La Prensa* reappeared in September 1987 after fifteen months of closure.

11. *Barricada*, February 25, 1987.

12. *Barricada*, March 6, 1987, 3.

13. "Zur Einschätzung der wirtschaftlichen Situation. Anlage zum Bericht," May 19, 1987, BArch DE/58122.

14. Ramírez, "Ströme von Milch."

15. The 1986–1987 Esquipulas agreements paved the way for peace in Central America. The second agreement was an initiative for a regional peace plan developed by the Costa Rican president, Oscar Arias. In August 1987 all heads of state agreed on an open political process with a free press and regular elections supervised by the United Nations and the Organization of the American States.

16. Martínez Cuenca, *Sandinista*, 73–74.

17. Dr. Bothe to Dr. Schürer, February 25, 1988, BArch DE 1/58122; Dijkstra, *Industrialization*, 136–39; Ocampo, "Collapse and (Incomplete) Stabilization."

18. Dijkstra, *Industrialization*, 136–39; "Anlage 3: Übersicht über die Maßnahmen zur Durchführung der Wirtschaftsreformen," October 10, 1988, BArch DE 1/58121; Ocampo, "Collapse and (Incomplete) Stabilization."

19. *Barricada*, September 1, 1988, 3, September 2, 1988, 3, also July 2, 1988, 3.

20. Translation from Spanish original. *Barricada*, August 20, 1988, 3.

21. Utting, *Economic Adjustment*, 39–42.

22. "Tesis Centrales del Plan de Ajuste Economico: Operacion-P-Plomo," BArch DE 1/58122.

23. Titles of *Barricada* articles from September 20, 1988, 11, September 28, 1988, 3, and February 26, 1989, 3.

24. Lancaster, *Life Is Hard*, 58–60.

25. Dr. Bothe, "Zusammenfassende Information zur bisherigen ökonomischen Entwicklung und den voraussichtlichen Ergebnissen des Jahres 1988," October 10, 1988, BArch DE 1/58121.

26. Equipo Envío, "New Economic Package"; Ricciardi, "Economic Policy," 264; Polakoff and La Ramée, "Grass-Roots Organizations," 194.

27. Investigative Team, "Survival Strategies," 26; Utting, *Economic Adjustment*.

28. Utting, *Economic Adjustment*, 64–65, 92–93; Soule, "Economic Austerity Packages," 40–43.

29. "Briefing Paper for Potential CARE Food Assistance Activities," April 4, 1990, box 1218, CARE Archives.

30. Utting, *Economic Adjustment*, 56–62.

31. *Washington Post*, "Hunger Becomes an Issue."

32. *Barricada*, June 4, 1987, 5, June 9, 1987, 6, June 19, 1987, 9; Selser, *Banderas y harapos*, 166.

33. Mendoza Fletes, *Distribución del ingreso*, 18; Ministerio de Agricultura y Ganadería and PAN, *Segunda Encuesta*, 40–44.

34. *Barricada*, June 12, 1987, 5.

35. Simon, "Probleme und Perspektiven," 128–48, 41–44.

36. According to PAN, OPS (Organización Panamericana de Salud) contributed with $733,700; UNICEF with $738,200. PAN, "Plan quinquenal."

37. Juch, "Unser revolutionärer Alltag," 13.

38. Translation from German original. Juch, "Unser revolutionärer Alltag," 8.

39. FAO, "Nicaragua," 27; "Löhne für politische Ämter," September 1988, BArch DE 1/58121; Utting, *Economic Adjustment*, 61–62.

40. Selser, *Banderas y harapos*, 164; Utting, *Economic Adjustment*, 61–62; Lancaster, *Life Is Hard*, 58–60.

41. Lancaster, *Life Is Hard*, 52–56.

42. Geiser, "Ni del uno ni del otro," 95–96; Kinzer, *Blood of Brothers*, 169.

43. Largaespada Fredersdorf, *Soy la última en comer*, 95–110.

44. Largaespada Fredersdorf, *Soy la última en comer*, 110–16, 132–35, 136 (quote), 139–41.

45. Spoor, *Agricultural Markets*, 91–92; Utting, *Economic Adjustment*, 7–8, 39, 42.

46. Translation from Spanish original. *Barricada*, May 6, 1987, 2.

47. *Barricada*, June 19, 1988, 2, May 31, 1988, 8, July 2, 1988, 5.

48. *Barricada*, August 3, 1988, 5, August 25, 1988, 3.

49. Translation from Spanish original. *Barricada*, October 1, 1988, 8.

50. Kinzer, *Blood of Brothers*, 166, 365.

51. Ramírez, *Adiós muchachos*, 30–31. For a similar analysis, see Selser, *Banderas y harapos*, 298–304; Ferrero Blanco, *De un lado*, 190, 292–93.

52. In Cuba the diplotiendas were accessible only to foreigners. They sold imported food products as well as fresh vegetables and milk. Collins, Scott, and Benjamin, *No Free Lunch*, 42.

53. Translation from Spanish original. *Barricada*, February 20, 1987, 3.

54. Lundgren, *Lost Visions*, 132.

55. Selser, *Banderas y harapos*, 169.

56. Rede von Daniel Ortega, February 20, 1988 (Auszugsweise Übersetzung), BArch DE 1/58122; Porter, "Fleeting Dreams."

57. Dr. Bothe, "Bericht zur ökonomischen Situation," December 4, 1988, BArch DE 1/58121; Ricciardi, "Economic Policy," 266–67.

58. "Botschaft Arbeitspapier, Zur Entwicklung in Nikaragua," December 12, 1988, BArch DE 1/58722.

59. Anderson and Dodd, *Learning Democracy*, 6–18, 152–53; Selser, *Banderas y harapos*, 297–305.

60. Equipo Envío, "From a Mixed-Up Economy"; Stahler-Sholk, "Structural Adjustment," 84–86; Close, *Nicaragua: Chamorro*, 128–29; Gibson, "Nicaragua," 445–46.

61. Lamberg, *Subsistenzökonomie*, 108–12. The IMF's financial contributions made up 30 percent of the Nicaraguan gross domestic product (GDP) during the first years of the Chamorro government. Although the Nicaraguan government established cooperation with the IMF soon after the 1990 election, they had to settle several conflicts before signing the first structural adjustment agreement in 1994. Solá Montserrat, *Un siglo y medio*, 103–4.

62. *Barricada*, May 10, 1990, 11; *La Prensa*, May 18, 1990, 16. ENABAS intervened twice in 1990, once in October 1992, and for the last time in May–June 1993. Equipo Envío, "Immovable Object."

63. Throughout the 1980s, state holdings and agrarian reform land had not been legalized and in many cases still ran on the names of former owners. In March 1990 the National Assembly passed two laws to legalize the transfers.

64. Ramírez, *Adiós muchachos*, 32; Zamora, "Some Reflections."

65. Martí i Puig, "FSLN and Sandinismo."

66. Arana, "General Economic Policy," 86; Prevost, "The FSLN," 157.

67. Ministerio de Agricultura and PAN, *Segunda Encuesta*, v–xi.

68. FAO and WHO, *Conferencia Internacional*, 9.

69. *Barricada*, August 21, 1990, 1, 5, August 30, 1990, 4, August 31, 1990, 1, 5.

70. *Barricada*, September 14, 1990, 3, June 4, 1990, 2, September 4, 1990, 1, October 6, 1990, 1, September 16, 1990, 11.

71. "Hora cero en occidente," *La Prensa*, March 30, 1993, 1, 12; "Hambre y desempleo acechan Chinandega," *La Prensa*, April 5, 1993, 2; "En Chinandega. Mueren 3 niños por desnutrición," *La Prensa*, June 23, 1993, 1, 20; "Preocupa desnutrición de infantes," *La Prensa*, August 4, 1993, 11.

72. Peter van Brunt, "Team TDY to Nicaragua," March 24, 1990, box 1218, CARE Archives.

73. *Barricada*, April 10, 1990, 4, April 21, 1990, 9, May 5, 1990, 1; FAO, "Nicaragua," 27; FAO and WHO, *Conferencia Internacional*, 35.

74. Nicaragua and Comisión Nacional de Nutrición, *Plan quinquenal*; World Bank, "Republic of Nicaragua," 14; FAO, Representación en Nicaragua, "Informe Anual: Julio 92 a junio 93," 3–4, 18; FAO, "Informe Terminal," 1–2.

75. FAO, "Food and Agriculture Data"; Baumeister, "Politics of Land Reform," 257.

76. Jonakin, "Agrarian Policy"; Baumeister, "Politics of Land Reform."

77. This program was based on the Food for Progress Act of 1985. It was limited to states that the United States perceived as emerging democracies and to states fostering free enterprise in agriculture. FAO and WHO, *Conferencia Internacional*, 17.

78. World Food Programme, "Food Aid Information."

79. Mintz, "Zur Beziehung," 64–66.

80. Ministerio de Agricultura and PAN, *Segunda Encuesta*, 28–29, 39, 76.

81. Translation from Spanish original. Arancibia Mujica, Gutiérrez Castro, and Zelaya Ramírez, "Manual de alimentación," 21.

82. *Gente*, December 20, 1991, 8–10; *Barricada*, December 23, 1991, 1; Babb, *After Revolution*, 131–37.

83. *La Prensa*, August 24, 1991, 6; *Barricada*, February 14, 1991, 13; *La Prensa*, September 30, 1991, 27.

84. León, Espíndola, and Schejtman, "Pobreza, hambre y seguridad," 46; FAO and WHO, *Conferencia Internacional*, 28–29.

85. The shopping center is owned by the Salvadoran enterprise Grupo Robles, which had constructed the first center in 1974. In the 1990s the firm invested in its expansion and reopened it in 1998.

86. *La Prensa*, October 24, 1991, 4, December 17, 1991, 3.

87. Núñez, *De la ciudad al barrio*, 234–36; Geiser, "Ni del uno ni del otro," 95–96.

88. Trentmann, "Modern Genealogy," 50.

89. *La Prensa*, August 16, 1991, 4.

90. *Gente*, weekly supplement in *Barricada*, May 24, 1990, 5.

CHAPTER SEVEN: CARIBBEAN TRANSITIONS

1. Vernooy, *Starting All Over Again*, 163.

2. Vernooy, *Starting All Over Again*, 162, also 156–68.

3. Mintz, "Zur Beziehung," 64–66.

4. The official name has now changed to Bilwi, the Miskito name of the city.

5. Wilk, "Real Belizean," 252.

6. Coronel Urtecho, "Elogio de la cocina nicaragüense," 30.

7. Ramírez, *Tambor olvidado*, 233–54.

8. Potthast, *Mosquitoküste*, 282–303; Pineda, *Shipwrecked Identities*, 57. In Lat-

in America the term "Creole" first referred to people of Spanish descent born in the colonies. Later on it acquired a more general meaning as a reference to traditional elements in national culture such as "creole cuisine." By contrast, in the Caribbean, the term was applied either to the combination of French, English, indigenous, and African languages or to people of mixed descent, including descendants of Spanish, French, or African forebears. Stewart, "Creolization."

9. Wheelock Román, *La comida nicaragüense*, 215–19.

10. Gordon, *Disparate Diasporas*, xi.

11. Sollis, "Atlantic Coast," 484–87, 494–95. During the nineteenth century, the British had promoted the Moravian Church, a Protestant denomination based in German Saxony. The church experienced a rupture when Germany's leadership was replaced by the United States during the First World War.

12. Gabbert, *Creoles-Afroamerikaner*, 251–54; Gordon, "Creoles und die Revolution," 172; Pineda, *Shipwrecked Identities*, 92–95.

13. Pineda, *Shipwrecked Identities*, 120–25; Wheelock Román, *La comida nicaragüense*, 215–19.

14. Pineda, *Shipwrecked Identities*, 127–30.

15. Bulmer-Thomas, *Political Economy*, 58.

16. *La Información*, February 23, 1930 (translation from Spanish original). See also *Excelsior*, September 3, 1930, quoted after Vernooy, *Starting All Over Again*, 233.

17. Carr, "Pioneering Transnational Solidarity," 142.

18. Schroeder and Brooks, "Rebellion from Without"; Wünderich, "Sandino an der Atlantikküste," 136–39; Dozier, *Nicaragua's Mosquito Shore*, 232–35.

19. Vernooy, *Starting All Over Again*, 236–40; Gabbert, *Creoles-Afroamerikaner*, 251–54; Sollis, "Atlantic Coast," 482, 502–6.

20. Helms, *Asang*, 110–15.

21. Sujo Wilson, *Oral History*, 32.

22. Pineda, "Chinese Creoles," 215; Dennis, *Miskitu People*, 32–33; Sujo Wilson, *Oral History*, 32–34.

23. Cardoso and Faletto, *Dependencia*. With dependency theory, Latin American social scientists and economists offered an alternative explanation for unequal relations between North and South, or center and periphery, in the global economy. They argued that the expansion of capitalism had transferred wealth to the capitalist centers of the world economy and the periphery faced "underdevelopment."

24. This period was interrupted by a crisis during the mid-1920s and early 1930s prompted by the unstable political situation in Nicaragua and the worldwide economic downturn. Helms, *Asang*, 110–15.

25. Hutton utilizes the term "restorative nostalgia," which was coined by the novelist and professor of Slavic languages Svetlana Boym in contrast with "reflec-

tive nostalgia." "Restorative nostalgia" implies the idealization of an earlier period while "reflective nostalgia" allows for questioning and even criticism of the past. Hutton, "Reconsiderations of the Idea"; Boym, "Nostalgia."

26. Data collected by Nicaraguan health authorities in 1975 estimated rural literacy in the Caribbean at 24.1 percent while the national average was 30.3 percent. On the national level 71.9 percent of the population had access to potable water; in Caribbean towns it was only 35.3 percent. Poyner and Strachan, "Nutrition Sector Assessment," 24.

27. Vilas, *State, Class, and Ethnicity*, 70, also 60.

28. Dozier, *Nicaragua's Mosquito Shore*, 231–32; Kinzer, *Blood of Brothers*, 253–57.

29. Vilas, *State, Class, and Ethnicity*, 70–71; Gabbert, *Creoles-Afroamerikaner*, 274–79; Vernooy, *Starting All Over Again*, 177.

30. Sollis, "Atlantic Coast," 491–92; Soto Joya, *Ventanas en la memoria*, 25–27.

31. "Assistance Agreements 1970–1978, CARE, Agrarian Institute of Nicaragua," box 859, CARE Archives.

32. "Discursive Report," September–November 1966, box 657; "Discursive Report," September–December 1972, box 841, CARE Archives.

33. Randall E. Trudelle, "Medico Program, CARE-Nicaragua," box 1074, CARE Archives.

34. Ralph Foulke to Mary Anderson, October 16, 1974, box 402; Glenn Porter, "Description on the State of Nutrition in Nicaragua for the Conferees of the Latin America Nutrition Planning Workshop, Bogota, Colombia," May 20–31, 1975, box 184; Cam McIntyre, "Community Information and Opinions on Family Planning, Nutrition and Medicine in Rigoberto Cabezas," March 1974, box 184, all in CARE Archives.

35. Vilas, *State, Class, and Ethnicity*, 76; Gabbert, *Creoles-Afroamerikaner*, 281.

36. Lagueux, "Marine Turtle Fishery," 29–30; Nietschmann, *Between Land and Water*, 196–200.

37. Nietschmann, *Between Land and Water*, 107, 206–11, 256–58; Helms, *Asang*, 146, 110–15; Cattle, "Nutritional Security," 38, 51, 85.

38. Meringer, "Local Politics," 5.

39. Richter, "ALPROMISU"; Meringer, "Local Politics."

40. FSLN, *El programa histórico*, 24–25; Sollis, "Atlantic Coast," 482–83, 500–501.

41. Hale, *Resistance and Contradiction*, 14–15.

42. Soto Joya, "De sueños"; Dozier, *Nicaragua's Mosquito Shore*, 232–35; Gabbert, *Creoles-Afroamerikaner*, 291–92.

43. Gabbert, *Creoles-Afroamerikaner*, 291–92; Sollis, "Atlantic Coast," 502–6.

44. Sollis, "Atlantic Coast," 500–501; Vilas, *State, Class, and Ethnicity*, 110–14; Colburn, *My Car*, 87–97.

45. Vilas, *State, Class, and Ethnicity*, 113. See also Sollis, "Atlantic Coast," 498; Gabbert, *Creoles-Afroamerikaner*, 299.

46. Yih and Hale, "Mestizen, Creoles," 261–63; Hale, "Der Konflikt der Miskito," 262–65.

47. Arbeitsgruppe des CIDCA "Vom Rio Coco," 234.

48. González and Figueroa, "Regional Autonomy," 164–66; Arbeitsgruppe des CIDCA, "Vom Rio Coco," 219–53.

49. *Barricada*, April 24, 1980, 9.

50. Translation from Spanish original. *Barricada*, September 24, 1980, 1, 5.

51. *Barricada*, April 18, 1984, 7; Dozier, *Nicaragua's Mosquito Shore*, 232–35; Gabbert, *Creoles-Afroamerikaner*, 301.

52. *Barricada*, June 3, 1987, 9.

53. *Sunrise*, no. 35 (June 1986): 10; Vernooy, *Starting All Over Again*, 136.

54. *Sunrise*, no. 7 (December 1983): 6, no. 9 (January 1984): 8–9.

55. *Sunrise*, no. 39 (November 1986): 13.

56. Translation from Spanish original. *Sunrise*, no. 7 (December 1983): 6.

57. *Sunrise*, no. 29 (November 1985): 9.

58. *Sunrise*, no. 4 (September 1983): 13.

59. *Sunrise*, no. 13 (June 1984): 14.

60. *Pinolera* refers to the adjective *pinolero*, which is used in Nicaraguan Spanish as a colloquial expression to refer to Nicaraguans. In this quote, the author uses it to refer explicitly to Pacific Nicaraguans. Translation from Spanish original. *Sunrise*, no. 7 (December 1983): 6.

61. *Sunrise*, no. 7 (December 1983): 6.

62. *Sunrise*, no. 38 (October 1986): 12.

63. *Sunrise*, no. 29 (November 1985): 8–9, no. 14 (July 1983): 4–5, no. 42 (February 1987): 13.

64. Translation from Spanish original. *Barricada*, May 30, 1986, 5.

65. *Barricada*, June 3, 1987, 4.

66. *Barricada*, May 29, 1987, 6, and November 2, 1986, 6.

67. Vernooy, *Starting All Over Again*, 33–38; CEPAL, "Damage," 32; Equipo Envío, "Ay Nicaragua"; Equipo Envío, "Just the Facts."

68. Vernooy, *Starting All Over Again*, 136; *Barricada*, March 29, 1990, 1, October 22, 1990, 1, 5.

69. Torres and Vernooy, "Mujeres comerciantes"; *Barricada*, November 12, 1990, 2, April 17, 1991, 1.

70. Vernooy, *Starting All Over Again*, 129–49.

71. González, "Gigante que despierta"; González, "Unmaking of Self-Determination," 307.

72. Soto Joya, *Ventanas en la memoria*, 49–50. She refers especially to the Siuna region.

73. Rueda Estrada, "El campesinado migrante," 181–84; Soto Joya, *Ventanas en la memoria*, 24, 49–50.

74. Morris, "Toward a Geography of Solidarity," 358; González and Figueroa, "Regional Autonomy," 174–79.

75. González and Figueroa, "Regional Autonomy," 168–72.

76. Sujo Wilson, *Oral History*; Alvarez and Escobar, *Pedazos de historia*; Heldke, "But Is It Authentic?"

77. Translation from Spanish original. *Bluefields Creole Kitchen*, 8.

78. Beushausen, Brüske, Commichau, Helber, and Kloß, "Caribbean (on the) Dining Table," 14.

79. Castillo Aramburu, *Cocina nicaragüense*; López Guzmán, *Cocinando con María Esther*.

80. Kauffmann et al., *Arte culinario*, 15. This research was conducted by the regional governments in cooperation with BICU University.

EPILOGUE: NICARAGUA'S ROLE IN THE DEBATES

1. Sáenz, "Hay hambre."

2. *La Voz del Sandinismo*, "Destaca Rosario"; *La Voz del Sandinismo*, "Gobierno Sandinista."

3. In this epilogue I have incorporated short extracts from Berth, "Nicaraguan Food Policy." Thanks go to the University of London Press for granting permission.

4. Boyer, "Food Security"; Froidevaux, "Grassroots Movements," 141–42.

5. United Nations, "Department of Economic," Dataquery.

6. Froidevaux, "Grassroots Movements," 123; Edelman, "Food Sovereignty."

7. Edelman, "Transnational Peasant Politics," 53.

8. Holt-Giménez, *Campesino*, 13–61; Froidevaux, "Grassroots Movements," 202–9.

9. Froidevaux, "Grassroots Movements," 20–21.

10. Froidevaux, "Grassroots Movements," 20–21; Holt-Giménez, *Campesino*, 61.

11. See, for example, the 2016 definition on La Vía Campesina's homepage: "Food sovereignty prioritizes local food production and consumption. It gives a country the right to protect its local producers from cheap imports and to control production. It ensures that the rights to use and manage lands, territories, water, seeds, livestock and biodiversity are in the hands of those who produce food and not of the corporate sector. Therefore the implementation of genuine agrarian reform is one of the top priorities of the farmer's movement," accessed February 18, 2020, https://web.archive.org/web/20150323045941/http://viacampesina.org/en/index.php/organisation-mainmenu-44.

12. Equipo Nitlápan-Envío, "Time for a Pact"; Rocha and Cristoplos, "Las ONGs"; Marti i Puig and Baumeister, "Agrarian Policies."

13. Asamblea Nacional de la República de Nicaragua, "Iniciativa de ley."

14. Godek, "Institutionalization," 175–81.

15. Spalding, *Contesting Trade*, 208.

16. Spalding, *Contesting Trade*, 208–10; Marti y Puig and Baumeister, "Agrarian Policies."

17. Müller, "Loss of Harmony"; Godek, "Challenges."

18. Godek, "Tale of Two Food Sovereignties."

19. Martí i Puig and Close, "Nicaraguan Exception?" 299–300. The AL-BA-TCP was founded in 2004 by Venezuela and Cuba as an alternative alliance to the Free Trade Area of the Americas (FTAA). The two nations agreed on petroleum trade and intensified exchange in the areas of health and education. Later on, Bolivia (2006), Nicaragua (2007), Ecuador (2009), and several Caribbean nations joined ALBA.

20. Spalding, *Contesting Trade*, 233. On the role of food security in Brazilian foreign policy, see Coelho and Inoue, "When Hunger Meets Diplomacy."

21. Kester, *Informe evaluativo*, 17; Spalding, "Poverty Politics."

22. Grupo Venancia, "Hambre Cero."

23. Shillington, "Right to Food"; FAO, "Urban and Peri-urban."

24. Translation from Spanish original. *El Nuevo Diario*, "Preparan feria"; *El Nuevo Diario*, "Jalapa con su maíz."

25. Transcription from my sound recording at the event, April 2011.

26. Bornemann, Cuadra, Narváez Silva, and Solorzano, *Desafíos*, 34; Martí i Puig and Baumeister, "Agrarian Policies," 389.

27. FAO, "Suite of Food"; FAO, OPS, WFP, and UNICEF, *Panorama*, 8.

28. For the controversy on child malnutrition, see *La Voz del Sandinismo*, "Declaraciones de la compañera Rosario Murillo"; López, "Los últimos datos." The 2018 UNICEF report seems to support Rosario Murillo's interpretation of decreasing child malnutrition: According to the document, chronic child malnutrition had decreased from 17.3 percent (2011–2012) to 12.4 (2018). However, the UNICEF report provides no information on statistical sources. It is possible that Nicaraguan authorities provided manipulated data.

GLOSSARY

achiote	A spice made from the red seed of the annatto tree.
bami	A flatbread based on cassava flour. It was important in Caribbean Garífuna communities, but there are also Creole styles of preparation.
Barricada	The FSLN newspaper published between 1979 and 1998.
buñuelo	Fried paste balls made out of cassava or maize. The paste also contains cuajada, eggs, or banana.
Buzón popular	This was a section in *Barricada* that answered to complaints on everyday problems affecting the Nicaraguan population during the 1980s.
chayote	A vegetable that is widespread in Central America and Mexico (botanical name: *sechium edule*).
comisariato	Stores distributing basic goods at workplaces during the 1980s.
Creole	A term used in the Caribbean for people of mixed descent and mixed European African languages. In Nicaragua, the term was used for people of Afro-Caribbean descent but was not exclusively limited to this group.
cuajada	A cheese (milk curd), made from cow's milk. In Nicaragua, it is one of the most frequently consumed dairy products.
diplotienda	Another name for the dollar shops that sold imported goods for foreign exchange during the 1980s.
duswa	Miskito expression for a root, a variety of dasheen, used as basic food in the Nicaraguan Caribbean (botanical name: *Xanthosoma spp.*).

expendios populares   Small shops distributing basic products after the Sandinista revolution.

fresco   Short for *refresco*. A cold fruit drink based on water or milk to which sugar is added.

fritanga   Nicaraguan street food stands or simple restaurants frequently offering fried plantains, cheese, or grilled meat.

gallo pinto   A dish of rice and red beans. Both Nicaragua and Costa Rica claim it as the national dish.

Garífuna   Descendants of black and indigenous populations in the Central American Caribbean.

Green Revolution   A term to describe the spread of new agricultural technologies and high-yielding seeds to increase global food production since the 1940s.

indio viejo   A typical Nicaraguan dish with meat, tomatoes, bell peppers, and wet-ground tortillas.

Johnny cake   A Caribbean dish whose name is derived from journey cake. A cake made out of wheat flour, coconut milk, sugar, egg, butter, and baking powder.

manzana   A unit of area measurement used in Central American countries. In Nicaragua it is equivalent to 7,050 square meters.

Mayangna   An indigenous group at the Nicaraguan Caribbean Coast also referred to as Sumu.

mestizo   A term used in Latin America for persons of mixed race, mainly a mixture of either Spanish or Portuguese and Latin American indigenous groups. In many Latin American countries, this became a general term for distinguishing Spanish-speaking groups from indigenous groups during the twentieth century.

Miskito   An indigenous group at the Nicaraguan Caribbean Coast.

nacatamal   A typical Nicaraguan dish, a tamal filled with pork meat, rice, tomatoes, onions, garlic, and achiote.

piñata   Figures made out of papier-mâché filled with candy that are used for games at children's birthday parties in Latin America. The piñata hangs on a string from above and blindfolded participants have to hit it with a stick until the sweets fall out.

pinol	A traditional Nicaraguan drink made out of toasted cornmeal dissolved in water to which sugar is added. Nicaraguans sometimes refer to themselves as *pinoleros*.
pulpería	A small neighborhood store.
Rama	A small indigenous group at the Nicaraguan Caribbean Coast.
rondón	A Caribbean dish whose name derived from the Jamaican Rundown. It is a fish dish frequently including cassava, plantains, garlic, and coconut milk.
Semana Santa	Easter Week.
sopa de queso	Cheese soup.
tamales	A Central American and Mexican dish with a maize dough as filling wrapped in corn or banana leaves. Fillings can be sweet or savory.
tiste	A traditional Nicaraguan drink made out of toasted cornmeal mixed with cocoa. In some regions, pieces of tortilla are soaked in water and ground to generate the cornmeal.
wabul	A vegetable stew in the Nicaraguan Caribbean, the simple version consists of green bananas and coconut milk.

BIBLIOGRAPHY

ARCHIVAL SOURCES

Bundesarchiv Bern, Switzerland
DEZA Relance et développement de la production alimentaire dans la région des Segovias
Hilfswerk der Evangelischen Kirchen der Schweiz
Bundesarchiv Berlin-Lichterfelde, Germany
DC 20 Ministerrat der Deutschen Demokratischen Republik
DE 1 Staatliche Planungskommission
DN 10 Staatsbank der DDR
CARE records, Manuscript and Archives Division. New York Public Library. Astor, Lenox, and Tilden Foundations.
Assistant Executive Director's Files
Assistant Director's Files
Country Files, Nicaragua
Country Project Files, Nicaragua
Country Correspondence, Nicaragua
CARE Canada, Project Files, Nicaragua
Nutritionists' files
Food and Agriculture Organization (FAO) Archives, Rome, Italy
ESH
World Food Days (WFD) IN 4 9 NIC, World Food Days Nicaragua
Office of Director-General (ODG) Old
FA 6/1 DG, Trips and Tours, Nicaragua
FA 13/1 Food Security Assistance Scheme, General Matters
DP 9/1 Projects, General Matters, Nicaragua
TA 9/1 Projects, Policy and General Matters, Nicaragua
Office of Director-General (ODG) New
Country Office (CO) Nicaragua
CO-A Nicaragua

      Projects 1989–1996
   Office for Special Relief Operation (OSRO)
      FP 5/3 Emergency Projects
      SP 50/21 Countries, Nicaragua
   Yriat Files: Nicaragua, 1980–1981
   IODG 8: FA 4/4 Emergency Aid
Instituto de Historia de Nicaragua y Centroamérica (IHNCA), Managua,
   Nicaragua.
   Government documents on the supply situation, 1984–1986
The Political Archive of the Federal Foreign Office (PA AA), Berlin, Germany
   B33 Länderakten Nicaragua, Entwicklungshilfe
USAID: Development Experience Clearinghouse

NEWSPAPERS AND PERIODICALS

Barricada, Managua, 1980–1992
Envío, 1981–1995
Excelsior, 1930
Gente, 1990–1991
La Información, 1930
nicaráuac, 1981
La Prensa, Managua, 1970–1973, 1990–1994
Revista Conservadora, 1960–1970
Semana Cómica, 1983–1985
Somos, 1982–1986
Sunrise, 1983–1989

AUTHOR'S INTERVIEWS

I have changed all the names of interviewees to maintain their privacy.
Marlen Jimena Guillén Mora, Managua, August 2012
Ximena Cubero, León, September 2012
Gabriel Diego, León, September 2012
Rina Méndez Osorno, León, September 2012
Emilce María Vega Sandoval, León, September 2012
Philip Ulman, Geneva, September 2013

PUBLISHED SOURCES

Aguilar Antunes, Alexander, Esteban de Gori, and Carmen Elena Villacorta, eds.
   Nicaragua en crisis. Buenos Aires: Sans Soleil, 2018. http://biblioteca.clacso
   .edu.ar/clacso/gt/20190813034645/Nicaragua_en_crisis.pdf.
Alvarez, Cristóbal, and Glennis Escobar, eds. *Pedazos de historia Puerto Cabezas*.
   Colección Centenario. Managua: URACCAN, 2004.

Álvarez Montalván, Emilio. "Requerimientos y deficiencias de la dieta popular en Nicaragua." *Revista Conservadora* 1, no. 2 (1960): 19–24.

Anderson, Cheasty Kristin. "Health Care Reform in Sandinista Nicaragua, 1979–1990." PhD dissertation, University of Texas, Austin, 2014.

Anderson, Leslie, and Lawrence C. Dodd. *Learning Democracy: Citizen Engagement and Electoral Choice in Nicaragua 1990–2001.* Chicago: University of Chicago Press, 2005.

Antonio Ramírez, Marco A. "Comercio de alimentos en el Mercado Común Centroamericano y en el de Panamá." *Separata de la Revista de la Universidad de San Carlos* 68 (1966): 39–83.

Arana, Mario. "General Economic Policy." In Walker, *Nicaragua without Illusions*, 81–96.

Arancibia Mujica, María C., Amparo Gutiérrez Castro, and Aura L. Zelaya Ramírez. "Manual de alimentación y nutrición: Guía para docentes, lideres comunales y gremiales." INCAP-OPS, MINSA-MED, Managua, 1991.

Arbeitsgruppe des CIDCA. "Vom Rio Coco nach Tasba Pri: Chronik einer gescheiterten Umsiedlung." In *Mosquitia—die andere Hälfte Nicaraguas: Über Geschichte und Gegenwart der Atlantikküste*, edited by Klaus Meschkat, Eleonore von Oertzen, Ernesto Richter, Lioba Rossbach, and Volker Wünderich, 219–53. Hamburg: Junius, 1987.

Argüello Hüper, Alejandro. "La ciudad de Managua: Historia y desarrollo hasta 1979." Objektbezogene Stadtplanung im Forschungsschwerpunkt, Arbeitsfeld Planen und Bauen in Entwicklungsländern 21, TU Hamburg-Harburg, Hamburg, 1986.

Arnove, Robert F. *Education and Revolution in Nicaragua.* New York: Praeger, 1986.

Asamblea Nacional Constituyente. "Constitución Política de 1987." https://www.enriquebolanos.org/constitucion/constitucion-original-1987/.

Asamblea Nacional Constituyente. "Constitución Política de Nicaragua 1939." https://www.enriquebolanos.org/articulo/constitucion_nicaragua_1939.

Asamblea Nacional de la República de Nicaragua. "Iniciativa de ley 'Ley de Seguridad Alimentaria.'" Unpublished manuscript, 1998.

Austin, James, Jonathan Fox, and Walter Kruger. "The Role of the Revolutionary State in the Nicaraguan Food System." *World Development* 13, no. 1 (1985): 15–40. https://doi.org/10.1016/0305-750X(85)90064-6/.

"Avances en el mejoramiento de la utilización de la ayuda alimentaria en Centroamérica y Panamá: Seminario Subregional sobre programas de alimentación a grupos en Centroamérica y Panamá. Nicaragua—Documento País." Managua, November 1988.

Ayala, Víktor. "Iguana en amaranto." Accessed March 3, 2015. http://www.trincheraonline.com/2014/08/15/iguana-en-amaranto/.

Babb, Florence E. *After Revolution: Mapping Gender and Cultural Politics in Neoliberal Nicaragua.* Austin: University of Texas Press, 2001.

Banco Central de Nicaragua. *Informe anual 2018.* Managua: Banco Central de Nicaragua, 2018.

Barraclough, Solon L. *A Preliminary Analysis of the Nicaraguan Food System.* Geneva: United Nations, 1982.

Barraclough, Solon L., and Peter Utting. "Ernährungssicherung in Lateinamerika Erfahrungen u. Trends." *Lateinamerika. Analysen und Berichte* 10 (1986): 102–86.

Barraclough, Solon L., Ariane van Buren, Alicia Garriazzo, Anjali Sunderam, and Peter Utting. *Aid That Counts: The Western Contribution to Development and Survival in Nicaragua.* Amsterdam: Transnational Institute, 1988.

Barrett, Christopher B., and Daniel G. Maxwell. *Food Aid after Fifty Years: Recasting Its Role.* Priorities in Development Economics. London: Routledge, 2005.

Barrientos Tecún, Dante. "Acerca de las concepciones de Desarrollo y Modernidad vistas desde los discursos poéticos de Centroamérica." *Mesoamérica: Una Revista Multidisciplinaria* (2015): 99–116.

Barry, Tom, and Deb Preusch. *The Soft War: The Uses and Abuses of U.S. Economic Aid in Central America.* New York: Grove Press, 1988.

Baumeister, Eduardo. "Agrarian Reform." In *Revolution and Counterrevolution in Nicaragua,* edited by Thomas W. Walker, 229–45. Boulder, CO: Westview Press, 1991.

Baumeister, Eduardo. *Estructura y reforma agraria en Nicaragua (1979–1989).* Managua: Ediciones CDR-ULA, 1998.

Baumeister, Eduardo. "The Politics of Land Reform." In Close, Martí i Puig, and McConnell, *Sandinistas and Nicaragua,* 245–68.

Belli, Gioconda. *The Country under My Skin. A Memoir of Love and War.* London: Bloomsbury, 2002.

Bendaña, Alejandro. *Una tragedia campesina: Testimonios de la resistencia.* Managua: Edit-Arte, 1991.

Berth, Christiane. "Nicaraguan Food Policy: Between Self-Sufficiency and Dependency." In Francis, *Nicaraguan Exceptionalism,* 61–85.

Beushausen, Wiebke, Anne Brüske, Ana-Sofia Commichau, Patrick Helber, and Sinah Kloß, eds. *Caribbean Food Cultures: Culinary Practices and Consumption in the Caribbean and Its Diasporas.* Postcolonial Studies 18. Bielefeld: transcript Verlag, 2014.

Beushausen, Wiebke, Anne Brüske, Ana-Sofia Commichau, Patrick Helber, and Sinah Kloß. "The Caribbean (on the) Dining Table: Contextualizing Culinary Cultures." In *Caribbean Food Cultures: Culinary Practices and Consumption in the Caribbean and Its Diasporas,* edited by Wiebke Beushausen, Anne Brüske,

Ana-Sofia Commichau, Patrick Helber, and Sinah Kloß, 11–24. Postcolonial Studies 18. Bielefeld: transcript Verlag, 2014.

Beverley, John, and Marc Zimmerman. *Literature and Politics in the Central American Revolutions.* Austin: University of Texas Press, 1990.

Biltekoff, Charlotte. "Critical Nutrition Studies." In *The Oxford Handbook of Food History*, edited by Jeffrey M. Pilcher, 172–90. Oxford: Oxford University Press, 2012.

Biondi-Morra, Brizio N. *Revolución y política alimentaria: Un análisis crítico de Nicaragua.* Mexico DF: Siglo XXI Editores, 1990.

Bluefields Creole Kitchen: A Taste of the Caribbean. Managua: Oficina de Coordinación Programa RAAN, 2004.

Bobrow-Strain, Aaron. "Making White Bread by the Bomb's Early Light: Anxiety, Abundance, and Industrial Food Power in the Early Cold War." *Food and Foodways* 19, nos. 1–2 (2011): 74–97.

Booth, John A. *The End and the Beginning: The Nicaraguan Revolution.* 2nd ed. Boulder, CO: Westview Press, 1985.

Bornemann, Guillermo, Oscar Neira Cuadra, Carlos Narváez Silva, and José Luis Solorzano. *Desafíos desde la seguridad alimentaria y nutricional en Nicaragua.* Managua: Oxfam-UCA-Crece, 2012. http://www.oxfamblogs.org/lac/wp-content/uploads/2013/05/Desaf%C3%ADos-desde-la-seguridad-alimentaria-y-nutricional-en-Nicaragua.pdf.

Boyer, Jefferson. "Food Security, Food Sovereignty, and Local Challenges for Transnational Agrarian Movements: The Honduras Case." *Journal of Peasant Studies* 37, no. 2 (2010): 319–51. https://doi.org/10.1080/03066151003594997/.

Boym, Svetlana. "Nostalgia and Its Discontents." *Hedgehog Review* (Summer 2007): 7–18. http://www.iasc-culture.org/eNews/2007_10/9.2CBoym.pdf.

Brands, Hal. *Latin America's Cold War.* Cambridge, MA: Harvard University Press, 2010.

Brenner, Edith. "'Sie sollen sich immer an uns und unser Völkchen erinnern': Ethnologische Feldstudie mit Frauen über Beziehungs- und Machtstrukturen in einem marginalen Quartier von Managua, Nicaragua." Dissertation, University of Zürich, 1987.

Brockett, Charles. "The Right to Food and United States Policy in Guatemala." *Human Rights Quarterly* 6, no. 3 (1984): 366–80.

Bulmer-Thomas, Victor. *The Political Economy of Central America since 1920.* Cambridge Latin American Studies 63. Cambridge: Cambridge University Press, 1987.

Cardenal, Ernesto. *La revolución perdida.* Memorias vol. 3. Managua: Anama Ediciones, 2003.

Cardenal, Roberto. *Lo que se quiso ocultar: 8 años de censura sandinista.* San José, CR: Libro Libre, 1989.

Cardoso, Fernando Henrique, and Enzo Faletto. *Dependencia y desarrollo en América Latina: Ensayo de interpretación sociológica.* México, DF: Siglo XXI Editores, 1969.

Carr, Barry A. "Pioneering Transnational Solidarity in the Americas: The Movement in Support of Augusto C. Sandino 1927–1934." *Journal of Iberian and Latin American Research* 20, no. 2 (2014): 141–52.

Carrión, Luis. "Austeridad: Principio y norma de nuestro pueblo." Managua: Departamento de Propaganda y Educación Política del FSLN, 1981.

Castillo Aramburu, Ligia. *Cocina nicaragüense.* Managua: Editorial Hispamer, 2004.

Castro, Josué de. *The Geography of Hunger.* Boston: Little, Brown, 1952.

Cattle, Dorothy J. "Nutritional Security and the Strategy of Purchasing: The Coastal Miskito Indians, Eastern Nicaragua." Dissertation, University of New Mexico, 1973.

CEPAL. "Nicaragua: The Floods of May 1982 and Their Effects on Social and Economic Development." Mexico City, 1982. https://repositorio.cepal.org/bitstream/handle/11362/26468/S8299999_en.pdf?sequence=3/.

CEPAL. "Damage Caused by Hurricane Joan in Nicaragua: Its Effect on Economic Development and Living Conditions, and Requirements for Rehabilitation and Reconstruction." Santiago de Chile, 1988. http://cidbimena.desastres.hn/docum/crid/Octubre2004/pdf/eng/doc56/doc56.htm.

CEPAL. "Preliminary Overview of the Economics of Latin America and the Caribbean, 2018." Santiago de Chile: United Nations, 2019.

Chernyshova, Natalya. *Soviet Consumer Culture in the Brezhnev Era.* BASEES/Routledge Series on Russian and East European Studies 90. London: Routledge, 2013.

Christiaens, Kim. "Between Diplomacy and Solidarity: Western European Support Networks for Sandinista Nicaragua." *European Review of History: Revue européenne d'histoire* 21, no. 4 (2014): 617–34. https://doi.org/10.1080/13507486.2014.933184/.

CIERA, ed. *Distribución y consumo popular de alimentos en Managua.* Colección Comandante Germán Pomares Ordóñez. Managua: CIERA, 1983.

CIERA, ed. *El hambre en los países del tercer mundo.* Colección Comandante Germán Pomares Ordóñez. Managua: CIERA, 1983.

CIERA, ed. *La reforma agraria en Nicaragua 1979–1989: Sistema alimentario.* Colección 10 Aniversario, vol. 2. Managua: CIERA, 1989.

CIERA, PAN, and CIDA, eds. *Informe del primer seminario sobre estrategia alimentaria: (CIERA-PAN-CIDA) realizado en Managua, Nicaragua Libre del 21 al 25 de febrero, 1983.* Colección Comandante Germán Pomares Ordoñez. Managua: CIERA, 1983.

CIERA and UNRISD. *Managua es Nicaragua: El impacto de la capital en el sistema alimentario nacional.* Managua: CIERA, 1984.

Close, David. *Nicaragua: The Chamorro Years*. Boulder, CO: Lynne Rienner, 1998.

Close, David. *Nicaragua: Navigating the Politics of Democracy*. Boulder, CO: Lynne Rienner, 2016.

Close, David, Salvador Martí i Puig, and Shelley A. McConnell, eds. *The Sandinistas and Nicaragua since 1979*. Boulder, CO: Lynne Rienner, 2012.

Coelho, Natália Bandeira Ramos, and Cristina Yumie Aoki Inoue. "When Hunger Meets Diplomacy: Food Security in Brazilian Foreign Policy." *Meridiano 47—Journal of Global Studies* 19 (2018):1–20.

Colburn, Forrest D. *Post-revolutionary Nicaragua: State, Class, and the Dilemmas of Agrarian Policy*. 2nd ed. California Series on Social Choice and Political Economy 7. Berkeley: University of California Press, 1986.

Colburn, Forrest D. *Managing the Commanding Heights: Nicaragua's State Enterprises*. Berkeley: University of California Press, 1990.

Colburn, Forrest D. *My Car in Managua*. Austin: University of Texas Press, 1991.

Collins, Joseph D. *Nicaragua: Was hat sich durch die Revolution verändert? Agrarreform und Ernährung im neuen Nicaragua*. With the assistance of Frances Moore Lappé, Nick Allen, and Paul Rice. 2nd ed. Wuppertal: Edition Nahua, 1986.

Collins, Joseph D. *Nicaragua: What Difference Could a Revolution Make? Food and Farming in the New Nicaragua*. 3rd ed. A Food First book. San Francisco: Grove Press, 1986.

Collins, Joseph D., Michael Scott, and Medea Benjamin. *No Free Lunch: Food and Revolution in Cuba Today*. New York: Grove Press, 1986.

Conroy, Michael E. "Nicaragua: The Economic Dilemmas of Peace and Democracy in 1988." *Texas Papers on Latin America*, no. 88-05 (1988). http://lanic.utexas.edu/project/etext/llilas/tpla/8805.pdf.

Cooper, David: "Grassroots Verticalism? A Comunidad Eclesial de Base in Sandinista Nicaragua." In Francis, *Nicaraguan Exceptionalism*, 145–64.

Cooper, Frederick. "Writing the History of Development." *Journal of Modern European History* 8 (2010): 5–38. https://doi.org/10.17104%2F1611-8944_2010_1_5/.

Coronel Urtecho, José. "Elogio de la cocina nicaragüense." *Revista Conservadora* 3, no. 20 (1962): 30–34.

Cuadra, Pablo A. *El nicaragüense*. 13th ed. Managua: Hispamer, 1997.

Cullather, Nick. "Development? It's History." *Diplomatic History* 24 (2000): 641–53. https://doi.org/10.1111/0145-2096.00242/.

Cullather, Nick. "The Foreign Policy of the Calorie." *American Historical Review* 112, no. 2 (2007): 337–64. https://doi.org/10.1086/ahr.112.2.337/.

Cullather, Nick. *The Hungry World: America's Cold War Battle against Poverty in Asia*. Cambridge, MA: Harvard University Press, 2010.

Dennis, Philip A. *The Miskitu People of Awastara*. Austin: University of Texas Press, 2004.

Diederich, Bernard. *Somoza: And the Legacy of U.S. Involvement in Central America.* 3rd ed. Princeton: Markus Wiener, 2007.

Dijkstra, Geske. *Industrialization in Sandinista Nicaragua: Policy and Practice in a Mixed Economy.* San Francisco: Westview Press, 1992.

Dore, Elizabeth. "The Great Grain Dilemma: Peasants and State Policy in Revolutionary Nicaragua." *Peasant Studies* 17, no. 2 (1990): 96–120.

Dore, Elizabeth. *Myths of Modernity: Peonage and Patriarchy in Nicaragua.* Durham, NC: Duke University Press, 2006.

Dosal, Paul. "Accelerating Development and Revolution: Nicaragua and the Alliance for Progress." *Inter-American Economic Affairs* 38, no. 4 (1985): 75–96.

Douglas, Mary, and Baron Isherwood. *The World of Goods: Towards an Anthropology of Consumption.* London: Routledge, 1996.

Dozier, Craig L. *Nicaragua's Mosquito Shore: The Years of British and American Presence.* Alabama: University of Alabama Press, 1985.

Drinot, Paulo. "Food, Race and Working-Class Identity: Restaurantes Populares and Populism in 1930s Peru." *The Americas* 62, no. 2 (2005): 245–70. https://doi.org/10.1353/tam.2005.0160/.

Eckstein, David, Marie-Lena Hutfils, and Maik Winges. "Briefing Paper Global Climate Risk Index 2019: Who Suffers Most from Extreme Weather Events? Weather-Related Loss Events in 2017 and 1998 to 2017." Germanwatch, Bonn, December 2018.

Edelman, Marc. "Transnational Peasant Politics in Central America." *Latin American Research Review* 33, no. 3 (1998): 49–86.

Edelman, Marc. "Food Sovereignty: Forgotten Genealogies and Future Regulatory Changes." Food Sovereignty: A Critical Dialogue, Conference Paper 72, Yale University, September 2013.

El Nuevo Diario. "Preparan feria del maíz en Jalapa." *El Nuevo Diario*, August 28, 2008.

El Nuevo Diario. "Jalapa con su maíz . . . orgullo de Nicaragua." *El Nuevo Diario*, September 17, 2009.

Enríquez, Laura J. *Harvesting Change: Labor and Agrarian Reform in Nicaragua 1979–1990.* Chapel Hill: University of North Carolina Press, 1991.

Equipo Envío. "Nicaragua's Floods: Digging Out from Disaster." *Envío*, no. 13 (1982). http://www.envio.org.ni/articulo/3369/.

Equipo Envío. "The Economic Costs of the Contra War: Nicaragua's Case before the World Court." *Envío*, no. 51 (1985). http://www.envio.org.ni/articulo/3408/.

Equipo Envío. "Ay Nicaragua Nicaragüita. El desafío del huracán." *Envío*, no. 86 (1988).

Equipo Envío. "The New Economic Package." *Envío*, no. 86 (1988). http://www.envio.org.ni/articulo/3062/.

Equipo Envío. "From a Mixed-Up Economy toward a Socialist Mixed Economy." *Envío*, no. 94 (1989). http://www.envio.org.ni/articulo/2702/.

Equipo Envío. "Just the Facts: Damage Figures from Hurricane Joan." *Envío*, no. 90 (1989). http://www.envio.org.ni/articulo/2778/.

Equipo Envío. "Immovable Object Meets Irresistible Force." *Envío*, no. 125 (1991). http://www.envio.org.ni/articulo/2851/.

Equipo Nitlápan-Envío. "Toll Rises from Hurricane Joan: Emergency as Daily Life." *Envío*, no. 90 (1989). http://www.envio.org.ni/articulo/2831/.

Equipo Nitlápan-Envío. "Time for a Pact or Time for a Reflection?" *Envío*, no. 204 (1998).http://www.envio.org.ni/articulo/1378/.

Ernst, Jutta, and Florian Freitag. "Einleitung: Transkulturelle Dynamiken—Entwicklungen und Perspektiven eines Konzepts." In *Transkulturelle Dynamiken: Aktanten-Prozesse-Theorien*, edited by Jutta Ernst and Florian Freitag. Mainzer Historische Kulturwissenschaften 19. Bielefeld: transcript Verlag, 2015.

Escobar, Arturo. *Encountering Development: The Making and Unmaking of the Third World*. Paperback reissue. Princeton, NJ: Princeton University Press, 2012.

Fagen, Richard R. *The Transformation of Political Culture in Cuba*. Stanford Studies in Comparative Politics 2. Stanford, CA: Stanford University Press, 1969.

FAO. "Office for Special Relief Operations. Report no. 02/83/E, Republic of Nicaragua. Report of the FAO/WFP Mission. Assessment of Basic Food Production and Availability during 1982–83 in Areas Affected by Floods and Drought." Rome: FAO, 1983.

FAO. "Report of the Seventeenth FAO Regional Conference for Latin America: Managua, 30 August to 10 September 1982." Rome: FAO, 1983.

FAO. "Nicaragua. Situación alimentaria en 1989 y lineamientos de política para la seguridad alimentaria." Managua: FAO, 1990.

FAO. Representación en Nicaragua. "Informe anual: Julio 92 a junio 93." Managua: FAO, 1993.

FAO. "Informe terminal: Apoyo al programa alimentario nicaragüense para la planificación de la seguridad alimentaria." Rome: FAO, 1994.

FAO. "Urban and Peri-urban Agriculture in Latin America and the Caribbean." Last modified 2015. https://web.archive.org/web/20181123104314/http://www.fao.org/ag/agp/greenercities/en/GGCLAC/managua.html/.

FAO. "Food and Agriculture Data." FAOSTAT. http://www.fao.org/faostat/en/.

FAO. "Suite of Food Security Indicators." FAOSTAT. http://www.fao.org/faostat/en/#data/FS/visualize/.

FAO, and CIERA. "Nicaragua. Estudio sobre campesinos pobres." Rome, 1985.

FAO, IFAD, UNICEF, WFP and WHO. *The State of Food Security and Nutrition in the World 2019: Safeguarding against Economic Slowdowns and Downturns*. Rome: FAO, 2019.

FAO, and Ministerio de Agricultura y Ganadería. *Proyecto FAO: Formulación de políticas agrícolas en el marco del ajuste macroeconómico: Diagnóstico del sector agropecuario, forestal y agroindustrial de Nicaragua 1970–1991*. Managua: FAO, 1991.

FAO, OPS, WFP, and UNICEF. *Panorama de la seguridad alimentaria y nutricional en América Latina y el Caribe 2019.* Santiago de Chile: FAO, 2019.

FAO, and WHO. *Conferencia Internacional sobre Nutrición: Informe de Nicaragua.* Managua: FAO, 1992.

Ferguson, James. *The Anti-politics Machine: "Development," Depoliticization, and Bureaucratic Power in Lesotho.* Cambridge: Cambridge University Press, 1990.

Ferrero Blanco, María Dolores. *La Nicaragua de los Somoza 1936–1979.* Huelva: Universidad de Huelva, 2010.

Ferrero Blanco, María Dolores. "Daniel Ortega y Mijail Gorbachov: Nicaragua y la URSS en los últimos años de la Guerra Fría (1985–1990)." *HISPANIA NOVA, Revista de Historia Contemporánea* 13 (2015): 26–53.

Ferrero Blanco, María Dolores. *De un lado y del otro: Mujeres contras y sandinistas en la Revolución Nicaragüense (1979–1990).* Granada: Editorial Comares, 2018.

FIDA. "Informe de la Misión Especial de Programación a Nicaragua." Rome: FIDA, 1980.

FIDEG. "Encuesta de hogares para medir la pobreza en Nicaragua." Managua: FIDEG, 2018.

FitzGerald, E.V.K. "Una evaluación de los costos económicos de la agresión estadounidense para Nicaragua, 1980–1984." In *La economía política de la Nicaragua revolucionaria,* edited by Rose Spalding, 238–60. México DF: Fondo de Cultura Económica, 1989.

Flores, Marina. "Estudios dietéticos en Nicaragua: II. Barrio de San Luis, Ciudad de Managua." In *Boletín Sanitario: Edición especial dedicada a labores de INCAP en Nicaragua* (July 1956): 31–51.

Flores, Marina. "Food Patterns in Central America and Panama." In *Tradition, Science and Practice in Dietetics: Proceedings of the 3rd International Congress of Dietetics, London, July 10–14, 1961,* 23–27. Bradford: Byles and Sons, 1961.

Flores, Marina, Telma H. Caputti, and Zela Leytón. "Estudios dietéticos en Nicaragua: I. Municipio de San Isidro, Departamento de Matagalpa." In *Boletín Sanitario: Edición especial dedicada a labores de INCAP en Nicaragua* (July 1956): 2–21.

Flores, Marina, María T. Menchú, Marta Yolanda Lara, and Moisés Béhar. "Dieta adecuada de costo mínimo para Nicaragua." Guatemala City: INCAP, 1970.

Francis, Hilary. "The Difference the Revolution Made: Decision-Making in Liberal and Sandinista Communities." In Francis, *Nicaraguan Exceptionalism,* 127–44.

Francis, Hilary. "Introduction: Exceptionalism and Agency in Nicaragua's Revolutionary Heritage." In Francis, *Nicaraguan Exceptionalism,* 1–19.

Francis, Hilary, ed. *A Nicaraguan Exceptionalism? Debating the Legacy of the Sandinista Revolution*. London: University of London Press, 2020.

Frens-String, Joshua. "Communists, Commissars, and Consumers: The Politics of Food on the Chilean Road to Socialism." *Hispanic American Historical Review* 98, no. 3 (2018): 471–501. https://doi.org/10.1215/00182168-6933567/.

Friedman, Harriet. "The Political Economy of Food: The Rise and Fall of the Postwar International Food Order." *American Journal of Sociology* 88, Supplement (1982): S248–S286. https://doi.org/10.1086/649258/.

Friedman, Jonathan. "The Hybridization of Roots and the Abhorrence of Bush." In *Spaces of Culture: City, Nation, World*, edited by Mike Featherstone and Scott Lash, 231–56. Theory, Culture and Society. London: Sage, 1999.

Friedman, Max Paul. *Nazis and Good Neighbors: The United States Campaign against the Germans of Latin America in World War II*. Cambridge: Cambridge University Press, 2003.

Froidevaux, Alice. "Grassroots Movements as Transnational Actors: The Case of CLOC-La Vía Campesina in Central America." PhD Dissertation, University of St. Gallen, 2018.

FSLN. *El programa histórico del FSLN*. 4th ed. Managua: Departamento de Propaganda y Educación Política del FSLN, 1984. http://www.asamblea.gob.ni/bibliotecavirtual/Libros/70502.pdf.

Gabbert, Wolfgang. *Creoles-Afroamerikaner im karibischen Tiefland von Nicaragua*. Kontroversen 1. Münster: Lit Verlag, 1992.

Gambone, Michael D. *Eisenhower, Somoza, and the Cold War in Nicaragua*. Westport, CT: Praeger, 1997.

Gambone, Michael D. *Capturing the Revolution: The United States, Central America, and Nicaragua, 1961–1972*. Westport, CT: Praeger, 2001.

Ganuza, Enrique, and Carlos M. Vilas. "Nicaragua. I. Scientific Research in a Revolutionary Setting: The Case of Nicaragua II. Research Cooperation between Sweden." SAREC Documentation, Research Surveys, Stockholm, 1988.

Garst, Rachel. *La ayuda alimentaria al istmo centroamericano*. Colección Temas de Seguridad Alimentaria 13. Panama: CADESCA, 1992.

Garst, Rachel, and Tom Barry. *Feeding the Crisis: U.S. Food Aid and Farm Policy in Central America*. Lincoln: University of Nebraska Press, 1990.

Geiser, Sepp. "Ni del uno ni del otro . . . soy de mi familia: Eine ethnologische Untersuchung zu Alltag und Politik in einem Unterschichtquartier von Managua/Nicaragua." Dissertation, University of Zürich, 1995.

Gerlach, Christian. "Die Welternährungskrise, 1972–1975." *Geschichte und Gesellschaft* 31 (2005): 546–85.

Gibson, Bill. "Nicaragua." In *The Rocky Road to Reform: Adjustment, Income Distribution, and Growth in the Developing World*, edited by Lance Taylor, 431–56. Cambridge, MA: MIT Press, 1993.

Gobat, Michel. *Confronting the American Dream: Nicaragua under U.S. Imperial Rule.* American Encounters/Global Interactions. Durham, NC: Duke University Press, 2005.

Gobat, Michel. "Reconstrucción histórica de la revolución Sandinista de Nicaragua." *Mesoamérica* 54 (2012): 142–47.

Godek, Wendy. "The Institutionalization of Food Sovereignty: The Case of Nicaragua's Law of Food and Nutritional Sovereignty and Security." PhD Dissertation, State University of New Jersey, 2014.

Godek, Wendy. "Challenges for Food Sovereignty Policy Making: The Case of Nicaragua's Law 693." *Third World Quarterly* 36, no. 3 (2015): 526–43. https://doi.org/10.1080/01436597.2015.1005437/.

Godek, Wendy. "A Tale of Two Food Sovereignties." *ReVista Harvard Review of Latin America*, Spring/Summer (2019). https://revista.drclas.harvard.edu/book/tale-two-food-sovereignties/.

González, Miguel. "El gigante que despierta (The Awakening Giant): Parties and Elections in the Life of the Autonomous Regional Councils." In *National Integration and Contested Autonomy*, edited by Luciano Baracco. New York: Algora, 2011.

González, Miguel. "The Unmaking of Self-Determination: Twenty-Five Years of Regional Autonomy in Nicaragua." *Bulletin of Latin American Research* 35, no. 3 (2016): 306–21. https://doi.org/10.1111/blar.12487/.

González, Miguel, and Dolores Figueroa. "Regional Autonomy on the Caribbean Coast." In Close, Martí i Puig, and McConnell, *Sandinistas and Nicaragua*, 161–84.

González de la Rocha, Mercedes, Elizabeth Jelin, Janice Perlman, Bryan R. Roberts, Helen Safa, and Peter M. Ward. "From the Marginality of the 1960s to the 'New Poverty' of Today: A LARR Research Forum." *Latin American Research Review* 39, no. 1 (2004): 183–203.

González-Rivera, Victoria. *Before the Revolution: Women's Rights and Right-Wing Politics in Nicaragua, 1821–1979.* University Park: Pennsylvania State University Press, 2011.

Gordon, Edmund T. "Die Creoles und die Revolution von 1979." In *Mosquitia— die andere Hälfte Nicaraguas: Über Geschichte und Gegenwart der Atlantikküste*, edited by Klaus Meschkat, Eleonore von Oertzen, Ernesto Richter, Lioba Rossbach, and Volker Wünderich, 165–87. Hamburg: Junius, 1987.

Gordon, Edmund T. *Disparate Diasporas: Identity and Politics in an African Nicaraguan Community.* New Interpretations of Latin America Series. Austin: University of Texas Press, 1998.

Gould, Jeffrey L. *To Die in This Way: Nicaraguan Indians and the Myth of Mestizaje, 1880–1965.* Durham, NC: Duke University Press, 1998.

Gould, Jeffrey L. *Aquí todos mandamos igual: Lucha campesina y conciencia política en Chinandega, Nicaragua, 1950–1979.* Managua: IHNCA-UCA, 2008.

Gould, Jeffrey L. "Ambivalent Memories. A Reflection on Nicaragua." ReVista (2019). https://revista.drclas.harvard.edu/book/ambivalent-memories/.

Grandin, Greg. *Empire's Workshop: Latin America, the United States and the Rise of the New Imperialism.* New York: Metropolitan Books, 2006.

Grupo Venancia. "Hambre Cero. Cómo les va a las mujeres." *Envío* no. 396 (2015). https://www.envio.org.ni/articulo/4972/.

Hale, Charles R. "Der Konflikt der Miskito mit dem nicaraguanischen Staat 1979–1985." In *Mosquitia—die andere Hälfte Nicaraguas: Über Geschichte und Gegenwart der Atlantikküste,* edited by Klaus Meschkat, Eleonore von Oertzen, Ernesto Richter, Lioba Rossbach, and Volker Wünderich, 255–75. Hamburg: Junius, 1987.

Hale, Charles R. *Resistance and Contradiction: Miskitu Indians and the Nicaraguan State, 1894–1987.* Stanford: Stanford University Press, 2004.

Harsch, Ernest. *Thomas Sankara: An African Revolutionary.* Ohio Short Histories of Africa. Athens: Ohio University Press, 2014.

Harwood, Jonathan. "Peasant Friendly Plant Breeding and the Early Years of Green Revolution in Mexico." *Agricultural History* 83, no. 3 (2009): 384–410. https://doi.org/10.3098/ah.2009.83.3.384/.

Heldke, Lisa. "But Is It Authentic? Culinary Travel and the Search for the 'Genuine Article.'" In *The Taste Culture Reader: Experiencing Food and Drink,* edited by Carolyn Korsmeyer, 385–94. Sensory Formations Series. Oxford: Berg, 2005.

Helm, Christian. *Botschafter der Revolution: Das transnationale Kommunikations-Netzwerk zwischen der FSLN und der bundesdeutschen Nicaragua-Solidarität 1977–1990 (Studien zur Internationalen Geschichte 39).* Berlin: de Gruyter, 2018.

Helms, Mary W. *Asang: Adaptations to Culture Contact in a Miskito Community.* Gainesville: University of Florida Press, 1971.

Henriksen, Thomas H. "The People's Republic of Mozambique: Perestroika in the Tropics?" *Africana Journal* 17 (1998): 147–63.

Hernández, Julio R. "La ayuda alimentaria en Nicaragua, 1980–1989: El marco institucional del manejo de las donaciones, y su impacto en el consumo y la producción nacional." Informe de consultoría, UTN-Nicaragua, Managua, 1991.

Herren-Oesch, Madeleine, Martin Rüesch, and Christiane Sibille. *Transcultural History: Theories, Methods, Sources.* Berlin: Springer, 2012.

Herrera León, Fabián. "El apoyo de México al triunfo de la revolución sandinista. Su interés y usos políticos." *Anuario Colombiano de Historia Social y de la Cultura* 38, no. 1 (2011): 219–40.

Higman, B. W. *Jamaican Food: History, Biology, Culture.* Jamaica: University of West Indies Press, 2008.

Higman, B. W. *A Concise History of the Caribbean.* Cambridge: Cambridge University Press, 2011.

"La Historia de Supermercados La Colonia. Entrevista al Sr. Felipe Mántica Abaunza." *CCIN Boletín Informativo*, no. 3 (2010). Accessed December 25, 2019. https://web.archive.org/web/20160711224025/http://italcam.org.ni/BoletinIIIccin.pdf.

Holt-Giménez, Eric. *Campesino a campesino: Voces de Latinoamérica, Movimiento campesino para la agricultura sustentable.* Managua: SIMAS, 2008.

Horton, Lynn R. *Peasants in Arms: War and Peace in the Mountains of Nicaragua, 1979–1994.* Monographs in International Studies. Latin America Series 30. Athens: Ohio University, 1998.

Hutton, Patrick H. "Reconsiderations of the Idea of Nostalgia in Contemporary Historical Writing." *Historical Reflections* 39, no. 3 (2013): 1–8. https://doi.org/10.3167/hrrh.2013.390301/.

INCAP. "Recomendaciones nutricionales para las poblaciones de Centro América y Panamá." *Boletín de la Oficina Sanitaria Panamericana* 35, no. 1 (1953): 119–29.

INCAP. *Evaluación nutricional de la población de Centro América y Panamá: Nicaragua.* Guatemala City: INCAP, 1969.

INCAP. "Informe anual: 1° de enero–31 de diciembre de 1968." San Salvador, 1969.

INCAP. "Informe anual: 1° de enero–31 de diciembre de 1974." Guatemala, 1975.

INCAP and ICNND. *Nutritional Evaluation of the Population of Central America and Panama 1965–1967.* Guatemala City: INCAP, 1971.

INIDE. *Reporte de pobreza y desigualdad EMNV 2016.* Managua: INIDE, 2016.

INIDE and MINSA. "Encuesta Nicaragüense de Demografía y Salud 2011/12. Informe preliminar." Managua: INIDE/MINSA, 2013.

Inter-American Commission on Human Rights. "Special Monitoring Mechanism on Nicaragua Newsletter." January 2020. https://www.oas.org/es/cidh/actividades/visitas/2018Nicaragua/Newsletter-MESENI-January2020.pdf.

Investigative Team, School of Sociology, UCA. "Survival Strategies in the Popular Sectors of Managua." *Critical Sociology* 15, no. 1 (1988): 5–32.

Isbester, Katherine. *Still Fighting: The Nicaraguan Women's Movement, 1977–2000.* Pittsburgh, PA: University of Pittsburgh Press, 2001.

Jachertz, Ruth. "'To Keep Food Out of Politics': The UN Food and Agriculture Organization, 1945–1965." In *International Organizations and Development, 1945–1990*, edited by Marc Frey, Sönke Kunkel, and Corinna R. Unger, 75–100. Palgrave Macmillan Transnational History Series. Basingstoke, UK: Palgrave Macmillan, 2014.

Jonakin, Jon. "Agrarian Policy." In Walker, *Nicaragua without Illusions*, 97–113.

Jones, Adam. *Beyond the Barricades: Nicaragua and the Struggle for the Sandinista Press, 1979–1998.* Athens: Ohio University Press, 2002.

Juch, Harald. "Unser revolutionärer Alltag: Teil 2. Tagebuch Comics Zeichnungen Fotos." Managua, 1989. Photocopied manuscript.

Junta de Gobierno de Reconstrucción Nacional de la República de Nicaragua. "Ley de Defensa de los Consumidores. Decreto No. 323." http://legisla cion.asamblea.gob.ni/normaweb.nsf/($All)/72779EB4D1E24898062570A1 0057BE7B?OpenDocument/.

Junta de Gobierno de Reconstrucción Nacional de la República de Nicaragua. "Ley para Regular Informaciones de Contenido Económico. Decreto No. 512." https://nicaragua.justia.com/nacionales/decretos-ley/ley-para-regular -informaciones-de-contenido-economico-sep-17-1980/gdoc/.

Kaimowitz, David. "Nicaragua's Experience with Agricultural Planning: From State-Centred Accumulation to the Strategic Alliance with the Peasantry." *Journal of Development Studies* 24, no. 2 (1988): 115–35.

Kaimowitz, David, and David Stanfield. "The Organization of Production Units in the Nicaraguan Agrarian Reform." *Inter-American Economic Affairs* 39, no. 1 (1985): 51–77.

Kampwirth, Karen. *Feminism and the Legacy of Revolution: Nicaragua, El Salvador, Chiapas.* Latin American Series 43. Athens: Ohio University Press, 2004.

Kauffmann, Marciela et al., eds. *Arte culinario tradicional: Identidad y patrimonio de las culturas de la Costa de Caribe de Nicaragua.* Managua: CRAAN, 2012. http://unesdoc.unesco.org/images/0022/002283/228337S.pdf.

Kay, Cristóbal. "Reflexiones sobre la contribución de Solon L. Barraclough a los estudios rurales: Algunas impresiones personales." *Cuadernos de Desarrollo Rural* 56 (2006): 9–28.

Kester, Paul. *Informe evaluativo (2007–2008): Programa Productivo Alimentario (PPA) "Hambre Cero."* Managua: Embajada del Reino de los Países Bajos, 2009.

Kinzer, Stephen. *Blood of Brothers: Life and War in Nicaragua.* New York: Putnam, 1991.

König, Wolfgang. *Kleine Geschichte der Konsumgesellschaft: Konsum als Lebensform der Moderne.* Stuttgart: Steiner, 2008.

Kornbluh, Peter. *Nicaragua: The Price of Intervention—Reagan's Wars against the Sandinistas.* Washington, DC: Institute for Policy Studies, 1988.

Krujit, Dirk. *Guerrillas: War and Peace in Central America.* New York: Zed Books, 2008.

Kühn, Wolfram. *Agrarreform und Agrarkooperativen in Nicaragua.* Spektrum 6. Saarbrücken: Breitenbach, 1985.

Lagueux, Cynthia J. "Marine Turtle Fishery of Caribbean Nicaragua: Human Use Patterns and Harvest Trends." PhD Dissertation, University of Florida, 1998.

Lamberg, Sigrid. *Subsistenzökonomie in Nicaragua: Perspektiven in einer sich transformierenden Gesellschaft.* Wissen & Praxis 157. Frankfurt am Main: Brandes and Apsel, 2010.

Lancaster, Roger N. *Life Is Hard: Machismo, Danger, and the Intimacy of Power in Nicaragua*. Berkeley: University of California, 1992.

Lappé, Frances M., and Joseph Collins. *World Hunger: Ten Myths*. San Francisco: Institute for Food and Development Policy, 1978.

Lappé, Frances M., and Joseph Collins. *Now We Can Speak: A Journey through the New Nicaragua*. San Francisco: Institute for Food and Development Policy, 1982.

Largaespada Fredersdorf, Carmen. *Soy la última en comer: Crisis económica y familiar de las mujeres trabajadoras de Managua*. Managua: Editorial Nueva Nicaragua, 1993.

Laure, Joseph. "Nicaragua: Salarios mínimos desvaneciéndose: Relación de la casi desaparición de los salarios mínimos con desplome de su poder de compra tanto general como alimentario." Guatemala City, 1991. Manuscript.

Lee, David J. "De-centering Managua: Post-earthquake Reconstruction and Revolution in Nicaragua." *Urban History* 42, no. 4 (2015): 663–85.

Leogrande, William M. "Making the Economy Scream: US Economic Sanctions against Sandinista Nicaragua." *Third World Quarterly* 17, no. 2 (1996): 329–48.

León, Arturo, Rodrigo Martínez, Ernesto Espíndola, and Alexander Schejtman. "Pobreza, hambre y seguridad alimentaria en Centroamérica y Panamá." Serie políticas sociales 88. Santiago de Chile: CEPAL, 2004.

Linkogle, Stephanie. "Soya, Culture and International Food Aid: The Case of a Nicaraguan Communal Kitchen." *Bulletin of Latin American Research* 17, no. 1 (1998): 93–103.

López, Lidia. "Los últimos datos sobre nutrición infantil en Nicaragua son desde 2012." *La Prensa*, November 6, 2019. https://www.laprensa.com.ni/2019/11/06/nacionales/2607704-los-ultimos-datos-sobre-nutricion-infantil-en-nicaragua-son-desde-2012/.

López Guzmán, María E. *Cocinando con María Esther: Cocina nicaragüense y algo más . . .* Managua: Ediciones Mundo, n.d.

Luciak, Ilja A. *The Sandinista Legacy: Lessons from a Political Economy in Transition*. Gainesville: University Press of Florida, 1995.

Lundgren, Inger. *Lost Visions and New Uncertainties: Sandinista Professionals in Northern Nicaragua*. Stockholm Studies in Social Anthropology. Stockholm: Department of Social Anthropology, 2000.

Mackenbach, Werner. *Die unbewohnte Utopie: Der nicaraguanische Roman der achtziger und neunziger Jahre*. Frankfurt am Main: Verveurt, 2004.

Martí i Puig, Salvador. "The Origins of the Peasant-Contra Rebellion in Nicaragua, 1979–87." *Research Papers* 54, Institute of Latin American Studies, London, 2001.

Martí i Puig, Salvador. "The FSLN and Sandinismo." In Close, Martí i Puig, and McConnell, *Sandinistas and Nicaragua*, 21–44.

Martí i Puig, Salvador. "Nicaragua: The Roots of the Current Crisis." *ReVista Harvard Review of Latin America* (Spring/Summer 2019). https://revista.drclas.harvard.edu/book/nicaragua-roots-current-crisis/.

Martí i Puig, Salvador, and Eduardo Baumeister. "Agrarian Policies in Nicaragua: From Revolution to the Survival of Agro-Exports, 1979–2015." *Journal of Agrarian Change* 17, no. 2 (2017): 381–96. https://doi.org/10.1111/joac.12214/.

Martí i Puig, Salvador, and David Close. *Sandinista Economies in Practice: An Insider's Critical Reflections.* Cambridge, MA: South End Press, 1992.

Martí i Puig, Salvador, and David Close. "The Nicaraguan Exception?" In Close, Martí i Puig, and McConnell, *Sandinistas and Nicaragua*, 287–307.

Martínez Cuenca, Alejandro. *Sandinista Economies in Practice: An Insider's Critical Reflections.* Cambridge: South End Press, 1992.

Mattelart, Armand, ed. *Communicating in Popular Nicaragua.* New York: International General, 1986.

Mattelart, Armand. "Communication in Nicaragua between War and Democracy." In *Communicating in Popular Nicaragua*, edited by Armand Mattelart, 7–27. New York: International General, 1986.

McGanity, William J. "The Story of the Interdepartmental Committee on Nutrition for National Defense's North American Activities (1958–1970)." *Journal of Nutrition* 135, no. 5 (2005): 1268–71.

Melo Contreras, Leonardo. "Las Juntas de Abastecimiento y Precios: Historia y memoria de una experiencia de participación popular: Chile 1970–1973." Tesis de Licenciatura, Escuela de Historia, Universidad Academia de Humanismo Cristiano, Santiago de Chile, 2012.

Mendoza Fletes, Orlando. *Distribución del ingreso y seguridad alimentaria en un ambiente de ajustes cambiarios: los precios relativos en Nicaragua (1986–1992).* Managua: Escuela de Economía Agrícola, 1992.

Meringer, Eric R. "The Local Politics of Indigenous Self-Representation: Intraethnic Political Divison among Nicaragua's Miskito People during the Sandinista Era." *Oral History Review* 37, no. 1 (2010): 1–17. https://doi.org/10.1093/ohr/ohq038/.

Milanesio, Natalia. "The Guardian Angels of the Domestic Economy: Housewives' Responsible Consumption in Peronist Argentina." *Journal of Women's History* 18, no. 3 (2006): 91–117.

Ministerio de Agricultura y Ganadería, and PAN, eds. *Segunda Encuesta de Consumo Aparente: Región III, Managua, diciembre 1991.* Managua: Ministerio de Agricultura y Ganadería, Programa Alimentario Nicaragüense, 1992.

Ministerio de Salud. "Apoyo nutricional a programas de atención primaria de salud en zonas determinadas: Manual de normas y procedimientos del proyecto PMA-Nic 2536 (Ampliación)." Managua, 1987. Manuscript in Ministerio de Salud Library.

Minks, Amanda. "Reading Nicaraguan Folklore through Inter-American Indigenismo, 1940–1970." *Latin American and Caribbean Ethnic Studies* 9, no. 3 (2015): 197–221.

Mintz, Sidney W. "Zur Beziehung zwischen Ernährung und Macht." *Jahrbuch für Wirtschaftsgeschichte* 35, no. 1 (1994): 61–72.

Mitchell, Kenneth. "Democratisation, External Exposure and State Food Distribution in the Dominican Republic." *Bulletin of Latin American Research* 28 (2009): 204–26.

Mitchell, Timothy. *Rule of Experts: Egypt, Techno-politics, Modernity.* Berkeley: University of California Press, 2002.

Molyneux, Maxine. "Mobilization without Emancipation? Women's Interest, the State, and Revolution in Nicaragua." *Feminist Studies* 11, no. 2 (1985): 227–54. https://doi.org/10.1057/9780230286382_3/.

Montes Orozco, Rosario. *Una pizca de amor y sabor.* Managua: Hispamer, 2000.

Mora Castillo, Luis, ed. *Participación popular y Democracia en Nicaragua: De los Comités de Defensa Sandinista (CDS) al Movimiento Comunal Nicaragüense (1979–1991).* Part 1. Managua: Instituto Nicaragüense de Investigaciones Económicas y Sociales, December 1991.

Mora Olivares, Alberto. *Nicasio 2.* Managua: N.p., 1975.

Morris, Courtney Desiree. "Toward a Geography of Solidarity: Afro-Nicaraguan Women's Land Activism and Autonomy in the South Caribbean Coast Autonomous Region." *Bulletin of Latin American Research* 35, no. 3 (2016): 355–69. https://doi.org/10.1111/blar.12490/.

Müller, Birgit. "Favores, ayuda y robo: Peasants' Views of Continuity in Systemic Change in Nicaragua." *Anthropologica* 52, no. 2 (2010): 1–14.

Müller, Birgit. "The Loss of Harmony: FAO Guidance for Food Security in Nicaragua." In *The Gloss of Harmony: The Politics of Policy Making in Multilateral Organisations,* edited by Birgit Müller, 202–26. Anthropology, Culture and Society. London: Pluto Press, 2013.

Nalibow Ruxin, Joshua. "Hunger, Science, and Politics: FAO, WHO, and UNICEF Nutrition Policies, 1945–1978." PhD Dissertation, University College London, 1996. http://discovery.ucl.ac.uk/1317860/1/288630.pdf.

Nestle, Marion, and Malden Nesheim. *Why Calories Count: From Science to Politics.* California Studies in Food and Culture 33. Berkeley: University of California Press, 2012.

Nicaragua and Comisión Nacional de Nutrición. *Plan quinquenal de acción para la nutrición.* Managua: El Gabinete, 1994.

Nicaragua guía oficial de turismo. Managua: n.p., 1968.

Nietschmann, Bernard. *Between Land and Water: The Subsistence Ecology of the Miskito Indians, Eastern Nicaragua.* New York: Seminar Press, 1973.

Núñez, Juan C. *De la ciudad al barrio: Redes y tejidos urbanos: Guatemala, El Sal-*

vador y Nicaragua. Guatemala City: Universidad Rafael Landívar and Coop-eración Externa Francesa, 1996.

Ocampo, José Antonio. "Collapse and (Incomplete) Stabilization of the Nicara-guan Economy." In *The Macroeconomics of Populism in Latin America*, edited by Rudiger Dornbusch and Sebastian Edwards, 331–68. Chicago: University of Chicago Press, 1991.

Ochoa, Enrique C. *Feeding Mexico: The Political Uses of Food since 1910*. Wilming-ton, DE: Scholarly Resources, 2000.

Ommen, Eline van. "The Sandinista Revolution in the Netherlands: The Dutch Solidarity Committees and Nicaragua (1977–1990)." *Naveg@america* 17 (2016): 1–22.

Organización de los Estados Americanos and Comisión Interamericana de Dere-chos Humanos. "Nicaragua. Mecanismo especial de seguimiento para Nic-aragua. MESENI Boletín." https://www.oas.org/es/cidh/actividades/visitas /2018Nicaragua/Boletin-MESENI-Enero2020.pdf.

Olivares, Iván. "Hambre y pobreza ronda a los nicas." *Confidencial*, April 22, 2019. https://confidencial.com.ni/hambre-y-pobreza-ronda-a-los-nicas/.

PAN. "Plan quinquenal de alimentación y nutrición. Plan de acción 1988." Mana-gua, 1987.

Pasos, Matilde de. *Cocina nicaragüense*. 4th ed. Managua: La Prensa, 1938.

Pastor, Robert A. *Condemned to Repetition: The United States and Nicaragua*. Princ-eton, NJ: Princeton University Press, 1987.

Patten, George G. "Dairying in Nicaragua." *Annals of the Association of American Geographers* 61 (1971): 303–15.

Peña Torres, Ligia M. *Historia de la salud pública en Nicaragua: Del protomedicato a la dirección general de sanidad 1859–1956*. Managua: IHNCA-UCA, 2014.

Pérez, Louis A. *On Becoming Cuban: Identity, Nationality, and Culture*. H. Eugene and Lillian Youngs Lehman Series. Chapel Hill: University of North Carolina Press, 1999.

Perla, Héctor. "Heirs of Sandino: The Nicaraguan Revolution and the U.S.-Nicaragua Solidarity Movement." *Latin American Perspectives* 36, no. 6 (2009): 80–100.https://doi.org/10.1177%2F0094582X09350765/.

Perla, Héctor. *Sandinista Nicaragua Resistance to US Coercion: Revolutionary Deter-rence in Asymmetric Conflict*. Cambridge Studies in Contentious Politics. New York: Cambridge University Press, 2016.

Pernet, Corinne A. "Developing Nutritional Standards and Food Policy: Latin American Reformers between the ILO, the League of Nations Health Or-ganization, and the Pan-American Sanitary Bureau." In *Globalizing Social Rights: The International Labour Organization and Beyond: Reformist Networks and the International Labor Organization*, edited by Sandrine Kott and Joëlle Droux, 249–61. Basingstoke, UK: Palgrave Macmillan, 2013.

Pernet, Corinne A. "L'UNICEF et la lutte contre la malnutrition en Amérique Centrale dans les années 1950: Entre coopération et compétition." *Relations Internationales* 161, no. 2 (2015): 27–42. http://www.cairn.info/revue-relations-internationales-2015-2-page-27.htm.

Pernet, Corinne A. "FAO from the Field and from Below: Emma Reh and the Challenges of Doing Nutrition Work in Central America." *International History Review* 41, no. 2 (2019): 396–406. https://doi.org/10.1080/07075332.2018.1498799/.

Pezzullo, Lawrence, and Ralph Pezzullo. *At the Fall of Somoza*. 2nd ed. Pitt Latin American series. Pittsburgh, PA: University of Pittsburgh Press, 1994.

Pilcher, Jeffrey M. "Industrial Tortillas and Folkloric Pepsi: The Nutritional Consequences of Hybrid Cuisines in Mexico." In *Food Nations: Selling Taste in Consumer Societies*, edited by Warren James Belasco and Philip Scranton, 222–39. New York: Routledge, 2002.

Pilcher, Jeffrey M. "Introduction." In *Food History: Critical and Primary Sources: Contemporary Transitions*, vol. 4, edited by Jeffrey M. Pilcher, 1–20. London: Bloomsbury, 2014.

Pineda, Baron. "The Chinese Creoles of Nicaragua: Identity, Economy, and Revolution in a Caribbean Port City." *Journal of Asian American Studies* 4, no. 3 (2001): 209–33.

Pineda, Baron. *Shipwrecked Identities: Navigating Race on Nicaragua's Mosquito Coast*. New Brunswick, NJ: Rutgers University Press, 2006.

Polakoff, Erica, and Pierre M. La Ramée. "Grass-Roots Organizations." In Walker, *Nicaragua without Illusions*, 185–201.

Polèse, Mario. "Ciudades y empleos en Centroamérica." In *Economía y desarrollo urbano en Centroamérica*, edited by Mario Lungo and Mario Polèse, 11–45. San José, CR: FLACSO, 1998.

Porter, Amy L. "Fleeting Dreams and Flowing Goods: Citizenship and Consumption in Havana Cuba." *PoLAR: Political and Legal Anthropology Review* 31, no. 1 (2008): 134–49. https://doi.org/10.1111/j.1555-2934.2008.00009.x/.

Porter, Theodore M. *Trust in Numbers: The Pursuit of Objectivity in Science and Public Life*. Princeton, NJ: Princeton University Press, 1995.

Potthast, Barbara. *Die Mosquitoküste im Spannungsfeld britischer und spanischer Politik, 1502–1821*. Lateinamerikanische Forschungen 16. Köln: Böhlau, 1988.

Poyner, George, and Catherine Strachan. "Nutrition Sector Assessment for Nicaragua." Managua: USAID, 1976.

Preston-Werner, Theresa. "Defending National Foodways: Laying Claim to Tradition in Costa Rica." In *Rice and Beans: A Unique Dish in a Hundred Places*, edited by Richard Wilk and Livia Barbosa, 181–201. New York: Berg, 2011.

Prevost, Gary. "The FSLN." In Walker, *Nicaragua without Illusions*, 149–64.

Prevost, Gary, and Harry E. Vanden, eds. *Democracy and Socialism in Sandinista Nicaragua*. Boulder, CO: Lynne Rienner, 1993.

La Prensa. *85 años: Al servicio de la verdad y la justicia*. Managua: Editorial La Prensa, 2011.

"Primer Congreso Nacional de Alimentación: 13 al 15 de Mayo 1970, Managua." Managua: n.p., 1970.

Programa Mundial de Alimentos. "Informe de evaluación y apreciación del proyecto PMA Nicaragua 2536: Asistencia a niños pre-escolares y mujeres lactantes y gestantes." Managua: n.p., 1986.

Rabe, Stephen. *The Killing Zone: The United States Wages Cold War in Latin America*. New York: Oxford University Press, 2012.

Radell, David R. "Historical Geography of Western Nicaragua: The Spheres of Influence of Leon, Granada and Managua, 1519–1965." PhD Dissertation, University of California, 1969.

Ramírez, Sergio. "Ströme von Milch und Honig." In *Die Revolution ist ein Buch und ein freier Mensch: Die politischen Plakate des befreiten Nicaragua 1979–1990 und der internationalen Solidaritätsbewegung*, edited by Otker Bujard and Ulrich Wirper, 150–64. Köln: PapyRossa-Verlag, 2007.

Ramírez, Sergio. *Tambor olvidado*. San José, CR: Santillana, 2007.

Ramírez, Sergio. *Adiós muchachos: A Memoir of the Sandinista Revolution*. Durham, NC: Duke University Press, 2012.

Ramírez, Sergio. *Lo que sabe el paladar: Diccionario de alimentos de Nicaragua*. Managua: Hispamer, 2014.

Ramiro Arcia, J. "La desnutrición." *Revista Conservadora* (June 1962): 16–19.

Randall, Margaret. *Todas estamos despiertas: Testimonios de la mujer nicaragüense de hoy*. México, DF: Siglo XXI Editores, 1980.

Ricciardi, Joseph. "Economic Policy." In *Revolution and Counterrevolution in Nicaragua*, edited by Thomas W. Walker, 247–73. Boulder, CO: Westview Press, 1991.

Richter, Ernesto. "ALPROMISU: Die Entstehung einer neuen ethnischen Bewegung 1970–1979." In *Mosquitia—die andere Hälfte Nicaraguas: Über Geschichte und Gegenwart der Atlantikküste*, edited by Klaus Meschkat, Eleonore von Oertzen, Ernesto Richter, Lioba Rossbach and Volker Wünderich, 141–63. Hamburg: Junius, 1987.

Rinke, Stefan. *Begegnungen mit dem Yankee: Nordamerikanisierung und soziokultureller Wandel in Chile (1898–1990)*. Köln: Böhlau, 2004.

Ritzer, George. *The McDonaldization of Society*. 5th ed. Los Angeles: Pine Forge Press, 2008.

Rocha, José Luis. "Agrarian Reform in Nicaragua in the 1980s: Lights and Shadows of Its Legacy." In Francis, *Nicaraguan Exceptionalism*, 103–25.

Rocha, José Luis, and Ian Cristoplos. "Las ONGs ante los desastres naturales: Vacíos y oportunidades." *Envío*, no. 212 (1999). http://www.envio.org .ni/articulo/974/.

Rojas Bolaños, Manuel. "La política." In *Historia General de Centroamérica: De la posguerra a la crisis (1945–1979)*, edited by Héctor Pérez Brignoli and Edelberto Torres Rivas, 85–163. Historia general de Centroamérica 5. Madrid: Ediciones Siruela, 1993.

Romero, Luz. "El inventor de la Kola Shaler." *La Prensa, Magazine*, May 29, 2011.

Rueda Estrada, Verónica. "El campesinado migrante: Políticas agrarias, colonizaciones internas y movimientos de frontera agrícola en Nicaragua, 1960–2012." *Tzintzun: Revista de Estudios Históricos* 57 (January–June 2013): 155–98.

Rueda Estrada, Verónica. "Sandinismo y pragmatismo político: Generaciones militantes en Nicaragua, 1979–2016." *Palimpsesto* 8, no. 11 (2017): 147–71.

Rushdie, Salman. *Das Lächeln des Jaguars: Eine Reise durch Nicaragua*. Reinbek: Rowohlt, 2009.

Sáenz, Enrique. "Hay hambre en el país del 'Hambre Zero.'" *Confidencial*, December 13, 2017. https://confidencial.com.ni/hambre-pais-del-hambre-cero/.

Saldaña-Portillo, María J. *The Revolutionary Imagination in the Americas and the Age of Development*. Durham, NC: Duke University Press, 2003.

Sasson, Tehila. "Milking the Third World? Humanitarianism, Capitalism, and the Moral Economy of the Nestlé Boycott." *American Historical Review* 121, no. 4 (2016): 1196–224. https://doi.org/10.1093/ahr/121.4.1196/.

Saulniers, Alfred H. "State Trading Organizations in Expansion: A Case Study of ENABAS." In *Nicaragua: Profiles of the Revolutionary Public Sector*, edited by Michael E. Conroy, 95–126. Boulder, CO: Westview Press, 1987.

Scott, James C. *Seeing like a State: How Certain Schemes to Improve the Human Condition Have Failed*. Yale ISPS series. New Haven, CT: Yale University Press, 1998.

Scrimshaw, Nevin. "Los problemas nutricionales de Centro América con referencia especial a la República de Nicaragua." *Nicaragua Médica* 8, no. 11 (1952): 1–18.

Schroeder, Michael J., and David D. Brooks. "Rebellion from Without: Foreign Capital, Missionaries, Sandinistas, Marines & Guardia, and Costeños in the Time of the Sandino Rebellion, 1927–1934." In *National Integration and Contested Autonomy: The Caribbean Coast of Nicaragua*, edited by Luciano Baracco, 45–87. New York: Algora, 2011.

Selser, Gabriela. *Banderas y harapos: Relatos de la revolución en Nicaragua*. Managua: Gabriela Selser, 2017.

Shaw, John D. *The UN World Food Programme and the Development of Food Aid*. Basingstoke, UK: Palgrave, 2001.

Shaw, John D. *The World's Largest Humanitarian Agency: The Transformation of the UN World Food Programme and of Food Aid*. Basingstoke, UK: Palgrave Macmillan, 2011.

Shillington, Laura J. "Right to Food, Right to the City: Household Urban Agriculture and Socionatural Metabolism in Managua." *Geoforum* 44 (2013): 103–11. https://doi.org/10.1016/j.geoforum.2012.02.006/.

Siegel, Benjamin Robert. *Hungry Nation: Food, Famine, and the Making of Modern India*. Cambridge: Cambridge University Press, 2018.

Siegrist, Hannes. "Konsum, Kultur und Gesellschaft im modernen Europa." In *Europäische Konsumgeschichte: Zur Gesellschafts- und Kulturgeschichte des Konsums (18. bis 20. Jahrhundert)*, edited by Hannes Siegrist, 13–48. Frankfurt am Main: Campus, 1997.

Simon, Heide. "Probleme und Perspektiven von Frauenförderung vor dem sozio-ökonomischen Hintergrund Nicaraguas: Das Fallbeispiel der "nutricionistas populares" von Ciudad Sandino." Diplomarbeit, Soziologie, Freie Universität Berlin, July 15, 1991.

Soares, John A. Jr. "Strategy, Ideology, and Human Rights: Jimmy Carter Confronts the Left in Central America, 1979–1981." *Journal of Cold War Studies* 8, no. 4 (2006): 57–91. https://doi.org/10.1162/jcws.2006.8.4.57/.

Solá Montserrat, Roser. *Un siglo y medio de economía nicaragüense: Las raíces del presente*. Managua: Universidad Centroamericana, 2007.

Sollis, Peter. "The Atlantic Coast of Nicaragua: Development and Autonomy." *Journal of Latin American Studies* 21, no. 3 (1989). https://doi.org/10.1017/S0022216X00018526/.

Sonnenfeld, David A. "Mexico's 'Green Revolution,' 1940–1980: Towards an Environmental History." *Environmental History Review* 16, no. 4 (1992): 28–52. https://doi.org/10.2307/3984948/.

Soto Joya, Fernanda. *Ventanas en la memoria: Recuerdos de la revolución en la frontera agrícola*. Managua: UCA, 2011.

Soto Joya, Fernanda. "De sueños de 'colonización individual' al trabajo colectivo: La experiencia de campesinos en la región de Siuna durante los años ochenta." *Monograma: Revista Iberoamericana de Cultura y Pensamiento* 2, no. 1 (2018): 61–76.

Soule, John W. "The Economic Austerity Packages of 1988 and Their Impact on Public Opinion." *International Journal of Political Economy* (Fall 1990): 34–45.

Soynica. "Historia Soynica." Accessed September 20, 2010. http://www.soynica.org.ni/qs_rhist.php/.

Spalding, Rose J. "Poverty Politics." In Close, Martí i Puig, and McConnell, *Sandinistas and Nicaragua*, 215–43.

Spalding, Rose J. *Contesting Trade in Central America: Market Reform and Resistance*. Austin: University of Texas Press, 2014.

Spalding, Rose J. "Los empresarios y el estado posrevolucionario: El reordenamiento de las élites y la nueva estrategia de colaboración en Nicaragua." *Anuario de Estudios Centroamericanos* 43 (2017): 149–88.

Spicer Nichols, John. "The Media." In *Nicaragua: The First Five Years*, edited by Thomas W. Walker, 183–99. New York: Praeger, 1985.

Spoor, Max. *State and Domestic Agricultural Markets in Nicaragua: From Interventionism to Neo-liberalism.* New York: St. Martin's Press, 1995.

Stahler-Sholk, Richard. "Stabilization, Destabilization, and the Popular Classes in Nicaragua 1979–1988." *Latin American Research Review* 25, no. 3 (1990): 55–88.

Stahler-Sholk, Richard. "Structural Adjustment and Resistance: The Political Economy of Nicaragua under Chamorro." In *The Undermining of the Sandinista Revolution*, edited by Gary Prevost and Harry E. Vanden, 74–113. London: Macmillan, 1999.

Stahler-Sholk, Richard, and Max Spoor. *La política macroeconómica y sus efectos en la agricultura y la seguridad alimentaria: Caso Nicaragua.* Panama: Poligráfica SA, 1990.

Staten, Clifford L. *The History of Nicaragua.* Greenwood Histories of the Modern Nations. Santa Barbara, CA: Greenwood, 2010.

Stewart, Charles, ed. *Creolization: History, Ethnography, Theory.* Walnut Creek, CA: Left Coast Press, 2007.

Stewart, Charles. "Creolization: History, Ethnography, Theory." In *Creolization: History, Ethnography, Theory*, edited by Charles Stewart, 1–25. Walnut Creek, CA: Left Coast Press, 2007.

Streeter, Stephen M. "The Failure of 'Liberal Developmentalism': The United States's Anti-Communist Showcase in Guatemala, 1954–1960." *International History Review* 21, no. 2 (1999): 386–413. https://doi.org/10.1080/07075332.1999.9640864/.

Sujo Wilson, Hugo. *Oral History of Bluefields.* Colección Autonomía. Managua: CIDCA-UCA, 1998.

Tagle, María Ángelica. "Cambios en los patrones de consumo alimentario en América Latina." *Archivos Latinoamericanos de Nutrición* 38, no. 3 (1988): 750–65.

Tapia Barquero, Humberto. *Nicaragua: Maíz y folklore.* Managua: Papelera Industrial de Nicaragua, 1981.

Téfel, Reinaldo A. *El infierno de los pobres: Diagnóstico sociológico de los barrios marginales de Managua.* 3rd ed. Managua: Ediciones el Pez y la Serpiente, 1976.

Tomka, Béla. *A Social History of Twentieth-Century Europe.* Hoboken: Taylor and Francis, 2013.

Tomlinson, John. *Cultural Imperialism: A Critical Introduction.* London: Pinter, 1991.

Torres, Gabriel, and Ronnie Vernooy. "Mujeres comerciantes y política: Reconstrucción social del mercado de Bluefields." *Wani* 13 (November 1992): 68–91.

Trentmann, Frank. "The Modern Genealogy of the Consumer: Meanings, Identities and Political Synapses." In *Consuming Cultures, Global Perspectives: Historical Trajectories, Transnational Exchanges*, edited by John Brewer and Frank Trentmann, 19–69. Cultures of Consumption Series. Oxford: Berg, 2006.

US Agency for International Development. "U.S. Overseas Loans and Grants: Obligations and Loan Authorizations, July 1, 1945–September 30, 2017." https://explorer.usaid.gov/reports/.

United Nations. "Report of the World Food Conference, Rome, 5–16 November 1974." New York, 1975. https://digitallibrary.un.org/record/701143/.

United Nations. "Department of Economic and Social Affairs Population Dynamics." Last modified August 28, 2019. https://population.un.org/wpp/DataQuery/.

United Nations. "Department of Economic and Social Affairs Population Dynamics." Accessed December 15, 2019. https://population.un.org/wpp/Download/Standard/Population/.

Utting, Peter. "Introducción." In *La reforma agraria en Nicaragua, 1979–1989: Sistema alimentario*, 3–15. Colección 10 Aniversario II. Managua: CIERA, 1989.

Utting, Peter. "La oferta interna y la escasez de alimentos." In *La economía política de la Nicaragua revolucionaria*, edited by Rose Spalding, 158–83. México DF: Fondo de Cultura Económica, 1989.

Utting, Peter. *Economic Adjustment under the Sandinistas: Policy Reform, Food Security, and Livelihood in Nicaragua*, edited by UN Research Institute for Social Development. UNRISD report 91.1. Geneva: UNRISD, 1991.

Utting, Peter. *Economic Reform and Third-World Socialism: A Political Economy of Food Policy in Post-revolutionary Societies*. Basingstoke, UK: Macmillan, 1992.

Utting, Peter. "The Political Economy of Food Pricing and Marketing Reforms in Nicaragua, 1984–87." *European Journal of Development Research* 4, no. 2 (1992): 107–31.

Valenze, Deborah M. *Milk: A Local and Global History*. New Haven, CT: Yale University Press, 2011.

Vázquez Olivera, Mario, and Fabián Campos Hernández, eds. *México ante el conflicto centroamericano, 1978–1982*. México DF: Centro de Investigaciones sobre América Latina y el Caribe/Bonilla Artiga Editores, 2016.

Vernooy, Ronnie. *Starting All Over Again: Making and Remaking a Living on the Atlantic Coast of Nicaragua*. PhD Dissertation, Landbouwuniversiteit Wageningen, 1992.

La Vía Campesina. "Homepage." https://web.archive.org/web/20150323045941/http://viacampesina.org/en/index.php/organisation-mainmenu-44/.

Vilas, Carlos M. *I. Scientific Research in a Revolutionary Setting: The Case of Nicaragua*. SAREC Documentation, Research Surveys, Stockholm, 1988.

Vilas, Carlos M. *State, Class, and Ethnicity in Nicaragua: Capitalist Modernization and Revolutionary Change on the Atlantic Coast*. Boulder, CO: Lynne Rienner, 1989.

Vivas, Angelica. *Cocina Nica*. Colección popular. Managua: Ministerio de Cultura, 1985.

Vogl Baldizón, Alberto. *Nicaragua con amor y humor*. 2nd ed. Managua: Ministerio de Cultura, 1985.

Voss, Klaas. *Washingtons Söldner: Verdeckte US-Interventionen im Kalten Krieg und ihre Folgen*. Hamburg: Hamburger Edition, 2014.

La Voz del Sandinismo. "Gobierno Sandinista aplica estrategia nacional de seguridad y soberanía alimentaria." *La Voz del Sandinismo*, July 27, 2011.

La Voz del Sandinismo. "Destaca Rosario labores por la soberanía alimentaria." *La Voz del Sandinismo*, June 21, 2012.

La Voz del Sandinismo. "Declaraciones de la compañera Rosario Murillo, Vice Presidenta de Nicaragua." *La Voz del Sandinismo*, August 29, 2019. https://www.la vozdelsandinismo.com/nicaragua/2019-08-29/declaraciones-de-la-companera -rosario-murillo-vice-presidenta-de-nicaragua-29-08-2019-texto-integro/.

Walker, Thomas W. *Nicaragua: Living in the Shadow of the Eagle*. 4th ed. Boulder, CO: Westview Press, 2003.

Walker, Thomas W., ed. *Nicaragua without Illusions: Regime Transition and Structural Adjustment in the 1990s*, 81–96. Wilmington, DE: Scholarly Resources, 1997.

Walter, Knut. *The Regime of Anastasio Somoza, 1936–1956*. Chapel Hill: University of North Carolina Press, 1993.

Washington Post. "Hunger Becomes an Issue in Nicaragua." *Washington Post*, October 3, 1988. https://www.washingtonpost.com/archive/politics/1988/10/03/ hunger-becomes-an-issue-in-nicaragua/62d515ba-3101-444e-9eaf-8934f1d b827a/.

Weinreb, Amelia Rosenberg. *Cuba in the Shadow of Change: Daily Life in the Twilight of the Revolution*. Gainesville: University Press of Florida, 2009.

Welsch, Wolfgang. "Transculturality: The Puzzling Form of Cultures Today." In *Spaces of Culture: City, Nation, World*, edited by Mike Featherstone and Scott Lash, 194–213. Theory, Culture and Society. London: Sage, 1999.

Wheelock Román, Jaime. *La comida nicaragüense*. Managua: Editorial Hispamer, 1998.

Whisnant, David. E. *Rascally Signs in Sacred Places: The Politics of Culture in Nicaragua*. Chapel Hill: University of North Carolina Press, 1995.

Whitted, Stephen F. "Analytical Description of the Dairy Industry of Nicaragua with Recommendations." USAID, 1973.

Wieters, Heike. *The NGO CARE and Food Aid from America, 1945–80: "Showered with Kindness"?* Manchester, UK: Manchester University Press, 2017.

Wilk, Richard R. "'Real Belizean Food': Building Local Identity in the Transnational Caribbean." *American Anthropologist* 101, no. 2 (1999): 244–55.

Wilk, Richard R. "Consumer Goods as Dialogue about Development." In *Consumption: Critical Concepts in the Social Sciences: Vol.3, Disciplinary Approaches to Consumption*, edited by Daniel Miller, 34–54. London: Routledge, 2001.

Wilk, Richard R. *Home Cooking in the Global Village: Caribbean Food from Buccaneers to Ecotourists.* New York: Berg, 2006.

Wilk, Richard, and Lívia Barbosa. "A Unique Dish in a Hundred Places." In *Rice and Beans: A Unique Dish in a Hundred Places*, edited by Richard Wilk and Lívia Barbosa, 1–17. New York: Berg, 2011.

World Bank. "Republic of Nicaragua: Review of Social Sector Issues." Report No. 10671 NI, February 3, 1993.

World Food Programme. "Food Aid Information System—FAIS." https://www.wfp.org/fais/.

Wünderich, Volker. "Sandino an der Atlantikküste, 1927–1934." In *Mosquitia—die andere Hälfte Nicaraguas: Über Geschichte und Gegenwart der Atlantikküste*, edited by Klaus Meschkat, Eleonore von Oertzen, Ernesto Richter, Lioba Rossbach, and Volker Wünderich, 99–139. Hamburg: Junius, 1987.

Wünderich, Volker. *Sandino: Eine politische Biographie.* Wuppertal: Peter Hammer, 1995.

Yates-Doerr, Emily. "Intervals of Confidence: Uncertain Accounts of Global Hunger." *BioSocieties* 10, no. 2 (2015): 229–46. https://doi.org/10.1057/biosoc.2015.9/.

Yih, Katherine, and Charles R. Hale. "Mestizen, Creoles und Indianer: Die ethnische Hierarchie in Zelaya Sur." In *Mosquitia—die andere Hälfte Nicaraguas: Über Geschichte und Gegenwart der Atlantikküste*, edited by Klaus Meschkat, Eleonore von Oertzen, Ernesto Richter, Lioba Rossbach, and Volker Wünderich, 189–203. Hamburg: Junius, 1987.

Zalkin, Michael. "Nicaragua: The Peasantry, Grain Policy, and the State." *Latin American Perspectives* 15, no. 4 (1988): 71–91.

Zamora, Augusto. "Some Reflections on the Piñata," *Envío*, no. 180 (1996). http://www.envio.org.ni/articulo/3019/.

INDEX

Note: Page numbers in *italics* refer to figures.